CLAUSEWITZ

CLAUSEWITZ

HIS LIFE AND WORK

DONALD STOKER

OXFORD
UNIVERSITY PRESS

OXFORD
UNIVERSITY PRESS

Oxford University Press is a department of the University of Oxford.
It furthers the University's objective of excellence in research, scholarship,
and education by publishing worldwide.

Oxford   New York

Auckland   Cape Town   Dar es Salaam   Hong Kong   Karachi
Kuala Lumpur   Madrid   Melbourne   Mexico City   Nairobi
New Delhi   Shanghai   Taipei   Toronto

With offices in

Argentina   Austria   Brazil   Chile   Czech Republic   France   Greece
Guatemala   Hungary   Italy   Japan   Poland   Portugal   Singapore
South Korea   Switzerland   Thailand   Turkey   Ukraine   Vietnam

Oxford is a registered trademark of Oxford University Press
in the UK and certain other countries.

Published in the United States of America by
Oxford University Press
198 Madison Avenue, New York, NY 10016

Library of Congress Cataloging-in-Publication Data
Stoker, Donald J.
Clausewitz : his life and work / Donald Stoker.
pages cm.
Includes bibliographical references and index.
ISBN 978–0–19–935794–9
1. Clausewitz, Carl von, 1780–1831.   2. Napoleonic Wars, 1800–1815—Campaigns—Russia—
Biography.   3. Prussia (Kingdom). Armee—Officers—Biography.   I. Title.   II. Title:
Clausewitz, his life and work.
DD422.C5S76 2015
355.02092—dc23
[B]
2014016786

1 3 5 7 9 8 6 4 2

Printed in the United States of America
on acid-free paper

To my students who fought the Global War on Terror.

Sound tactics win battles.
Sound operational art wins campaigns.
Sound strategy wins wars.
Sound policy wins the peace.
For all of these, judgment is the key.

Contents

List of Illustrations

Maps

Figures

Acknowledgments

I have incurred many debts in the course of writing this book, not the least to my wife Carol, who has had to take up the parental slack during my all too frequent absences. Thank you, my love. My daughter Sarah has also been understanding. Thank you, Sarah.

I am deeply beholden to Michael Leggiere of the University of North Texas, an old friend from graduate school. Mike answered my endless queries, graciously pointed me to sources, and allowed me to read parts of three books he was writing (most of us only write one at a time). He also took the time to read the entire manuscript and make valuable suggestions and corrections. Thanks, Mike. I owe you one. Alexander Mikaberibzde helped me navigate the Russian microfilm collection on the Napoleonic period—in which I found a drop of new material on Clausewitz—and also answered many questions. Niels Nielsen translated Clausewitz's works on 1813 and 1814, as well as some other things, and checked many of my own translations. Marc Guarin provided a translation of Clausewitz's *Strategie*. I am grateful for the help of both and we hope to soon publish these three works, none of which exists in a complete English translation. Regina Kuehn helped refresh my slumbering German and deciphered some of the colloquialisms I encountered. Nils Bartholdy and the staff of the Rigsarkivet, Copenhagen, supplied the Clausewitz-related documents I requested. The staff of the British Library proved very helpful with my inquiries on the Sir Hudson Lowe papers, in which I found a previously unpublished letter by Clausewitz, and the British National Archives provided a copy of a heretofore forgotten map that Clausewitz helped draw in 1813. Vanya Eftimova Bellinger and Christopher Bassford kindly supplied illustrations from their own collections (I look forward to reading Vanya's biography of Marie von Clausewitz). Other professional help and advice came from George Baer (who was always encouraging), Harold Blanton (who read much of the manuscript), John Dunn, the late Michael Handel (to whom I am indebted for my first analytical introduction to Clausewitz's work),

Peter Hofschröer, Michael Jones (who also read parts of the text), Kevin McCranie, Alfred Mierzejewski, Dan Moran (with whom I had an informative lunch), and Charles White. The staff and leadership of the College of Distance Education of the U.S. Naval War College were also helpful and encouraging. My thanks go out to Stan Carpenter, Fred Drake, Rose Drake, Jay Hickey, Doug Smith, and Walt Wildemann. Chiaki Gayle receives my special thanks as she provided much needed assistance photocopying and scanning critical material. The ideas and opinions expressed in this book are solely my own and do not represent those of the U.S. government, the Department of Defense, or the U.S. Naval War College.

Two of the other keys to this work's completion were Zooey Lober and Irma Fink. They are the interlibrary loan gurus at the Naval Postgraduate School's Dudley Knox Library. They worked very hard to track down what were sometimes very obscure sources. Thank you again, ladies.

The idea for a short biography of Clausewitz originated with my agent at POM, Inc., Dan Green. Tim Bent at Oxford proved supportive and worked over the draft manuscript with his customary competence and thoroughness. As always, I benefited from the diligent, hardworking professionals at Oxford University Press, particularly Lauren Hill, Jonathan Kroberger, Keely Latcham (who worked particularly hard to help pull together the maps and illustrations), Alana Podolsky, Christian Purdy, and Elyse Turr. Sunoj Sankaran provided excellent copy editing. Thank you all. *SDG*

Abbreviations Used in the Notes

"1806"   Carl von Clausewitz. "Notes on the Jena Campaign." Includes "Notes on Prussia in Her Grand Catastrophe of 1806" and "Prince August's Battalion in the Battle of Prenzlau." Conrad H. Lanza, ed. and trans. Command and General Staff School. *Jena Campaign Sourcebook*. Fort Leavenworth: The General Service Schools Press, 1922.

"1812"   Carl von Clausewitz. "From the Campaign of 1812 in Russia." In *Historical and Political Writings*. Peter Paret and Daniel Moran, ed. and trans. Princeton: Princeton University Press, 1992, 110–204.

1812   Carl von Clausewitz. *The Campaign of 1812 in Russia*. Foreword by Sir Michael Howard. New York: Da Capo, 1995.

1813   Carl von Clausewitz. *The Campaign of 1813 to the Armistice*, Niels Nielsen, trans. (Unpublished Manuscript, 2013). This is a translation of: Carl von Clausewitz. "Der Feldzug von 1813 bis zum Waffenstillstand." *HW* (1862), 7:215–72.

"1814"   Carl von Clausewitz. "Strategic Critique of the 1814 Campaign." Niels Nielsen, trans. (Unpublished Manuscript, 2012). This is a translation of Carl von Clausewitz. "Strategische Kritik des Feldzuges von 1814 in Frankreich." *HW* (1862), 7:307–404.

HPW   Carl von Clausewitz. *Historical and Political Writings*. Peter Paret and Daniel Moran, ed. and trans. Princeton: Princeton University Press, 1992.

HW   Carl von Clausewitz. *Hinterlassene Werke des Generals Carl von Clausewitz über Krieg und Kriegführung*. 10 vols. Berlin, 1832–37; 2nd ed., 1857–63.

Karl und Marie   Carl and Marie von Clausewitz. *Karl und Marie von Clausewitz: Ein Lebensbild in Briefen und Tagebuchblättern*. Karl Linnebach, ed. Berlin: Warneck, 1916.

Leben   Karl Schwartz. *Leben des Generals Carl von Clausewitz und der Frau Marie von Clausewitz*. 2 vols. Berlin: Dümmlers, 1878.

"Observations" Carl von Clausewitz. "From 'Observations on Prussia in Her Great Catastrophe.'" In Peter Paret and Daniel Moran, ed. and trans. *Historical and Political Writings*. Princeton: Princeton University Press, 1992, 32–84.

Pertz-Delbrück, *Gneisenau* G. H. Pertz and Hans Delbrück. *Das Leben des Feldmarschalls Grafen Neidhardt von Gneisenau*. 5 vols. Berlin: Reimer, 1864–80.

Schriften Carl von Clausewitz. *Schriften—Aufsätze—Studien—Briefe*. Werner Hahlweg, ed. 2 vols. in 3. Göttingen: Vandenhoeck & Ruprecht, 1966–90.

Author's Note

One of the pieces of so-called conventional wisdom about Clausewitz is that he was "just a staff officer," meaning he never saw much—if any—combat. Clausewitz certainly spent much of his time as a staff officer—though carrying this office during the Napoleonic era did not mean safe duty in the rear—and as a young soldier Clausewitz had also not yet put on this mantle. Clausewitz had an enormous amount of combat experience (he was involved in perhaps three dozen battles), as did the literally millions of men who bore arms during the era of the French Revolution and Napoleonic Wars, one of the most intense periods of continuous, large-scale warfare in history. My primary focus has been upon reconstructing Clausewitz's role in the various campaigns in which he served between 1793 and 1815. For understandable reasons, the bulk of the writing related to Clausewitz concerns his ideas and their development. Most previous works also march quickly over his combat experience, particularly that of 1813, 1814, and 1815. But, as we will see, reconstructing his battle experiences at places such as Göhrde, Sehestedt, Wavre, and others has much to teach us about Clausewitz as a soldier and a man. Clausewitz—who wrote profusely—was less prolific in regard to his own personal experiences. I have made use of what has come down to us, and added flesh to bone using accounts of those he served with or under, while placing him in the historical context of the campaigns in which he fought. While doing this I have also tapped his historical and analytical works to give his later assessments of individuals and their actions—especially their military decisions—in order to broaden our picture of his views of the campaigns. This also allows us to utilize some of his analysis and theoretical ideas in connection with events. His various works are touched upon along the way to mark the development of his ideas on his road to writing *On War*. The hope is that the result provides a basic introduction to Clausewitz's life, as well as what he left us, and a map for those who wish to learn more. Peter Paret brilliantly traced

Clausewitz's intellectual development in his *Clausewitz and the State*, and those interested in deepening their understanding of Clausewitz and his age will be richly rewarded by his work.

It is self-evident that Clausewitz's extensive military experience—combined with much study and thought—fed his theoretical writings, but drawing conclusive lines from any one event to an argument in *On War* is risky. However, studying his military experiences, when possible in toto, deepens our picture of the events that shaped Clausewitz's mind and perhaps guided his pen.

Donald Stoker
Monterey, California
July 2014

Introduction
The Point of It All

We must not consider every possibility, but only probabilities.

July 29, 1831, Posen, Prussia (Now Poznan, Poland)

"If I should die, dear Marie," Carl von Clausewitz wrote to his wife, "that is simply how things are in my profession. Do not grieve too much for a life that had little left to undertake in any event.... I cannot say how great is my contempt for human judgment in leaving this world."[1] Three aspects of Clausewitz's personality reveal themselves here, all constants in his adult life: frustration with the political situation of his time, melancholy (occasionally tinged with fatalism), and his abiding love for his wife.

The year before Clausewitz wrote his note, revolution and riot had engulfed much of Europe. The French ousted Charles X, the brother of the king they had guillotined in January 1793. Uprisings erupted in Germany, Italy, and Spain. The Belgians rose against the Dutch, the Poles against the Russians. It was the latter that brought Clausewitz to Posen as the chief of staff of the Prussian forces posted on an unstable frontier. Across the border, the Russian army fought the hapless Poles.

Eighteen-thirty was the year of revolution. Eighteen-thirty-one was the year of cholera. Clausewitz's fatalism proved prescient. The disease didn't take him immediately, but it did take him, on November 16, 1831. On August 23 it had claimed his longtime friend and mentor, the Prussian field marshal August von Gneisenau. The philosopher Hegel succumbed two days before Clausewitz. On June 31 it had killed Field Marshal Hans Karl von Diebitsch, the commander of the Russian army suppressing the Poles; Clausewitz had served under him in 1812. Tens of thousands more joined them as the epidemic burned its way from Asia, to Europe, then to the New World.

Clausewitz left only a deeply bereaved Marie, their union having produced no heirs, which always pained them. But Marie, an intelligent and exceedingly well-read woman—discussions of literature and art sprinkle their correspondence—played an indispensable role in creating a different kind of legacy for her husband. In the spring of 1830 Clausewitz had transferred to the artillery from his post as director of Prussia's War College. Knowing he would no longer have time for scholarly pursuits, Marie wrote later, "he arranged his papers, sealed them in individual packages, gave each one a label, and bid a sad farewell to this activity, which he held so dear."[2] The bundles contained a number of works, among them histories of the Napoleonic campaigns of 1806, 1812, 1814, and 1815. One held a manuscript titled *Vom Kriege*, known to the English-speaking world as *On War*.

After her husband's death, Marie worked with Major Franz August O'Etzel, who taught military geography at the War College, and her brother, Major General Friedrich Wilhelm von Brühl, to organize Clausewitz's works. The ten volumes appeared from 1832 to 1837. *On War* encompassed the first three (1832–1834). The Berlin publisher Ferdinand Dümmler, like Clausewitz a veteran of what the Prussians called the Wars of Liberation (1813–1815), printed the texts, accompanied by maps drawn by O'Etzel. The firm has remained Clausewitz's publisher since.[3]

Initially, *On War* caused only a small tremor in its narrow literary circle. The author of an 1832 review in a military journal judged it tough going, though worth the slog. Its "crystalline waters stream over particles of pure gold," he wrote. In other words, one had to study the book—not merely read it—to grasp its merit. The work failed to impress Baron Antoine-Henri Jomini—the most important military theorist of the day—who branded it "too pretentious for a didactic discussion" due to its lack of clarity. He grudgingly admitted to pulling an occasional nugget from it, but criticized Clausewitz for being overly skeptical of established military theory.[4]

Nearly two centuries later, few beyond a narrow band of scholars and hobbyists read Jomini's works, which is unfortunate, as he has much interesting and useful to say. Clausewitz, in contrast, has become a global brand, one constantly refreshed by a flow of books and articles debating his ideas. All or part of *On War* appears in an array of translations from Arabic to Vietnamese. Military staff colleges the world over assign Clausewitz's text, largely to prepare their officers for staff positions and higher command. *The Economist* magazine titled its defense blog "Clausewitz."

On War is not without critics. Sir Basil Liddell Hart, the British soldier and theorist, branded Clausewitz the "evil genius of military thought"
while blaming his work and its devotees for the slaughter of the First World
War's Western Front. Others have attacked his grandiosity. In the mold of
Thucydides, Clausewitz determined to write a book on war that would not
be soon forgotten, claiming that readers of the first six books of *On War*
"may even find they contain the basic ideas that might bring about a revolution in the study of war."[5]

Clausewitz's work has certainly not been forgotten. Far from it. The
question is, how did it come to be written? That is what this book will seek
to answer.

I

Boy Soldier (1780–1795)

Great things alone can make a great mind, and petty things will make a
petty mind unless a man rejects them as completely alien.

In the late spring of 1792, a man wearing the uniform of a minor
Prussian civil servant appeared at the garrison gate of the Prince
Ferdinand Infantry Regiment in Neuruppin. He had served in the
Nassau-Usingen infantry regiment and fought at Kolberg in the closing
days of the Seven Years War (1756–1763). Prussia frequently rewarded
its veterans by appointing them to government posts, and the king,
Frederick the Great, had named him a royal tax collector. His post was in
the small town of Burg, nearly due west of the Prussian capital of Berlin.
It was a low-paying job; he never made more than 300 talers a year—a
Berlin schoolteacher could earn 800. The man, Friedrich Gabriel von
Clausewitz, had in tow a melancholy boy of eleven, whom he intended to
sign on with the regiment.[1]

Carl von Clausewitz never forgot this moment. Twenty-nine years later,
he recognized the house in which he and his father had stayed in Potsdam
on their journey to join the regiment. The experience churned up emotions, and even nearly three decades later he still had a clear vision of the
misery gripping him that day, something, he insisted, that "never really
left me." But amid his gloom he also saw that the journey to Potsdam had
"laid the first stone" of a life that he considered very lucky, and upon which
Providence had smiled.[2]

Clausewitz's boyhood entry into Prussian service was far from unusual.
Prussian officers started very young, sometimes as early as nine. Frederick
the Great described them as "snatched from their mother's breast," but did
nothing to change the practice. Two of Clausewitz's older brothers had

Figure 1.1. Clausewitz's Boyhood Home in Burg.
Courtesy of Vanya Eftimova Bellinger.

earlier entered the service when little more than babes. One, Wilhelm
Benedikt, was in the same regiment. Wilhelm and his older brother,
Friedrich, eventually had distinguished military careers in their own right,
both retiring as generals.[3] Prussia was not alone in recruiting children for
service, as other nations had similar practices. British naval officers, for
example, commonly went to sea before the age of ten.

After leaving the army and taking up his post as royal tax collector,
Friedrich von Clausewitz had married Friederike Dorothea Charlotte
Schmidt, the daughter of another official. They had six children—Gustav,
Friedrich, Wilhelm, Charlotte, Carl, and Johanna—all born in Burg,
about eighty miles west of Berlin. Carl von Clausewitz was born on July
1, 1780. Traditionally, June 1 became his accepted birth date. As is clear
in their letters, Clausewitz and Marie celebrated this day; it is also on his
grave. But the parish register in Burg gives July 1, 1780. The reason for this
discrepancy is unknown; there is some speculation that the date was altered
to ease Clausewitz's entry into the army. The details of his name are also
contested. It is often rendered "Carl Philipp Gottlieb von Clausewitz," but
"Carl Philipp Gottfried" von Clausewitz is on his headstone.[4]

The validity of the "von" in the Clausewitz name—the traditional sig-
nifier of Prussian nobility—is also debated. Despite claims to the contrary
from Clausewitz's father, and Carl's apparently sincere beliefs, the family
had staunchly bourgeois roots: pastors, professors, teachers—these were
the professions of Clausewitz forbears. The *von* was an affect, possibly an
attempt by Clausewitz's father to improve his own career possibilities, as
well as those of his sons. What tenuous connection there was to aristocratic
blood came through the second marriage of Clausewitz's widowed grand-
mother to Gustav Detlof von Hundt, who commanded the 34th Infantry
Regiment when Wilhelm entered as an officer cadet in 1787. Clausewitz
could not have joined a distinguished Prussian infantry regiment as an officer cadet without such a noble link.⁵

The fragile claim worried Clausewitz and Wilhelm, as the Prinz
Ferdinand Regiment only accepted nobles as officers. Clausewitz later
confessed to fearing that they would be considered "usurpers" or impos-
tors. He and his brother had made no attempt to deceive, Clausewitz later
maintained, and if anyone dared charge them with mendacity, "we would
have given him an answer with the sword," meaning a challenge to a
duel. Wilhelm fretted enough about their situation to consider seeking a
renewal of their noble status, but he was dissuaded by his friends, as well
as his superior, Ernst Friedrich von Rüchel, who assured him that no one
doubted their nobility and that to raise it at that moment (in the middle of
the Revolutionary War of 1793) would be branded petty.⁶

We know little of Clausewitz's childhood before he entered the army.
He attended the local school in Burg, where he learned, among other sub-
jects, the rudiments of Latin. He also picked up a working knowledge of
French somewhere, which he later brought to fluency while a prisoner of
war in France. He described his overall education, however, as "mediocre."
His father could provide scant help here. "Fortune," Carl once wrote to
Marie, "was my teacher."⁷

What we do know is that even as a child, Clausewitz lived in a military
world. "I am a son of the camp," he had noted. Burg was the home of his
father's old regiment, and writing about himself, Clausewitz insisted that
"he grew up in the Prussian army." His father, a former Prussian officer,
was animated "with the prejudices of his class," and "in his parents' house
he saw almost no one but officers, and not the best educated and most ver-
satile at that." "Until 1800," Clausewitz continued, he "was suckled on no
other opinions than those prevailing in the service: that the Prussian army

and its methods were of surpassing excellence. In short, from the beginning, *national* feeling and even *caste* sentiment were as pronounced and firmly rooted in" him "as the lessons of life can make them."[8] Clausewitz was a Prussian officer to his core.

The Prussian army that Clausewitz entered had rested heavily upon its hard-won laurels of the Seven Years War. Prussia owed its very existence to its army. Carved from disparate provinces scattered from the Rhineland to the too-often sandy reaches of what used to be northern Germany and East Prussia, after 1640 Prussia's rulers counted upon force to keep them independent and expand their domains. The province of Brandenburg formed its core; the Hohenzollern dynasty provided its rulers. The Junkers (nobility) came to provide the officer corps, their peasants the rank and file. The French philosopher Voltaire famously said "Whereas some states possess an army, the Prussian army possesses a state."

When Frederick II came to the throne in 1740, he wasted no time using the army his forefathers had created to expand Prussian power. In December of that year he invaded Austria, where the young Maria Theresa had succeeded to the Habsburg throne, to seize Silesia. The Austrians counterattacked in the spring, and his troops defeated a Habsburg force southeast of Breslau at Mollwitz on April 10, 1741, and at Chotusitz (now Chotsice, east of Prague) on May 17, 1742. The conflict spread after this, becoming the War of Austrian Succession as a coalition of states sought dismemberment of the Habsburg Empire. The separate peace Frederick made with Austria in 1742 won him Silesia. He fought a second round with Vienna beginning in 1744. Launching what he deemed a necessary preventive war to protect Silesia, he scored victories at Hohenfriedberg, Soor, and Kesseldorf. In 1745 he again made peace with Austria in exchange for reconfirmation of his Silesian holdings. The successes of Frederick's tiny Prussia against the formidable Austrians—particularly the speed with which he conducted his operations—stunned Europe.[9]

Tensions between Britain and France erupted into the Seven Years War beginning in 1756. Sloppy diplomacy by Frederick, and the Austrian desire for revenge, congealed to form an anti-Prussian coalition of France, Austria, and Russia. Instead of waiting to be attacked, Frederick struck first, seizing in August 1756 the key German state of Saxony, south of Berlin. The resulting struggle became a war of survival for Prussia as Austria sought to destroy it. British money, coalition mistrust, and what came to be acknowledged as Frederick's own genius enabled Prussia's preservation. At

Rossbach (November 5, 1757) and Prague (May 6, 1757), Frederick, utilizing his superb infantry to make tactically innovative oblique (or flanking) attacks on the enemy, rolled up the troops of his foes at a much lower cost to his own men. Though during this war he suffered as many battlefield defeats as victories, his creativity and energy helped him keep Prussia—and its army—active in what became a long war. The death of the Russian empress Elisabeth in 1762 brought a change of Russian policy, and the signing of a peace the next year.[10]

Later in his reign, Frederick the Great, as he was now known, had decided that as few productive citizens as possible would man his regiment's ranks; they had more important things to do than drill or die in battle. Prussia had a recruiting system in which each canton provided men, but Frederick depended upon foreigners and mercenaries to fill his legions. Nothing changed after his death in 1786 and the succession of his nephew Frederick William II. Nearly half of the fully mobilized Prussian army of 1804 hailed from other lands. The soldiery also had limited preparation. Newly inducted draftees received ten weeks' training, but to save money the state habitually granted all of them extended leaves. The soldiers in garrison were often foreigners whose low pay drove them to take jobs outside their posts.[11]

The officer corps, drawn almost entirely from the nobility, many of whom were non-Prussian, generally placed little value on education. The practice of sending Prussian nobles into the army as children exacerbated this. There were efforts to redress this via the establishment of military schools and a reform of cadet institutions, but the small number of graduates could not change the Prussian army's culture. The few reformers—calling for better education and training—found no audience among their military and political betters. The attitude of Field Marshal Joachim Heinrich von Möllendorf was typical. He responded to the reformers' thrusts with: "This is altogether above my head." Clausewitz later wrote that the Prussian army of 1792 bore little resemblance to that of Frederick the Great. "Its generals and commanding officers had not grown gray in arms, but old and soft in peace," he said, adding: "Military experience had mostly faded, Frederick's spirit no longer coursed through the whole." Clausewitz thought the army decrepit and later branded it one of the least admirable parts of the state.[12]

But such acerbic criticism would not come until much later. Clausewitz did not begin his military career as an officer. Like the other young aspirants, he entered service as a cadet, or lance-corporal. One of his jobs was to carry the unit's colors, but being of fairly slight build, he couldn't bear their weight on the march. Only when the regiment marched through a city would the colors be given to him. In later years he still recalled onlookers staring at "the half-grown boy" laboring under his load.[13]

"My entrance into the world occurred at the scene of great events, where the destiny of nations was decided," Clausewitz later wrote his future wife Marie.[14] In July 1789, three years before Clausewitz entered the army, revolution had erupted in France. Angry crowds famously stormed Paris' Bastille fortress, and in the political upheaval that followed the French went from being subjects of a king to citizens of a republic, and then of an empire. The Revolution would leave no European social or political institution untouched, including, as we shall see, their armies, and it would forever alter how nations fought wars.

The Prussia of 1789 did not immediately see this new, emerging France as a threat. Austria, not France, aroused Prussian fears. "Germany" in this era was a geographical expression, referring to a patchwork of principalities, dukedoms, and kingdoms (many of them loosely organized into the Holy Roman Empire), an arena for political competition among the Great Powers of the day. France was the strongest of these, while the Austrian Empire carried the most influence among the lesser German states. Prussia, however, was the weakest of the three, and saw in the new French regime an opportunity to build an alliance against their traditional Austrian Habsburg foe, weaken Vienna's influence in Germany, and gain commensurate territorial compensation while the Austrians and Russians made gains at the expense of the Ottoman Turks.[15]

The new Austrian emperor, Leopold II, facing disorder in Hungary, as well as in the Austrian-controlled areas of the Low Countries, decided *rapprochement* with Prussia was Austria's wisest course. His efforts led to a treaty, signed on July 27, 1790, that ended half a century of antagonism between the two dominant German states, while providing the catalyst for shifting Prussia against the French. The Prussian king, Frederick William II, drew closer to Vienna, and on August 27, 1791, the two states signed the Declaration of Pillnitz, aligning them against the French.[16]

The French, in turn, saw a conspiracy forming among Prussia, Austria, and French Royalist émigrés based in the Rhineland—one aimed clearly at them—and feared an invasion. Actually, however, the Austrians and Prussians made plans to snatch up some of the smaller states on the western edge of the Holy Roman Empire, with Prussia planning to gain Jülich and Berg from the southwestern German state of the Palatinate. Pressure mounted in Paris to embark upon a foreign war and spread the Revolution. On April 20, 1792, the French declared war on Austria.[17] What became known as the War of the First Coalition had begun.

Overall, it was a slapdash affair on both sides. The French armies were at best improvised rabble, the Revolution having destroyed the pre-1789 force. After declaring war, the Assembly ruling France ordered the Army of the North into the Austrian Netherlands. They were quickly repelled. A three-month lull descended over the combatants. The French adopted a cordon defense consisting of four forces. The Army of the North covered the region from the Channel to the Meuse River; the so-called Army of the Center protected the area from the Meuse to the Vosges Mountains; the Army of the Rhine secured Alsace; and the southeast was held by the Army of the Midi.[18]

The coalition force of Austrians, Prussians, and a small French Royalist detachment proved equally incompetent and mistake-prone. Command of the Prussian units fell to Karl Wilhelm Ferdinand, Duke of Brunswick-Wolfenbüttel—better known as the Duke of Brunswick, one of the most distinguished military men of his day—whom the French had unsuccessfully attempted to recruit to lead their armies. Brunswick, a nephew of Frederick the Great, was a general cut from eighteenth-century cloth. His successful 1787 campaign of maneuver in Holland—one with very little fighting—had made his reputation as a commander (Clausewitz later wrote a history of the campaign). The coalition planned a three-pronged drive into France, but they were slow to start and the Austrians never produced the number of men they had promised. The offensive culminated at Valmy on September 20, 1792. Here, Brunswick's attacking force of 30,000 was repulsed by 64,000 French. Brunswick, after a council of war, said: "We will not strike here." The Prussians withdrew. His refusal to attack the French did not injure his reputation as it might have in a later era—imagine Napoleon, Lee, or Patton proposing the same thing. Brunswick's contemporaries, however, considered it completely logical. Nevertheless, Clausewitz later criticized the assumptions underlying the actions of Austria and Prussia. "We will hardly find a more erroneous standard of measurement in history than that applied in 1792. It was expected that a moderate auxiliary corps would be enough to end a civil war; but the colossal weight of the whole French people, unhinged by political fanaticism, came crashing down on us."[19]

The Allies had underestimated their enemy and failed to commit enough troops to the campaign. They were also weak at the decisive point, which Valmy proved to be; attrition had weakened the Prussians by the time they reached the battle. Moreover, Poland had heated up. The Russians sent in troops in May 1792, taking advantage of the Austro-Prussian distraction in the West. The Prussians lost their focus on France as they became involved in the partition of Poland, hoping to ensure that they received a generous portion of the spoils.[20]

The failure at Valmy indeed proved serious, as Clausewitz asserted, and the French victory and Allied withdrawal had far-reaching effects. "The wars of kings were at an end; the wars of peoples were beginning," French Field Marshal Ferdinand Foch wrote more than a century later about Valmy. The War of the First Coalition and the Allied failure resulted in the execution of the French king and queen, allowed the French to conquer Belgium and Holland, and inaugurated two-and-a-half decades of continuous European conflict.[21]

The French responded to the victory at Valmy with an immediate, three-pronged counteroffensive. On September 21, 1792, as the Allied armies began retreating from France, the French Army of the Midi attacked the Italian state of Sardinia-Piedmont. This led to the annexation of Savoy and Nice to France. Meanwhile, the Army of the Vosges (14,000 troops) invaded the Palatinate in what is now southwestern Germany, and kept going. The Rhine cities began to fall: Speyer on September 30, Worms on October 4, Mainz on October 21, followed by Frankfurt-am-Main on the 23rd (which the French held for five weeks). The French, however, didn't know what to do with their territorial gains. Having gone to war without any long-term political objectives in mind, they decided that they needed some, coming up with the notion that France's natural boundaries in the east were the Rhine and the Alps. By the spring of 1793 an extensive coalition had arrayed itself against the French and their territorial ambitions. Austria, Prussia, and Great Britain were chief among them, but Spain, Sardinia-Piedmont, Naples (the Kingdom of the Two Sicilies), most of Italy, the Dutch Republic, and the loose patchwork of German states under Austrian guidance joined as well.[22]

In January 1793 Clausewitz marched off to his first war as his regiment moved westward to meet the French forces on the Rhine. Clausewitz's regiment shelled the town of Ginsheim on the Rhine's eastern bank on February 2, Clausewitz's first taste of combat. He was twelve years old. Later, in *On War*, he gave a picture of the journeyman soldier's first experience of battle: "To someone who has never experienced danger, the idea is attractive rather than alarming. You charge the enemy, ignoring the bullets and casualties, in a surge of excitement. Blindly you hurl yourself toward icy death, not knowing whether you or anyone else will escape him. Before you lies that golden prize, victory, the fruit that quenches the thirst of ambition. Can that be so difficult? No, and it will seem even less difficult than it is. But such moments are rare; and even they are not, as is commonly thought, brief like a heartbeat, but come rather like a medicine, in recurring doses, the taste is diluted by time."[23]

The Prussians on the Rhine front (Clausewitz among them) served in an army some 99,000 strong, commanded by Brunswick. Aiming at Mainz, Brunswick's men pushed into the Rhineland on March 21, 1793. The French withdrew most of their troops from the region in April, but left a garrison of 22,000 holding the fortress city of Mainz. The Prussian king detached troops for a siege. Clausewitz's unit reached Mainz on March 23.[24]

Mainz sits on the western bank of the Rhine, cradled in a river bend that protects two sides of the town. A brick barrier flanked by two bastions sheltered its river side. The western defenses of the city rested upon a series of fourteen fortified, connected bastions, some protected by water-filled ditches, ramparts, and moats. Digging the zig-zag approaches common in siege warfare of the day would be difficult because in some places the fortifications dominated the terrain. A citadel added additional strength, as did the French possession of some of the surrounding villages such as Weissenau and Zahlbach, around which they hastily raised fortifications. Antoine-Henri Jomini, for one, judged Mainz difficult to take, as it offered few approaches for the attackers.[25]

On March 31 the Allies closed the ring around Mainz. But any assault was delayed as the necessary Austrian artillery went instead to the Belgium–Holland front, which Vienna considered more important. The Allies had approximately 33,000 men in the besieging force, though Jomini argued they needed 50,000 to do it properly. Nevertheless, the attackers did succeed in destroying the river locks as well as the mills that fed the garrison and Mainz's citizens. The French conducted an active defense, making frequent and often large-scale sorties against their besiegers. On the night of May 30 they sent 6,000 men—unsuccessfully—against the village of Marienborn at the center of the Allied lines, the site of the Prussian headquarters.[26]

The fighting around Mainz involved Allied efforts to reduce the French defense, which hinged on the fortified bastions and villages on the outskirts of the city. Clausewitz's regiment participated in at least one of the attacks designed to tighten the grip on the city. On June 6 the Prinz Ferdinand Regiment (Clausewitz's) successfully assaulted the trenches of Zahlbach in fighting that one author describes as "fierce."[27]

After two months of delays, the attack on Mainz began in earnest when on the night of June 19, after some initial abortive attempts, the Allied attackers began digging the first of three parallels of trenches to encircle and then undermine the city's defenses. The main attack came against Mainz's southwest.[28]

There is scant surviving information on the actions of Clausewitz and his unit at the fighting for Mainz, but much that relays the violence of the siege. This phase of Clausewitz's first war also had a particularly famous observer, Johann Wolfgang von Goethe. Goethe rode in the retinue of Duke Carl August, the ruler of his homeland of Saxe-Weimar, and the commander of a Prussian regiment. Goethe did not go eagerly; his patron insisted upon his company. On June 24 Goethe watched the French try to force out the sick and civilian inhabitants of the city to preserve their food supplies. "They were," he wrote, "just as cruelly turned back by our side." When not watching the fighting, he worked on *Reynard the Fox*, his version of the famous animal tale.[29]

On June 27, 1793, the Allied bombardment commenced. The cathedral's meeting house was immediately engulfed in flames. The shelling continued. By the next day the flames consumed the cathedral and the houses around it. "We watched this terrible spectacle from the redoubt in front of the Marienborn," Goethe wrote; "the night was absolutely clear and full of stars, the bombs seemed to vie with the heavenly lights, and there were moments when it was really impossible to distinguish between the two." The ongoing siege became a spectacle, and on Sundays and holidays the local peasants would visit one of the redoubts and watch the attackers' progress, dressed in their Sunday best and still carrying rosaries and prayer books.[30]

The first parallel (a trench line running in line with the enemy's works) was completed on July 4, allowing fifty-eight guns to intensify the bombardment. Soon, the shelling took a toll on the city. At the beginning of the night of July 6 the Prussians under General Franz Kasimir von Kleist

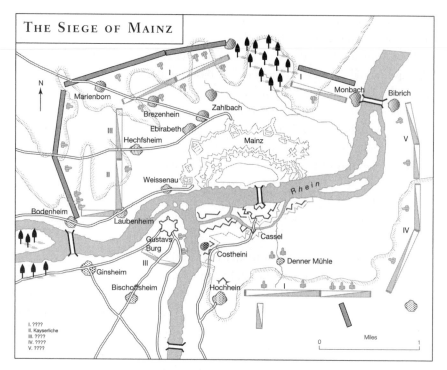

Map 1.1. The Siege of Mainz.

attacked the Zahlbach redoubt, which was taken and destroyed. "This operation permitted then the opening of the left of the second parallel, and assured this position for a flank and a redoubt." On July 7 Clausewitz's unit stormed the Zahlbach Heights.[31]

On the night of July 12 the second parallel was begun. On the 17th the Prussians assaulted the flèches—the most forward posts—of the Italian Trenches, as one part of the defenses was called. By this time much of the outer works had been wrecked and the continuous cannonade wrought great devastation upon the city. Flames illuminated the night. An etching based on a 1793 painting shows a column of flame rising from the city. "As Mainz was destroyed by fire," Clausewitz wrote a decade and a half later, "one that we had kindled; my own childish voice was added to the cheers of the rough soldiers."[32]

At Ginsheim, Clausewitz had seen shots fired in anger for the first time. The fighting around Mainz introduced him to the intensity of battle. Later, he ruminated on how this feels:

Let us accompany a novice to the battlefield. As we approach the rumble of guns grows louder and alternates with the whir of cannonballs, which begin to attract his attention. Shots begin to strike close around us. We hurry up the slope where the commanding general is stationed with his large staff. Here cannonballs and bursting shells are frequent, and life begins to seem more serious than the young man had imagined. Suddenly someone you know is wounded; then a shell falls among the staff. You notice that some of the officers act a little oddly; you yourself are not as steady and collected as you were: even the bravest can become slightly distracted. Now we enter the battle raging before us, still almost like a spectacle, and join the nearest divisional commander. Shot is falling like hail, and the thunder of our own guns adds to the din. Forward to the brigadier, a soldier of acknowledged bravery, but he is careful to take cover behind a rise, a house or a clump of trees. A noise is heard that is a certain indication of increasing danger—the rattling of grapeshot on roofs and on the ground. Cannonballs tear past, whizzing in all directions, and musketballs begin to whistle around us. A little further we reach the firing line, where the infantry endures the hammering for hours with incredible steadfastness. The air is filled with hissing bullets that sound like a sharp crack if they pass close to one's head. For a final shock, the sight of men being killed and mutilated moves our pounding hearts to awe and pity.[33]

On the night of July 14–15, Allied cannon fire from the opposite bank of the Rhine hit a munitions factory. The explosion shattered windows and shutters and toppled chimneys. In the midst of the fight, on July 20, 1793, Clausewitz received his commission as ensign; he was now technically a Prussian officer; he was barely thirteen years old.[34]

After an obstinate four-month defense, lacking medicine for the sick and fodder for his horses, and with a scarcity of food glaring at him, the French general, François d'Oyre, determined he could no longer continue. He arranged their capitulation with Generalleutnant Friedrich Adolf von Kalkreuth at the Allied camp at Marienborn on July 22, 1793, and surrendered the city, the castle, and all the fortifications to Prussia. The victors recognized the bravery of the defenders by granting them free passage with all military honors—as well as their weapons and baggage—under the condition that they would not serve against the Allied powers for one year. The French losses in killed, wounded, and missing were more than 5,000, the Allies' more than 3,000. The Prussians counted 88 officers and 1,579 men killed.[35]

The siege had ended, but the campaign continued. The Allied armies launched an offensive aimed at seizing the heavily wooded Saar region in present-day southwestern Germany. To support this, the Prussian army—Clausewitz's unit in its advance guard—plunged into the adjacent Vosges, the range of low mountains on the west side of the Rhine traversing some of the southernmost areas of the Franco-German frontier. Clausewitz found his surroundings uninteresting and later delighted in leaving them. "I still remember with much pleasure one such moment which I had in 1793 when the Prussian army left the Vosges Mountains. We were half a year in this very same extremely wooded and rough, poor, and melancholy mountain course, and with a kind of resignation the eye had already become accustomed to only seeing a few steps of the path we followed... An extremely limited horizon allowed the soldiers scarcely to look beyond the next hours of their existence, often meeting his ear is the voice of battle, close to him, yet invisible, and he goes toward his fate like a danger in the dark night."[36]

The Austrians and Prussians refused to coordinate their actions, a general weakness of the Allied coalition on all fronts. Indeed, this failure might have saved France. A campaign of skirmishes ensued amongst the hills, small peaks, and primeval woods, one in which the commanders on either side dared little. Operationally, one might call it a "War of Posts" or "War of Positions," as the Duke of Brunswick generally put his now 45,000 men to holding key spots in the Vosges and the area between the Rhine, Mosel, and Saar Rivers. Doctrinally, in some respects the execution of the campaign became an example of what eighteenth-century soldiers called *Petite Guerre*, "Little War," or as Clausewitz knew it, *kleiner Krieg, Kleinkrieg,* or *Parteigängerkrieg*.[37] An American or Englishman of the era would have dubbed it "Partisan War," implying modern guerrilla war, though they are not the same thing. "Partisan War" meant fighting on a small scale: units parry the enemy, nibble at him, rather than trying to annihilate him. The intent is to hit outposts, messengers, supply lines, and smaller enemy forces, wearing down the enemy. It was generally practiced by light infantry and cavalry units, though militia could be effective tools. If "Partisan War" is sometimes confused with modern guerrilla warfare today it is because the tactics can be similar. The eighteenth-century "Partisan" was generally a regular soldier, fighting in an established unit in a regular army within the confines of the many doctrinal manuals and practices of his day. The modern guerrilla, in contrast, is usually an irregular—a non-state actor—a revolutionary determined to overthrow a ruling system or someone resisting an occupying power. Clausewitz observed the birth of the modern guerrilla in Spain and other places in war-torn Europe, and as we will see, he became one of the first to blend the practices of both in plans for Prussia to resist French occupation. Later, when teaching tactics to junior officers, he lectured extensively on "Little War," sometimes drawing upon his experiences in his first campaign, as well as the memoirs of Germans who had served in the War for American Independence.[38]

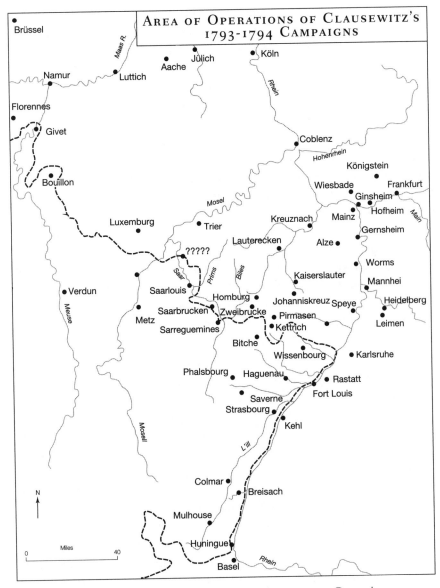

Map 1.2. The Area of Operations of Clausewitz's 1793–1794 Campaigns.

The Prussian campaign was but one challenge besetting the French at the end of the eighteenth century. August 1793 proved a pivotal month for the revolutionary regime's survival, as well as the history of warfare itself. Austrian armies based in Belgium had crossed the French frontier, while the Prussians, after reducing Mainz, invaded from the east. The Spanish had crossed the Pyrenees and scored victories on French soil. Counterrevolutionary forces in France had also arisen, particularly in the west, in the Vendée, where conscription had ignited an earlier explosion. Toulon, Marseilles, and Lyon had also fallen to opponents of the regime. The Revolutionaries became desperate. On August 23, 1793, the National Convention ruling France took the final step in the march to modern warfare it had embarked upon in 1792: it declared a *levée en masse*. From this point on, every resource, every person, every possession and animal in France became a tool of the state for the prosecution of the war. As historian T. C. W. Blanning put it succinctly: "by the summer of 1793 all the elements of revolutionary warfare were finally in place. To France it brought the Terror, to Europe it brought conquest, to the Revolution it brought salvation."[39]

The key element of the French decree was the establishment of a mass army based on conscription drawn from the entire population, an act contributing to the overturning of the traditional European military and social order. Eighteenth-century armies were small, generally professional organizations in the sense that those who served in them often did so for a long time. Noblemen dominated the officer class. Often—particularly in Prussia, as we've seen—"undesirables" and foreigners made up the enlisted ranks. The armies were tightly controlled to limit the rampant desertion that plagued all European armed forces.[40]

Before the Revolution the political objectives for which wars were fought were almost always limited, meaning something less than the overthrow of the enemy regime or the annexation of their nation. Raisons d'etat, not ideology, drove formulation of political objectives. The mark of superior generalship was the ability to fight a campaign of maneuver, and pitched battles were something to be avoided. Battles, when fought, were dominated tactically by volley fire from tight ranks of flintlock-armed men and by the bayonet. Casualties of 30 to 50 percent were not unusual, a fact fueling a general's reluctance to come to grips with the foe. If one scored a victory, there was seldom any significant pursuit of the defeated because the victor risked desertion in his own ranks just as he did on the march. The population of the nation—the people—were also not a factor in the calculations of rulers. War was the realm of kings, not of their subjects.⁴¹

The French Revolution and its *levée en masse* changed this. It unleashed what Clausewitz would later call the "passions of the people." Now the energy of the nation's inhabitants—especially their willingness to support and sacrifice for the war effort—became a critical element of its ability to wage war, as well as the manner. "Looking at the situation in this conventional manner," Clausewitz wrote about the French Revolution's alteration of the nature and practice of European warfare, "people at first expected to have to deal only with a seriously weakened French army; but in 1793 a force appeared that beggared all imagination. Suddenly war again became the business of the people—a people of thirty millions [*sic*], all of whom considered themselves to be citizens." This distinction is critical, as the people of the other European states were subjects—not citizens— which gave them less of a vested interest in the affairs of their ruling state, and sometimes even its very survival. Clausewitz continued: "The people became a participant in war; instead of governments and armies as heretofore, the full weight of the nation was thrown into the balance." "War," he wrote, "untrammeled by any conventional restraints, had broken loose in all its elemental fury. This was due to the peoples' new share in these great affairs of state; and their participation, in turn, resulted partly from the impact that the Revolution had on the internal conditions of every state and partly from the danger that France posed to everyone." The French Revolution intensified warfare by unleashing the passion of the people so long contained by governments that had sought only limited aims. The impact of the French Revolution upon Europe in this era and upon Clausewitz was profound, and proved the critical catalytic event for his theories on warfare.⁴²

Political change drove—indeed, made possible—the evolution of military tactics and doctrine, and resulted in much larger armies, organizational changes Clausewitz later analyzed in *On War*. The armies of the *Ancien Régime* (the pre-Revolutionary era) had large baggage trains; these started shrinking during the Revolutionary Wars as armies began abandoning tents. An army of 100,000 men had required 6,000 horses just to move its shelters. Additional artillery and cavalry were seen as better uses of horsepower. The baggage trains shrank even further when armies began foraging to fill much of their supply needs. Clausewitz points out that this did not increase the daily march rates from the wars of the eighteenth century—something one might expect—because since the men had to spend part of their day foraging, it could diminish its range. Moreover, traditionally, the baggage trains had moved on different routes from the armies, and thus did not affect the march rates, an argument Clausewitz buttresses by comparing those in the Seven Years War and the Napoleonic Wars, and finding no real difference. But the new method did confer advantages. Flexibility and mobility were increased, and armies no longer had to worry about protecting their baggage, which gave them more options when choosing where to fight.[43] Finally, and most importantly, armies also increased nearly exponentially in size, reaching a scale almost impossible to maintain under the old system.

The French Revolutionary armies also instituted important tactical changes. Before the Revolution, European infantry fought according to very similar linear tactics. The Great Powers deployed their units for battle in formations three-men deep that were essentially gigantic rectangles and concentrated fire on the opponent; the British used a formation only two ranks deep. But the large, often improvised armies of the French Revolution often lacked the training necessary to form, maneuver, and fight in these tight formations. The French responded by using many of their men as skirmishers in loose order. They would pour harassing and pinning fire into the enemy while other infantry, packed into tight columns, or drawn up in line, advanced behind them. The French would use the columns to mount attacks. Other nations eventually adopted various forms of French tactics (which were not static) and usually trained the third rank of their infantry to fight as skirmishers, but for a time the French possessed a tactical edge.[44]

The armies also included artillery and cavalry arms. They used artillery to soften up the enemy for an attack and to defend their own forces. The guns fired solid shot cannonballs, which could pass through a number of targets— i.e., people—and would bounce when hitting solid ground. Canister and grapeshot rounds turned cannon into giant shotguns, each spraying its victims with thousands of lead balls. Cavalry did reconnaissance and guarded the flanks, and was often held in reserve until it could be launched at the enemy at the key moment of a battle, preferably accompanied by its horse artillery. Infantry facing a cavalry charge would form into squares, counting upon their firepower, mass, and bayonets to protect them from the horsemen. But if the cavalry could bring up its guns, they could blast gaps in the squares and ride down the infantry. Cavalry also became indispensable for pursuing a defeated enemy army, making it theoretically possible to destroy a defeated foe. The three arms—infantry, artillery, cavalry—each also came to possess various subtypes developed for specific tasks.

As the war on Clausewitz's front continued, Brunswick's troops, including Clausewitz's regiment, soon took up a position at Pirmasens, on the western edge of the Vosges Mountains, about six miles northeast of the present-day German-French frontier. On August 16–17, 1793, they made a rare night march to attack a French brigade holding the Kettrich Heights two hours away. The Prussians opened fire at dawn, the enemy fleeing after the first cannonade. Brunswick returned to his camp in the Hüster Heights north of Pirmasens after destroying the entrenchments, leaving eighty men to hold Kettrich. These proved insufficient; the French attacked and retook the Kettrich Heights on the 20th. Clausewitz's regiment helped Brunswick chase them away the same day, before they could rebuild the works. The post was then occupied by an infantry brigade and the fortifications strengthened. Brunswick, in anticipation of further attacks, secured positions south and west of Pirmasens.[45] Such actions typified Clausewitz's first campaign.

By September, the French began pushing back, encouraged by the lack of Prussian activity (Brunswick had kept the right wing of his army sitting for seven weeks). On September 14 the French made a serious attempt against Pirmasens, hitting it with about 12,000 men. Brunswick, however, had predicted their move. The French attacked in three columns and were bloodily repulsed. The Prussians had about 7,000 men engaged in the fight, Clausewitz among them, and lost nine officers and 154 men. French losses were 800 dead and 1,800 prisoners.[46]

Afterward Brunswick began shifting his army to his intended winter quarters, spreading them in posts stretching roughly sixty miles—much of it through the Vosges—from Wissenbourg on the current Franco-German border in the south, through Kaiserslautern, to the village of Lauterecken fifteen miles north. Twenty-three thousand men of Brunswick's command reached Kaiserslautern on November 23, 1793. The French, having replaced their commanders in the theater, pushed against both Brunswick's Prussians and the Austrians farther south. They attacked the Prussians at the end of November at Kaiserslautern, where Brunswick dealt them another defeat. The French then decided to ignore the slow-moving Brunswick and concentrate on the Austrians. Under pressure, the Austrians abandoned Alsace. Clausewitz's unit fought three small actions at Lembach in December, and the Prussian army then pulled back to the west bank of the Rhine and went into winter quarters.[47]

Clausewitz's body suffered badly in the back-and-forth of the campaign. Two of his regiment's three young ensigns died because of its rigors and Clausewitz noted that it was generally believed that the third—himself—would soon join them. Clausewitz wrote later of his joy at making an escape from the region: "Finally, after a laborious march, we stood suddenly on one of the last of the Vosges chain and had the beautiful Rhine Valley from Landau to Wurms before and below us. At that moment life seemed to me to move from gloomy seriousness to friendliness, from tears to smiles."[48]

The campaign reopened in the spring of 1794, though the bulk of the fighting between the French and the coalition—as well as the most important—took place in Belgium and Holland. Clausewitz's unit fought at the battle of Kaiserslautern on May 23, an Allied success, and was probably in eight other actions by the end of July.[49]

On July 7, at Leimen (near Heidelberg), a vastly superior French force attacked the lead company of Clausewitz's regiment, which kept up its fire for several hours and held its post, then returned once again to the rough Vosges to fence with the French. The regiment's first battalion fought at Johanniskreuz on July 13, throwing back the superior attacking enemy until a general retreat took place. This was the regiment's last action of the war. Clausewitz later noted that in one of these July 1794 battles (which one is unclear), "I found myself in a fierce fight in a bad position from which I luckily escaped." He was only fourteen at the time.[50]

Nothing in this back-and-forth campaign affected the larger strategic picture. The *levée en masse* enabled French leaders to tap their nation's full financial and manpower resources and use the war machine created to crush their internal and external foes. Early 1795 saw Belgium and Holland in French hands, as well as the Rhine's left bank (the last Prussians crossed the river in late October 1794), with the Allies holding only the fortresses of Mainz and Luxembourg. Clausewitz wrote later that "The defensive outpost-and-cordon system was pushed to the limit in both campaigns. That the Prussian forces did not suffer more heavily for employing such a system was the fault of the poor quality of the armies that opposed them." In *On War* he wrote that the Allies' actions foreshadowed their future fate while demonstrating that they did not understand the forces the French Revolution had unleashed. "Not only did the allies, in the campaign itself, completely fail to recognize the powerful nature of the enemy offensive, trying to counter it with a paltry system of extended positions and strategic maneuver, but it is evident from the political squabbles between Prussia and Austria, and the foolish abandonment of Belgium and the Netherlands, that the governments involved had no idea of the fury of the oncoming torrent." Archduke Charles, a famous Austrian officer and writer, offered a similar after-action report. However, he believed the defeat of the 1793 coalition was due to the failures of the Allies, not the virtues of the French. "Austria and Prussia were divided not just by the conduct of the war in north-west Europe but also by their competition for the territory offered by the partition of Poland."[51]

The campaign also marked other coming changes. From 1792 to 1815 Europeans fought 713 battles. The previous three centuries had seen only 2,659. The French Revolutionary government of 1794 (the National Convention with its de facto executive branch, the Committee of Public Safety), and its 1794 insistence on the offensive, was one of the major reasons for this change in military intensity.[52]

Nonetheless, long before the campaign drifted to its end, Prussian king Frederick William II had revealed his lack of interest in the western war by departing the theater for Poland on August 29, 1793. The partition of Poland—and Prussia receiving its share, as we've seen—mattered far more. Only the Prussian commitment to their Allies kept them in the war in any way. They were even more eager to make peace with France after the dictator Robespierre was overthrown and "The Terror" was replaced by a more rational French regime in July 1794. The negotiations began in December, but went on until April, when a treaty was signed on the night of April 5–6, 1795. Prussia's defection led the Dutch and Spanish to follow suit in the spring and summer. For Berlin, the agreement brought peace with France for the next eleven years.[53]

Thirty years later, while writing *On War,* Clausewitz offered his own bitter assessment of the fecklessness of Prussian political behavior here and in the days following: "The energy needed for deceit and cunning, for consequential dishonesty, was lacking. Prussia concluded the Peace of Basel, left her former allies in the lurch, now and then fawned on the French but lacked the courage to make common cause with them."[54]

2

The Ambitious Student of War
(1795–1805)

Critical analysis is not just an evaluation of the means actually employed, but of *all possible means*—which first have to be formulated, that is, invented. One can, after all, not condemn a method without being able to suggest a better alternative.

Carl von Clausewitz was driven to succeed as a child, and this only intensified once he reached adulthood. He was blunt regarding his own abundance of "that vanity which we call ambition." This, he later told Marie, was one of only two active elements of his youthful inner life. The other began in the spring of 1795 when his regiment marched out of the Rhineland into Westphalia and into cantonment near Osnabrück in the county of Tecklenburg, there to await the peace. Here, he lived for three or four months, billeted upon a peasant family. "All of a sudden," Clausewitz wrote later, "removed from the scene of the war, put in the quiet of a country life in all its significance, for the first time my gaze turned inward." Proximity to Onasbrück meant books, and Clausewitz began to read. "Accidentally, some Illuminati writings and other books on the perfectibility of man fell into my hands. Here suddenly the vanity of the little soldier became intense philosophical ambition and then I found myself at the time as close to rapture as the nature of a mind that has no propensity toward this. Were this ember, however, better preserved and used by me, I would perhaps have become a good deal better than I am." Clausewitz had discovered the Enlightenment, and more importantly, his own intellect—but would have to wait for the chance to feed it to his liking.[1]

Figure 2.1. Napoleon Bonaparte (1769–1821).
LC-DIG-npcc-19687. National Photo Company Collection, Library of Congress Prints and
Photographs Division, Washington, D.C.

In the summer of 1795, sixteen-year-old Sekonde-lieutenant Clausewitz
(he had been promoted on March 5) returned with his regiment to their garrison in Neuruppin. Clausewitz didn't like being, as he put it, "squeezed"
into a small and isolated garrison and surrounded by those whom he considered quite ordinary. The only distinction he felt was his inclination toward
thought and literature, and his burning military ambition. This appeared
to him the last spark of an old fire, one that "seemed more of a hindrance
than beneficial in my inner development, as long as there seemed no means
to satisfy it." In reality, Neuruppin was not as physically and intellectually
isolated as Clausewitz later insisted. It had been the home of Frederick the
Great when he was Crown Prince and was only forty miles from Berlin.

A Prussian officer would have far preferred a posting to Neuruppin than one in the newly acquired Polish lands. Clausewitz wrote these comments in 1807 as a prisoner of war in France, a desperately unhappy time for him, of which we will soon learn more.[2]

Clausewitz soon settled into the routines of a junior officer of his day. He took his turn commanding the camp guards, and spent four to five hours daily drilling his men in core tactical routines such as practicing loading and reloading their smoothbore, muzzle-loading muskets to develop the ability to produce quick, uniform volleys of fire. Unusually, Clausewitz took the time to train his men in skirmish tactics, an innovation then on the rise, and a loose-order break with the severe linearism of the then current practice. Clausewitz also participated in the regular army maneuvers. Later, reflecting upon this time, especially in light of his combat experience in 1806, he pronounced Prussia's peacetime training unrealistic. "How then would it have been possible, with a little reflection, not to realize that the autumn maneuvers in Potsdam and Berlin were totally unlike the war we had fought?" These mock battles—a waste of time—were "carried out by the most distinguished men of the army . . . with an all-absorbing seriousness and intensity that bordered on weakness." He had, however, he maintained, begun to feel the "spirit of independent judgment" awaken in him.[3]

Clausewitz took leave for six weeks in the summer of 1797 to journey to Poland with his step-uncle, Major-General Johann Christian von Hundt. Here he saw Poles and Polish society for the first time, developing a prejudice against both that never left him. But in other respects, his intellectual development continued under the guidance of his superiors. Colonel Friedrich Wilhelm Alexander von Tschammer und Osten, the commander of Clausewitz's regiment, firmly believed in education for all under his care, even the sons and daughters of this regiment's men, for whom he set up a garrison industrial school to provide technical job training in skills such as spinning. Tschammer saw education as more than accumulating facts. In his view, a soldier lacking judgment was little better than a beast. In 1799 he established a course of instruction for his lance-corporals and ensigns; Clausewitz, though a lieutenant, attended some of these. The school was run by an educated officer named Major von Sydow, who, in a not-unusual discussion of his day, "distinguished between raw and educated courage." Clausewitz's discussion of military genius in *On War* has some similarities. His time in Neuruppin was also possibly Clausewitz's first introduction to the value of theory to the soldier, something critical in many of his works. Theory "is meant to educate the mind of the future commander," he later wrote, and he came to see the bond between the pair: "A critic should never use the results of theory as laws and standards, but only—as the soldier does—as *aids to judgment*."[4]

During his time in Neuruppin, Clausewitz's superiors developed high opinions of the youthful subaltern. His evaluation for 1799 deemed him "an excellent young man, useful and eager in service, [who] has intelligence, and seeks to gain knowledge of all kinds." The next year's noted that "his conduct is good, in every consideration [he] is a very good officer, has intelligence, and seeks to acquire knowledge." The one for 1801, though he had departed for Berlin, was similar: "His conduct is very good; he is a good officer who seeks to acquire knowledge."[5]

Between the time of Clausewitz's arrival in the Vosges in 1793 and his departure for Berlin in late 1801, the political and military landscape of Europe was irrevocably altered. A young French general of Corsican descent named Napoleon Bonaparte waged a stunning campaign in Italy in 1796–97. The War of the First Coalition ended in 1797, but the War of the Second Coalition against France (1798–1801)—one Prussia sat out—immediately followed. Despite an abortive campaign in Egypt beginning in 1798, Napoleon's previous military successes had raised him to the precipice of power. In 1799 he launched a coup against France's unpopular rulers, the Directory.

Napoleon immediately began consolidating his political position at home, but understood that his rule depended upon what happened on the battlefield. Harnessing the passion of the French citizen unleashed by the Revolution, his own political determination and drive to dominate, the efficient, innovative, and well-led tool that became known as *le Grande Armée*, and a little of his own military genius, Napoleon made France the dominant power in Europe, and himself emperor.

In 1800 Napoleon led the French army across the Alps and into Italy in a campaign that culminated in the defeat of the Austrians at Marengo in June. Afterward, in 1801 and 1802, Napoleon negotiated a pair of treaties that brought peace, but this was short lived. France next fought the War of the Third Coalition against Britain, Russia, and Austria. Napoleon conducted what is known as the Ulm campaign in the fall of 1805, which climaxed in his decisive victory over the Austro-Russian army at Austerlitz on December 2 of that year. The reordering of Italy and Germany followed, a political transformation that shifted the balance of power on the continent in France's favor. Austerlitz also ensured that Napoleon would always be remembered as one of history's greatest generals.

G.D.v.Scharnhorst.

Figure 2.2. Gerhard von Scharnhorst (1755–1813).
LC-USZ62-58870. Library of Congress Prints and Photographs Division, Washington, D.C.

The new century also brought with it a fresh opportunity for Clausewitz, and a bigger field for his own driving ambition: In the fall of 1801 he went to Berlin to attend the General Military College. Here he found his intellectual light: Gerhard Johann David von Scharnhorst. "He is," Clausewitz wrote, "the father and friend of my spirit."[6]

Scharnhorst, like many of those in Prussian service, was not Prussian by birth. He was born on March 12, 1755, in Bordenau, Hanover, the second child of a peasant farmer who had served as a Hanoverian supply sergeant during the War of Austrian Succession (1740–1748). Scharnhorst received no formal education until his entry in August 1773 into the military academy of Count Friedrich Wilhelm Ernst zu Schaumburg-Lippe-Bückeberg, in Wilhemstein. The count, born in England, was fluent in six languages and a veteran combat soldier. He was also very forward thinking. A writer on military affairs, he argued that the best way for small states to protect themselves was through universal conscription and alliances, particularly with states similarly small—revolutionary ideas in an age of absolutist rulers, but ones he applied to his own state of Schaumburg-Lippe, as a volunteer militia supplemented the army. His ideas suggest what was to come. He also taught Scharnhorst and his other students to think broadly about the profession of arms. The count's approach, Scharnhorst insisted, stayed with him throughout his life.[7]

Scharnhorst entered the Hanoverian army as an ensign in July 1778. He was lucky to serve under a commander who believed in education as well as practical experience and who almost immediately appointed the youthful Scharnhorst a teacher at the regimental school. In less than a year Scharnhorst headed instruction and went on to build a reputation as a military writer and intellectual, publishing journals as well as books on military affairs. Scharnhorst stressed the study of history, believing one can learn from past military experience, but also believed in practical, realistic military training and experience. Classroom instruction, personal study, realistic training, experience: to Scharnhorst, these made the soldier—not just the officer.[8]

Scharnhorst, like Clausewitz, saw his first combat in the War of the First Coalition. His experience convinced him of the necessity of the people being supportive of the war, a break from the view that war was the province of princes and kings and their armies. Scharnhorst's personal bravery in the war solidified his reputation, but his lack of noble status limited his options in Hanoverian service.[9]

After the war he pushed for reforms of the Hanoverian army. These included competitive exams for commissions and education for both the officers and non-commissioned officers, and officer promotion by merit. He also suggested many other reforms based upon the military changes being generated by the French Revolution. His superiors weren't interested, so Scharnhorst sought employment elsewhere. He entered Prussian service as a lieutenant-colonel of artillery on May 12, 1801. His ennoblement was part of the agreement, as only this gave him a chance to serve as an equal to other Prussian officers, as well as a possibility of pressing his ideas.[10]

Soon after taking up his new position, Scharnhorst asked to be given charge of the Berlin Institute in the Military Sciences for Young Infantry

Officers. There were only two permanent instructors: Professor Johann
Gottfried Kiesewetter, a devotee of the philosopher Immanuel Kant,
and Major Ludwig Christian Müller. The institute was one of six schools
founded in 1779 by Frederick the Great in the large garrisons for their
related military districts. They had no degree programs; officers attended
a variety of courses running from November to February on such top-
ics as mathematics and tactics. On September 5, 1801, Frederick William
III named Scharnhorst superintendent. Within a month, Scharnhorst proposed a plan to make the school Prussia's premier military college, which
Frederick William approved on October 6, 1801.[11]

Scharnhorst reorganized the curriculum so that the three-year course
ran from October to April. The school included practical courses on mathematics and artillery, including live-fire exercises, as well as instruction in
the tactical and strategic ideas and theories of the day and logic. Scharnhorst
determined to shape the practical and philosophical sides of his students.
He would teach them not only what to do as soldiers on the battlefield, but
more importantly, how to reason, think, analyze.[12] It is too great a stretch to
say that without Scharnhorst there would be no Clausewitz, but Clausewitz
might not have gone as far as he did in his thinking without the influence
of his mentor.

When Clausewitz began the fall 1801 course at the Berlin Institute for
Young Officers, he was twenty-one and "described at the time as being
of medium height, thin and erect...with full brown hair, to which, until
1806, he was obliged to tie in a short tail when on duty." Some of his fellow
students apparently regarded him as rough and too earnest, as he strove to
better himself through shaking off the dust of the provinces. The cost of
living in Berlin was much greater than in his small garrison town, something over which he fretted. Young officers generally received allowances
from their families to supplement their meager pay, but his father's poverty meant that he and his brothers never had any hope of financial help.
Clausewitz resorted to earning extra money by pulling guard duty for
other officers.[13]

The curriculum challenged Clausewitz. Initially, Marie later noted,
Clausewitz had a difficult time following the lectures because he lacked the
necessary fundamental knowledge. She credited Scharnhorst, especially
his "goodness and gentleness," for looking out for him and nourishing, as
she put it "all the seeds of his mental abilities." When the third and final
year of the program ended, Clausewitz graduated first in his class. "The

reward was inexpressibly sweet to me," he told Marie. Clausewitz considered this one of the two events in his life that brought him the most joy; the other was winning Marie's love. He had also earned Scharnhorst's lasting, fatherly affection (Scharnhorst was twenty-five years his senior), feelings strengthened by the death of Clausewitz's father in 1802. Their bond lasted until Scharnhorst's death.[14]

In a November 29, 1803, memo Scharnhorst sent to the king, he ranked only two students among the most distinguished: Clausewitz and Tiedemann, who became one of Clausewitz's closest friends. In his graduation assessment of his pupil, Scharnhorst noted: "The performance of Lieutenant von Clausewitz is characterized by an unusually good analysis of the whole and by a modest and agreeable style of presentation. Furthermore he possesses a thorough knowledge of mathematics and military science."[15]

We know that Clausewitz joined the Militärische Gesellschaft, or Military Society, while in Berlin, but little material survives from his time as a student. We do have a short tactical exercise, and another such 1803 document is held by the University of Münster library. We also have (beginning in 1803) the earliest examples of Clausewitz's writing on political and military matters. They are speculative jottings, originally penned in two now-lost notebooks (one ninety-eight pages, the other forty-seven) in which he sporadically scribbled until 1809, that were never intended for publication. They give us some insight, however, into Clausewitz's thinking at age twenty-three. He ponders whether or not the French of his time are like the ancient Romans ("yes, they *are* alike, as *much* alike as the difference in their eras allows"), muses on the relative geopolitical situations of various European states (especially the larger ones), compares Germany's development with that of France, Spain, and England, and discusses the balance of power system.[16]

He also composed an interesting piece on coalitions and warfare and already believed in 1803 that the only way to successfully oppose the strength of France was through a group of powers: "In politics there are two kinds of coalitions: one that aims expressly to defeat or coerce the enemy, and another that aims to *weaken*, to *preoccupy*, both the enemy *and* the state with which one is allied." From his point of view statesmen often made the mistake of forming coalitions to take advantage of both. This was dangerous for "weak states," and only the "self-sufficient" state can manage it, and even then when not "seriously threatened by the common enemy."[17]

Clausewitz reaches back to past wars in his evaluation of coalitions and their utility. He had thoroughly imbibed the history-based analytical method of Scharnhorst. It is clear that he had already read deeply in military history and theory, as his examples stretch from the medieval period to 1792. Among the authors into whose works he delved were Machiavelli, Montecuccoli, Maurice de Saxe, Puységur, Guibert, Lloyd, Turpin, Tempelhoff, Mauvillon, Feuquières, Santa-Cruz, Berenhorst, Prince de Ligne, Folard, Venturini, and de Silva. To these he added the memoirs of the campaigns of Condés, the Duke of Brunswick, Frederick the Great, and Turenne, as well as the histories of ancient warfare and the military art.[18] He was proving adept at drawing historical lessons and ties his examples to theory, using this to evaluate coalitions, the respective political objectives sought by their members, and whether or not they achieved them. It is a supremely modern method and one that the best military staff colleges and strategic studies programs use today.

Clausewitz's study of the extant military theory of his day convinced him of its mediocrity. In 1804 he began his own book. Writers like Heinrich Dietrich von Bülow, author of *The Spirit of the Modern System of War*, were "sophists," and Machiavelli was too preoccupied with the ancient world. The surviving draft of Clausewitz's early foray into military writing is titled *Strategie*, but the work (in thirty numbered sections) deals with a variety of military issues stretching from tactics, to the defense of mountains, to operations, to strategy, to command.[19] He will tread much of this same ground in *On War*.

Clausewitz draws upon other theorists such as Machiavelli, whom he says had "a very keen eye in matters of war," and in particular on his *Discourses*, a study of Roman war and politics. Hence we have the Roman general Fabius Cunctator (The Delayer), famous for taking up positions in traditional Roman fortified camps nearby to Hannibal but refusing to meet him in battle, preferring harassing the enemy and protracting the war in an effort to exhaust him. The Clausewitz of 1804 was not a fan of "hesitation in the spirit of Fabius," yet his criticism fell mainly upon Fabius's usage of fortified camps, arguing that it was far easier for a modern enemy to take fortified positions than it had been for Hannibal.[20]

Clausewitz also explores the utility of theory itself, perhaps not surprising since he is so critical of the other theoretical works. What theory had to teach a commander was "the evaluation of matters that are outside him. It can ensure that his faith in himself, his enterprising spirit, does not arise from ignorance." Clausewitz was already exploring not just what advice gets offered, but *why*. He understood the difficulty of "turning theory into practice." "The art of war speaks thusly" Clausewitz wrote; one must "proceed towards the greatest, most decisive object that you can reach," and "choose the shortest path to it that you trust yourself to follow."[21]

Strategie has sections on tactics, operations, and strategy. The tactical discussions cover a variety of subjects, from the defense of outposts to mountain warfare. Again, however, what is most interesting is Clausewitz's definitions, an element of what became a quest for a coherent methodology. "Tactics is the science of securing a victory through the employment of military forces in battle; strategy is the science of achieving the aim of the war," and "the science of employing the individual battles to further the aim of the war." Battle underpinned every use of military force. Two decades later, in *On War*, he would express the same basic principles: "tactics teaches *the use of armed forces in the engagement*; strategy, *the use of engagements for the object of the war*."[22]

His sense of strategy often encompasses what today we would call "operations." He even says as much. For example, in "The Operational Plan," the first sentence reads: "Strategic plans are a thing unique unto themselves." Moreover, the conduct of energetic, critical operations is seen as pivotal to military success. Clausewitz advises that in war one should embark upon the operation or operations that will bring victory even if the cost is great and insists that we must conduct "the most decisive operation within the scope of our powers." The conflation of strategy and operations was typical of the age. Jomini's later definition of strategy likewise covers what today we call the strategic and operational realms.[23]

Arguably, the most important insight from *Strategie* is in "The Operational Plan," for he provides a more cogent explanation of the two types of war than appears in the prefatory letter published with *On War*: "The political aim of war can be twofold. Either to annihilate the adversary entirely, to abolish the existence of his state, or impose conditions upon him in peacetime."[24]

Clausewitz's text shows the degree to which he had already broken with the practices of conventional warfare, a conclusion bolstered by his view on the utility of combat engagements. As we've seen, generals preferred maneuver, often believing this by itself could win a campaign. The French Revolutionaries, as we've also seen, had increased warfare's pace *and* intensity. Clausewitz understood this evolution: "In war everything turns on the engagement, which has either actually occurred or is merely intended by one side or even feigned. Engagement is therefore to strategy what hard money is to currency exchange."²⁵ In short, warfare meant not avoiding warfare.

In 1805, probably before the outbreak of the War of the Third Coalition in April, Clausewitz wrote a short essay—in French—on how to wage war against France. Here he outlined a multipronged plan, with each nation operating in its own theater, arguing that this is better than a scheme encompassing all the armies. Success was more likely if the members of an alliance against the French fought from a common template, but one that allowed flexibility. Underpinning his discussion of war with France is the acknowledgment that the coalition partners will have territorial goals (in other words, political objectives) for which they are fighting. The multi-theater nature of the plan, with coalition armies hitting France from many directions at once, is something with which the anti-Napoleon forces found ultimate success. Also interesting is Clausewitz's suggestion that one of the means of defeating France is with a great captain (in *On War* he calls him the man with a "Genius for War"), but he thought it would be only through chance that the coalition found such a leader.²⁶ There was likely but one Napoleon.

Clausewitz's first publications were probably a collection of reviews appearing in 1801 and 1802 in the journal *Neue Bellona*. His first significant work—published anonymously in the same journal in 1805—was a review essay on *The Spirit of the Modern System of War* (1799), a book on military theory by fellow Prussian Adam Heinrich Dietrich von Bülow (1757–1807). Clausewitz found little worthwhile here and wasted no time in showing it. Bülow "has given us nothing other than a new title," he announced in his second paragraph, and deemed Bülow's "pretension to a scientific approach laughable."²⁷

Clausewitz's attacks on Bülow parallel concepts he developed in *Strategie*, and lend weight to the idea that it was at least partially a reaction to Bülow's work. Importantly, Bülow's definitions of strategy and tactics were hopelessly vague. "Strategy is the science of military movements beyond the enemy's vision, tactics is within it," Bülow wrote—inexplicit classifications that Clausewitz found arbitrary. Clausewitz believed that failing to define the terms of one's argument was intellectually lazy and reminded readers that the meanings of terms change over time. In place of Bülow's weak definitions, Clausewitz would offer, as we've seen, his own. This early development of his thinking is very much in line with what he would later say in *On War*.[28]

Clausewitz defined himself in opposition to Bülow and other "sophists" and "charlatans" who built geometrical systems for victory, he later wrote, to which they "ultimately gave a veneer of mathematical elegance." Fixation on mathematical solutions and angles of attack were useless. To Clausewitz, war was never a chalkboard exercise. Earlier he had expressed some sympathy for geometrical attempts to measure strategic elements, but his experience as a soldier had convinced him that mathematical elegance did not reflect the messy reality of the battlefield.[29]

Clausewitz's attack on Bülow was heavy-handed; he ends his review by calling the book "the children's military companion." But the essay contains some nuggets: "There is a fairly prevalent but fundamentally false idea: That the art of war ought always begin with the development of the means, and where the means at hand would be inadequate, there remains nothing for the art of war to do but to advise peace.... This is an art of war for speculators, not for the general."[30]

Despite his harsh critique, Clausewitz also learned from Bülow. Clausewitz's view of war's inherent political nature was influenced by Bülow's writings, which are one source for Clausewitz's most celebrated line: "war is the continuation of politics by other means." Even at twenty-five, Clausewitz had moved beyond geometrical approaches and begun to think in far larger terms than Bülow or others.[31]

Clausewitz also wrote a number of histories during this period, all probably completed before 1806. The most substantial and analytical is a study of Gustavus Adolphus's campaigns of 1632–1634 during the Thirty Years War. The other works include a look at the Dutch War of Independence, 1568–1606; an examination of Turenne, the seventeenth-century French marshal during Louis XIV's regn; a study of the campaigns in Flanders from 1690–1694 of another of Louis XIV's marshals, François-Henri de Montmorency, Duke of Luxembourg (this is a more organized and systematic work); and a look at the War of Spanish Succession, 1701–1714. Overall, these primarily narrative, often blow-by-blow chronological accounts lack the deep analysis and the intense psychological portraits of his later works, though we do see the beginnings of such thought. They are, however, exceptionally remarkable for a twenty-five-year-old who had received little formal education before coming to Berlin as a student.[32] We also observe some patterns in Clausewitz's writing, particularly those related to theory: a belief in the necessity of defined terms for building a clear, philosophical underpinning for debate. As seen, this comes through particularly in his striving to define tactics and strategy. There is also an interest in the applicability of ancient warfare (especially its tactical elements) to the art of war in his era.

Clausewitz's experience mirrors what often happens in today's professional armies. After his education he began his service with practical training in the ranks, then graduated to the tasks and duties of a junior officer before continuing on to education designed to shape the manner of one's thought. The combination—when properly done—prepares the soldier not only for the rigors of the field, but for increasing responsibility. Moreover, like many officers today, Clausewitz, while attending the General War School, also had another assignment, one which proved particularly beneficial for his career.

Figure 2.3. Marie von Brühl (1779–1836).

From Karl Schwartz, *Leben des Generals Carl von Clausewitz und der Frau Marie von Clausewitz, geb. Gräfin von Brühl: Mit Briefen, Aufsätzen, Tagebüchern und anderen Schriftstücken* (Berlin: Ferd. Dümmlers Verlags-Buchhandlung, 1878). Courtesywww.clausewitz.com.

Because of Scharnhorst's recommendation, in the spring of 1803 Clausewitz became the adjutant to Prince August von Preußen. Prince August was the twenty-four-year-old son of the head of Clausewitz's regiment, and a cousin to the king. With this appointment, which became official on August 8, Clausewitz moved into Prussian high society. August commanded a grenadier battalion in the infantry and Clausewitz received quarters in Berlin's Wilhelmsplatz Palace. In June 1804 his salary was raised to 360 talers a year, and on February 11, 1805, he was given a brevet promotion to captain. This change in position introduced him to the leaders of Prussia, providing him with valuable contacts. It also gave him the opportunity to meet Marie von Brühl.[33]

3

Clausewitz at War

The 1806 Campaign

It is a sign of Philistinism when everyone does only what he is paid to do.

"My Fatherland needs war," Clausewitz wrote Marie in September 1806, "and—plainly speaking—war alone can lead me to happy goals." The young Captain Clausewitz, though steeped in Enlightenment rationalism, was also carried by the Romantic age. He was ambitious and a professional solider in a land that judged success in war as the highest achievement. He also realized that his best means of achieving success was by distinguishing himself in battle, and told Marie as much. "But," he added, "I still have to make great demands on my luck!"[1]

Clausewitz was far from the only Prussian who thought his nation needed war. The man leading the civilian charge against the growing hegemony of Napoleon's France was Karl vom Stein. Stein, an outspoken Prussian nobleman, became the king's finance minister in 1804. Unafraid to clash even with his sovereign, he disapproved of Berlin's persistent neutrality policy and criticized Prussia's broken and backward governmental system and the mediocrities running it. He found the king too much influenced by personal advisors instead of his professional government ministers.[2]

Stein and others pushed the king to take a harder line against France. King Frederick William III, however, simply lacked the willingness to do this. Paralyzed by indecision, the king, writes historian Christopher Clark "combined a sharp, if reticent, intelligence with a profound lack of confidence in his own abilities." In the 1820s Clausewitz's take was similar, describing Frederick William as someone with "serious and firm principles," but "too

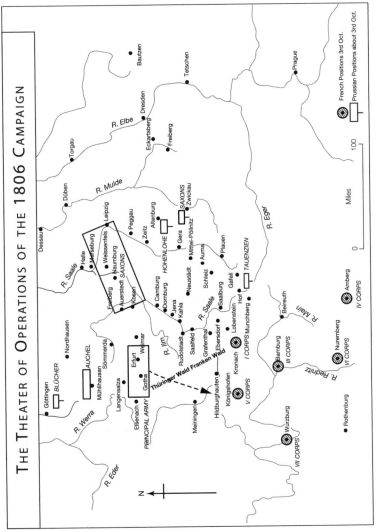

THE THEATER OF OPERATIONS OF THE 1806 CAMPAIGN

Bautzen

Tetschen

Prague

R. Elbe

Dresden

Eckartsberg

Freiberg

Torgau

R. Mulde

Düben

Dessau

Leipzig

Peggau

Altenburg

SAXONS

Zwickau

Zeitz

Gera

Mittel-Pöllnitz

R. Saale

Halle

Merseburg

Weissenfels

Naumburg

SAXONS

HOHENLOHE

Auma

Plauen

R. Eger

Göttingen

Nordhausen

BLÜCHER

Sömmerda

AUCHEL

Mühlhausen

R. Werra

Freiberg

Auerstadt

Kösen

Camburg

Dornburg

Jena

Kahla

Neustadt

Schleiz

Saalburg

Gafell

Hof

TAUENZIEN

Langensalza

Eisenach

Erfurt

Gotha

Weimar

R. Ilm

Rudolstadt

Saalfeld

Grafenthal

Ebersdorf

Lobenstein

Kronach

Munchberg

I CORPS

Bamburg

III CORPS

Amberg

IV CORPS

R. Eder

Meiningen

PRINCIPAL ARMY

Thüringer Wald Franken Wald

Hildburghauten

Königshofen

V CORPS

R. Rednitz

Nuremberg

VI CORPS

R. Main

Rothenburg

Wurzburg

VII CORPS

N

0   100

Miles

French Positions 3rd Oct.

Prussian Positions about 3rd Oct.

Map 3.1.   The Theater of Operations of the 1806 Campaign.

little trust in his own abilities and the abilities of others" and "too full of that cold, Nordic sense of doubt that undermines the spirit of enterprise, opposes enthusiasm, and inhibits every kind of creativity." The king's distrust of his advisors was driven by his "invincible tendency to doubt everything."[3]

To the older Clausewitz, the king's weakness was but a small part of his government's problems, which were exacerbated by the fact that its operation still reflected the character of Frederick the Great, a decidedly more forceful and determined ruler who had died in 1786. Frederick had decreed and the various ministers executed; they did not make policy, nor did they advise. But the state's size had doubled in the thirty years since "Old Fritz's" passing, and Frederick William was not his great uncle. The ministers could not freely bring matters to his attention and there was no prime minister. This produced an absence of leadership at the very top.[4] The Prussia of 1806 was sleepwalking into the modern age.

Much had changed since Prussia and France made peace in 1795. Prussia adopted a policy of neutrality for the next decade, one that did not serve the kingdom well. Meanwhile, of course, Bonaparte's star had ascended—as had France's—as Prussia watched. When the war of the Second Coalition broke out in 1798, Prussia stood aside. Napoleon's victories over Austria and Russia cracked the traditional Austrian domination of the German states of the dying Holy Roman Empire, and French power and diplomacy brought much of the region into Paris's orbit during 1801–1802. Prussia relished the weakening of its ancestral Austrian foe and saw in France's rise opportunities to expand via diplomatic means. This was not an incorrect assumption, as Napoleon's juggling and consolidation of many of the minor German states resulted in the Prussians being rewarded with chunks of Westphalia and Thuringia.[5]

But there were problems with Prussia's approach. What looked like success from Berlin's perspective appeared as weak complicity to Europe's other courts. The famous Austrian diplomat Clemens von Metternich found in Prussia "a conspiracy of mediocrities...united by the common terror of decisive action.... There is nobody to remind the king that his army might perhaps be utilized to greater advantage on the field of battle than on the plains of Berlin and Potsdam." In 1803 the French turned up the heat by taking Hanover, the ancestral home of Britain's ruling dynasty, and then still a possession of the British crown and in later negotiations even offered it to Berlin. This meant that because of the patchwork nature of Prussia's domain, the French army now separated Berlin from its possessions on the Rhine. Napoleon took advantage of the feebleness of Prussian foreign policy, particularly after making himself emperor in 1804. Prussia's doubts about its policy intensified, but not enough to force substantive change.[6]

It was the formation of the Third Coalition that finally dragged Berlin from its self-imposed slumber. In April 1805 Britain, Austria, and Russia united against Napoleon and the Russians demanded that Prussia join the alliance. Russia ratcheted up the pressure in September 1805 by demanding the right to move 100,000 troops across Prussia, and met Frederick William's refusal with a threat to do it anyway. Prussia mobilized and concentrated men along the banks of the Vistula in the east. Then the French had the nerve to do what the Russians only threatened: in October 1805 French Marshal Jean-Baptiste Bernadotte (a future king of Sweden) marched an army through the Prussian province of Ansbach in what is now south-central Germany.[7]

An enraged Frederick William met with Czar Alexander of Russia on November 3, 1805, and they signed the Treaty of Potsdam. The agreement was an odd one. Frederick William saw Prussia as an "armed mediator," bridging the gap between Napoleon and his enemies to the east. At the same time, the agreement made risibly unrealistic demands on France that included the abandonment of virtually all of the French territorial gains since 1792. If France refused, Prussia would then—truly—join the coalition against it.[8] In reality Prussian neutrality was now dead—which Frederick William didn't seem to realize—yet Prussia refused to fully commit to the coalition, trying to straddle the fence between neutrality and alignment.

Napoleon responded by going to war. He struck hard against the Austrian and Russian forces, scoring one of history's most decisive military victories at Austerlitz on December 2, 1805. Austria immediately made peace, and the Third Coalition collapsed. King Frederick William now had the misfortune of having to deal with a French ruler who had accurately taken his measure and knew he habitually vacillated. Napoleon also didn't fear war with Prussia and believed Frederick William would do everything to avoid it. When Bonaparte thought he could bully an opponent, he did so. The situation after Austerlitz gave him this chance; he seized it with gusto.[9]

Before the December 1805 Battle of Austerlitz, Frederick William had dispatched to Napoleon Count Christian von Haugwitz—an advisor and sometime foreign minister—with an ultimatum. Haugwitz unexpectedly found himself presenting congratulations to Napoleon for his victory. Clausewitz thought Haugwitz "unscrupulous" and "a man without conscience," later writing of him and Berlin's foreign relations: "Prussian policy between the Peace of Basel [1795] and the catastrophe of 1806 is marked by weakness, timidity, thoughtlessness, and on many occasions an undignified agility, all of which are qualities deeply rooted in Haugwitz's character."[10]

Meeting in Vienna, Napoleon forced upon Haugwitz the Treaty of Schönbrunn, which essentially pulled Prussia into the French orbit. Napoleon also ordered Prussia to annex the former British possession of Hanover, which the French had seized in 1803, in an obvious attempt to drive a wedge between the two states. Clausewitz wrote later that when Haugwitz returned from this meeting he was met with disbelief. He had gone to declare war on France and returned bearing a treaty of alliance. "No one had imagined that an emissary might pursue a completely contrary policy on his own, in effect forcing the government to return to a position that it had decided, after long deliberation and not without considerable distress, to abandon." Prussia faced a dangerous conundrum. Not annexing Hanover risked war with France; doing so risked war with Great Britain. Amazingly, Frederick William nonetheless hoped to get Britain's approval for the acquisition as a reward for arranging a Franco-British peace.[11]

Napoleon and Haugwitz met again in February 1806, this time in Paris. The French demanded more from Berlin, including that Prussia close its ports to British trade as part of Napoleon's "Continental Blockade" of Great Britain. Frederick William, unwilling to fight France, bowed. Britain went to war with Prussia on April 20, 1806.[12]

The press of events combined to slowly push Prussia into war with France as well. Berlin worried about continued French expansion, a fear fed by Napoleon's effort to install one of his relatives on every throne in Europe. Napoleon also drove a reorganization of the fragmented German states, which brought the demise of the ancient Holy Roman Empire and the establishment of the "Confederation of the Rhine," which would be under French influence. But the Prussians caught wind of an offer by France to give Hanover back to London if the British withdrew from Sicily. This fed the anti-French forces in Prussia, particularly in the court. One of the dominant figures opposing France was Queen Louise, Frederick William's strong-willed wife (Napoleon once referred to her as "the only real man in Prussia"). She drove the king to act. The internal resistance culminated in a September 2, 1806, memo from a number of important civilian and military elites (including members of the royal family), which accused the king of being indecisive and in the thrall of pro-French advisors. The revelations of secret French negotiations for an alliance with Britain fed the flames.[13]

Fredrick William, Clausewitz recorded, made the decision to go to war in early August, before receiving the memo, and ordered mobilization early the same month, one of many that had occurred over the course of the previous year. The army was in the field by the end of August. The Prussian army began massing in Saxony (in southern Germany) in early September.[14]

A state of war still existed between France and Russia, and though Czar Alexander was skeptical of Prussia's intentions, the two nations eventually agreed to act in concert against the French. Britain and Prussia also ironed out their issues, and London provided financial support. Thus, the Fourth Coalition was born. Unfortunately for Prussia, Frederick William proceeded to mishandle the crisis. For once, he should have acted slowly, awaiting promised Russian support, and instead sent Napoleon an ultimatum. Bonaparte was already at the Prussian border with his army when the message caught up to him at Bamberg on October 7, 1806. He marched the next day. The czar's army was too far away to support their new allies. This meant that Prussia, the least of Europe's "Great Powers," faced the French Empire with only tiny Saxony by its side.[15]

Throughout 1806 Frederick William had looked for an opportunity to deliver a solid blow against Napoleon. Doing so would buy time for the arrival of the Russians as well as the onset of winter; both would change the strategic equation. Nothing had gone as planned. Charles, Duke of Brunswick, commanded the Prussian forces, just as he had during Clausewitz's first campaign. Though Clausewitz—always a shrewd if sometimes harsh judge of character—later found Brunswick "intelligent, well educated, and experienced in war," he also believed the old soldier had "no trace of boldness and could not rise proudly above adversity." Brunswick was well connected, being Frederick the Great's nephew and having risen under his tutelage, and was considered Prussia's first soldier, but in Clausewitz's view "the failure of his campaign in France in 1792 and his inconclusive campaign the following year further reduced his self-confidence." "Much practice in the leadership of troops, experience of war, personal courage, a lively mind, calmness in the face of danger—these were qualities that, combined with his natural adroitness, would ordinarily have made him an excellent leader. However, the command of an entire army requires self-confidence and complete authority; the former he denied himself, the latter he was unable to wrest from other men."[16]

At Brunswick's headquarters in the fall of 1806 the Prussians considered three courses of action: attacking Napoleon when he crossed the Saale River (in southeastern Germany) and moved on the Prussians; harrying Napoleon's lines of communication in the event he did not attack them; or, if the circumstances allowed, moving quickly and catching the French at Leipzig. Brunswick submitted his operational plan to the king on September 25. He had chosen the third course, intending to launch an offensive, the expectation being that the Prussians would meet parts of the French army in the upper arms of the Main River—in Saxony—not Prussia. However, the Prussians intended for the war to start on October 8, fourteen days after the delivery of their ultimatum.[17]

Clausewitz later branded this ultimatum foolish, arguing that it undermined any strategy of surprise. The Prussians could have marched on September 25, when Brunswick submitted his operational plan, and against French corps that were not yet moving. "But the Duke feared the war, perhaps more than the King did," and hoped for peace when he should have pressed for action. The delay meant that there would be no surprise offensive and the Prussians missed their chance to defeat the French forces in detail by hitting the separated corps before they could unite. Moreover, Clausewitz wrote in *On War*, by the time the Prussians moved, Bonaparte had already begun to cross the Saale River. "In his vacillation, the Duke had fallen between two stools: he had left the area too late to *intercept* the enemy, and too early to fight a sound battle."[18]

The Prussians soon learned that Napoleon had 180,000 troops along a thirty-eight-mile stretch of their border. Brunswick, now believing he lacked the time to mount an offensive, elected to divide his army into three forces, one under his command (six divisions), another under Prince Frederick Ludwig von Hohenlohe (five divisions), and a third force under General Rüchel (three divisions). Clausewitz was in Brunswick's army in the corps of Friedrich Adolf von Kalckreuth, which served as the reserve, and in the division commanded by Johann Ernst von Kühnheim. Prince August, a great nephew of Frederick the Great, commanded a Grenadier battalion in the infantry brigade of August Wilhelm von Pletz. Together, Brunswick's units were responsible for a front of more than 190 miles. "The division into two principal armies was without doubt contrary to all principles of good sense," Clausewitz later wrote unsparingly. "Any division in command weakened it."[19] It also gave the French the opportunity to do what the Prussians had hoped to accomplish themselves: defeat the enemy in detail rather than attacking its main strength.

To Clausewitz, this decision to divide the army also further undermined the Prussian command system. Hohenlohe had no inclination to listen to Brunswick, and Clausewitz believed that giving Hohenlohe such a large force encouraged him to be even less cooperative. "The greater the force which the general second in command receives," Clausewitz wrote of this in the 1820s, "the more he wishes to be independent, as the energy of the high command loses its strength." This fed the inclination of the seventy-year-old Brunswick to not exercise his command, a problem exacerbated by the presence of the king and a number of his closest advisors with Brunswick's army. All of this conspired to produce operational indecision.[20]

Indecision did not afflict Napoleon. Launching from camps in southern Germany, Napoleon intended to place his army between the Prussians and their capital of Berlin, and then force the Prussians into a defensive battle. Advancing through the Thüringen Forest, Napoleon would push his army into Saxony in three mutually supporting columns led by Marshal Jean-de-Dieu Soult on the right (50,000), Marshal Jean Bernadotte in the center (70,000), and Marshal Jean Lannes on the left (40,000). These, plus reserves and other forces, gave him 180,000 men. He believed this would enable him to hit the Prussians with double their number wherever his soldiers encountered them. Supplementing these forces were troops advancing from Holland and probing from Mainz. Napoleon saw them as protecting France from any possible Prussian invasion, but additionally hoped they might draw away Prussian troops from the crucial theater while also potentially becoming a wall against which to drive the Prussians if they dared march into the area between Mainz and Bamberg.[21]

Napoleon began his offensive at dawn on October 8 by rushing six corps northward through the Saxon territory of Thuringia. His ability to move quickly, combined with Prussian sloth, allowed his plan to work. Writing immediately after the campaign, Clausewitz commented on the superiority of the French system of march, deeming it "unheard of in the history of warfare." The French could travel between 33 or 37 miles a day if needed; half of that was typical and covering 140 miles in eight days had been considered "a remarkable speed." It wasn't that soldiers were incapable of marching faster, but they were limited by the need to keep order and maintain the ability to fight.[22]

And so Clausewitz went to war for the second time. He had already endured the frustrations of recent war scares and the related mobilizations and demobilizations. Earlier in the year he had received a contract to publish a journal article, but wrote the editors in May thanking them for the opportunity and respectfully declining because he expected to soon be on the move and would not have access to his books.[23]

When the Prussians mobilized for the 1806 war, they did not immediately gather their troops in East Prussia or use them to strengthen their field army. Though defenders of the decision argued that it gave Prussia a reserve army, in his history of the campaign Clausewitz argued that the idea "entirely confused people's heads," producing one of the fundamental errors of military thinkers and the historians who study them: the muddling of the tactical and the strategic. "While tactical reserves are to be recommended," Clausewitz insisted, holding in strategic reserve forces that are ready to go "is contrary to good sense." His argument was that battles decided "the fate of the war." Employing tactical reserves preceded the choice to fight in them, "while the employment of strategical reserves follows the decision." He made a similar argument in *On War*.[24]

When Clausewitz took to the field, he found parting with Marie difficult. Their first meeting had occurred nearly three years before, in December 1803 at a dinner party hosted by Prince August's father, Ferdinand. As the adjutant to a member of the royal family, Clausewitz moved in circles that soon brought him other meetings with the socially well-connected Marie, such as when Prince August met with the queen mother a few days later, and the January wedding of the king's brother. The death of Marie's younger sister in childbirth interrupted the growth of their relationship, as the von Brühls withdrew from society for a time. By October 1805 Clausewitz and Marie had developed deep feelings for one another, but were too reserved to show them. Clausewitz's mobilization, however, goaded them both to action. By the time his unit rode out of Berlin in 1806, they had come to an understanding. She gave him a ring to wear and on his last morning in Berlin he rode by her house with hopes (quickly dashed) of spotting her.[25]

Marie's widowed mother did not approve. The prospect of her daughter being bound to a poor, landless army captain from a questionable family and with few obvious prospects did not warm Madame Sophia von Brühl's heart to Clausewitz, as he well knew. Though not wealthy, the von Brühls had a distinctly upper-crust lineage and distinguished roots. One of Marie's grandfathers had been Saxony's prime minister. Her father, Charles, became the crown prince's governor in 1786 and was promoted to full general in 1797. He died in 1802. Other uncles also held high positions in the Prussian military or civilian service. Madame Brühl was the daughter of an English businessman, William Gomm, who among other things had served as Britain's consul to St. Petersburg. She had met her future husband, Charles, when he visited the city. But her ancestors also included an English lord and a Baltic baron. Marie's parents married on August 17, 1778. Marie was born on June 3, 1779, a year before Clausewitz. Nonetheless, Marie's mother did allow the two to write when Clausewitz marched off to war. On September 11 Clausewitz received orders to go to Magdeburg to march to Halle. Clausewitz wrote Marie that possessing her undivided affection seemed to him like having robbed heaven. "Heaven take you under its care," he closed one of his letters, "and allow me to defend its cause on earth."[26]

Clausewitz's letters to Marie are the best reflections of his passions and beliefs. "When we march over the mountain and through the valley on the curved forest road in open, long rows, and music and song fill the air, my heart opens up, and I am filled with joyous hopes and anticipation," he wrote her. On September 20 he penned a note to Marie from Roßbach, the site of Frederick the Great's victory over a Franco-Austrian army in 1757. "[T]he insufferable arrogance of the French had been so very humbled," he noted, a typical example of his feelings toward the French. He had at first carried doubts regarding Prussia's ultimate success in the war, but these were now gone and he wrote a few days later that through the war fate had given Prussia a chance to "pour pale horror over all the French" and "plunge the arrogant Emperor into an abyss."[27]

On September 29 he again expressed to Marie his confidence in their ultimate success, but, in the same letter, talked about the difficulties under which his mentor Scharnhorst labored in trying to guide Prussian strategy and operations. Scharnhorst served as the quartermaster general on Brunswick's staff. In theory, this meant he should have a decisive impact on how the war was fought. In practice, Scharnhorst, a mere colonel, found himself in a den of generals and princes, all with more influence (and less knowledge) than he. Prussia, Clausewitz noted, had three field commanders and two quartermaster generals where there should only be one of each. "I have never in my life discovered a man more capable of overcoming the difficulties in the way as the man of whom I speak here," Clausewitz wrote of Scharnhorst. But he "is paralyzed by the unceasing friction of other opinions." Here, for the first time, Clausewitz uses the term "friction"—meaning virtually any uncontrollable factor making the waging of war more difficult. It was a term he would return to.[28]

Clausewitz nonetheless believed the advantage lay with Prussia. "In the next great battle we will be the winner," he boasted to Marie, and believed the probability of victory would become a certainty if he had the freedom to direct the war and the Prussian armies as he saw fit. "So close is the salvation of Germany and Europe," he declared, insisting that this opinion was held by all those with knowledge of the subject.[29]

He could not have been more wrong. Miscommunication on the Prussian side led to an advance force under Prince Louis Ferdinand— August's older brother, and one of the court's most vociferous hawks— fighting a battle near Saale on October 10 against forward elements of the French army. The prince was killed and the French shattered Louis's unit. The news stunned the Prussian high command. Worse was to come. On October 11 Napoleon's fast-moving troops stood between the Prussian army and Berlin, separating the Prussians from their capital, their sources of supply, and their lines of retreat. The French army turned westward to face the Prussians. Two corps aimed at Weimar, two others moved to the north of this, while the remaining pair swung even farther north with the intent of striking the Prussian rear.[30]

Clausewitz was by now convinced a big battle was nigh and wrote excitedly on October 12—to Marie of all people, "I myself look forward to this day as I would look forward to my wedding day!" This time he proved very correct, for that same day Napoleon ordered his forces to begin a swing to the left (westward). The Prussians realized that the French might break through and cut the Prussian army's communications. Hohenlohe began to withdraw, marching toward Jena with his 38,000 men. He had been ordered—with Rüchel in support—to hold the village of Capellendorf between Jena and Weimar while the bulk of the Prussian army took the road north past the city of Auerstedt, whereupon Hohenlohe would become the rearguard. Brunswick and the king concentrated their force at Weimar. They marched from the city on the 13th and bivouacked near Auerstedt that evening. Clausewitz's unit, which was part of the reserve force of Brunswick's army, did the same directly south of the village at about midnight.[31]

For his part, Napoleon was unaware that the Prussians were moving in two groups and thus not united; Hohenlohe would have been equally surprised to learn that he faced the mass of Napoleon's army. In any event, on October 14 Napoleon's forces attacked both Prussian armies. The French emperor himself hit Hohenlohe's men at Jena with four corps (96,000 men), routing the inferior Prussian force (35,000). The Prussians suffered 25,000 casualties (including 15,000 men captured) to France's 5,000.[32]

The night before (October 13), Marshal Davout called a halt to the march of his wing of Napoleon's advance near the small village of

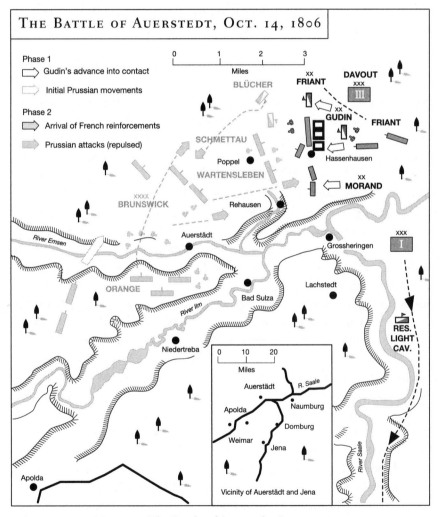

Map 3.2. The Battle of Auerstedt, Oct. 14, 1806.

Auerstedt. Fog exacerbated the difficulties of the French troops navigating the narrow roads and fed their uncertainty about the situation to their front. Intelligence from prisoners lightened their picture, however, indicating they faced Brunswick's army (63,000). Correspondingly, Prussian cavalry had taken French prisoners and discovered Davout's force (27,000). The fog still draped Auerstedt and its surroundings on the morning of October 14, as it did Jena, and as it had the battlefield of Austerlitz ten months before. Davout had his men on the road at 4:00 a.m. At 7:00, they made contact with Brunswick's Prussians near the village of Hassenhausen, driving them off with the lifting mist, and took up positions along the Lissbach rivulet to await reinforcements. What followed was an enormous meeting engagement as both sides poured troops into the fight.[33]

Clausewitz, in one of a trio of letters he wrote for publication after the campaign, and in his later history of the events of 1806, remarked that the Prussians, in spite of many mistakes, now had a great opportunity to score a victory because they could strike a portion of the French army with the bulk of theirs. Moreover, the French, "with their back against the closed-in valley of the Saale, found themselves in the worst position possible in war." Here, the steep banks of the Saale River increased the danger to the French as they had only a single path of retreat—the bridge at Kösen—which they couldn't cross "without being blown into the Saale," as Clausewitz put it.[34] His assessment was correct; it was up to Prussia's leaders to seize the chance.

By 8:00 a.m. the Prussian 3rd Division under Generalleutnant- Friedrich Wilhelm Karl von Schmettau, supported by Blücher's cavalry to the north, began massing against the smaller French force. Blücher's cavalry went in before the infantry was ready, suffering a repulse. Brunswick, who was with the lead division, as was King Frederick William, could have attacked at 8:00 a.m., but he waited until Generalleutnant Leopold Alexander von Wartensleben's 2nd Division came up. This gave the French time to bring up their own reinforcements, which included cavalry and artillery. The Prussian attack opened at 9:45. Schmettau's men in the center were bloodily halted, but Wartensleben's push to the south (the right) hit weaker French forces and routed them. Davout threw in his last reserves to staunch the Prussian advance. The Prussians failed to capitalize on their success and instead mounted four attacks against the village of Hassenhausen in the French center. In the last assault, the Duke of Brunswick was shot through both eyes while leading a regiment of grenadiers in the attack—not a task usually undertaken by army commanders. He died three weeks later. "The wound," Clausewitz wrote, "ended his life in a manner that was as painful as it was tragic."[35]

Brunswick's incapacitation proved decisive. Frederick William did not assume command himself, nor did he appoint a successor. More reinforcements arrived on each side at 11:00 a.m. The king ordered up the fresh division commanded by the Prince of Orange, but it was too late. The Prussians did not commit the new division en masse and instead the king split the force, sending one brigade to support each flank. Despite the fact that the Prussian attacks lost focus, they still came close to breaking the French lines. Wartensleben struck the French left, but withering enemy fire brought this to a halt. The French responded with a concentrated assault on Wartensleben's division. The Prussian right collapsed. Frederick William, commanding a vastly superior force, could have committed more troops to blunt the enemy but simply refused to do so. The French drove in the Prussian right (southern flank), while also hitting their left (northern flank), which too began to crumble. By half-past noon the Prussian army was in retreat.[36] However, unlike at Jena, it didn't break.

Clausewitz later wrote that Brunswick should have done better in the campaign, believing that "the natural strength of his position was so great that he should have been able to annihilate the right wing of the French at Auerstedt." Still, he recognized the difference between that battle and Jena. At Auerstedt "the Prussians did not dare to hold out for a *certain* victory; at Jena, where it was *completely impossible*, they thought they could count on it."[37]

★ ★ ★

At daybreak on the 14th, cannon fire awakened Clausewitz and his comrades. General von Kalckreuth's reserve corps, of which Prince August's units were a part, received their orders to move at 9:00 a.m. They marched through the steep, broken country that stretched from Auerstedt to the Ilm River. When Kalckreuth's two divisions arrived, the battle of Auerstedt had already been decided and the Prussian retreat had begun. The king, deciding to not risk Kalckreuth's men, used them as a rearguard to cover the Prussian exodus. Kalckreuth arrayed his troops along the bank of the Liesbach, supported by cavalry under Blücher. Clausewitz insisted later that had Kalckreuth's 18,000-strong reserve been committed "to turn the tide of battle," "a Prussian defeat would have been impossible."[38]

To buy time, the king ordered Prince August to launch a four-battalion thrust with his grenadiers at the village of Poppel and the French forces holding it. August took two battalions from Prince Orange's 1st Division (those under Reinbaden and Knebel) and one under Guadi from Alexander Wilhelm von Arnim's 2nd Division of the reserve to add to his own, and gave direct command of the two regiments of his battalion to Captain Schönberg. August deployed the Reinbaden and Knebel battalions about 1,000 paces from the village of Gernstädt and put Gaudi's near the village as a reserve, but had no cavalry to cover his planned line of retreat through the hamlet. He pushed up the Knebel and Reinbaden battalions to protect the army's weak left flank and put out Reinbaden's skirmishers to cover his right against the French skirmishers. As the Prussians advanced, they began to take cannon and small arms fire, and lost a significant number of men to French troops firing behind bush rows. Amidst the fury, August tried to mount a bayonet attack to push away the French, but the enemy fire was too heavy and loud for the men to understand his commands, and they weren't accustomed to responding to the rattle of their drums.[39]

August rode up and urged the men forward. He got one battalion to advance, but only through the effort of Major Reinbaden—who had stayed with his command despite being wounded in the mouth and foot—and led his battalion against the French. But they were still taking fire and stopped to return it after the attack had advanced only twenty or thirty paces. The Knebel battalion also surged forward against the French, and then August's own battalion arrived to join the fight. Clausewitz went in with them, at the head of the battalion's third rank. Prussian infantry fought in formations three men deep. In some units, such as August's, the third ranks were trained to fight in loose order as skirmishers. Clausewitz deployed these men into skirmish lines and used their fire to support the push, "a rare case of attempting to answer the French tactics in kind." The force of the Prussian attack carried them into Poppel.[40]

Twice they received orders to withdraw from the king's eighty-two-year-old advisor, Field Marshal Wichard Joachim Heinrich von Möllendorf. August, however, had great difficulty convincing his men to retreat. They took heavy cannon and canister fire, but lost few men. When they withdrew, August wrote, "My battalion, which had suffered the least, stayed about 100 paces behind to cover the retreat. We had to several times form a front in order to discourage the enemy skirmishers, which were superior to our skirmishers." Once the enemy stopped pressing, August halted, reformed his ranks, withdrew to Gernstädt in perfect order, and marched his battalion back to the heights to the right of Eckardsberge.

Realizing that the village of Auerstedt now divided the army—creating a dangerous position—August sent word to the king and Möllendorf and asked for instructions. After a quarter of an hour, he had received no reply. Knowing the Prussians had decided to retreat, he alerted the adjacent unit as to what he was doing and marched his men south through Auerstedt, putting the Gaudi battalion in the village to cover his own withdrawal.[41]

They had not marched far before the arrival of orders from Möllendorf to again occupy the Eckardsberge Heights, followed soon after by a command to retreat back through Auerstedt, and then yet another directive to remount the Heights. This back and forth gave the French time to bring up their artillery, and they began pouring canister and howitzer fire into both August's men and Auerstedt. Clausewitz and his comrades retreated through Auerstedt, a passage made under a hail of shots in which, miraculously, not a man was killed. Fires broke out in the village, adding to the chaos as wounded, horses, cannons, and limbers clogged the narrow streets in their now disordered retreat. August was glad the French cavalry weren't there to press them; it would have made things even worse. The Guadi battalion guarded their rear very well and kept the French fire off them as they escaped the burning hamlet.[42]

The rest of the army, meanwhile, marched away in perfect order. August's attack had stopped the French attempt to cut off the retreat of Schmettau's division, giving Schmettau's and Prince Heinrich von Preußen's troops time to withdraw and break contact. August himself suffered two contusions, one in his haunch from a canister round that proved particularly painful and made it difficult for him to walk and another in his back. Clausewitz escaped unscathed. At some point during the assault he took command of August's battalion when Schönberg was wounded, the largest combat command he ever held. Prince August later wrote glowingly of Clausewitz's behavior that day: "This is an extremely talented and scientifically trained officer, who acquitted himself very well during the war, and at Auerstedt—after Captain von Schönberg was wounded—it was through his good leadership my grenadier battalion was used to excellent advantage."[43]

Overall, Kalckreuth's units suffered heavy fire from the French, but bought enough time for the remnants of the three other Prussian divisions to break contact. They then began withdrawing westward. Davout continued to push, hitting both of Kalckreuth's flanks. The Prussians continued their retreat, but the army was beginning to come apart. Davout pursued his beaten foe until 4:30 p.m. Although he lacked the cavalry necessary to wreak the same level of destruction that Napoleon had upon the Prussians in the wake of Jena, Davout had done something that his emperor had not: defeated an enemy army that outnumbered his by two to one.[44]

Many years later, Clausewitz wrote of the feelings provoked by losing a battle. It is worth quoting in full:

> Those who have never been through a serious defeat will naturally find it hard to form a vivid and thus altogether true picture of it: abstract concepts of this or that minor loss will never match the reality of a major defeat.... When one is losing, the first thing that strikes one's imagination, and indeed one's intellect, is the melting away of numbers. This is followed by a loss of ground, which almost always happens, and can even happen to the attacker if he is out of luck. Next comes the break-up of the original line of battle, the confusion of units, and the dangers inherent in the retreat, which, with rare exceptions, are always present to some degree. Then comes the retreat itself, usually begun in darkness, or at any rate continued through the night. Once that begins, you have to leave stragglers and a mass of exhausted men behind; among them generally the bravest—those who have ventured out farthest or held out longest. The feeling of having been defeated, which on the field of battle had struck only the senior officers, now runs through the ranks down to the very privates. It is aggravated by the horrible necessity of having to abandon to the enemy so many worthy comrades, whom one had come to appreciate especially in the heat of battle. Worse still is the growing loss of confidence in the high command, which is held more or less responsible by every subordinate for his own wasted efforts. What is worse, the sense of being beaten is not a mere nightmare that may pass: it has become a palpable fact that the enemy is stronger. It is a fact for which the reasons may have lain too deep to be predictable at the outset, but it emerges clearly and convincingly in the end. One may have been aware of it all along, but for the lack of more solid alternatives this awareness was countered by one's trust in chance, good luck, Providence, and in one's own audacity and courage. All this has now turned out to have been insufficient, and one is harshly and inexorably confronted by the terrible truth.

Clausewitz makes an important distinction between the recognition of defeat and flight in the face of it: "All of these impressions are still far removed from panic. An army with spirit will never panic in the face of defeat; even others panic in the wake of a lost battle only in exceptional cases."[45]

After departing Auerstedt, Prince August, Clausewitz, and their men turned westward. A bitter and often hungry fourteen-day retreat followed

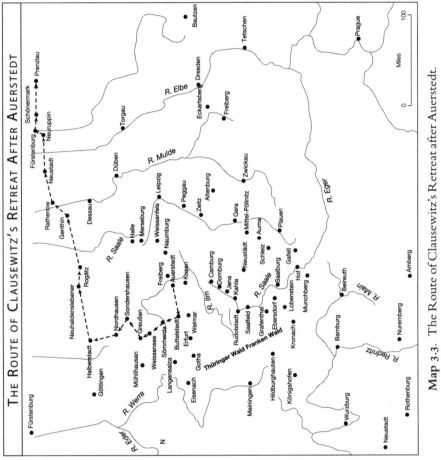

Map 3.3. The Route of Clausewitz's Retreat after Auerstedt.

their lost battle. "The spirit of the troops was[,] however, not changed by this," Clausewitz wrote in his history of the campaign, even though the men "had been without rations on the 14th and 15th, after the battle of Auerstedt." Following a short rest they were ordered to Weimar, but this changed after only a march of about an hour and a half because word came of French forces blocking the way. They were then ordered north, to Buttelstedt, but lost contact with friendly units along the way because the troops to their fore did not keep up their connection with those behind. Not knowing the way, they had no choice but to find a messenger to guide them, which they fortunately discovered in a nearby village not occupied by the French. They marched into the night—straight through the midst of the French forces—whose fires they could see burning nearby, often only 100 to 150 paces away. The French never called out to them, and they camped at Buttelstedt late that night.[46]

They marched again early on the morning of October 15. Down the road from Buttelstedt, August and Clausewitz watched the crews of an entire four-gun Prussian battery flee at the appearance of two French cavalrymen. They later found the crews and made them reclaim their guns. They continued on—northwestward—to Sömmerda, where they spent the night. "Since the soldiers had had nothing but bread to eat since noon on the 13th," Prince August said, "and no suitable preparations were made for their provisions, plundering could not be completely avoided." Here they learned that the king had left the army and put Kalckreuth in command.[47]

At daybreak on the 16th, they marched with the rest of the army for Weissensee. When they reached the heights at Weissensee they halted, finding French troops in the village. They waited for a long time and at one point were harangued by Colonel Christian Karl August Ludwig von Massenbach, who had been appointed Hohenlohe's quartermaster general; this made him Hohenlohe's chief advisor and assistant. "Massenbach," Clausewitz wrote, "made pathetic speeches on the duty of obedience, so that it was difficult to avoid hitting him on the head." One of August's officers who had been serving as an orderly to Kalckreuth tracked him down and reported that there was talk of surrender. August went to Kalckreuth and told him not to believe any such rumors. Kalckreuth replied: "We are surrounded by the French, the King has forbidden me from making an attack, and the troops are exhausted due to a lack of food. There remains no other choice to us but surrender." August argued with Kalckreuth, shaming and browbeating him into keeping up the fight.[48]

August convinced Kalckreuth to reconnoiter the area; they discovered that only small French cavalry units blocked their way. Kalckreuth,
however, was closer to correct about their being surrounded than
August realized. French pursuers pressed them from many directions,
and French cavalry had already occupied Weissensee, to their north
and on their line of retreat. Instead of fighting, Kalckreuth decided to
negotiate. Blücher, Kalckreuth's cavalry leader, convinced the French
commander in Weissensee that an armistice had been signed, and the
Prussians marched on.[49]

August and Clausewitz crossed the Helba near Greußen on the 16th,
destroying the bridge afterward. Their troops arrived, Clausewitz wrote
later, "dying with hunger. Prince August sent a detachment towards a
neighboring village to obtain rations. The peasants were astonished when
the soldiers arrived for this purpose. When rations were taken by force they
raised cries of distress."[50]

In Greußen, Kalckreuth also tried to negotiate with the pursuing French
forces led by Marshal Soult. Soult would have nothing of it and talked
only as long as it took for him to bring up his infantry. Kalckreuth ordered
August to form a square with his battalion (it ended up more of a rect-
angle, August noted later) and another put under his command, to cover
the retreat. The French mounted a heavy attack with cannon and howit-
zers against the bottleneck at Greußen and the city itself, setting the town
ablaze. The actions of other units in the rearguard, particularly the Oswald
infantry regiment, allowed Kalckreuth's little army to march unmolested
into the night.[51]

The rearguard reached Sondershausen at 6:30 on the morning of the
17th and found waiting orders from Kalckreuth—who had marched to
Nordhausen at 6:00 a.m. The preceding units had eaten the town bare.
Clausewitz and his comrades had received no bread since the 16th and had
had nothing for twenty-four hours. August wrote of his men: "They were
so tired from the incessant marching and lack of food that I, on my own
responsibility, dared to decamp an hour later. Since I had no money, I borrowed from my officers enough to buy some brandy for the grenadiers,
without this most of them probably would have broken down."[52]

They soon caught up with the other troops, who were marching slowly
because of their fatigue. August's unit remained in the rearguard, which
satisfied him, but he mentioned to General Hirschfeld that his men could
not keep up this post without rations. The general noted—oddly—that

it was not common to have the Guard and the King's Regiments as the rearguard, "and left it at that." [53] It seems that Kalckreuth took out his frustration with August by placing them constantly in the rearguard. Much of Clausewitz's combat experience in 1806 and in 1812 would be in this position—fighting defensive, delaying battles. This could have influenced his later thoughts regarding the superiority of the defense in *On War*, but claiming certainty on this is impossible.

Clausewitz's unit reached Nordhausen around 1:00 p.m. They had been there about half an hour when they heard cannon fire, and were ordered to form up. August, on his own initiative, decided that it was critical to hold the bridge outside the gate that led to Sondershausen and marched his two regiments there without orders. They arrived in time to see the Prussian cavalry in retreat, with nothing in the way of the French entering Nordhausen. Kalckreuth put his units on the heights above the town, with their back to the Harz Mountains to their north. August's battalion was put on high ground to the right of the road to Ilfeld to cover the army's flank.[54]

Under a heavy French bombardment, the Prussian retreat continued. The cavalry withdrew through the infantry, General Blücher going with the largest elements of it, as well as an infantry battalion and the heavy artillery, via Elbingerode and through the mountains. The rest of the army retired in fine order through Ilfeld and Hasselfelde, into the depths of the Harz. Clausewitz's unit again formed the rearguard, but the men were so exhausted from the quick marches and lack of food that August asked for help and Kalckreuth reinforced them with the Guadi battalion.[55]

They marched on, in darkness, into the Harz. Throughout Prussia other elements of the Prussian army endured retreat and privation as Napoleon's forces overran Clausewitz's homeland. The French didn't press August's men at this time, but the narrow and bad roads meant frequent stops. Units also got lost in the mountain blackness, Clausewitz's among them. Nervous firing from soldiers fed confusion bred by the night. Others added looting and plundering to chaos. Fatigue, confusion, darkness, rough terrain—in all of this August's units became intermingled. They stumbled on anyway, not stopping until five in the morning.[56]

August got separated from most of his men and was fortunate enough to find a wood cutter who led him to the village of Stiege. He rested there for two hours, figuring that the army would have to come this way, and arranged on his own for the purchase of vegetables and cattle because nothing had been done to feed the men. He discovered that Kalckreuth was in Blankenburg and went there to find him and get orders, though he had still not found the rest of his men. He ran into Captain Tiedemann of the General Staff, one of Clausewitz's best friends, and handed over to his care the improvised provisioning. He arrived in Blankenburg to find that Kalckreuth had already left for Halberstadt. August followed, finding the road along the way strewn with baggage and individual soldiers fleeing to Magdeburg. He soon found that Kalckreuth had also left Halberstadt, heading for Magdeburg. Since Nordhausen, they had not seen their divisional commander, nor received an order from him.[57]

With Kalckreuth gone, the corps had no leadership, and according to August was only held together by the mettle of some of the staff and most of the junior officers, and the goodwill of the bulk of the soldiery. "Toward evening Captain Clausewitz," August wrote, "whom I had abandoned in the Harz, arrived in Halberstadt and brought me the news that he and about 200 Grenadiers of my battalion had been sent to General Hirschfeld at Stiege, who would on the 19th, with all of the troops he had collected, go to Oschersleben."[58]

On the 20th the gathered remains of August's force marched to the neighborhood of Neuhaldenslebener, northwest of Magdeburg. They crossed the Elbe at Rogätz on the 21st and camped in several villages for two days, encountering no French troops. They learned here that Kalckreuth had been put in charge of the East Prussian troops and that Hohenlohe now commanded the units in the area of Magdeburg (he was given this job on October 18), which included theirs. Prince Hohenlohe's army was reorganized into three divisions on October 21 and August's men were now in a division commanded by General-Major Karl Friedrich von Hirschfeld.[59]

On the 22nd they marched to the area of Genthin. The next day, they trod on to the neighborhood of Rathenow, where they received bread for three days and each battalion got a cask of brandy. On the 24th they marched to Neustadt, then Clausewitz's former cantonment of Neuruppin on the 25th. There they found at least some preparations to feed the troops—ineffective ones.[60]

Up until this point their luck had held. They were hungry and exhausted but had avoided capture. Then things got worse. They left Neuruppin on the 26th, with 600 men. August's command was now a scratch unit made up of the remnants of his battalion and the Reinbaden Grenadiers. They arrived at Fürstenberg at night between 11 and 12 and most of the corps camped around the city. Many of the soldiers broke down from exhaustion.

The provisioning system had collapsed and the bulk of the men received nothing to eat. Prince August took it upon himself to forage in the surrounding villages, but most of the Grenadiers received only some potatoes.[61]

On the 27th they were told to march to Boitzenburg via Lychen, but French cavalry overran Boitzenburg before they reached it, capturing part of Hohenlohe's entourage. Two infantry battalions were sent to take back the town, which they did after a minor skirmish. August complained that instead of continuing straight on to Prenzlau, the army stayed about an hour and then decided to move that night to Schönermark. They marched continuously, for nine hours in the forests between Boitzenburg and Schönermark. Several times they became lost and finally reached Schönermark at 4:30 in the morning, where they slept for about an hour and a half. The lack of rations and rest began exacting an especially heavy toll on their men.[62]

Early on the 28th, at 6:00 a.m., Hohenlohe's army began to move toward Prenzlau. August's battalion again acted as the rearguard. They were twice ordered to hurry along and close up the distance to the main army by General Hirschfeld, the road now having been cleared of the hundreds of wagons previously separating them. Their march from Fürstenberg had been brutal on their unit. They had lost 516 men, and only 240 remained. Every day since the 14th (except for the 17th) they had been in the rearguard. His men exhausted, August sent his adjutant (probably Lt. von Hagen) to the reserve division commander, General Hirschfeld, asking to be replaced or reinforced.[63]

Count Stolberg of the King's Regiment delivered the second order to close up. August also received General Hirschfeld's reply that they would be reinforced by the King's Regiment, possibly by the same hand. As they were nearing Prenzlau, Prince August sent Clausewitz to reconnoiter the town in the company of the returning Stolberg. Just outside the city they spotted what Clausewitz estimated as three or four French cavalry regiments seemingly poised to attack Stolberg's regiment (The King's), which had just reached Prenzlau's gate.[64]

Stolberg insisted that Clausewitz join his regiment in a hasty retreat. He refused. "I replied that our duty here separated us, that he could regain his regiment in time by galloping, but that I would wait for Prince August at this place." As Clausewitz waited, he saw the Dohna Grenadiers and the Prittwitz Dragoons clash with the French cavalry. The French beat back the Dragoons, and then a melee between infantry and cavalry of both sides ensued before the city gate. August hurried his unit to the sound of the guns, arriving shortly with the battalion. Clausewitz gave his report, they discussed their options, and determined that their best course was to march around Prenzlau to the northwest and try to link up with Hohenlohe's army. They thought their exhausted men could handle little more, and believed the confusion would allow them to slip away unnoticed. Clausewitz later criticized their decision, chalking it up to the fact that "we had not learned by experience that a battalion of infantry can hold its own in the midst of hostile cavalry."[65]

They then noticed the Prussian Quitzow cuirassiers riding up behind them. Some French artillery that had come up on their right, across a stream flowing from the village of Boitzenburg, saw them too. The French gunners began throwing rounds into the horsemen, dispersing them, Clausewitz wrote, "like a handful of chaff thrown on the ground." Only Colonel Schubärt and fifty of his horsemen remained to support them. Clausewitz's unit waded a small stream, tramped through a vegetable garden, formed square, and began marching the course of the Uecker, which flowed about 1,000 paces away, heading roughly toward the village of Ellingen.[66]

After half an hour, about two miles from Prenzlau on the road to Pasewalk, they spotted cavalry on their left. At first they believed it the remnants of the Quitzow Regiment, but they quickly saw it was a bigger force. Colonel Schubärt said to August: "We're lost, there come the French." August told him to be quiet and not make the troops fainthearted with such talk, and also made it clear that they intended to defend themselves. "We hardly saw the French cavalry shimmer on the horizon," August wrote later, "and Colonel Schubärt had disappeared with his 50 horses." To his men the prince promised rewards of medals, money, and food, and encouraged them to keep their heads, defend themselves honorably, and not fire unless ordered. The French cavalry came on. "I thought for a moment to myself of the battle of Minden," Clausewitz wrote, "where the French cavalry charged two Hannover battalions; and when these failed to fire at the usual distance, they came gradually from a gallop to a trot and finally from a trot to a walk. Exactly the same thing happened here." Beaumont's 16th Dragoons rushed at the gallop, but when they drew up to 100 paces and had still not been fired on, they began slowing their horses until they reached a trot. At thirty paces, the Prussians volleyed. "Many fell," Clausewitz said of the French, and "the rest lay down in rear of their horses' necks, wheeled about and fled."[67]

The small victory enlivened the tired Prussians. "Now all our men were well in hand," Clausewitz wrote. "They seemed thoroughly astonished at the great success of the maneuver which they had often practiced on the drill ground and which they had usually considered as a sort of play." One dismounted Dragoon fled on foot. "The contrast between this anxious flight and the savage appearance of this dragoon with helmet and horse hair plume, made such an impression on the men that everyone laughed."[68]

They took up their march again, repelled another charge, and pressed on. But they immediately found the road blocked by French horsemen. Growing numbers of others pressed from behind, constantly threatening to charge. The Prussians sent their remaining skirmishers to the fore, and after a few shots they cleared the road and August's men marched on. The French kept on as well, however, mounting seven charges against Clausewitz and his comrades—usually in open line rather than column or squadron—and peppering them with fire from dismounted Dragoons shooting from hedges and bushes in a nearby village. In his description of the fight, Clausewitz mentions, significantly, that the French lacked artillery. Cavalry supported by artillery could more easily crush an infantry square because they would force it to disperse with cannon fire and then ride them down. "I acquired the conviction during this little cavalry fight, that infantry is very strong against cavalry," he wrote later. Clausewitz would find himself on the other side of this equation at Borodino in 1812.[69]

His men had endured a retreat of fourteen days and were physically exhausted and morally beaten down by their defeat in battle. Clausewitz later confessed his surprise at the steady performance of his men through what became three hours of combat and marching, strength manifested despite a numbing fatigue. These 240 enfeebled men held off what Clausewitz estimated as 1,500 cavalry. "The calmness maintained by its chief and his officers, and their continuous caution not to fire, and consequently retaining the fire until late, caused the success."[70]

Meanwhile, August sent three men on horseback to ask Hohenlohe or another Prussian commander for help. They had taken two farmers near Prenzlau as guides, who both fled when the French approached, but not before revealing that between Prenzlau and Pasewalk the swamps were impassable. Judging as too high the possibility of their ammunition running out or the strength or morale of their men breaking, Prince August decided to risk the marshes and make for Löcknitz or Pasewalk. To protect themselves from the cavalry—especially their artillery, which had now arrived to support the cavalry—they marched beside a swampy meadow, the marshes guiding a side of their square. But the farther they marched, the worse the ground became, and more gashed by broad, deep trenches.[71]

After an hour of this the terrain became so rough they could advance no more. They moved to the left, but encountered a yawning trench that most of the Grenadiers couldn't cross, and in which most of their horses got stuck. The French cavalry couldn't follow, but the Prussians endured a fearsome march. "Frequently we met large ditches full of water and so deep that the water came up under the arms," Clausewitz wrote. Nearly 100 men fell out from exhaustion along the way. They left behind their saddle horses, except August's, an especially strong English mount. But the harsh route exhausted it as well; it broke free, leapt into the river, and swam along beside them, resisting every effort to rescue it. August himself nearly drowned twice.[72]

The French had also not forgotten them. Their artillery had arrived and began firing into the swamp, though with no real effect. After crossing a particularly enormous, water-filled trench, the Prussians found firmer ground. This, Clausewitz said, meant they would not escape. The French cavalry could now reach them, albeit slowly, and proceeded to do so. The men were ordered to form square, but the constant French artillery fire made it impossible. Forced to use their muskets like staves to cross ditches, often in water reaching their arms, their weapons were dirty and water-logged, and their cartridge cases soaked. "They foresaw the impossibility of defending themselves," Clausewitz wrote, and "threw down their arms and voluntarily permitted the hostile cavalry to take them."[73]

The prince surrendered as well, and Clausewitz with him. About 100 men remained with them; others still in the swamp made their way back to Prenzlau. A few more got away across the river after a musket duel with the French. A few weeks later Clausewitz wrote to Marie of their end: "Finally, after three hot hours, fate showed the beautiful prize nearer. To the question repeated to me: 'Do you think we'll get through?' I could for the first time answer: 'Now I believe it. We are saved from the fire,' was the answer. But the fourth act was a tragedy in which we, thinking to escape danger, went into the snares of evil chance that doom disgorged. Destiny was tired of the game; it denied us the last wager to win back what was lost."[74]

Their captors took them to Prenzlau (after returning August's horse). Clausewitz and the prince arrived about 4:00 p.m. to find that Hohenlohe had surrendered the city. Joachim Murat, the famous French cavalry marshal, had told Hohenlohe that the city was surrounded by 100,000 men. It was a bluff, but Hohenlohe bit, and gave up the 10,000-man garrison.[75]

In Prenzlau, the French ushered Clausewitz and Prince August into Murat's presence. Murat was, Clausewitz noted, "making up a report to the Emperor on a sheet of open paper with very large oblique letters and a miserable handwriting." Murat flattered the prince and told him he would be taken to Berlin that night. They actually reached Berlin on the afternoon of the 29th. The French ushered Prince August immediately into Napoleon's presence. In addition to his pair of earlier wounds, the prince's horse had also trod on his foot at Prenzlau. He couldn't wear boots and had to appear before the emperor in slippers and the same clothes he wore in the swamp. "As to me," Clausewitz recalled, "I was allowed to remain with my much worn uniform in the midst of the brilliant uniforms of the Emperor's aides, who seemed slightly to dislike me." The prince's audience lasted only five minutes. Napoleon allowed him to remain in Berlin with his parents to recover from his wounds, but to have no correspondence with anyone or

Figure 3.1. Prince August's Battalion Firing at French Dragoons at Prenzlau.
From Emir Bukhari, *Napoleon's Dragoons and Lancers*. Men-At-Arms Series, No 55. (Oxford: Osprey Publishing, 1976).

make any speeches. Two months later, General Henri Clarke, the governor of Berlin, sent him to Nancy in France. Clausewitz accompanied him.[76]

In the wake of Jena and Auerstedt, utter disaster unfolded for the Prussians; Prenzlau's fall was but a minor note. The French had taken Berlin on October 25. A few days later they marched many of their captives through the city's streets. Napoleon ordered the Prussian Guard to parade past the French embassy, on the steps of which they had defiantly sharpened their swords only a few weeks before. On October 29 Stettin's commander folded the Prussian flag without a shot, handing the French another 5,000 prisoners. Blücher—Scharnhorst with him—was forced to surrender 10,000 men who had taken refuge in the neutral Danish city of Lübeck on November 5. A Swedish division sent to help their Prussian ally arrived just in time to become French prisoners themselves. Magdeburg surrendered on November 10; Napoleon took another 22,000 prisoners. The remnants of the broken Prussian force staggered toward the Oder River to join the advancing Russians.[77]

In seven weeks Napoleon had inflicted 25,000 casualties on the Prussians and taken 140,000 prisoners, eliminating the bulk of the Prussian army's manpower, as well as its reputation. Historian David Chandler rightly observed that "Seldom in history has an army been reduced to impotence more swiftly or decisively."[78]

4

A Political Education
(1807–1812)

If we know how to fight and how to win, little more knowledge is needed.

Clausewitz's war ended at Prenzlau; Prussia's did not. Frederick William withdrew northward to Memel (now Klaipėda, Lithuania), gathering another army. As we saw earlier, Czar Alexander had also decided to come to Prussia's aid, and the Russian army entered East Prussia on November 1, 1806. Napoleon's forces crossed into Prussian Poland four days later. Napoleon bided his time, building supply magazines to support a winter campaign. In late December the French began to move. The Russians withdrew as Napoleon came on. The Russians then surprised Napoleon with a counteroffensive that saw the French emperor scrambling to concentrate his forces and then counterattacking into East Prussia. The Russians fell back again. The armies of the two emperors clashed at Eylau on February 7–8, with Prussian forces supporting Alexander. A bloody fight ensued amidst a snowstorm. The defeated Russians retreated northward, toward Königsberg, leaving the French a field strewn with 40,000 casualties, more than half French. The war went on. Prussia's major fortresses had already fallen, often to inferior French forces; those in Silesia held out. Clausewitz later attributed this staggering series of surrenders to poorly prepared defenses; ancient, tired generals holding their respective reins; and the Prussian will to resist cracking under the weight of defeat.[1]

After a winter pause, the war resumed. The Prussian Baltic coast city of Danzig fell at the end of May, and in April Napoleon pushed his army deeper into East Prussia. On June 14, 1807, French and Russian forces clashed at Friedland (now Pravdinsk in Russian Kaliningrad). French troops broke the Russians, who retreated eastward. The defeat convinced Czar Alexander to change course.[2]

Napoleon and Alexander then had their famous meeting upon a raft anchored in the midst of the Niemen River on June 25, 1807. Napoleon had no interest in treating Prussia as a great power, and the French and Russian emperors proceeded to cut a deal beneficial to themselves, but disastrous for Prussia, which had little choice but to accept it. Two treaties followed, with the July 9 Franco-Prussian Treaty of Tilsit costing Prussia half of its land and people and strapping it to a large indemnity to pay for a French occupation force. In September 1808 Frederick William submitted to another humiliating agreement. This neutered Prussia, limiting its army to 42,000, and forbidding it a militia and the use of conscription.[3]

When Prince August had rejoined his parents in November 1806, Clausewitz returned temporarily to his regiment's cantonment in Neuruppin, awaiting the moment when he would accompany the prince to France as a prisoner. His situation was not unusual under the conventions of the day. A captured officer released in wartime under his own recognizance—especially a royal like August—would have limited freedom as long as he did not take up arms again until officially exchanged. Clausewitz, as the prince's adjutant, followed in his master's train. Clausewitz resumed his correspondence with Marie and also wrote three extended letters on the 1806 campaign that soon appeared—unsigned—in the magazine Minerva. The text published in February 1807 is important for the development it reveals in his theories, particularly as an early demonstration of his awareness of the non-material elements of war. "Nothing seems to me more petty than if one counts only upon flesh and blood and powder and lead, and gives no consideration to the moral forces."[4] In this letter he addresses the German nation—not just Prussia; he was becoming a German nationalist.

One of the many effects of the French Revolution and Napoleon's establishment of his empire was the intensification of the nationalist impulse throughout Europe. "Germany" was a geographical expression in Clausewitz's day. French expansion and power fueled the idea of a unified Germany, one that transcended political bounds. The passions of German Romanticism, the hearkening to the classical age, fed upon and powered nationalist ideas among many German intellectuals. Clausewitz read the works of these writers—Goethe and Fichte being perhaps the most important—and soaked up the intellectual passions of his age. His own zealous temperament seems to have made their ideas particularly attractive to the young Clausewitz.

The campaign and Prussia's humiliation dealt heavy psychological blows to Clausewitz, something his letters make plain. "I have had painful experiences, and bloody wounds have been struck against my mind," he wrote Marie. He had hoped, indeed *needed*, to win fame in battle, and believed his Fatherland required success as well. But no victory laurel came. At one point in the campaign (probably at Prenzlau), he felt they were "abandoned by Fate, thrown into the arms of Despair, and playing with their loaded dice for death or an immortal deed." But he still had faith in the future, both for himself and his country, for he considered their destinies intertwined. He struggled to remain modest—"a human life is just a small dot on the scale with which the Almighty orders the destinies of nations"—but, as he told Marie, "I must say that I was not unworthy of the humblest of hopes that you had in me."[5]

On December 30, 1806, the French sent Prince August to Nancy in France; Clausewitz accompanied him. Clausewitz's treatment as a prisoner of war will strike many modern readers as unusual. He did not face the terrors of Andersonville or a British prison hulk. The worst thing he endured was boredom—the POW's perennial problem.

As he and Prince August traveled across Germany to France, Clausewitz passed through the areas where he fought his first war in 1793, seeing ruins from the campaign as well as the still shattered city of Mainz, and encountered Prussian prisoners from the battle of Auerstedt. It was, he said, a most unpleasant moment when they departed Germany and heard nothing spoken but French. The change made him homesick and his notes to Marie during his journey are filled with mourning over his nation's fate—and sometimes his own. "I am healthy in body," he wrote Marie, "but not in spirit." "I am very, very unhappy."[6]

Reaching Nancy in mid-January made him no more joyful and even the prospect of seeing Paris did not cheer him. News of friends lost in the war added to his ill feelings. Word of Scharnhorst's survival brightened him, but he found no German friends to whom he felt particularly drawn. "Your letters and their answering are my only recreation," he told Marie. During his imprisonment he decided against learning a musical instrument to pass the hours, deeming the return not worth the investment, but he did make some use of his days writing in the aforementioned lost notebooks, sharpening his skills at mathematics and French, achieving a fluency in the tongue that would serve him throughout his career.[7]

Clausewitz also reported to Marie an unfortunate incident with a French officer, one that shows not only his scorn of French arrogance, but his view of German superiority: "I found myself in the company of a young French Colonel, the director of the school of engineering in Metz, and thus holding a very important post. In a conversation in no way prompted by me, he treated me as if I had no more value than the least of his pupils." Clausewitz's response was to leave off conversation with the officer and begin a playful conversation with a lady. "I remember this incident with pleasure because it is part of the national character and because I can rightly ask: What German would treat a stranger with this ridiculous presumption if he knows nothing about him?"[8]

At the end of February the prince received orders to leave Nancy and choose one of four small towns near Paris: Senlis, Beauvais, Meaux, or Soissons. August chose Soissons, and they left Nancy on March 1. Clausewitz, who considered the spirit of intrigue an essential element of French character, was suspicious of the move and wondered if the French had composed a plan for using August to do yet more injury to Prussia. On the way they visited Rheims, and admired the cathedral (Clausewitz habitually commented on the architecture during his travels). They left Soissons on March 14 and visited Paris for fourteen days. August traveled under the name "Müller" as the two prisoners toured the painting and art galleries, attended the theater, and visited several well-known salons. "God knows how little this trip fits my mood!" Clausewitz told Marie.[9]

When they passed through Rheims, Clausewitz called its cathedral's bells, and those of the other cathedrals he visited, "the sublime voice of the herald of our devotion" to the Christian religion. But to claim this as an expression of Christian faith would be a stretch. Whether or not Clausewitz shared the Christian believer's faith in Jesus Christ is something for which he left little definitive evidence. A French biographer of Clausewitz doubted he had faith in a personal God, but this also cannot be proven. In his "Notes on History and Politics" written during this period, Clausewitz makes some comments on religion, but nothing here that could be clearly identified as conventionally Christian. He certainly does mention God in his letters at various points, though perfunctorily: "I will always strive as long as the Lord allows me to remain," for example. In a note to Marie of October 5, 1807, Clausewitz remarks that "Religion should not distract our gaze from this world; it is a divine force which enters into a covenant with what is noble in this life, and a religious feeling has never pervaded and strengthened me without cheering me on to a good deed, to a great desire, indeed even giving me hope." Still, as he added, he could and would not "turn my eyes away from the earth."[10]

Clausewitz did not greatly enjoy his time in Paris and complained to Marie about what he termed the prince's "pleasure-seeking life." The introverted Clausewitz and the more relaxed and adventuresome prince did not make the best companions. Clausewitz believed that August was wasting his youth, although this judgment seems overly harsh considering their recent experiences. Enforced inactivity led the ambitious Clausewitz to frustration. "I feel within me a particular striving for a noble purpose," he told Marie. Prussia's war with France continued, and he chafed to be back in active service. But he also reflected upon his experience in the war, where he had "seen nothing that is not bad and pitiful." Nonetheless, he could not banish thoughts of victory; it had for him "an indescribable allure," even though he felt the Prussian army had not shown in battle the ability to attain it. "Of everything that I have learned of the art of war, I have not seen the least bit that has been executed by us." He viewed leadership, youthful, dynamic leadership *à la* Napoleon, as one of the keys to victory: "I know that calculated audacity, innovation, swiftness provide justified belief in victory (and therein lie the advantages of a young general—that he surprises the opponent with all the originality and innovation of his talent)." Indeed, he hoped that one day he might be such a general: "and now I am going nowhere and one day perhaps one will entrust to me as so many others the fortunes of the state and the leadership of the army when my arm shakes due to old age."[11]

It is little wonder that Clausewitz remained melancholy during his exile; Marie's letters were one of the few things that brought him happiness. Prussia's war with France went on and he saw the world collapsing around him and felt that he could do nothing. Shortly before the signing of the Treaties of Tilsit, which ended the struggle, he wrote: "I fear nothing more than peace; the more one has the desire to bring it about, the more dangerous it is." Shortly after his twenty-seventh birthday, he wrote Marie that because of the sporadic nature of his education, and the environment in which he had grown up and since lived, he considered himself intellectually "a piece and patchwork, and for that reason a very imperfect work."[12]

On August 1 the Prince and Clausewitz were allowed to leave Soissons, but they still had to wait two months for the necessary passports before going home. In the meantime they traveled first to Switzerland (a French possession at the time), arriving in Geneva on August 5. The wandering Prussians went to Savoy to see the glacier on the 8th, then came on the 11th via Geneva to Lausanne and then to Coppet for a lengthy stay in the literary salon of Madame de Staël.[13]

Unlike the rest of his POW experience, Clausewitz very much enjoyed his time with Madame de Staël, who impressed him with her learning. For her part, she came to call Clausewitz and the prince "the two excellent Germans," of which, Clausewitz wrote, "we are both very proud." Clausewitz was far from the first man to fall under her spell. He was less taken, however, by the presence of Madame Recamier, a famous beauty of the day. He denounced her as "a very common flirt," a response no doubt related to Prince August's infatuation with her and subsequent unrequited love. The prince did very little for three weeks to obtain the passports they needed to leave France after the peace was signed; this irritated Clausewitz even more. In any case, he continued his soul-searching, both on a personal level and in regard to the weakness of the German spirit and lack of character, which war could overcome. "In war a vast field of energetic means is opened," he declared, "and if I utter the secret thoughts of my soul I am for the most violent of all; by whipping I would awaken the lazy beast and teach it to break the chains that it has so cowardly and fearfully allowed itself to wear."[14]

During their time in Switzerland, Clausewitz and August visited an innovative school run by Johann Heinrich Pestalozzi. Pestalozzi's methods stimulated Clausewitz intellectually, so much so that he wrote an essay about his observations there. Pestalozzi abandoned the traditional practice of having the student recite to the teacher by rote and instead would pose questions to a class of students, building upon their answers with further questions, thus creating—through what was an essentially Socratic method—an active, inquiring learner. Clausewitz maintained a lifelong interest in educational and instructional methods. In Paris he had visited the city's institute for educating the deaf and much admired the educational practices he observed there. He also came to know and like the writer Karl Wilhelm Friedrich Schlegel, a well-known member of the German Romantic movement. In all this enforced inaction Clausewitz nonetheless tried to manage his career. He no longer relished serving as Prince August's adjutant and wrote to his mentor Scharnhorst about tacking to a different course. Doing so required "a small intrigue" because the king would demand reasons for the change. Clausewitz also considered leaving the army and following in the footsteps of the Roman general Cincinnatus, retiring to the country to "study history and the art of war, and quietly await the moment when it would be time to step back into the service."[15]

On October 7, 1807, the passports finally arrived. A visit to Italy, which would have included Rome, was abandoned, and Clausewitz and August began the trip home. They arrived in Berlin at the beginning of November, after a ten-month absence. They returned to a city transforming into a hotbed of German Romanticism, one teeming with intellectuals such as the philosopher Johann Gottlieb Fichte and the poet and writer Ernst Moritz Arndt, whom Clausewitz would later number among his friends. The Romantic movement was a reaction against what many considered the sterile, even atheistic, rationalism of the Enlightenment. Yes, reason and science still mattered, but men were also creatures of feeling, passion, and spirit. And the past mattered as well. But the German version of Romanticism was awash in anti-French feeling. Many young Germans—the Prussians included—saw the Enlightenment as the French occupier's alien culture, one lacking a soul, and a distinctive "Germanness."[16]

Defeat had deeply affected Clausewitz, but it also shocked the Prussian military and political systems, helping give rise to a reform movement dedicated to improving and strengthening both. Clausewitz was caught up in that movement. War, defeat, and imprisonment had expanded his viewpoint. "The author was a Prussian officer in every sense of the word," he later wrote of himself, "and if he soon came to think differently about Prussia's military institutions than most of his comrades, this was simply the result of reflection." He was, he said, "driven to uncover its weaknesses" and help "renovate the building before it collapsed."[17] In Clausewitz's mind this struggle to build a new Prussian army, and thus a new Prussian state—for Prussia was nothing without its army—was an act of filial love.

At the top of the Prussian pyramid sat the king, Frederick William III, who, as we've seen, was a man riven by caution and indecision. He did have strengths, however. Critically, Frederick William did not accept Prussia's defeat as the last word, and simply refused to become another minor German ruler scraping by under Napoleon's thumb. This made him willing to accept changes that ran counter to his most heartfelt beliefs. But Frederick needed able men in his government to drive change, and a forceful, determined personality to take the necessary steps. Frederick William brought Karl vom Stein back into office as a de facto first minister. This ensured progress on the political front, though employing Stein was not without its challenges.[18]

Heinrich Friedrich Karl vom und zum Stein was outspoken, as noted earlier, and known for possessing "a furious rage." Frederick William had already fired him once before for being "refractory, insolent, obstinate and disobedient." He was the complete opposite of Scharnhorst, who led the military reformers and preferred to push for changes in more subtle ways. But both Stein and Scharnhorst agreed that the people felt no particular love for their state and that this had to change. "The chief idea," wrote Stein in 1807, "was to arouse a moral, religious and patriotic spirit in the nations, to instill into it again courage, confidence, readiness for every sacrifice in behalf of independence from foreigners and for the national honor, and to seize the first favorable opportunity to begin the bloody and hazardous struggle."[19] They intended to harness the passion of the Prussian people in the service of their state as Napoleon and the Revolutionaries had done in the service of France.

Reformers like Stein and Scharnhorst were keenly aware that they had to make drastic societal changes to get the average Prussian peasant and member of the middle class to care about the fate of what many viewed as an oppressive state that too often treated them little better than chattel. Stein brought about the abolition of serfdom in 1807, and an element of devolution via the independence of local city government in 1808, though he failed to get approval for any form of national, representative assembly.[20]

Scharnhorst's stock rose dramatically after the war due to his courage at Auerstedt and staunch leadership during the Prussian retreat. Frederick William decided to rely on Scharnhorst to build a new Prussian army. In July 1807 the king formed the Military Reorganization Commission. After a bumpy start, Scharnhorst emerged as its head. The commission went through a number of members, all of them army officers. Many of them, including Scharnhorst, August Neidhardt von Gneisenau, Hermann von Boyen, and Carl Wilhelm Georg von Grolman, had not held influential positions in the Prussian government or army before 1806. Their appointments also broke the dominating hold of the nobility in Prussia. Scharnhorst's father was a sergeant; Grolman's father was an ennobled judge; Gneisenau couldn't prove the title he claimed (nor for that matter could Clausewitz, who became Scharnhorst's assistant). They were solidly from the middle class.[21]

The members of the commission realized that Prussian subjects had no real link to the government, meaning that the all-important support of the people had been denied their nation in its contest with France, something they would work to overcome. The commission recognized, as did Clausewitz, the political and social forces unleashed by the French Revolution, and wanted to tap into them. "Through the power and energy of its principles and the enthusiasm that it inspired in the French people," Clausewitz wrote later, "the Revolution had thrown the whole weight of the nation and its strengths into a balance that had formerly weighed only small standing armies and limited state revenues."[22] Military reform was paramount—and the key to saving Prussia from France—but this could not succeed in isolation from social change in Prussia, which in turn had no hope of success unless it came from the political elite.

In short, Scharnhorst knew that to remake the army they must remake the state. "We must kindle a sense of independence in the nation," he wrote Clausewitz in November 1807. "We must enable the nation to understand itself and take up its own affairs; only then will the nation acquire self-respect and compel the respect of others." Scharnhorst would enjoy much success, and Clausewitz later explained why. He was not one of those reformers "who verge on charlatanism or use their genius like a club to flatter themselves that their ideas are wholly new and unprecedented." What Scharnhorst did was to reassure people that everything he planned was not revolutionary, in fact, but "only slightly modified and rationalized." Clausewitz also admired the clarity of Scharnhorst's judgment, and his dedication to historical data to support his thoughts and conclusions.[23]

Scharnhorst directed the attack on the hidebound Prussian military, and one of the first places he struck was at the composition and construction of the noble-dominated officer corps. The Junkers—Prussian nobles who filled the ranks of the officer corps—needed to give way to officers of talent from the middle class. "What can we expect from the inhabitants of these sandy steppes," Stein wrote of the Prussian officer caste, "these artful, heartless, wooden, half-educated men—who are really capable only of becoming corporals or book-keepers?" The king would not perhaps have agreed with Stein's depiction, but he agreed with the theory behind it, and his order of August 6, 1808, opened the officer corps to those with the requisite education in peacetime or those who proved themselves in battle in wartime. Would-be officer recruits now had to be seventeen and pass an examination for entry into a regiment.[24]

One of the first suggestions the reform committee received was from Prince August, who was still a French captive at the time. Clausewitz helped in its composition. Among the things August advised were adopting

Scharnhorst's recommendation to divide the Prussian army into artillery, cavalry, and infantry branches; lightening the soldier's load; improving the logistics system; and better integrating the light troops and line infantry at the tactical level. He questioned the use of corporal punishment, but stopped short of pushing its abolition, something the reformers deemed necessary, as one could not appeal to a man's honor and sense of personal dignity and self-worth if that man was subject to beatings from his superiors. Eventually the reformers did eliminate corporal punishment for minor infractions while establishing a fairer structure of military justice. Scharnhorst achieved the reorganization of the military schools via an August 1808 order, and soon the Prussians had schools in Berlin, Königsberg, and Breslau with a nine-month course to prepare officers. He also founded an advanced military school in Berlin for select officers, which later became the Kriegsakademie. It had a three-year curriculum and from its top graduates, the *Selekta*, the General Staff recruited.[25]

The Prussians also had to rethink how they recruited and organized the rank and file. As we have seen, in the 1700s the Prussian army had relied upon enlisting foreigners and upon levies from the nation's cantons, a regiment assigned to each. Defeat in 1806 and Napoleon's expansion broke this system. Foreign recruitment became impossible, and some of the reformers hated the limitations on popular participation in the army imposed by the canton system. The reform commission declared that all men were defenders of the kingdom and some of its members pushed for universal service— one tied to and supported by a militia drawn from the rest of the male population. This was, they felt, at the very heart of what was necessary for national rebirth.[26]

But they did not get this in 1808, for two reasons. First, the 1808 treaty with Napoleon limited the Prussian army to 42,000 and forbade a militia. Second, the king refused to grant the reformers universal conscription—fearing, among other things, that it would result in the replacement of the professional army. He also did not approve their militia, seeing this as "inimical to royal authority." The king pled penury because of the high cost, as well as the restrictions of the treaty with the French, whose demands exerted influence over Prussia. The canton system remained, greatly restricting the size of the army. Scharnhorst responded by developing what was known as the *Krumper* system to train wartime replacements. Units released some of their men each year and replaced them with recruits. The system, launched in 1807, was only applied to the whole army in 1809, and ended in 1811, producing, overall, limited success. In 1813 the Prussian army only had a trained reserve of 65,675. Moreover, the army's size, fixed at 42,000, meant that Prussia could only build an army based around six brigades, not the six divisions the commission wanted.[27]

However, the army received newer and better equipment, and the Prussians developed more facilities to produce it. There were also a number of tactical innovations introduced. The concept that *all* light infantry should be trained to fight as skirmishers was institutionalized by 1811, though some began pushing for light troops to also be trained to fight in attack columns just as the line infantry, effectively removing most differences between the light and line units. Scharnhorst oversaw the writing of new manuals for the infantry, artillery, and cavalry. Clausewitz would eventually help write the one for the infantry, which appeared in 1812.[28]

March 1809 saw the establishment of a new Ministry of War— Allgemeine Kriegsdepartement—which, finally, united all of Prussia's military activities under one administrative bureau. The king, most probably because he feared surrendering too much military power to one man, did not appoint a minister of war. Scharnhorst served as the leader of the General Department, one of the War Ministry's two departments, while Friedrich Karl von Lottum became the head of the Military Economy Department. Both would be given access to the king. Their forerunners were dissolved or folded into these operations.[29]

The traditionalists, of course, pushed back. Some feared losing their own rights and those of their sons. Others believed the new regulations emphasized theoretical training at the expense of traits that were, they felt, so important to making a good soldier, such as duty and calm under duress. The king responded by reasserting his right to appoint commanders in March 1809.[30]

During his time in France, Clausewitz had already begun working to have himself reassigned. When he and Prince August returned home in November, Clausewitz remained his adjutant, but wheels were turning. In November and December 1807 Scharnhorst wrote Clausewitz to be patient. Scharnhorst intended to do everything possible that Prussia's "current weak, sick condition allowed" to plant the seeds for its rebirth. They were building a new system and part of their effort was creating a new General Staff where Scharnhorst hoped to use Clausewitz.[31]

On April 1, 1808, Clausewitz arrived with prince August in Königsberg, where most of the royal family had gathered. The prince had a great interest in the expected reform of the artillery and went to Königsberg to aid in its development. Clausewitz was happily reunited with Scharnhorst. He also met for the first time someone else with whom he would develop a close relationship, a member of the reform commission, August Neidhardt von Gneisenau. In a letter to Marie, written when he was in Switzerland, Clausewitz confessed that he had deep affection for only two people in his life—Marie and Scharnhorst—and doubted ever finding a third to equal them.[32] Gneisenau would become this third.

Clausewitz met Gneisenau shortly after arriving in Königsberg. Unlike most of his comrades—but like most of the reformers—Gneisenau also carried a questionable "von" before his surname. Born in Saxony, the son of a non-noble soldier, he entered Prussian service as an artillery officer in 1786. He was twenty years older than Clausewitz, and a lieutenant-colonel, when Clausewitz returned to duty in 1807. Gneisenau had been a captain when the 1806 war began, and was promoted to major in October. He made a name for himself after unexpectedly ending up in command of the Baltic coast fortress of Kolberg, which he held against the French until July

Figure 4.1. August Neidhardt von Gneisenau (1760–1831). Courtesy of www.123rf.com.

2, 1807. Gneisenau stood firm when so many other Prussian commanders had folded. Marie wrote later that almost from the moment of their first meeting, Clausewitz's relationship with Gneisenau was as close as that with Scharnhorst.[33]

In Königsberg, Clausewitz moved in the nation's most powerful circles. He spent time in the company of Prince Anton Heinrich Radziwill and his wife, Princess Louise, the sister of Prince August and a woman of education and erudition. Clausewitz also mingled with the men who would return Prussia to its former glory—Stein; the one-time Prussian chancellor Karl August von Hardenberg; the philosopher, educational reformer, and diplomat Wilhelm von Humboldt; and others.[34]

While in Königsberg, Clausewitz became aware of a plot to have Marie marry someone else. Out of friendship with Marie's mother, Stein pushed to have Marie wed Count Alexander zu Dohna. This annoyed Clausewitz, though at the same time he understood Countess von Brühl's interest— the Dohnas were one of Prussia's most powerful and important families and firm members of the landed aristocracy. Alexander's brother, Carl Friedrich, served with Clausewitz on Scharnhorst's staff and married Scharnhorst's daughter, Julie. Later, when Stein left his post as the minister of the interior, Alexander zu Dohna replaced him.[35]

Marie had no intention of going along and the issue became their private joke. When Marie learned that Clausewitz had developed a relationship with Stein she was happy to hear about it. Her mother had a high opinion of Stein and—she quipped—a single word from him in Clausewitz's favor "would perhaps produce a great revolution" in her mother's opinion. Until this time Madame von Brühl had remained unmoved. "With Mama, nothing is changed," Marie wrote Clausewitz in the last week of August 1808. She encouraged him to be patient until things evolved, adding that she believed her mother's resistance was weakening.[36]

Meanwhile, Clausewitz continued his campaign for a new post and fretted over his future. August had asked Scharnhorst about formally promoting Clausewitz to captain, which Scharnhorst said wouldn't be difficult, especially since the prince would soon be moved to an artillery command. To Clausewitz, however, this meant the prince intended to keep him in his service, something that he was determined to avoid. With Scharnhorst unwilling to go against August's wishes, Clausewitz decided to write to the king, emphasizing how bad it was for any officer's development to be in the same post for almost six years—one with no military responsibilities—and that the prince's posting to the artillery would rob him of the chance of acquiring any. "What I feared, however," he related to Marie, was being categorized with the other officers "who are without positions and on half-pay." He saw no reason why the king should not lump him with all the other officers to whom nothing special was owed and who also had done nothing wrong.[37]

Clausewitz's concern was not misplaced. Not only did he face the reality of a postwar drawdown resulting from treaty provisions that shrunk the army, but the Prussians themselves had embarked upon a rigorous self-examination of the causes of the debacle. Part of this investigation centered upon the officer corps. The Military Reorganization Commission eventually forced 208 officers from the service, including 103 of their 142 generals. Almost three-quarters of the officer corps was pushed out, an astounding number.[38]

Clausewitz wrote his letter to the king and determined to send it as soon as the prince took up his new command. He told Marie he would be trading a promotion and a raise for being free again. Although Scharnhorst wasn't particularly supportive of the move, Clausewitz remained confident that Scharnhorst would help him when he could because the general spoke to him in confidence about a number of critical matters. "For the first time in my life," Clausewitz wrote Marie, "I am pulled by my mental faculties out of the narrow circle of personal life."[39]

Clausewitz's letter went to the king and Scharnhorst stressed to Frederick William the perfect reasonability of Clausewitz's request. The king replied on August 19, 1808, that if Prince August later named an artillery officer as his adjutant, as would be expected, they could revisit Clausewitz's request. Clausewitz went back to waiting. "I remain undiminished in the Kitchen Department," he joked to Marie. Yet though he could laugh at his situation, it still vexed him, and as he worried for the future, his old melancholy descended. "Great, indescribably great is this time," he told Marie, but feared that most people, even the wisest, didn't realize this. With perhaps a bit too much self-important Romanticism, he wrote, "Think of my prophecy, Marie, there will come a much blacker sky over us, and we will be wrapped in night and sulfur fumes before we realize it."[40]

Even though officially he was still August's adjutant, Clausewitz worked unofficially for Scharnhorst and the Commission in Königsberg. In September 1808 Scharnhorst, while consoling him with promises of the future, employed Clausewitz as his literary amanuensis writing such

things as the new Prussian Articles of War, other regulations, and articles
for newspapers and scholarly journals. He was also tasked with gathering
the best achievements of individuals during the war to make a small propaganda book "to awaken the public mind." Sometimes the things that he
wrote Scharnhorst would simply sign and send along; for others he offered
revisions. At times Clausewitz found his activities insignificant, but he
believed they generally served a useful purpose, and the work was proof to
him of Scharnhorst's friendship.[41]

Though Scharnhorst's influence was important, no one's position in the
Prussian government was entirely secure. Prussia's problems with Napoleon
were far from ended, and in late 1808, Bonaparte forced the Prussian government to remove some of its most effective (and sometimes vociferously
anti-French) members. One of the first to go was Stein. Marie mourned
his departure from the Prussian government because of his great talents.
"A moral rebirth of the state was the only hope we had left," she wrote
Clausewitz, adding, "I don't know from whom we can expect it when he is
wrested from us." But she also had hoped that Clausewitz's working with
Stein would lead to her mother softening her resistance. "Perhaps this was
all just a beautiful dream," she wrote, "but the loss of an illusion is always
painful and it is all the more so in a moment where real hopes are so few."[42]

Late October 1808 saw the arrival of the Russian czar in Königsberg
on his way to Erfurt, and the far worse news of the Prussians signing the
treaty with France that included the aforementioned limits on the army
and saddled Prussia with a harsh indemnity and a foreign occupation.
Clausewitz and many others found this heartbreaking. "All the people here
look sick and miserable," Clausewitz told Marie, Stein and Scharnhorst
among them. French pressure also made Scharnhorst's position untenable
and Clausewitz thought—correctly—that he would soon be forced to go.
He wanted to have confidence in the future, but the more he considered
Prussia's circumstances in late 1808, the more it bothered him: "The greater
the care with which I climb into this dark pit to dig out a sparkling gem,"
he wrote Marie, "the poorer I return."[43]

But not all was bad news, at least for Clausewitz. Gneisenau had relayed
to him Scharnhorst's remark that of his staff, Clausewitz was the best among
them. The elated Clausewitz told Marie, "You can't believe how proud I
feel because of this personal trust." Marie also reassured and encouraged
Clausewitz. "The deep love that unites us is the beneficent balm heaven
has given us for all of life's wounds," she told him, and urged him to

have confidence in the future. In January 1809 Clausewitz learned from Scharnhorst that the general had cleared things with Prince August to allow Clausewitz to come to work on the General Staff, having told the prince he could find no one else suitable. "God be praised," he wrote Marie, "this is truly a load off my mind!" He officially took up his post on February 21, 1809. The prince let him go and recommended to the king Clausewitz's promotion to captain. The transfer was Scharnhorst's doing and he ensured that the promotion order detailed Clausewitz to the War Department. Clausewitz believed the prince wasn't happy with the change, though they parted on good terms. He also wasn't sure whether the prince realized that Clausewitz had helped engineer his own departure, though August never raised a single "indelicate" question on the matter. If he had, Clausewitz confessed, it would have caused him much embarrassment. With the promotion came a raise and his salary—after deductions—would be 900 talers a year, a comfortable sum. He told Marie: "To me it is as if I stepped from a cold tomb back into life on a beautiful spring day!"⁴⁴

In 1808 Napoleon invaded Spain. The French emperor quickly defeated the opposing regular army, but resistance to French rule arose from the civilian population. Their armed opposition as *guerrillas* gave us our modern terms for the type of war the Spanish waged and its irregular combatants. Napoleon's "bleeding ulcer" of Spain convinced the Austrians that it was time to regain some of their lost position in Europe. The War of the Fifth Coalition began on April 9, 1809. This marked the first attempt to make the struggle against Napoleon a German nationalist war, as the Austrians tried to gather the other German states to oppose France. Pressured by Russia to remain neutral, Prussia refused to intervene on the Austrian side, though Scharnhorst and others urged the king to go to war. Frederick William feared Prussia's annihilation. "A political existence of some kind, no matter how small it be, is better than none," he wrote. Preservation meant "at least some hope remains for the future, but none would remain if Prussia disappeared entirely from the community of states." Considering the military and political situation, and the reality that it would be very hard for Prussia and Austria to defeat Napoleon without Russian help, the king probably made the best choice, though many of his most important officers and officials heartily disagreed.⁴⁵

Blücher, for one, was enraged by the king's refusal to act, and retreated to the bottle. Clausewitz's path often intertwined with this key Prussian military commander. Gebhard Lebrecht von Blücher (1742–1819) is one of those historical figures described with the cliché "larger than life." Witty and insanely brave, Blücher possessed a firm judgment under fire and an inner mental strength that enabled him to shake off battlefield defeat with the nonchalance another man might show dusting off a cloak. But he was also prone to personal excesses, and soon stories emerged from his head-quarters at Stargaard that Blücher thought he had been impregnated by an elephant and that French secret agents were heating the floor of his head-quarters so much that he couldn't walk on it.[46]

Clausewitz envisioned in war with Austria not only an opportunity for Prussia, but also for himself. He saw the French stretched by their war with Spain (which was turning into a vicious and unending series of irregu-lar actions) and then with Austria, thought the mood in Germany ripe for action, and hoped French defeats would awaken the Germans against Napoleon. The situation could not be resolved with a few hard blows, Clausewitz knew, but rather by forcing upon France an extended strug-gle that would bring it down.[47] We see here a line of thought breaking with Ancien Régime military views of short wars fought for limited aims, while demonstrating an awareness of the manner in which the French Revolution and modernity changed warfare. The pace and intensity of warfare had increased, and wars were no longer fought by armies detached from the mood of the people. Clausewitz would come to see a protracted war (though he did not use this term) as a viable strategic approach, espe-cially for a weaker power.

But in the spring of 1809 other matters pressed. Clausewitz feared that Prussia would be forced to side with Napoleon against Austria—a real pos-sibility as Prussia was technically allied with France and could be required to dispatch an expeditionary corps in support of one of Bonaparte's wars. He declared to Marie that he would not serve against Germany. He would leave the army first, something he confessed held some attraction for him, even if he also desperately wanted to join the fight against France. He wrote for Gneisenau a plan for a British-funded Prussian Legion of 4,500 to serve under the Austrian flag, and another for an uprising in North Germany with British help. He also continued his work in the War Department, which included giving briefings twice weekly on the course of Europe's latest conflict.[48]

Though the thought of seeking Austrian service occurred to Clausewitz in April 1809, he seems to have only begun acting upon it in June, when he approached an Austrian official in Königsberg and gave to him a letter for the Archduke Charles, the commander of the Austrian army. "I am very happy with the thought that I will finally once again see murderous balls dispatched against the arrogant, hated Frenchmen," he wrote Marie. He received no reply before the Austrians suffered a devastating defeat by Napoleon at Wagram on July 5–6. Clausewitz rightly feared this would change things and considered offering his services to the British to fight in northern Germany.[49]

Clausewitz had been overly optimistic about Austrian success. After Wagram, Clausewitz determined that peace would be made before he would have a chance to join the fight. "Nothing is easier—and more befitting human weakness—than to give up hope all at once," he wrote Marie. France's victory in the war led to a Franco-Austrian rapprochement that included Napoleon marrying the daughter of the Austrian emperor. This left Prussia even more diplomatically isolated.[50]

On December 23, 1809, the royal couple and the court returned to Berlin. Clausewitz and Scharnhorst returned also to their former place of residence and more or less the same duties they had had in Königsberg. Overall, Clausewitz believed the time he spent in Königsberg had been valuable as self-evaluation and reflection. Much of it had been spent reading history and politics. In October Clausewitz had written that he intended to use his remaining weeks there to study English.[51]

In January 1810 Napoleon began to pressure Prussia to make early payment of its indemnity, bringing yet more pain to Clausewitz's homeland. Bonaparte gave Prussia the choice of giving up Silesia or reducing the army to 6,000 men in order to pay. Hardenberg, who had returned to the king's service after Stein's forced removal in November 1808, convinced the French that Prussia would come up with the money. But the reformers also paid a price; Scharnhorst was forced to step down as head of the War Department in June 1810, yet another Prussian sacrifice to Napoleon.[52]

The king moved Scharnhorst to the general staff and Clausewitz went with him, the pair essentially carrying on their same tasks but with a different placard on the door. Clausewitz sometimes found his military reform work frustrating. He complained to Gneisenau that he attended a lot of meetings from which little emerged because the attendees lacked clear views. Gneisenau, meanwhile, continued to form high opinions of the young officer: "If you write to Clausewitz," Gneisenau told his wife, "say to him that you share with me the profound respect for him with which you know I am imbued." He also praised Clausewitz's intelligence, his strength of mind, and the fact that he "with rare friendship sticks by me."[53]

Clausewitz had suffered from fevers in Königsberg, but when he returned to Berlin he suffered another illness common to soldiers who spent countless hours in the saddle: hemorrhoids. Their severity meant a surgery—with its contingent risks—and a painful recovery. He took a long leave during August 1810 to take the waters at Landek. Clausewitz had suffered bouts of ill health since 1807, but his fevers grew more frequent as he reached his thirtieth year.[54]

Despite his poor health, this was one of the happiest periods of Clausewitz's life. Working for Scharnhorst meant involvement in a variety of tasks, from assisting in the writing of the aforementioned military manuals, to the production and selection of new weapons and equipment, to the security of Prussia's fortresses, unit organization, and myriad other things. Marie wrote later that to Clausewitz, working for Scharnhorst, because of the depths of their relationship, "would have made him happy indefinitely if the situation of the fatherland at the time had not clouded the happiness of every individual, and caused the two friends in particular so many hard and anxious hours." Scharnhorst and Clausewitz, she felt, "understood each other almost without words."[55]

French pressure had forced Scharnhorst to step down as the de facto minister of war, but he retained a directorship over military education. As we have seen, the military reformers were attempting to remake Prussia into a modern state. An order of May 2, 1810, reorganized the officer education system, establishing three institutes to prepare cadets for commissioning as ensigns, as well as another for more advanced instruction. The War School for Young Officers, or General War School, opened to students on October 15. Scharnhorst considered it so important to properly shape the intellectual tenor of the officer corps that he added teaching to his mass of responsibilities. Scharnhorst's control of military education also meant that he determined the faculty, and he appointed his two best students from his time at the General War School (later the War College): Karl von Tiedemann and Carl von Clausewitz. Clausewitz wrote to Gneisenau about the appointment a few months before he took up the new job. "Half against my will I have become a professor; indeed with Tiedemann I'm to teach tactics at the future War School; my pursuits are almost as peaceful as planting cabbages."[56]

Instruction began on September 1 and ended on March 21. Clausewitz only lectured during the two winter semesters of 1810–1811 and 1811–1812. In their first year, he and Tiedemann each gave more than 150 hours of lectures. Clausewitz taught "Little War"—the tactical use of small, detached light or irregular forces—where he elaborated on how this supported conventional fighting and touched lightly upon how it could be used to wage guerrilla war, or "People's War," as part of a general uprising. Rebellions in the Tyrol, the Vendée, and Spain supplied the historical guerrilla warfare examples of Clausewitz's day, and George Washington even makes an appearance (though as "General Wassington"). In his two years at the War College he acquired a reputation as an excellent teacher.[57]

His superiors also gave Clausewitz a collateral duty: tutoring the fifteen-year-old crown prince (the future Frederick William IV). In 1811 his cousin, Prince Friedrich of the Netherlands, and Frederick Wilhelm's younger brother—both of whom were two years the prince's junior—would join them. By October 1810 Clausewitz was teaching at the General War School four hours each week and spending another three with the prince (to whom he generally taught tactics, organization, and campaign analysis) while still working for Scharnhorst, who continued to guide the military reforms. "The teaching has been far less unacceptable to me than I would have believed," he wrote Gneisenau, "however it is almost too much time at the desk for me and I look forward to the summer."[58]

The end of 1810 brought Clausewitz a happy change. On June 7, 1810, he became a general staff officer, and his promotion to major followed on August 29. Even more significantly, the advancement in his career made Clausewitz a safer prospect in the eyes of Marie's mother, and they were finally allowed to become engaged. They married at St. Mary's Church on December 17, 1810, after a seven-year courtship. The newlyweds immediately took a trip to Silesia and Saxony to visit relatives. They returned to Berlin on the evening of December 31 to their new apartment and surprise gifts from their friends. Clausewitz once wrote that the two happiest moments of his life were graduating first in his class from the General War School and winning Marie's love.[59]

The Clausewitzes were fortunate to have generous friends, as they had little in the way of financial means. Their spartanly furnished apartment had half a dozen calico-covered chairs, a sofa, and some other items of furniture. They subsisted almost entirely on Clausewitz's salary, as Marie's family had an astounding pedigree but little wealth. Madame von Brühl lived on a government pension and Marie had very little income of her own. Clausewitz also helped support his widowed mother until she died in 1811. He received a substantial raise to 1,150 talers upon his promotion to major, which placed his pay at roughly 25 percent less than a high-ranking professor at the University of Berlin. He had to pay for his own horse and its upkeep, but the army provided its hay and oats, as well as an orderly, and supplemented his pay with a housing allowance. As a general staff officer he was paid 25 to 30 percent less than his comrades in other branches, but he could expect quicker promotion.[60]

They were poor but happy, as the saying goes. Marie was in every way Clausewitz's intellectual equal, and, one could argue, a better writer. Their correspondence is filled with discussions of authors and their works, particularly the most important of their era: Johann Friedrich von Schiller, Johann Gottlieb Fichte, works by Goethe such as *The Sorrows of Young Werther*, Laurence Sterne's *The Life and Opinions of Tristram Shandy, Gentleman*, and on and on. Clausewitz himself sometimes composed poems that he occasionally sent to Marie, a practice begun as a young man that he continued until his death. Their letters discuss art, architecture and travel, politics (endlessly), history, and friends. There are passionate love letters, but also complaints, at least from Clausewitz, about his job, his superiors, and the general weakness of the German people and its leaders, and their collective refusal to stand up and fight.

Clausewitz was by this point developing a reputation for being something of a misanthrope—serious, perhaps overly so, and unyielding in his judgment of others. One of Marie's relatives by marriage, Caroline von der Marwitz, deemed Clausewitz's personality "unfortunate in every respect," and said "there was something cold and negative in his demeanor, which often went so far as to imply disdain of others." While she admired his passion and ambition, Caroline wondered if his close friends "expected and hoped more from him than he was able to achieve—whether because of fate, circumstances, or his off-putting personality." Stein called Clausewitz "a brave man but cold and methodical." He was known to walk up to groups of subordinates, say nothing, and simply walk away. Such things led to a reputation for detachment. Yet among close friends he could be boisterous and laugh to in extremis.[61]

In any case, Clausewitz remained disillusioned about the political situation and suspected that Prussia would be drawn into some disaster within a year or so, from which only an accident could save it from "complete destruction." His attachment to German Romanticism and his thirst for glory remained strong. If Prussia was destroyed, he wrote Gneisenau in January 1811, who was in Stockholm on a diplomatic mission, he hoped to go down honorably with it, "or at least to sacrifice my life." By early 1811 he had come to fear for Prussia's survival: "What wealth, culture, and trade have gathered over centuries in this sandy desert will now perhaps be scattered in a decade."[62]

In August 1811, as part of his quiet planning for Prussia's defense, Gneisenau dispatched Clausewitz to Silesia to learn the mountains and waterways, among other things. Clausewitz told Gneisenau that his trip did not give him the knowledge of the country that he wished, and continued tongue-in-cheek, "I have, of course, no choice but to return to Berlin and read lectures and preach to the Crown Prince's deaf ears." His visits led to a proposal for defending Silesia, assessing how many men could be realistically raised and armed in the province (30,000, and 3,000 cavalry) and suggesting various means of defense (largely fighting from fortresses). In the proposal, however, Clausewitz goes beyond his examination of Silesia, returning partially to former ideas for resisting Napoleon in Germany. One was the landing of a British expeditionary force. This, he says, could be supported by a volunteer German Legion, which was similar to the previously discussed idea of a Prussian Legion. This force would form the nucleus of a revolutionary army. In response, Gneisenau composed a plan for a German Legion, which Clausewitz wrote up. Gneisenau—over optimistically—believed landing a British army in Germany could produce the same result as that of a British army in Spain, a veritable "Spain in Germany."[63]

The Spanish example, as well as the April 1809 revolt in the former Austrian possession of Tyrol against their new Bavarian overlords, began to exert increasing influence over the imagination of Prussian officers eager to raise their swords against Napoleon. The idea of fighting a "People's War" (meaning a revolt of the population) in Germany united Clausewitz and Gneisenau, who, as we have seen, looked at this as a means of throwing off the French yoke. Clausewitz's Silesia study was part of Gneisenau's ongoing examination of the possibility of fighting a People's War. In the summer of 1811, as it became apparent that Russia and France were drifting toward blows, Gneisenau drew up a letter to the king, urging him to raise the Prussian nation to fight when this occurred. Frederick William penned two comments on its margins: "Nobody would come!" and "Good—as poetry!" Gneisenau wrote, not without some bitterness: "Religion, prayer, love of one's ruler, love of the fatherland—these things are nothing else than poetry. There is no lifting of the heart that is not attune to poetry.

The man that acts only in accordance with cold calculation becomes an inveterate egoist. Upon poetry is founded the security of the throne."[64] Gneisenau, Clausewitz, Yorck, Blücher—and the others pressing for war— would have to wait.

In the period from the time of his release as a prisoner of war through 1812, Clausewitz poured much of his life into his writing: heaps of correspondence (both personal and professional) piled upon essays on military and political matters (almost none written for publication), lectures for his classes, and finally, a small manual on the art of war for his student, the crown prince. Clausewitz seems to have written little but letters while interned in France, but he did pen additional scripts on history and politics in the pair of now lost notebooks. He continued, for example, a discussion of the "Balance of Power" in Europe, insisting that its destruction would see small states losing their independence because this system helped them survive.[65]

In November 1807, after his return to Prussia, Clausewitz wrote an essay not published until long after his death, titled "The Germans and the French." In it he blames German national character for Prussia's 1806 defeat in an emotional piece reflecting the ethnic views manifesting in some of his letters to Marie, and lacking the rational, even-handed approach of his other—particularly later—works. His national portraits are at best chauvinistic and at worst the self-justificatory scribbling of a young and injured mind searching for answers as to why his idol—the Prussian state—was shattered by a people so obviously inferior.[66]

In addition, Clausewitz wrote various notes on political issues, both historical and current to his day. These introduce two elements of the "trinity" he will later present in On War: passion and chance (though he says "luck" here). The third would be rationality. He was always trying to make order out of chaos, and searching for the inner core in life and particularly in ideas. This applied equally to his views on politics, where Clausewitz constantly urges action, seizing the initiative, and energy. Machiavelli's work was also something much on Clausewitz's mind. He studied the Italian author's writings—not just The Prince, but other works as well, including The Art of War and Discourses. Clausewitz's own discussions of chance and luck certainly drew upon Machiavelli, who discussed "fortune." Clausewitz wrote in 1809 that "Fortune favors the brave." He did not credit Machiavelli with this, although Machiavelli wrote similarly in his Discourses in a section on Fabius and Hannibal, which Clausewitz discusses in an anonymous 1809 letter he penned to the German philosopher and nationalist Johann Gottlieb Fichte, one including an early mention of "friction." The surviving fragment of a piece he wrote on art theory during this period (one dedicated to architecture) further demonstrates the breadth of Clausewitz's intellectual interests.[67]

Between November 1807 and March 1808 Clausewitz drew up a plan for a future Prussian war with France. Here he first utters ideas that appear in his famous political declaration of 1812. "As long as there are means and ends," Clausewitz wrote, "and there is also a rational connection between both, there is nothing more to the art of war." He also insists upon the preservation of the means—the army—even at the expense of losing the state itself. The army is the symbol of the state, and having some military force left at the end of the war can mean the restitution of the kingdom. We are not far here from his later idea of the army as a center of gravity, a core national strength. Clausewitz writes that the purpose of the offensive army would be determined by the government, something repeated later in a more developed form. He talks of the potential benefit if the person commanding the army is also the ruler determining the end being sought. This makes it nearly impossible for the enemy to know the commanders' will, "even if the entire army is spiked with spies." "In war," he says, "however, surprise is the soul of luck." He notes the potential impact of the fate of the army on public opinion, but thinks little of the state of German and European public views at the time of his writing.[68] All of these concepts return in On War.

In 1808 Clausewitz added to his 1804 Strategie. The criticality of theory underpins his discussion. "The more I think about this area of the art of war," he wrote, "the more convinced I become that the theory can postulate few or no abstract propositions; but not, as common opinion would have it, because the matter is so difficult, but because one would succumb to triviality." He laid the foundation for his later discussion in On War of "People's War," and introduced his use of "genius." The latter term was a fixture of some Romantic literature, including Goethe's Sorrows of Young Werther.[69] He returned to Strategie briefly in 1809, but abandoned it after this.

As we have seen, Clausewitz always insisted upon precise definitions when discussing ideas. He made an effort during this period to more precisely define both "tactics" and "strategy." Though he defines tactics as "the study of combat," he goes on to differentiate between lesser tactics and

higher tactics: "Just as elementary tactics concerns itself with the deployment and movement of elementary parts of an army, higher tactics concerns itself with the deployment and movement of larger parts, entire corps
and armies in combat." Jomini also sought a distinction between "Grand
Tactics"—how armies fought in combat—and "Minor Tactics," meaning
the tactical methods utilized by the different arms: the infantry, cavalry,
and artillery. Clausewitz continued this definitional struggle in *Strategie*
and linked the terms: "Tactics organizes the army in combat such a way
as to employ it appropriately for the purpose of obtaining a victory, while
strategy does the same thing in war in order to make the best use of the
individual engagements."[70]

In an 1811 letter to Gneisenau, Clausewitz broke with the
eighteenth-century view of the decisive battle determining the conflict's
outcome by describing what today we would define as operational warfare: "If I now consider that each war is not a single uninterrupted battle,
but rather is composed of multiple battles separated by time and place, and
then I see not one *demonstration*, they are all battle *combinations*." But battle
still mattered.[71]

He then took the next step and tied all of this to politics. In early 1812 he
penned what is generally referred to as his "Political Declaration" (about
which we will learn more shortly). His exposition on these issues is succinct
and more exacting, his concepts clearer: "Since war is no longer decided by
a single battle as in barbarous nations, the Art of War is divided into two
parts distinguished from one another by purpose and means. The first is the
art of fighting. (Tactics). The second part of the Art is to combine several
individual battles into a whole (for the purpose of the campaign, the war).
(Strategy). The distinction between offensive and defensive war applies to
both elements, and extends even into politics. The defense can thus be tactical, strategic, political."[72] Clausewitz's use of the term "Strategy" generally combines today's operational and strategic realms.

He treads some of the same ground yet again in two other extensive draft
manuscripts composed between 1809 and 1812, ones more developed than
his earlier *Strategie*. Together they form part of the intellectual foundation
of *On War* and show he was starting to resolve what Clausewitz saw as
one of the problems with writing about military theory: finding a coherent methodology. These provide important background on Clausewitz's
development as a theorist and in them he is inching toward his famous definition of war: "It is the science of the use of armed forces for the assigned

aim," which is political. "From these political aims follow directly the military ones: such [as] a weakening of [the] enemy strength so that the enemy cannot continue the war without risking his entire existence. This aim is achieved through the destruction of his state power and armed forces, and this destruction—continuing to the degree mentioned above—is the real aim of the art of war." The second covers some similar turf, ruminating on the political aims of war and not just its execution: "War is the manifest use of violence against others in order to force them to conform to our will, in other words it is the use of the available means applied to the aim of the war. The theory of the art of war is the science of the use of available means for the aim of the war." Clausewitz's splitting of war's aims into two categories—destruction of the enemy state or forcing a treaty upon it—is an argument expressed very similarly in his note of July 10, 1827, usually published with *On War*. The essence of war as violence—or force—to bend an enemy "to our will" can be found on the first page of his masterwork.[73]

In addition to defining the differences between tactics and strategy, Clausewitz goes on to argue the need for a new theory, one that can transcend the confusion of terms and the lack of quality in available works on military history. The challenge was that the relevant theory was "still in its infancy" and that as a result the excesses and quirky ideas in the current works should be considered "a kind of childhood disease."[74]

Critical to this were solid analytical tools. Clausewitz acquired some of his method of analysis from the approach of Immanuel Kant, to whose writings he was exposed in 1804 or 1805 via the Berlin lectures of his teacher Johann Gottfried Kiesewetter. Clausewitz conducted his inquiries into the essence of warfare along parallel lines, one objective, the other subjective. Via this method Clausewitz sought objective truths (principles that are always true) as well as subjective truths (principles that vary by circumstance or condition). All of this had to then fit within an accepted hierarchy of the day. Politics furnished this for Clausewitz.[75] This gave him a logical, consistent approach for examining the phenomenon of war.

The need to define concepts and ideas related to warfare and then clarify them was for Clausewitz a constant intellectual pursuit. But he also admired action, vigor, self-sacrifice, even to the point of romanticizing the last of the three. These drives—for clarity of vision *and* clarity of action—culminated in a critical decision made in the spring of 1812, as we shall soon see.

Overall the reformers won big on the military front, achieving dramatic modernization of Prussia's army along tactical, doctrinal, and

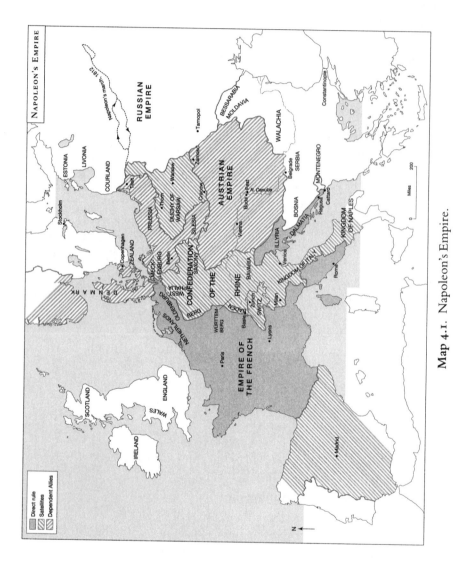

Map 4.1. Napoleon's Empire.

organizational grounds. Clausewitz's work with Scharnhorst and lectures at the War College were an example of the shift. But they had lost in regard to what Clausewitz viewed as the larger aim of war, the political struggle. They were building an army to fight the French and wanted an alliance with Russia. Frederick William instead bowed to the French and signed on to an anti-Russian war.[76] Clausewitz would get the opportunity he craved to win glory—but not the one he imagined.

5

War and Words

The Campaign of 1812

The summit of the Fatherland's misfortune has been reached, because its rulers are slaves, who, at the behest of their masters, use the sword against themselves.

In 1811, with war clouds forming over Russia and France, King Frederick William III came under pressure from his advisors to seek an alliance with Russia as a way of breaking Prussia free from the French yoke. The ever cautious Frederick William saw the ghost of 1806 in any dealings with Russia and reminded his advisors of the disaster that was the Franco-Prussian Treaty of Tilsit, in which Prussia had lost half its territory.[1]

Despite the criticism leveled against him then and since, Frederick William did prefer a struggle—even one with little chance of success—to permanent thralldom to France. But he also doubted Prussia's fortunes here and feared his subjects would not fight the kind of "People's War" Gneisenau, Clausewitz, and others suggested. Nevertheless, the Prussians began secretly rearming, as well as mobilizing forces beyond what their agreements with France allowed, actions in which Clausewitz, as Scharnhorst's assistant, was deeply involved. Frederick William also dispatched Scharnhorst—secretly—to seek Russian support. These preparations intensified in late August when the Prussians picked up signs of Paris's shift to an anti-Russian line. Even before Scharnhorst could fulfill his mission Napoleon struck. He ordered Frederick William to cease rearming and shrink his army to its treaty limits or face immediate invasion. Frederick William bent.[2]

Napoleon then further tightened the screws. On February 24, 1812, he imposed yet another treaty on the hapless Prussians, making them an ally in

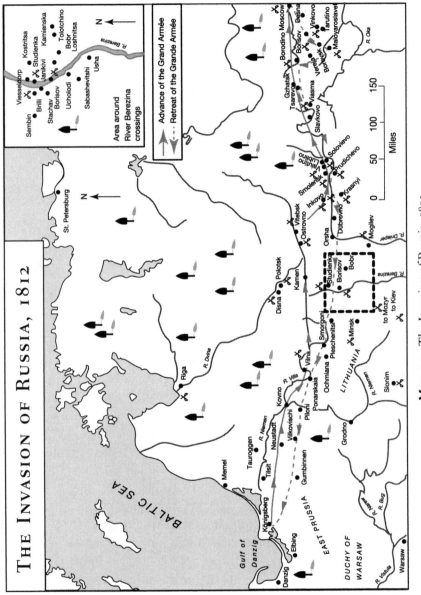

Map 5.1. The Invasion of Russia, 1812.

France's war against Russia and committing them to providing 20,842 men and great amounts of *matérial* support. The Prussian elite were indignant. Soon, more than two-dozen Prussian officers—including many of Clausewitz's friends—handed in their papers. Some went to Russia. Others left for Britain and Spain. "We shall receive the fate we deserve," lamented Gneisenau in the face of the resignations. "We shall go down in shame, for we dare not conceal from ourselves the truth that a nation is as bad as its government. The king stands ever by the throne on which he has never sat."[3]

Clausewitz, of course, also found the treaty profoundly disillusioning: "I believe, I must confess," he wrote with some Romantic excess, "that the shameful blot of a cowardly capitulation is never wiped away; that this drop of poison in the blood of a people is transmitted to posterity and will cripple and undermine the energy of later generations." He noted with dismay that few in Prussia beyond the dissenters associated with Scharnhorst regretted the accommodation with the hated French. Those not in the camp of Clausewitz's mentor, he wrote, regarded the disaffected as suffering from "semi-madness." He was among those who resigned. As we've seen, it was something he had considered before—and for similar reasons. He did not want to fight alongside France—even under the Prussian banner—and had decided this as early as 1809.[4]

Clausewitz left Prussian service in spectacular fashion, composing a 20,000-word document, often referred to as his "Political Declaration," though he himself gave it no title. Consisting of a three-part essay, the work was partially a statement of the political views of the Prussian elite opposed to alliance with France and partially a plea to fight accompanied by a strategy for doing so. In its construction he takes what many see as a dialectical approach, presenting reasons for and against various actions. His anti-French friends Boyen and Gneisenau made revisions of Clausewitz's work, and its subsequent dissemination intensified the hatred between both political camps. The work is nothing less than a full-throated incitement to violence against France and a demonstration of his (incorrect) conviction that Napoleon had decided to destroy Prussia. If Clausewitz could have proven this, he might have made a stronger argument. In any case, he directs his anger toward Prussia's rulers. "The upper classes are corrupt; court and government officials are the most corrupt." Though he calls Frederick William "above all an upright man," one doubts whether the king could see here anything other than self-righteous insubordination by someone who had forgotten his place and his duty. Even if "the king is deposed and the people are subjugated," wrote Clausewitz, they would "both retain their honor, the mutual love and respect for each other."[5] This is perhaps not the wisest appeal Clausewitz could have made; no king likes to lose, and one can imagine Frederick William would be generally averse to being deposed. The king knew very well that he had lost half his realm in the 1806 war. Another fight with France might see Prussia's annihilation. Clausewitz was willing to risk this for honor's sake; Frederick William was not.

Clausewitz, however, did not make the mistake of criticizing Prussia's course of action without offering one of his own. He believed Prussia should fight by building a mass army based upon universal conscription and supported by a civil defense force (*Landsturm*) organized by province and drawn from all men ages eighteen through sixty not already under arms. Prussia would hold eight fortresses and three entrenched camps and raise between 150,000 and 200,000 men, while counting on the Russians, who were in better shape than in 1806. He cited the revolt in the Austrian Tyrol as well as the French Revolutionary War rebellion in France's Vendée as precedents, and reminded the reader of the Spanish resistance to Napoleon. He urged a People's War on the lines of which he and Gneisenau had been studying (though he has expanded beyond his Silesia plan), and some of the declaration resembles his later discussion of "The People in Arms" in *On War*. He also reminds the king that one must keep the moral element in mind in "war's calculus," something also developed in *On War*.[6]

Clausewitz tried to bolster his case with concepts later fleshed out in his masterwork. He argued the strengths of the defensive—particularly of an active one. Included among its advantages was that they would be awaiting the attack and could thus strike only when they wished, that they had the support of the local population, and that they were close to their resources. Clausewitz naturally examines the tactical and strategic defense, but also adds a distinctive element—the political defense: "The political defense, which therein consists of a nation fighting for its preservation and not for conquest (irrespective of what form, by the way) is not relevant to the actual war, even though it has a significant influence on the spirit of the army and in this regard may become important."[7]

Would Clausewitz's plan have worked? Its success would have hinged upon two factors: the will of the Prussian people to rise up and fight against a superior enemy and Russian assistance. Both of these the Prussian crown could not control. The Prussian willingness to fight would certainly be influenced by the French reaction, which, considering the scale of resources Napoleon had amassed to invade Russia, one must assume would be heavy and fierce. How the Prussian populace reacted would also be affected by the Russian choice. There were Russian leaders who wanted to fight an offensive war—they even planned for one—but there were others who balked at the idea. If the Russians had launched an attack into Prussia or Poland against the French, Napoleon would have probably simply ignored the Prussian uprising, massed against the Russians—which he would have outnumbered—and broken their army. He could then have reduced the Prussians at his leisure—if the blow against the Russians did not convince the Prussians to quit.

Based upon the five criteria Clausewitz gives for a successful rising in his section on "The People in Arms" in *On War*, the plan meets three of the criteria for success: the war would "be fought in the interior of the country"; it would probably not be decided with one blow (at least against the Prussians); and in light of the reaction of the Prussians in 1813, one could argue that the people had the requisite "national character" (though they lacked the religious zeal of Spain's guerrillas). But the remaining pair of planks would be problems. The theater of operations was large, but not too large for the forces available to the French, and the country's terrain was not severe enough to hinder the enemy.[8]

In general, Clausewitz went too far even for many of those who agreed that they should risk war. "Will these beliefs win me and those who think as I do the contempt and derision of our fellow citizens?"[9] Clausewitz asked. Among many, and, especially the inhabitants of the court, they would. Clausewitz's willingness to die gloriously for the cause of his nation and the German people was not a Romantic notion King Frederick William III shared.

When Clausewitz left for Russia he did what he had been urging others to do: fight against France, for Prussia's independence and for that of Germany as well. Clausewitz's decision seems even more daring when one remembers he was still newly married and enjoying a comfortable life teaching in what was, as we have seen, at the time a great cultural center. One of Clausewitz's best friends, Major Karl Tiedemann, left as well. "That Tiedemann and Clausewitz departed is a great loss," Scharnhorst wrote later. "They promised much for the future." In any case, Clausewitz left Berlin on March 31, 1812, heading to Liegnitz to join Scharnhorst, who had also quit the capital (with the king's permission) because he believed he wasn't safe from the French. Clausewitz had to scrape together the money for the trip and to support Marie while he was gone. He gratefully accepted a loan from Gneisenau and expected to receive something from his student the crown prince, which he did, and hoped enough remittances reached him by May 1 so that he wouldn't be impoverished when he crossed into Russia.[10]

Clausewitz arrived in Frankfurt at midnight, visited his brother Friedrich and sister Johanna early in the morning, then reached Liegnitz on the evening of April 1. He had a miserable trip, he wrote Marie, suffering from a headache much of the way, and "cursing every stone I drove over." But he also grew melancholy, remembering fondly the time spent with her the previous few years. "God willing," he wrote, their separation would be as short as possible. In Liegnitz, he and Scharnhorst visited the churches and all the monuments, as well as the battlefield of Wahlstatt, the site of the famous 1241 fight with the Mongols. On April 3 they continued on to Frankenstein (now Ząbkowice Śląskie, Poland), traveling southeastward, accompanied by Scharnhorst's daughter Julie and his son-in-law, Carl Friedrich zu Dohna, who had also resigned and was going to Russia. Clausewitz lingered in Frankenstein with Scharnhorst and the Dohnas for about three weeks, making frequent trips to the surrounding area.[11]

In mid-April he was still in Frankenstein, hoping the rest of his money would arrive. He also wrote his request to resign on the 12th and mailed it from Frankenstein four days later. While waiting he hurriedly scribbled a piece meant for his student, the crown prince. He told the prince he hoped to leave the young man some solid advice for when he was a soldier, though to Marie he expressed the hope that the work "breathed a spark" into the young man's soul.[12]

The work has come down to us as a little book called—in English—*Principles of War*. It first appeared as an appendix to *On War*, but it really should be called "The Most Important Principles of the Conduct of War, to Supplement my Lessons to His Royal Highness, the Crown Prince." A Russian translation appeared in 1888, and Hans Gatzke's well-known English version appeared in 1942 in the midst of the Second World War.[13]

Clausewitz told the prince that its contents were "not so much to give complete instruction to Your Royal Highness," but rather that they would "stimulate and serve as a guide for your own reflection." This phrase is the essence of Clausewitz's entire approach to the study of theory. He goes on to offer principles for tactics and strategy, discussing defense and offense in each realm, and then delivering lessons in application. The first page of the text belies the term "Principles" in the title, as Clausewitz's immediate concern is to establish what theory is for. "The theory of warfare tries to discover how we may gain a preponderance of physical forces and material advantages at the decisive point. As this is not always possible, theory also teaches us to calculate moral factors: the likely mistakes of the enemy, the impression created by a daring action...yes, even our own desperation." As Peter Paret points out, to Clausewitz, a true examination of war goes beyond mere "Principles" learned and taught by rote. Theory is not a *diktat*; it is to train the mind, to develop judgment. He continues: "any person who may present this matter differently to Your Royal Highness is a pedant, whose views will only be harmful to you." Clausewitz echoes this in *On War*: "theory is meant to educate the mind of the future commander." That last point is key, acting as a foundation for his later discussion of military genius—an idea he first touched upon in *Strategie*. "Theory leaves it to the military leader, however, to act according to his own enterprise, and his self-confidence. Make your choice, therefore, according to this inner force; but never forget that no military leader has ever become great without audacity."[14]

The tactical section covers the positioning of units, the use of the terrain, leadership, offense and defense, and other things important to fighting a battle in the Napoleonic era. In this section Clausewitz is not shackled to the idea of a decisive battle, "for only a combination of successful engagements can lead to good results. The most important thing in war will always be the art of defeating your opponent in combat." In fighting battles he urges the prince to "pursue one great decisive aim with force and determination." He also encourages daring: "For great aims we must dare great things." He stresses the importance and value of a surprise attack, but also elaborates on the difficulty in bringing one about.[15]

In the strategy section of his book for the crown prince, Clausewitz lays out three "General Principles" for action, foreshadowing counsel in *On War* on how to strike an enemy's "center of gravity." He advises attacking the army as well as the enemy's material resources, which means striking cities, fortresses, and so forth. Second, he argues that public opinion—the will to fight—can be undermined by military victories and seizure of the enemy's capital. And he stresses acting with great energy; the importance of the "moral impression" resulting from one's actions (a hint of the "moral forces" of *On War*), and of concentration; the essential factor of time (never waste it) and surprise (it "plays a much greater role in strategy than in tactics"—something, we will see, also repeated in *On War*); and the importance of pursuing an enemy defeated in battle.[16]

Clausewitz also discusses waging a strategic defensive and says this is generally only done if you are weaker than the enemy. He once again suggests the defense is stronger than the offense, something he revisits in *On War* that has occasionally invited fierce criticism. He defends his contention thus: "Finally, it should be observed that strategic defensive, though it is stronger than the offensive, should serve only to win the first important successes." He also gives an exception to one of his "Principles" (a pattern repeated in *On War* that demonstrates his interest in realistic theory and resistance to theoretical pedantry), arguing that there are circumstances when it would be better to destroy the enemy's supply base rather than his army.[17]

To Clausewitz, the principles of the art of war are "in themselves extremely simple and quite within the reach of sound common sense." That does not mean they are easy to apply, however. In explaining this to the crown prince, he returns to the concept of friction, which he first mentioned in 1806. "The conduct of war resembles the workings of an intricate machine with tremendous friction, so that combinations which are easily planned on paper can be executed only with great effort," he explains. "Many good ideas have perished because of this friction, and we must carry out more simply and moderately what under a more complicated form would have given greater results." He discusses friction's causes, noting that "it may be impossible to enumerate exhaustively the causes," but they generally boil down to uncertainty (regarding the enemy situation as well as your own), self-doubt and a lack of confidence on the part of the commander, and limited provisions. How does one overcome the problems encompassed by friction? With quality leaders who have "that appearance of mind and character which is called firmness."[18] Clausewitz later develops his concept of friction much further.

Clausewitz also emphasizes to the prince the importance of learning from the past: "these difficulties, therefore, demand confidence and firmness of conviction. That is why the study of military history is so important, for it makes us see things as they are and as they function. The principles which we can learn from theoretical instruction are only suited to facilitate this study and to call our attention to the most important elements in the history of the war." He urged the prince to check these principles (theory) against history, just as he does in *On War*, as "only the study of military history is capable of giving those who have no experience of their own a clear impression of what I have just called the friction of the whole machine."[19]

The book also reflects Clausewitz's concerns at the time. First, he touches upon the impossibility of small states "waging wars of conquest" in his day. He suggests, instead, that they can wage a defensive war if they constantly put forces in the field and "use all possible means of preparation," which hints at his People's War inclinations. He also examines the use of national militias in mountain warfare, insisting they are perfect for such combat because they act independently.[20] The connection to his writing on Silesia and the revolt in the Tyrol, as well as his "Political Declaration," is not a difficult one to make.

Second, it demonstrates his political concerns and even duplicates some of what he expressed in the "Political Declaration." This is made clear by his urging the crown prince that "we must therefore familiarize ourselves with the thought of an honorable defeat." If nothing else, an honorable defeat provided seeds for the future, and was better than not fighting at all.[21]

On April 19 Clausewitz and Scharnhorst arrived in Breslau (now Wroclaw, Poland) from Frankenstein, spending the first evening having supper with Prince August, whom Scharnhorst had immediately sought out at the inn. In Breslau Clausewitz finally received the money he was waiting for, as well as some good news in the form of two letters from Count Christoph von Lieven. Lieven had been St. Petersburg's ambassador to Berlin and had arranged Clausewitz's entry into the Russian army. One note informed him his salary would be 1,900 talers annually—a significant increase from his previous salary of 1,300. The other named him a lieutenant-colonel.[22]

In late April Clausewitz received official notification that the king had accepted his resignation. "So the decisive step has been taken," he wrote Marie, and suspected ungraciousness in the king's one sentence reply (though one wonders how he could have expected anything else). "The standard which I've followed with love and devotion for twenty years, I am no longer allowed to bear," he continued to Marie. "A melancholy feeling did indeed slowly come over me with these ideas, but it did not sadden me." Indeed, Clausewitz insisted, "I have not drawn a bad lot," and believed it to be the best he could hope for "in this troubled time." He did not worry about the future, but approached what would come his way with calmness, telling Marie that "only the union with you is necessary for my happiness."

If the war does not soon drag me forth into its whirlwind, I'll soon get homesick for you, you dear woman of my heart's desire!"[23]

From Breslau, Clausewitz struck out through the Grand Duchy of Warsaw. His passage went smoothly until, he said, he encountered "the indescribably petty, childish, arrogance and impertinence" of the Polish area commanders and read great disdain in the gestures and looks of the Polish officers he encountered. They lived, he said, in "gray earth huts with dirty gray people crawling around like lice on a sore."[24] Considering that Clausewitz's homeland had helped destroy Polish independence two decades before, he should not have been so surprised by the behavior of the Polish officers.

On one leg of the journey Clausewitz's coachman told him that between Hohensalza and Bromberg (now Inowracław and Bydgoszcz in northwestern Poland), three days before he passed through, several houses had been broken into and looted. The community gathered and found the thieves in the local woods, but they escaped after jumping their guards. "Fortunately," he wrote Marie, the coachman had told him the tale after daylight's arrival, "otherwise I would have spent the night less carefree." But in Breslau he bought a money belt to wear under his clothes and a pair of pistols. He hung one on each side of his carriage, nightly taking the precaution of putting fresh powder in the pans, and told Marie that "a couple of times, when we were driving through thick brush . . . I took one in hand to shoot in the head the first person to enter the carriage." He found the carriage comfortable, but couldn't shake the headache he'd had since leaving Berlin, and seems to have added rheumatism to his ailments. "As long as I'm sitting completely upright in the carriage I feel nothing; but the moment I recline, the pain begins and grows each moment. On the whole, however, the headache has recently lessened and hopefully will soon completely disappear." Regrets over his separation from Marie would not lessen, however. "I will bravely endure this next storm of life that lies ahead of us, but how, if the ship wrecks and I am not buried in the waves, where I shall then get the courage to meet new uncertain fortunes which will remove me even further from you for even longer, this I do not know."[25]

By now Clausewitz was heading for Vilnius, where Czar Alexander had established his headquarters for the coming war. He crossed into Russian territory at Tauroggen in what is now Lithuania. There he stayed with a Cossack colonel and his family in a shabby farmhouse in which they occupied a couple of rooms. "In the middle of one sat in vegetable-like proximity with folded arms and legs a big, strong, young (I suppose also beautiful) Circassian woman, dressed in silk and costly furs, but a night hat like the ones our old men wear covering completely the head. She was like a fattened capon encased in white, fatty meat," but "looked very good-natured." Clausewitz added that the wives of Cossacks were supposed to do little more than have lots of children, so they were often fat, and their skin white. Clausewitz showed her Marie's picture and she wished him luck, embracing him twice when he left.[26]

He thought very little of his experience in Poland, telling Marie that his first Polish dinner, and the best for four days, "was a soup of half ham, half raw pork, followed by another soup of half beef and half veal." The poor state of most of the people he encountered in Poland during his passage convinced him that partition was a good idea and that fate had redeemed the Polish people from their lengthy suffering. "The whole life of the Poles is as if it were tied together and held together with torn ropes and rags." He also told her about the Jews he encountered, commenting upon their "incomprehensible German," and the fact that they married so young that they would be grandmothers in their thirties. What followed was a description that, in the light of more recent German history, is deeply troubling: "Filthy German Jews, who teem like vermin in filth and misery, are the country's patricians. A thousand times I have thought, if only fire would destroy this entire crop, so this impenetrable filth would be transformed by the cleaning flame neatly into ashes. That I have always found a salutary notion."[27]

There is no avoiding the implications, though Clausewitz scholar Peter Paret, for one, notes that this passage is unusual for Clausewitz in its content as well as its violence. Indeed, there are exceedingly few remarks about Jews in Clausewitz's voluminous writings. Paret also points out that others of Clausewitz's day wrote similar descriptions of the region and notes that Clausewitz had friendly relations with men who had Jewish wives, including Franz August O'Etzel, a brother officer who helped publish Clausewitz's works. Clausewitz's attitudes toward Jews seemed to hinge on whether or not they had converted and assimilated into German society.[28]

On May 20 Clausewitz reached Vilna, where he was reunited with two fellow officers, Ludwig August Friedrich Adolf von Chasot and his mentor and friend Gneisenau. Gneisenau's presence there was short, as he had already decided to head for Britain. His lack of Russian meant he would not receive an active command, and his equal absence of French precluded

him from participating in the court intrigue that would have been necessary to influence the czar as one of what Clausewitz termed the numerous "distinguished idlers" of the emperor's headquarters. Clausewitz also
met General Karl Ludwig von Phull, a former Prussian officer and one of
Clausewitz's instructors at the War School, who had entered Russian service after Jena-Auerstedt.[29]

Clausewitz went to the emperor's suite armed with letters of recommendation from Scharnhorst, which were so effusive in their praises for him
that Clausewitz said it made him nauseous. Gneisenau also lauded him to
the emperor, writing that Clausewitz had "one of the best minds and is full
of deep knowledge of the art of war." He also praised Clausewitz's recent
literary ambition, referring most likely to the little work for the crown
prince: "He has written in a few pages an instruction for generals which
surpasses all that has been published in this field and deserves to be translated into Russian."[30]

By the end of May the war had still not begun, which surprised
Clausewitz. "I have never seen a war break out so calmly," he wrote Marie
on May 28, and predicted it would start within fourteen days. They had
received news of Napoleon arriving in Dresden, and Clausewitz thought
it "not likely he'll wander around Germany for long." He also thought the
first campaign would not last very long because the Russian climate made a
winter war impossible. On June 24, 1812, Napoleon invaded Russia.[31]

What were Napoleon's objectives in invading Russia? Napoleon himself
remarked that he simply wanted to force the Russians back into supporting his Continental Blockade against Britain. He told the Austrian foreign
minister Klemens von Metternich that he planned to just seize Belorussia,
build a new Poland, and use this as a base for an 1813 invasion of Russia, a
move that some Russians considered potentially disastrous for them if made.
But on some occasions Napoleon professed a desire to knock the Russians
completely out of Europe. Moreover, a successful campaign against Russia
could place continental domination completely in Napoleon's hands. This
was undoubtedly the objective. Czar Alexander believed Napoleon sought
the complete destruction of Russian power and felt that his empire had been
placed on what Sun Tzu called "death ground": they could fight or they
could die; no other choice had been left to them. This steeled Alexander to
mount a bitter resistance.[32]

For Napoleon, strategy boiled down to massing an overwhelming force
against the Russian armies, defeating them—as quickly as possible—and

then forcing a peace upon Alexander. He planned for a short war and believed he could break the Russians in a matter of weeks by fighting the necessary battles close to the frontier. He made extensive preparations in the way of supplies and depots because he had learned in his earlier campaign in Poland about the difficulties of fighting in thinly populated areas, where foraging was more difficult. Napoleon planned and wanted a short war. Russian intelligence fed this desire through a double agent, who also convinced Napoleon that the Russians planned to fight for Vilna. That they did not surprised the emperor. Napoleon massed 600,000 troops on the Russian border, half from French allies and client states. He had attempted to get Sweden and Turkey involved to tie down Russia on its flanks, but had no success. The Swedes allied instead with Russia, and the Russians beat the Turks and made peace with them in June of 1812. Like others, including Metternich and even prominent Russians, Napoleon believed Alexander was weak. The 1812–1815 fighting would prove them wrong.[33]

By May 1812 the Russians had drawn up a plan to meet the invasion with three armies: The First Army under Mikhail Barclay de Tolly (around Vilna); the Second Army under Pytor Bagration (south of this); and farther south, the Third Army under Aleksandr Tormasov (which was assigned to block the routes into northern Ukraine). Combined, these gave the Russians around 242,000 men to oppose the invaders directly. Around 142,500 other men served in Russian armies, but they were either too far away to be used in 1812 or fighting the Persians in the Caucasus. Reserve units of various types would also join the fray. Beyond these Alexander could reach into the deep wells of Russian manpower; eventually Moscow called more than one million men to the colors during the war. Preserving the active, regular troops—particularly an experienced cadre—was critical to Russia's survival. One significant factor that kept down the size of Russian armies before and during the war was a shortage of skilled noncommissioned officers (NCOs) and officers. In all, the Russians had an army of maybe 650,000 soldiers scattered across their empire.[34]

Russian planning benefited from their often excellent intelligence on France and its intentions. One report General Barclay de Tolly received included remarks from disaffected French officers about how best to counter a French invasion. These officers believed (correctly) that Napoleon would try to win quickly through large battles and that therefore the Russians shouldn't give him any. The Frenchmen recommended that the system the Russians "should follow in this war is the one of which Fabius and indeed Lord Wellington offer the best examples." They believed that if the Russians could fight three campaigns (meaning essentially three years), that they would emerge victorious even if they won no battles. A Russian agent wrote: "Napoleon's goal and his hopes are all directed towards concentrating sufficient strength to deliver crushing blows and decide the matter in a single campaign. He feels strongly that he cannot remain away from Paris for more than one year and that he would be lost if this war lasted for two or three years."[35]

Russian strategy had firmed up by the summer of 1811. Alexander would fight on the defensive, a decision he explained to Prussian and Austrian diplomats, and which meant these two powers would join Napoleon against him—albeit half-heartedly. Alexander would withdraw into Russia, destroying everything of use to the invaders. Supplies were pre-positioned and reserve forces organized. Alexander explained his strategy to Frederick William III in May 1812: "It seems to me that this strategy has to be one of carefully avoiding big battles and organizing very long operational lines which will sustain a retreat which will end in fortified camps, where nature and engineering works will strengthen the forces which we use to match up to the enemy's skill. The system is the one which has brought victory to Wellington in wearing down the French armies, and it is the one which I have resolved to follow." Alexander would fight the long war, not the short one. The question in the mind of cognoscenti was whether or not Alexander could keep his nerve to do this. Russian mobilization was delayed by the state's poverty, and Alexander banked—literally—upon raising "voluntary" contributions, as historian Dominic Lieven put it, to support the nation's defense against invasion, yet another reason he had to fight a defensive war.[36]

The roots of the strategy lay in a March 1810 memorandum composed for the czar by Barclay de Tolly. He argued that since Russia's frontier was essentially indefensible against a larger invading force, their only alternative was a fighting retreat through Belorussia and Lithuania, eating or destroying everything in their path useful to the invader. A defensive line would be set up along the Dvina and Dnieper Rivers, one strengthened by fortresses and fortified camps. Barclay forecast a primary enemy offensive along the line of Kiev, but also thought a northeastern thrust into Courland and Livonia a threat. No matter the route the enemy chose, he would be opposed by an army making a fighting withdrawal, but one that would refuse a major battle. This force would retreat into fortified camps while others hit the enemy's rear. Barclay did not see any danger of an enemy invasion along the Minsk-Smolensk route, but were this to happen the endangered force would withdraw and the two main Russian armies would gnaw the invaders' rear and flanks. Barclay had no plan should the enemy breach the line of the Dvina and Dnieper Rivers.[37]

The Russians also realized what was most important for their own survival: the preservation of their army. In April 1812 Lieutenant-Colonel Peter Chuikevich, who worked in the Ministry of War's Secret Chancellery, wrote a key strategy memo addressed to Barclay. Chuikevich observed that "we must remember that we have no formed reserve units behind our front-line forces and the complete destruction of the First and Second armies could have fateful consequences for the Fatherland. The loss of a few provinces must not frighten us because the state's survival depends on the survival of its army." This note also supports the idea that the Russians were playing the long game. Both Barclay and Alexander saw the events unfolding in 1812 "as merely the first act in a longer war designed to destroy Napoleon's domination of Europe."[38]

The Russian operational planning to support their strategy went awry. Before the war, General Johann Ludwig von Wolzogen—another Prussian officer who had entered Russian service after 1806—proposed defending the Russian frontier with two armies. If the French aimed at one, it would withdraw to prepared fighting positions deep in Russia along the Dvina, Dnieper, or another river. The second army would hit the French lines of communication. Wolzogen's idea seems to have caught the eye of Clausewitz's old teacher General Karl Ludwig von Phull, who expanded upon it. Phull argued that since the Polesye swamp cut the western frontier in half, the Russians should put one army north of it and one south. If Napoleon attacked in the north, the army would retreat to the fortified camp of Drissa. If the French struck in the south, the Russians there would retreat to Zhitomir and Kiev. The army not attacked would strike French communications and hit Napoleon's rear. Alexander agreed with Phull's operational plan and the First Army began its war in the north, around Vilna, with the intention of withdrawing to Drissa to try to hold the French on the Dvina— exactly what Phull advised, and an action based upon Barclay's original plan. Doing this would leave the primary Russian armies separated, something exceedingly dangerous to do against a commander like Napoleon, a man whom Clausewitz once called "the God of War himself" and deemed "the most determined general the world has ever seen."[39]

Phull advised a significant withdrawal away from the border before fighting. This, in addition to placing the Russians nearer their reinforcements, would win them time and give them the opportunity to weaken the French by forcing them to make detachments, while also leaving the French vulnerable to Russian attacks against their flanks and rear. Alexander liked this "because it reminded him of Wellington's Portuguese campaign of 1811," Clausewitz revealed in his history of the campaign. But though Clausewitz thought the Russians wise to mount their main resistance in the interior, he believed the Dvina reinforcements, being 100 miles from the border, were out of place and useless, and the fortified camp impossible to defend. He also felt the distance the French had to traverse to reach this spot was fairly small and thus wouldn't weaken them much (Clausewitz was wrong about this; Napoleon's army suffered greatly on the march). He thought General Pytor Bagration's force could be easily pinned by Napoleon, and that the separation of the Russian forces gave the French the interior position and thus the opportunity to defeat the Russians in detail. Most importantly—though Clausewitz doesn't mention this—Phull did not ask what would happen if Napoleon attacked in both areas, and with superior forces in each, which is exactly what he did. Napoleon began crossing the Niemen on June 23. The First and Second Russian armies began withdrawing in the face of the French offensive.[40]

In Vilna, about two weeks before, on June 6, 1812, Clausewitz had finally put on Russian green. General Phull welcomed Clausewitz to Vilna, but Clausewitz had no confidence in his former instructor. He respected the general's learning and said fine things of his character, but he was, in Clausewitz's words, "a man of much understanding and cultivation, but without a knowledge of actual things." In other words, he was an excellent book soldier but devoid of any awareness of how things truly worked (or more likely did not) once the machine of war was wound up. Worse, he possessed a potentially disastrous tendency to lose his head at the slightest setback. Clausewitz attributed Phull's retention in Russian service to Alexander's inability to judge men.[41]

Clausewitz found himself placed under the command of Lieutenant-Colonel Wolzogen. On June 23 Wolzogen dispatched Clausewitz to Drissa with a Russian companion to inspect the camp as well as to map out the army's stopping points for the march. His mission is one typical of a quartermaster-general officer of the era. When he reached Drissa—which is on the banks of the Dvina River a bit south of the meeting point of the present Lithuanian, Russian, and Belarussian borders—armed with orders written in French by General Phull (many of the Prussian officers, not knowing Russian, used French), the Russian officer commanding the position thought he was a spy. Clausewitz managed to convince him otherwise.[42]

His inspection of the camp left him dissatisfied. Clausewitz found extensive works—too extensive, he concluded—and often impractical, though the position was strong. Worse yet, much still needed to be done, including the construction of seven bridges. The important provisions were also not secured, even from the weather. Overall, he was convinced of the position's tactical poverty. It could be easily encircled by the French, resulting in the loss of an entire army. Phull, Clausewitz insisted later, was looking for what is today known as a "force multiplier" for his inferior force, but was needlessly complicating the fact that the Russians needed "to follow the simple path of direct resistance."[43]

In Drissa, Clausewitz wrote to his friend Tiedemann, who had also joined the Russians and was on the staff of General Ivan von Essen in Riga. "I am well," he informed him, adding that "the Emperor has treated me very kindly"; but he would have felt a lot better if he had been doing something more constructive, and complained that he had not yet heard a shot fired. Clausewitz was also disappointed by what he saw of the Russian command system in Riga, and remarked that in Drissa, "no one knows what he has the right to do or is allowed to do," and no one seemed really sure what to do with the entrenched camp. "We have about 110,000 men altogether," he wrote of the czar's army, adding, "whoever is afraid doesn't understand the craft."[44]

Clausewitz rejoined the czar's party on June 28. They were at Swanziani. The war had begun, as had the Russian retreat. Clausewitz now faced a distasteful task: reporting what he had seen to the emperor and Phull, something made more difficult by Phull having warmly welcomed Clausewitz, and by the fact that Clausewitz was Phull's adjutant. Writing later about himself, Clausewitz recalled: "the importance of the crisis, the deficiencies and errors which in an enlarged view he had discovered, weighed so heavily on his mind, that he felt the strongest necessity to expose the dangers into which the parties and the cause were being hurried." These conflicting factors led Clausewitz to decide, in both his written and oral reports, "to confine himself to the terms of his commission," meaning to relay the state of the fortifications, "but to touch also lightly on the difficulties which might be expected to occur. The result of the conference was, that the Emperor conceived fresh suspicion that he might find himself embarked in a transaction which had not been maturely considered."[45]

Later, the Prince of Oldenburg, the czar's brother-in-law, told Clausewitz that Alexander thought Clausewitz hadn't spoken his mind. The emperor was right; Clausewitz half-answered the query, telling the prince that he had tried to point out the things that mattered the most, "which were yet to be considered." He then opened the door for more—if anyone was interested—noting that "many difficulties yet presented themselves to his imagination, which he concluded must already have suggested themselves to the framers of the scheme, in order to not be surprised by them." Prince Oldenburg responded that the emperor wanted to talk to Clausewitz alone, but then nothing came of this. Others in Alexander's entourage had already begun to expose the problems with Drissa—"officers better known to him," Clausewitz wrote, "who declared their opinions with less reserve."[46]

The retreat toward Drissa continued, and Clausewitz was dispatched several times to General Barclay to push him along (the emperor and his staff preceded the retreat of the army). Barclay had a nasty habit of stopping where he was not supposed to, and Phull worried about Napoleon beating Barclay to Drissa. Barclay didn't appreciate the prodding. Clausewitz performed this distasteful task, noting that he was "ill received." He liked Barclay's "repose and apparent self-possession," but the general's habitual disobedience to orders, as well as his poor treatment of others, "gave him uneasiness."[47]

At the town of Videsky, roughly midway between Vilna and Drissa, the czar received news that the French "had out-flanked the army on its left, and that in consequence the order of march must be altered, unless we wished to see on the morrow single columns overwhelmed by superior forces." Alexander called for Phull and told him to bring Clausewitz along. Phull and Clausewitz met in an anteroom with members of the czar's retinue, Alexander being in an adjacent chamber. One of the czar's staff, Petr Mikhailovich Volkonsky, gave the Prussians the news, and said they had summoned Clausewitz because he had charted the army's route to Drissa. They wanted to know how to respond.[48]

Phull began by blaming Barclay for his constant refusal to obey orders. Volkonsky didn't protest this, but wisely pushed the meeting back to the subject at hand: what should be done? Phull paced the room where they met, proclaiming that since his "advice had not been followed, he could not undertake the remedy." This exasperated Clausewitz, who, he wrote later, "was at his wits' end" with Phull. Part of this was his frustration with Phull's immense stupidity, but it was just as much a factor of pride and reputation. Clausewitz was one of Phull's men. Thus, what others thought of Phull was also automatically thrust upon Clausewitz. If the teacher is blamed, so are his students. He found the experience "humiliating," but also realized that it mattered not at all in relation to the larger affairs unfolding.[49]

Much discussion about what to do followed among Clausewitz, Count Vasili Orlov-Denisov, and Colonel Karl von Toll as they pored over the maps. Clausewitz didn't think the situation that serious, even if the reports proved true—something he doubted. Clausewitz thought they should stay their course and see how events unfolded. "It is usual, in a council of war," he wrote later, "that he who advises doing nothing carries his point, and this was no exception." Colonel Toll agreed with Clausewitz and they advised the czar so. The next day they discovered the report was false. These events shook Clausewitz's confidence.[50]

On July 8 the Russians reached the Drissa camp. Phull and Clausewitz were sent for to join the group touring the works. The czar and his staff were not pleased. Colonel Alexandre Michaud de Beauretour, a skilled engineer and veteran of the Sardinian forces who served as aide-de-camp to Alexander, pronounced the post terrible and this set the czar against it. The Russians knew that the path of Napoleon's advance meant that instead of hitting Drissa he could pass between the two northern Russian armies. If the Russians sat in this pre-built position, Napoleon could easily amass his forces against Bagration's Second Army, perhaps destroying it, and then drive on Moscow. Or he could simply bag Barclay's First Army at Drissa, using his superior numbers to surround it. All of this was topped off by the fact that Drissa was simply badly constructed.[51]

On the March to Drissa, Clausewitz had pointed out to Phull how the general had lost Alexander's trust, and tried to help him regain it. He suggested Phull advise the czar to put the entire army under Barclay so they had unity of command and one voice guiding their movements. Though Clausewitz had little faith that Barclay could defeat Napoleon in battle, he found him "calm and determined" and "a thorough soldier." After the debacle of the czar's viewing of the camp, he went to Phull again, pointed out the poverty of the general's position with the emperor, and pressed him to follow his advice regarding Barclay. Reluctantly, Phull agreed. Alexander received him graciously, "and appeared in his resolve only to follow the advice of the general," but Clausewitz did not believe the decision had been made based upon Phull's recommendation because Alexander would have met fierce resistance for following his now discredited advisor.[52]

The Russians decided to retreat to Vitebsk, and began withdrawing from Drissa on July 17. Clausewitz noted later that this was along the main road to Smolensk, which then joined that going to Moscow, providing "a natural line of retreat," as well as the chance to join hands with Bagration's army and reinforcements marching toward the front. On the 19th Alexander heeded his advisors and left the army, putting Barclay in command of First Army. Since Barclay was also minister of war, he now controlled Second Army as well. When the czar gave command of the Russian forces to Barclay, he told him to keep in mind that this was the only army Russia had. A letter to Bagration reminded him to preserve Russia's ability to resist and remember that "Our entire goal must be directed towards gaining time and drawing out the war as long as possible. Only by this means can we have the chance of defeating so strong an enemy who has mobilized the military resources of all Europe." Bagration was not happy with the instructions; he preferred to fight. "Russians ought not to run away," he wrote; "we are becoming worse than the Prussians." Clausewitz, however, "felt himself relieved, and rejoiced when he saw affairs taking the turn of a retreat in this direction." But he still worried about the condition of the Russian army, as well as the military situation in general. Barclay dispatched 20,000 men under General Peter Wittgenstein to cover the approaches to St. Petersburg, and then marched for Smolensk. Meanwhile, Bagration, the commander of Second Army farther south, also pushed his men toward Smolensk, fighting a number of actions against the French on the way.[53]

Clausewitz wrote to Marie on July 18, telling her they had left Drissa. He was still with General Phull and not happy about it. He also complained about his service thus far. "I still have not heard a shot," he said, and lamented the fact that his lack of Russian made him useless. His whole purpose for going was to see the war and win a reputation for himself. Their three weeks of marching had fatigued the army—even the headquarters staff with whom he rode had slept largely in stables and barns. The troops suffered even more. "Sometimes I think to myself about this entire period of absence from you which I still have before me as a long journey back to you on which I have found myself, which is the most pleasant, comforting thought that I can make of this for my heart and imagination."[54]

The next day, July 19, Clausewitz's job with Phull ended, leaving him unsure of where he would land next. Clausewitz took advantage of the presence of Colonel Lieven (who had sponsored his entry into the Russian army) to get an appointment to the general staff. This caused some consternation among several of its members, Clausewitz noted. Because of this, and with some help from Wolzogen, Clausewitz managed to get what he really wanted: a posting to the rearguard commanded by General Count Peter Pahlen. Their assignment was "to cover the retreat along the right bank of the Dvina." Pahlen was a cavalry officer in command of the 3rd Cavalry Corps, one of Russia's best, and, Clausewitz told Marie, "the most prestigious cavalry general we have."[55]

Clausewitz had sought a combat posting because only here, he believed, could he make a name for himself. Indeed, over the next three weeks he fought in what he told Marie were "several skirmishes." But Clausewitz soon discovered the appointment was not what he thought. Torpedoed by what he deemed enemies on Barclay's staff who were responsible for his appointment, he was named Pahlen's chief of staff, the first quartermaster. This made him responsible for the movement of the units and its dispositions in camp and in battle. As Clausewitz spoke no Russian, he was in his own opinion unqualified for the post. He had asked for posting as an aide-de-camp, and tried to convince Pahlen to use him so. The general "declined" and Clausewitz had no choice but to take up the given task. Clausewitz wrote that he found himself "at once in a false position, and nothing remained for him but the determination to gain the respect of the Russians by avoiding neither fatigue nor danger."[56]

To buy time for Bagration's army to move to meet his own, and to keep Napoleon off Bagration, Barclay decided to stand and fight. On July 23 he reached Vitebsk, roughly eighty miles from Smolensk, and began deploying for battle. He also sent a detachment to slow Napoleon's drive. But on the 26th Barclay received word that Bagration could not reach him because the French blocked his path. This fact did not dissuade Barclay from seeking a fight with Napoleon, but some of his generals managed to do so by pointing out the weakness of their position at Vitebsk and the fact that Napoleon had more than twice as many men. Barclay decided to withdraw.[57]

Clausewitz was much relieved by this. He had been "in despair at this idea" of Barclay fighting at Vitebsk. Pahlen's unit had been serving as Barclay's rearguard since they retreated from Polotsk about sixty miles to the west (both locations are in Belarus today). They had seen very little of the French because they had mostly kept to the Dvina's left bank. Clausewitz reached Vitebsk on the night of July 26, "after a severe march," and at dawn they moved to the Senno road, south of Vitebsk, where they were reinforced.[58]

The 27th saw Barclay renew his retreat. Pahlen commanded the rear-guard and Clausewitz got to see the combat he wanted. "General Pahlen," Clausewitz wrote in his history, "took up a position some two miles from Vitebsk, with his right flank on the Dvina, and his front covered by an insignificant rivulet. He placed his main force of cavalry, not very judiciously, on the right wing; because in that quarter, between the river and the wooded edge of the valley, there was a small plain; and a plain, according to the received rules, is the ground for cavalry. The space, however, was so limited, that it was necessary to adopt a chess-square formation in three or four ranks; and the cavalry, in consequence, suffered much from the artillery fire." To Clausewitz, Pahlen's units also had too much ground to cover and thus formed only a thin screen, while the left flank had no anchor. They had no reserves, no depth, and no way to secure their left against an enemy effort to turn it. At 5:00 a.m. they engaged with units of the French vanguard from the divisions of Broussier and Bruyère. The fighting went on until three in the afternoon. Clausewitz contributed its length—during which his unit held the position—to a slow French advance. Pahlen later pulled back behind the Lutchess to the spots Barclay had just evacuated, uneasy about fighting the advancing French from his initial post. Napoleon chose not to press them because it would be evening before his forces were concentrated.[59]

This was one of several actions in which Clausewitz was involved during his time with Pahlen, and one of the few of which he left any known record. For his bravery under fire here he received the Cross of St. Vladimir, 4th Class, with ribbon.[60]

Clausewitz, though, remained unhappy with his position with Pahlen, and his feelings were only intensified by what had happened in the battle. He had only been on Pahlen's staff for a week before seeing action, and knew because of this he could expect to exert little influence on his superior. But events during the action drove home to him a more severe problem. He had disagreed with Pahlen's troop deployments before the action, particularly the fact that the various arms were not positioned to support one another. He also gave Pahlen low marks for managing the fighting. But as happened to him many times in 1812, Clausewitz found that his inability to speak Russian prevented him from giving advice. He "felt himself so utterly useless, that he would rather have served as a subaltern in the line," and was very happy when arriving with their reinforcements on July 27 was a higher ranking officer that supplanted Clausewitz from his quartermaster post, making him "no longer responsible for the consequences of dispositions over which he could have no influence."[61]

Clausewitz also saw the successful orderly retreat of the Russian army as critically important. "In this case it may be said that the Russian army was here a second time saved from destruction," he later wrote, adding that he "felt himself delighted, and in a frame of mind to thank God on his knees for this having diverted our steps from the mouth of an abyss." Barclay de Tolly praised Pahlen for his performance covering the First Army's retreat from Vitebsk to Smolensk, while many of the French felt they had been denied an opportunity to inflict a severe defeat on the Russians.[62]

In the end, Clausewitz's posting with Pahlen only lasted three weeks, as the general fell ill and the Russians dissolved his command. Clausewitz went back to the Russian headquarters for eight days before being put at the disposal of the quartermaster general. This position made him fairly happy, though he continued to bemoan his lack of Russian. This shortcoming brought a level of constant annoyance and he described his situation as that of a deaf mute. He became convinced it would prevent him from accomplishing anything of significance.[63]

By August, Napoleon's strategy was in tatters. The Russian armies had not only escaped; they had succeeded in concentrating at Smolensk on August 2, 1812. The Russians now had 120,000 men facing Napoleon's 180,000. Desertion, sickness, combat, fatigue, and the Russian summer had already begun the grinding attrition of Napoleon's force. Clausewitz wrote in his history of the campaign: "whatever critics may say of particular moments of the transaction, the entire destruction of the French army is to be ascribed to the unheard-of energy of the pursuit, the results of which imagination could hardly exaggerate."[64]

Facing pressure from the public, his political masters, and his brother officers to do something other than retreat, Barclay agreed to attack. At Smolensk on August 6, the Russians launched a three-pronged offensive. But intelligence reports (later proved false) indicating that Napoleon was advancing to the north of Smolensk caused Barclay to idle First Army for several days. By the time he had a more accurate picture of events, Napoleon was ready, and the Russians called off their assault.[65]

Napoleon now saw a chance to land a blow on the Russians at Smolensk by taking the city and cutting their communications. He struck on August 14, but heroic resistance offered by troops in Krasnyi and their subsequent fighting retreat destroyed Napoleon's plan and bought valuable time for the Russians. The main Russian forces beat Napoleon to Smolensk, stopping the French attacks on August 15–16. The fighting burned most of Smolensk to the ground and both sides suffered approximately 10,000 casualties.[66] Clausewitz was at Smolensk, but we have no record of his actions there.

The retreat continued. "From this day on it was said at every march that we would take up a strong position and therein await the attack of the enemy," Clausewitz wrote, but the Russians did not do this, or even try to. "So it went, halfway to Moscow." Napoleon again tried to cut their line of retreat, and the Russians fought another battle at Valutina Gora (or Lubino), on August 19, but Barclay again battered his way out of Napoleon's grip. He then sent officers to scout a favorable position for a battle. "Thus the two armies converged towards the point of equalization," Clausewitz wrote later.[67]

The continuous movement and combat wore upon the men of both sides. "The hardships of the campaign are extraordinary," Clausewitz told Marie in an August 19 letter. "For nine weeks daily on the march, for five weeks having taken off no piece of clothing from the body, heat, dust, abominable water and often very considerable hunger. Until now I've spent every night except a few under the open sky because most areas have been abandoned by all of the inhabitants and the wretched huts have been laid waste." Despite such conditions, he wrote, "I find myself happier than in Berlin. The gout torments me at times, almost constantly I suffer from a toothache and since Vilna I've developed three hollow teeth; my hair is falling out—my hands, which have lacked gloves for the last 14 days, look like yellow leather." Still, Clausewitz did not consider his sufferings too terrible: "I have only been sick once, one day especially; I was so exhausted and attacked by the gout that I had to be lifted from my horse. In a farm behind the front I drank a few cups of your mother's bouillon, lay down near the fire, slept nine hours, and the next morning sat down healthy on my horse just as the rear guard was coming through."[68]

While he still had hopes and ambitions for the future, the situation wore on him. "If the war lasts another campaign I hope to be more useful in the next because I will learn Russian in the winter; then I will also be more cheerful because now, I confess it only to you, I am very sad." He had enjoyed the company of other Prussian officers until now, but this was coming to an end. Chasot was supposed to leave in a couple of days to go to the coastal provinces where the German Legion was being formed, and as he had made no other friends, he would be "entirely orphaned." He hoped Gneisenau would somehow rescue him.[69]

Most of all, he missed Marie. "My entire life seems to me mostly so confused and without results that I've come back to this a thousand times before: Your possession is the greatest thing that I've achieved—and this single and highest good I have to do without. On the other hand, I tell myself that if all goes badly and only this one thing remains to me, I am still an enviable man. But if everything comes to grief, where will we meet again?" "God keep you for me, and if it can be, I do not want to leave this world without having seen and embraced you again."[70]

Thoughts of serving in the newly forming Russo-German Legion became a small lifeline for Clausewitz during his time in Russia. The immediate concept for this unit had grown out of the czar's headquarters before the outbreak of the war. The Prussian exiles, under the leadership of Stein, latched onto a scheme already birthed by Wilhelm Daniel von Arentschildt for a Russo-German Legion to fight under the Russian flag. Alexander supported the idea, which initially entailed forming the units in Riga and sending out officers such as the former Prussian soldier Alexander Wilhelm von der Goltz to encourage desertion among the Germans fighting under Napoleon's banner. Stein and Georg von Oldenburg were part of the German Committee established to oversee it, but Stein soon took control of the political element while Oldenburg began organizing the Legion itself. By late October the Legion had about 2,200 men, mostly Prussians and Swiss. Goltz and Clausewitz were among those that feared its potential for growth would be restricted by a lack of Russian money. Clausewitz thought British funding a necessity.[71]

The Russian forces reached Dorogobuzh, about thirty-five miles east of Smolensk, on August 24. The retreat continued the next day, but the Russian high command was beginning to fracture. The relationship between Barclay and Bagration had never been good. The debacle of Smolensk made it worse. The city's loss, combined with the constant retreats, led to a virtual mutiny among the brass against Barclay's command. Alexander's advisor recommended appointing sixty-five-year-old General Mikhail Kutusov to replace Barclay. On August 20 Alexander signed the order. He did so not because he wanted to, but because he felt he had no better alternative. Kutusov did possess immense military experience, supplemented by a useful charisma and not a little slyness, but his age and diminished energy counted against him. Kutusov was the popular choice of the Russian people, though not of the Russian leaders.[72]

On August 29 Barclay began building works at Tsarevo-Zaimische and prepared to fight. But the same day Kutusov arrived to take up his post of commander-in-chief of the Russian forces. "In the army there was great joy over his arrival," Clausewitz wrote later. "In the opinion of the Russians, everything up to then had gone very badly; any change therefore held out hope of improvement." But, Clausewitz said, "the system of war, however, remained the same," and Kutusov "shuddered back every time the head of Medusa showed itself near him." The Russian army marched east from Tsarevo-Zaimische. On September 3 it set up camp near a small village. Colonel Toll chose the spot, and Kutusov agreed after seeing it himself. "And so we came to Mozhaisk [Borodino]," Clausewitz wrote, "where we finally gritted our teeth and braved a mediocre position."[73]

The battlefield at Borodino conferred some advantages on the Russians. Several streams that twisted to the Moscow River cut the hilly terrain. This river and the Kolocha marked the battlefield's north, or right flank, and the villages of the Old Smolensk Road marked the southern, or left flank. The ground here was hilly, but not as much as the rest of the nearby earth. The Russians had a strong position in the center, one studded with high ground and cut by gullies and steep-banked creeks, as well as the village of Borodino itself. The Russians stiffened the position by building field fortifications. The Maslovo Flèches helped anchor their right. Rayevsky's Redoubt (or the Grand Redoubt) dominated the center; the Bagration Fleches and Shevardino Redoubt supported the Russian left (the Russians were forced out of this position before the main battle on September 5, after bitter fighting). The right flank of the Russian position, as Clausewitz observed, was certainly the strongest, made so by the terrain. This virtually dictated a French attack on the Russian left.[74]

The Russian army stretched in a line along the Kolocha River, one Clausewitz later criticized because it assisted the French attacks on the weak Russian left, did not give the Russians a direct line of retreat, and ignored a second road that ran to the rear of their position. The placement of the Russian army in a type of arc that made the left flank weak—and drew the enemy there—also essentially placed the Russian right flank forces out of the fight. In Clausewitz's opinion, "it would have been better

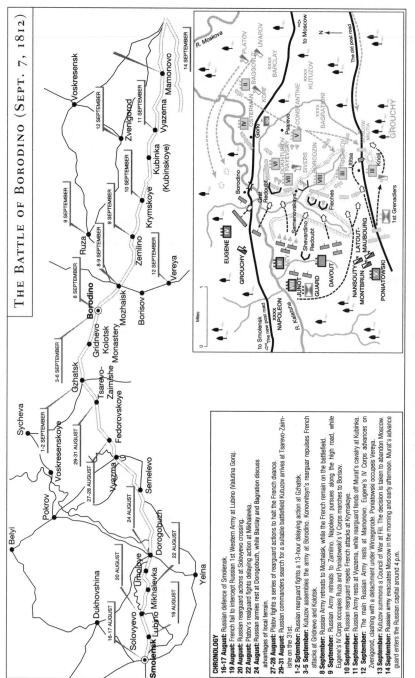

Map 5.2. The March from Smolensk and the Battle of Borodino (Sept. 7, 1812).

for the Russians to have extended the right wing along the Kolocha to the neighborhood of Gorky, and the rest of the terrain running to the Moskva River might have been occupied with a few units, or merely observed." He approved of the short frontage, which produced a dense, layered defense that he believed contributed to the staunchness of the Russian resistance. But Clausewitz preferred even greater depth, insisting that it would have been better to have the reserves as well as the cavalry even farther back, beyond the enemy's view, 3,000 to 5,000 paces, because major battles develop slowly and further depth offers the opportunity to throw in the reserves at the decisive moment. He thought the Russian cavalry and reserves too close to the rear of the infantry, and thus exposed unnecessarily to enemy fire without utilizing their combat power.[75]

Napoleon planned to open his attack with a heavy cannonade (he had 587 guns, almost twice his number at Waterloo). A heavy frontal assault would then strike the Russian center, supported by diversions on each flank. In the north, the troops of his stepson, Eugène de Beauharnais, were to capture the village of Borodino and then slide rightward, crossing the Kolocha and taking the Rayevsky Redoubt. This would also pin Russian forces so they couldn't be used elsewhere. Meanwhile, Józef Poniatowski's men were to march around the Russian flank on the Old Smolensk Road and threaten their left. Napoleon's primary attack would be made in the center with Davout's forces. Now, approximately 125,000 Russians awaited the attack of roughly 130,000 French troops. Both sides banked on brute force and attrition.[76]

Not long after 6:00 a.m. on September 7, 1812, the French artillery commenced the bombardment. The French drums beat, and Napoleon's troops moved to attack. Eugène's troops quickly took Borodino and pushed on, while Poniatowski swung around the Russian left, driving the Russians out of the village of Utitsa. Davout's men dove into the Russian center, seizing the Bagration Fleches. The Russians counterattacked at approximately 7:00 a.m., throwing back Eugène's forces into Borodino, stopping Poniatowski cold, and pushing Davout from the hard-won fleches. An intense fight for Davout's position ensued as both sides poured troops into the cauldron. By 8:30, Napoleon had been forced to commit all of his reserves except the Imperial Guard to this flank. Eugène pushed forward, launching a failed assault on the Rayevsky Redoubt. Napoleon massed forces in the center and at around 10:00 a.m. tried again. Both sides threw enormous amounts of artillery fire into the morass. Some of the Russians gave way, but reformed with a ravine to their front. A series of French cavalry charges failed to dislodge them. Napoleon would not commit his guard—his last reserve—despite the pleas of his marshals. Kutusov reinforced his weakened center and the attrition went on. Napoleon began planning a new assault.[77]

It is at this point that Clausewitz's involvement in the battle intensifies. After Pahlen fell ill, Clausewitz had found himself assigned as the senior quartermaster general to General Fedor Uvarov's First Cavalry Corps, which anchored the Russian right (or northernmost point). When General Matvei Platov, the Cossack commander on this flank, forded the Kolotscha, he was stunned to find no French troops where he had expected many. He watched as Eugène weakened this force to support his effort around Borodino and hit upon the idea that launching a flank attack could win the Russians much. He sent word to his superiors.[78]

At the time (between 8 and 9 am), Clausewitz was with the men of Uvarov's staff in Gorky village behind the Russian lines among Kutusov and his retinue. Colonel Toll, Kutusov's chief quartermaster, arrived with word that everything was secure on the Russian right when a report came in that the Russians had captured Eugène during the fighting for the Rayevsky Redoubt. The report was later proven false, but initially after this news, Clausewitz said, "enthusiasm rose up like blazing straw." At this moment, Toll relayed Platov's idea to Kutusov and suggested the 2,500 men of 1st Cavalry Corps as the support. Kutusov, Clausewitz said, "who had been listening to the reports and discussions like someone who did not have his head screwed on straight," thought such a diversion might even win the battle, and agreed.[79]

In his history of the 1812 campaign Clausewitz is critical of this attack. He believed such an action should be launched late in the day and also thought that using such a small force early in a battle against an enemy with abundant numbers had little hope of dramatic success. It also should have had infantry support because the Russians could certainly expect to meet enemy infantry as well as cavalry, and cavalry alone could not expect to triumph over two of the other service arms fighting in unison.[80]

Kutuzov dispatched half of Platov's Cossacks (at most about 2,700 men) and the 1st Cavalry Corps commanded by Uvarov (Clausewitz with them), which had roughly 2,440 men and a dozen guns. Uvarov splashed across the Kolocha River on the north flank of both armies around Maloye Selo, the artillery in the rear. They wove through the marshy but steep-banked rivulets feeding the Kolotscha and shifted left toward Borodino. Sometime between 11 and 12 o'clock they reached the Voina, a stream flowing past Borodino and into the Kolotscha. The Voina hosted a dam, which created a small lake a bit south of Bezzubovo, a dot of a village almost due north of Borodino that marked the north of the French line. A bridge near the dam crossed the Voina, and a small mill stood nearby. As Uvarov's men moved, Platov's forces swept to the north of Bezzubovo and deeper behind the French lines.[81]

When the Russian cavalry appeared, the French dispatched word to their corps commander, Eugène. The flank attack worried him enough that he called off his new attack on the Rayevsky Redoubt, dispatched an update to Napoleon, and took a horse to investigate. He reached the front in time to be swept up in Uvarov's attack and forced to seek safety in a French infantry square.[82]

Clausewitz described the unfolding scene:

> On the near side of the brook stood two regiments of French cavalry and a body of Italian infantry, perhaps a regiment or a reinforced battalion. The cavalry at once withdrew over the dam that crossed the brook about two thousand paces above Borodino, but the infantry [four regiments] was bold enough to remain and formed a square with its back to the brook. General Uvarov ordered his men to attack. In vain the author [Clausewitz] suggested that the square first be placed under fire by the light artillery; the Russian officers feared it would then retreat and they would not get any prisoners. The hussars of the Guard were therefore called forward and ordered to charge. They made three ineffectual attacks; the [French and Croatians] maintained discipline and their tight formation and returned a steady fire. As is usual in such cases, the hussars turned back some thirty paces from the square and drew out of range. General Uvarov discontinued these not very brilliant attempts, ordered the artillery to open fire, and at the first volley the enemy withdrew across the brook. The whole business came to an end.[83]

The Russian horsemen suffered heavily attacking the squares, and the French moved in more troops to oppose them. Eugène also called for cavalry reinforcements, which General Emmanuel de Grouchy dispatched. The Russian cavalry tried to fight its way over the dam, but French canister and musket fire made that impossible. The Russian guns drove off the French battery, but the Russians simply lacked the strength to break through. Uvarov and Clausewitz soon realized that the mass of enemy troops facing them meant they could not attack Borodino itself, and they also grew increasingly aware that "the whole weight of the giant [Napoleon's army] was beginning to press upon them." Russian general staff officers began appearing among Uvarov's command to see what this move could accomplish, including Toll. Clausewitz wrote that "Under these circumstances the author thanked God for having been reduced to a zero. He was not even able to take part in the exchanges in Russian between General Uvarov and the various officers that were sent to him. From the outset he had been convinced that this diversion would fail, and now saw that if anything at all was to be salvaged it could be done only by a young fire eater who had his reputation to make, not by General Uvarov." Others felt similarly. Russian observers later criticized Uvarov's advance as too slow, branding him a poor leader who missed a fine opportunity to damage the enemy.[84]

It became apparent to Uvarov, Clausewitz, and others that the French had too many reserves for much to come out of the situation. Heavy fire from across the stream on the French left eventually interrupted several hours of wrangling back and forth about what to do. Clausewitz and his comrades discovered that Platov's Cossacks were hitting the French. "Soon we could see these troops [the Cossacks]—remarkable in that sometimes they are exceptionally brave and at other times exceptional cowards— careening about between enemy infantry and stands of trees without making a serious charge," Clausewitz wrote. "The enemy units opposite us feared that the Cossacks might force them into the swamp and marched off to one side. At this, the Cossacks of the Guards, who were attached to Uvarov's corps, could restrain themselves no longer. They streamed over the dam like a rocket with a long tail, and like lightning were among their brethren in the woods on the other side."[85]

Clausewitz and Uvarov held their position. Uvarov kept up the pressure on the left flank, feigning attacks to keep the enemy from pulling forces from here to use in the center. They watched parts of the battle unfold until they received an order from Kutusov at three o'clock to return to their starting position. At between four and five they gathered behind Gorky. Uvarov's and Platov's superiors were not pleased—especially Kutusov. They thought spectacular results could have arisen from this attack if its leaders had properly executed it. Platov, who had a reputation for spending too much time with a bottle, was accused by several participants of being drunk when the attack was made.[86]

Uvarov's and Platov's attack had an effect that Clausewitz didn't understand at the time (or even later). Napoleon was about to send the Young Guard to bolster his units fighting around Semeyonovskoe and the

Rayevsky Redoubt, but the heavy firing from across the Voina (where the attack was going in) convinced him to wait. Worried about the potential threat to his baggage and communications, the emperor personally ordered forces to support Eugène and rode to the Kolocha River to examine his left. It was as much as two hours before he returned to his headquarters. The affair purchased the Russians two or three hours to reform and strengthen their center, which had suffered heavy French blows.[87]

As the bloody day drew to a close, "a fog soon covered the battlefield," a Russian officer wrote, "and complete stillness descended. Only now we were able to calmly discuss the events of this memorable day. None of us considered the battle lost." Indeed, Kutusov intended to fight a second day, but as the casualty reports came in he reconsidered. The Russians had suffered heavy losses, more than the French, though they could not have known this at the time, and the encroaching French threatened their line of retreat. With nothing to be gained, and his forces still in solid order—wisely, Clausewitz observed later—Kutusov ordered a retreat, which began after midnight.[88]

That night a wind kicked up, and a cold rain began to fall on the charnel house that was Borodino. Between them the armies had suffered approximately 65,000 casualties, 108 for every minute of battle. Indeed, this was the bloodiest one-day fight of the Napoleonic era, and the daily loss rate eclipsed that of Verdun and Stalingrad. Tens of thousands of dead and wounded lay on Borodino's hills, and thousands more would die in improvised field hospitals over the next few days, often from hunger and thirst. The French suffered fewer casualties, but the slight difference mattered little.[89]

Napoleon has often been criticized, at the time and since, for not committing his last reserves at Borodino and thus destroying the Russian army, and for not ordering a pursuit. Clausewitz, for his part, defended the emperor on both counts. Doing the first, he says, could have weakened Napoleon's army to the point where he could not have reached Moscow, which Napoleon believed necessary for forcing a peace (though he would be proved wrong about this). On the latter criticism, Clausewitz points out that when the battle had been decided, at 4:00 p.m., the Russians were strongly upon the field, had not yet decided to leave, and would have inflicted heavy casualties on the French.[90]

Kutusov announced their victory, and then told Alexander that their casualties had been too heavy to hold a position as large as the one at

Borodino. This necessitated their withdrawal to Mozhaisk, "where he hoped to receive reinforcements and fight another action." He also told Alexander that winning battles was not his objective; he sought the destruction of the French army. Alexander recognized that Kutusov's decision to withdraw had been the right one, but he also knew that announcing the battle as a victory and not mentioning the withdrawal was smart politics. He promoted Kutusov to field marshal and gave rewards and decorations to many others. Clausewitz later received a golden sabre inscribed with "For Bravery" for his service as Uvarov's quartermaster general at Borodino and other places.[91]

The Russians, in an orderly manner, spent the next seven days withdrawing the eighty miles from Borodino to Moscow. In the retreat, Platov initially commanded the rearguard, which included Uvarov's cavalry, with Clausewitz still serving as quartermaster. The Russian army reformed behind Mozhaisk, about ten miles to the east, on September 8. Murat's cavalry led the French pursuit. They reached the Russians that afternoon, and made some light attacks, but failed to break into the city. Reinforced, the French hit harder the next morning and Platov abandoned the town. Upset that Platov had allowed the French to so easily take Mozhaisk—which housed so many Russian wounded—Kutuzov replaced him with Mikhail Miloradovitch. The Russians continued their retreat on the 9th, after which, Clausewitz noted later, a pattern emerged on their march to Moscow.[92]

The French cavalry—Murat's force—followed lightly, the sides usually skirmished faintly in the afternoon, but with little result beyond a continued Russian withdrawal, whereupon both sides then encamped.[93] "Only one day proved an exception," Clausewitz wrote of this rearguard campaign, and it occurred when they were at the village of Krymskoye about fifty miles west of Moscow:

> On September 10 Miloradovitch had moved to within two miles of the main body of the army when, an hour before sundown, the French appeared with infantry and artillery as well as cavalry. Miloradovitch could not take evasive action without uncovering the main camp, and because the ground seemed not unfavorable he decided to risk battle. The Russian infantry, drawn up among trees on a low ridge, defended itself vigorously, and after it was forced to withdraw it continued to fight for another hour in a very unfavorable position at the foot of the ridge. Here too the French attacks, though initiated with great energy, had a feeble quality about them. The engagement lasted until eleven o'clock, and Miloradovitch retained a position close behind the battlefield.[94]

Clausewitz described this to Marie as "a fierce rearguard action which lasted until late in the night," and during which his horse was wounded.[95]

In the rearguard, Clausewitz and his comrades endured almost daily combat, but the rigors of retreat itself proved nearly as threatening. The rearguard, Clausewitz said, "usually found all wells dry and the smaller streams fouled and had to rely on whatever rivers and small lakes might be in the area." It was even worse for the French, of course, who came behind even them. "The author still vividly recalls the oppressive lack of water during this campaign," Clausewitz wrote later. "Never had he suffered such thirst; the filthiest puddles were emptied to quench the fever, and washing was often out of the question for a week. How this affected the cavalry can be imagined, and as we have said, the French must have suffered doubly. It is well known in what wretched condition the French cavalry reached Moscow." During the entire retreat (fourteen weeks by the time it was over, Clausewitz told Gneisenau), he never slept in a town or village.[96]

Though they struggled to find water—a problem exacerbated by the summer being hotter and dryer than normal—the Russian supply system kept them fed. "It is true that bread was usually lacking and that one had to content oneself with very bad biscuits, which however were not unhealthy and proved as nourishing as bread would have been. Porridge, meat, and spirits were plentiful. There was seldom grain for the horses, but Russian horses are used to feeding on hay," Clausewitz wrote to Marie.[97]

Both armies relied to at least some extent on foraging to feed both animals and men (the French more so than the Russians, whose line of retreat housed many supply depots). When the rearguard entered a village, they consumed any food and forage and then burned or tore down the buildings. "What had at first been thoughtlessness and carelessness gradually became policy," Clausewitz recalled, "which was often extended to small and large towns as well." In his three months in the rearguard he saw almost nothing but scenes of fire. They destroyed the bridges and cut the numbers from the mileposts. "These difficulties impeded the French advance and burdened and wasted the energies of man and beast."[98]

After a council of war on September 13, Kutusov took the side of the generals urging retreat and abandoning Moscow to the French. Clausewitz thought Borodino had decided Moscow's fate and wrote Gneisenau shortly after the battle that "I find that the evacuation of Moscow is neither a crime nor an error." He believed Kutusov had to choose between saving Moscow or the army and made the right choice, as a second battle would have likely meant a total Russian defeat.[99] Kutusov preserved the Russian army. Because he did, the war went on.

6

The Road to Tauroggen (1812)

Fear cripples the intellect, courage inspires it.

"On September 14 the Russian army passed through Moscow,"
Clausewitz wrote, "and the rearguard was ordered to follow the
same day." General Miloradovitch asked the French for time to evacuate
the city, and had orders to fight if they refused. Murat, the French cavalry commander, declined to meet with him, sending General Sebastiani
instead. They came to a deal, Miloradovitch asking that "Moscow might
be spared as far as possible." Clausewitz, who happened to be riding near
the pair, heard Sebastiani say: "Sir, the emperor will place his Guards at
the head of his army to make any sort of disorder absolutely impossible."
Four times he heard Sebastiani commit himself to protecting Moscow.
Clausewitz "thought it worth notice, because these words implied the
strongest wish to take control of an undamaged city."[1]

Clausewitz estimated that it was three or so in the afternoon when he
and his unit entered Moscow, "and between five and six when we took up
positions beyond the city." Miloradovitch had to have some of his cavalry
clear a path through the wagons thronging the streets. "The most painful sight was long rows of wounded soldiers, who lay along the houses and
were vainly hoping to be moved away. All of these unfortunates probably
died in the city." Famously, fires began engulfing Moscow as the Russians
retreated and the French entered. Moscow's governor Fedor Rostopchin
believed it better to set the city ablaze than leave it to the French. Clausewitz
wrote to Marie: "We held ourselves close behind the city and saw it burning at every corner during the night."[2]

Clausewitz by now found himself in a minor position on Miloradovitch's
staff since Uvarov had taken sick and the Russians rolled his command

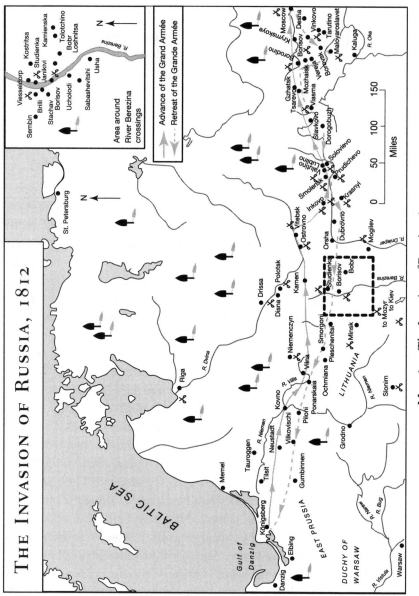

Map 6.1. The Invasion of Russia, 1812.

into Miloradovitch's. To his great joy, he learned while marching through Moscow that the army was retreating south, a move he favored. Colonel Toll had remarked to Clausewitz several times since Borodino that south was the best route, though he had different reasons, and told Clausewitz of his fear that the commanders would block his choice. It was also a topic of discussion among the junior general staff officers. "The march toward Kaluga, which subsequently became famous as a peak of intellectual brilliance, did not suddenly spring from the head of the commanding general or of one of his advisors like Minerva from Jupiter's helmet. In any case we have always believed that ideas in war are usually so simple and obvious that the merit of devising a strategy cannot constitute the essence of generalship."[3]

His experiences in the campaign led Clausewitz to another conclusion: "in Russia one could play hide and seek with the enemy, and by always retreating might in the end return to the frontier together with him." The size of the country made it impossible for Napoleon "to cover and strategically control the areas behind him simply by advancing. In developing this idea, the author had reached the conclusion that a very large western country could be conquered only with the help of internal dissension." In his study of the campaign, Clausewitz analyzed it in terms similar to those used in *On War*. "Everything in war is simple, but the simplest thing is difficult. The military instrument resembles a machine with tremendous friction, which unlike in mechanics, cannot be reduced to a few points, but is everywhere in contact with chance," and goals that seem plausible on paper prove unachievable in the field.[4]

The abandonment of Moscow disillusioned many in Kutosov's army. It had weakened their confidence in the Russian government, and many thought peace the only option. They did not know that Alexander had refused all offers of settlement from Napoleon, which Clausewitz saw as without question the correct choice. "We can see from this how little the army understood the meaning of these great events," he wrote in his history of the campaign, "and yet we were already near the culminating point of the French offensive, near the moment when the entire burden that the French had lifted but could not carry would fall back on them." After the French occupied Moscow, Kutusov took his army south of the city, setting up camp at Tarutino. This allowed him to draw supplies and men from untouched southern regions of Russia. He rebuilt his army and encouraged guerrillas to operate against the French and their lines of communication—creating friction—and he also hit them with cavalry. Meanwhile, Napoleon waited in Moscow for a message of surrender from Alexander that never came.[5]

Clausewitz had by now been appointed to yet another position in Russian service. A different unit had assumed the post of rearguard after they departed Moscow, leaving Clausewitz without a job. He reported to the Russian headquarters for reassignment and found a letter waiting for him from the emperor appointing him chief of staff to General Essen, the garrison commander of Riga. The order had lain fallow for weeks, surfacing only because a junior officer told Clausewitz of its existence. Clausewitz received the appointment because he was a German; his predecessor and old friend, Lieutenant Colonel Karl von Tiedemann, had been killed on August 22, and the emperor thought it fitting to replace one German with another. Tiedemann's death upset Clausewitz greatly. "My friend Tiedemann is dead," he wrote Marie a few weeks later, killed near Riga by a pistol shot from a Prussian hussar. "I have wept for him as I would weep for a brother. Even now I can hardly think of his loss without tears." But the change in position undoubtedly gave him great psychological relief because of his continued inability to see himself used in a manner he defined as satisfactory, a situation arising from his inability to speak Russian.[6]

Clausewitz looked forward to his new assignment and set off by mail coach on September 24. At Serpuchov, on his way to St. Petersburg, he was arrested by Russian militia, who, because he didn't speak Russian, suspected him of being French. He couldn't convince them otherwise, so they sent him back whence he came in the tow of a Russian officer. He decided to wait at headquarters before trying to make the trip again, this time in the company of a courier. He left a few days later with a group that included his old comrade Chasot and a former Saxon officer, Baron von Bose, both of whom were heading to St. Petersburg to help lay the groundwork for the Russo-German Legion. Even with a Russian guide they were arrested in a number of villages, which helped make the trip particularly harrowing. These arrests, and Chasot's poor health, meant the journey took more than two weeks and delayed their arrival in St. Petersburg until mid-October.[7]

In St. Petersburg Clausewitz spent at least part of his time in a stone inn on the banks of the Neva River, where Stein had set up headquarters. His company included other Prussian officers who had served in the recent campaign and who had gathered to birth the Russo-German Legion: his old friend Hermann von Boyen, Ferdinand Wilhelm von Stülpnagel, Chasot, and the poet and German nationalist writer Ernst Moritz Arndt. But Clausewitz also received bad news on several fronts. He discovered that King Frederick Williams's government had launched legal proceedings against him to confiscate his assets. Marie wrote later that when Clausewitz went to Russia, he hoped that the king would "see in this bold step only new proof of his loyalty."[8] Clearly, he did not. "That the king must do something against us I realize," Clausewitz wrote Marie, "but that he should mark me for his anger makes me very bitter, for I have done nothing to deserve it." He insisted he only worried about it because it might cause trouble for Marie and for his two brothers serving in the Prussian army. He told Marie that they had to console themselves with the fact that they had done the right thing, and not out of self-interest. He thought a drastic change in the political situation would see the proceedings suppressed, but if not, they would find themselves exiles.[9]

Next, Clausewitz learned, to his disappointment, that there was little possibility of his advancing in the Russian army. St. Petersburg was extremely expensive and he related to Marie that they could not hope to live there on their income. This stiffened his conviction that his best hope of advancement lie with the Russo-German Legion, and he determined to transfer immediately. Something undoubtedly feeding this dissatisfaction was his belief that since he didn't speak Russian he had been badly treated and also had had no chance to make a name for himself under fire; these joined with the war's harshness. "I cannot describe how unpleasant are the impressions I've had of this time, and how few joyful moments," he wrote Gneisenau. Nevertheless, Clausewitz refused to let regret overtake him. Although he wanted to serve in a German unit (preferably one commanded by Gneisenau), a post in the Legion would suffice.[10]

In a further piece of bad news, Clausewitz found that Essen had been replaced at Riga by Marquis Philip Osipovich Paulucci, whom he had met in Barclay's headquarters at the beginning of the war. Clausewitz found Paulucci "peculiar," and to have "a good deal of ill nature." Simultaneously, word came that the French had begun to retreat, which meant Riga would now become a military backwater. He convinced the Duke of Oldenburg to appoint him the senior staff officer to his newly forming Russo-German Legion, (he had been previously considered for this post), and also asked the czar to second him to the corps commanded by Ludwig Adolf Peter zu Sayn-Wittgenstein until Oldenburg finished raising his force. Alexander approved both requests and Clausewitz received his orders on November 11. Four days later he departed St. Petersburg for Czaśniki (today in Belarus about 120 miles northeast of Minsk), traveling via Pskov and Polotsk.[11] The war had changed. Napoleon was now the prey.

When Napoleon occupied Moscow he hoped it would bring the Russians to terms; it had the opposite effect. Alexander determined to fight on in extremis, even if it consumed his empire. "Napoleon or me," Alexander announced. "I or him, we cannot both rule at the same time; I have learned to understand him and he will not deceive me." After receiving Kutusov's missives from Borodino, the czar began planning a multipronged Russian counteroffensive. The Russian armies in the north and south of Napoleon's lines of communications through Belorussia were to push and sever them. Admiral Pavel Chichagov pushed from the south, Wittgenstein from the north, and Kutusov from the west. Subsidiary operations by smaller forces pinned the French troops under Marshal Jacques MacDonald in the Courland region of modern-day Latvia and kept the Austrians in the south under Karl Philipp zu Schwarzenberg from interfering with Chichagov. Alexander planned to have 160,000 men block Napoleon's potential retreat routes across the Berezina and Ulla Rivers by October 27. Meanwhile, the peasants, encouraged by the regime, rose against the invader and waged a "People's War," while Cossacks and other units fought a partisan war against French detachments and supply lines, the latter something of which Russian generals had been previously unaware.[12]

Napoleon abandoned Moscow on October 19. Alexander and the Russians had done everything to encourage him to stay there. The French emperor had received substantial infantry reinforcements since taking the city, boosting his numbers to about 100,000. On October 5 Kutusov's army had only 63,000 infantry, but of this number 7,500 were raw recruits and 15,000 Moscow militia. He did have 620 guns, which would slow his pursuit of Napoleon. Kutusov also had far more cavalry. His Cossack reinforcements alone amounted to 15,000. Napoleon had waited six weeks in Moscow, and the first snows had begun to fall. Kutusov planned to use the oncoming winter, pressure from his Cossacks, hunger, and the gradual erosion of discipline in the French ranks to defeat Napoleon's army.[13]

By November 6 snow had both armies in its grip. The winter was not cold by Russian standards; the last half of November was actually unseasonably warm. This melted the ice over the Berezina River, which had disastrous consequences for the French. The Russians also suffered from the winter and the rigors of the march; the realities of war always torture both sides. Kutusov's infantry strength eroded as he advanced.[14]

Napoleon reached Smolensk on November 9. Indiscipline had begun tearing his units apart. They marched out of the city on the 12th. Kutusov had a chance to put his army between Napoleon and his route of retreat to Orsha but he refused to take the risk. Had he done so he might have destroyed Napoleon's army there, but he was intentionally giving Napoleon a way out. Moreover, he did not want his own army broken by the time it reached the Russian frontier, something indeed a danger, as the farther Kutusov marched the more difficult it became to feed his forces.[15]

Kutusov also knew that Chichagov was marching to Minsk, which held Napoleon's primary Belorussian food supply. Almost fifty miles from here stood Borisov and its bridge over the Berezina River. Chichagov's advance units seized Minsk (along with its food stores) as well as the bridge over the Berezina at Borisov, and the situation began to appear as it might deliver Alexander's dream: the capture of Napoleon. But Chichagov couldn't quickly get sufficient reinforcements to Borisov. He needed help to decisively block the French retreat. This had to come from Wittgenstein, Clausewitz's new superior.[16]

Since early in the war, Wittgenstein had protected St. Petersburg from French thrusts, and done so very well, stopping a numerically superior force while losing no territory. "General Wittgenstein was a man of some forty years," Clausewitz recalled, "full of good will, with an enterprising, adventurous spirit. Only his judgment was not unfailingly clear, and his energy sometimes flagged." His chief of staff was a fiftyish former Saxon officer, Major General Friedrich d'Auvray, who had long served the czar, and always had the state's best interests at heart. "The prime mover in Wittgenstein's command," recalled Clausewitz, was a Prussian who had entered Russian service as a youth, Major General Johann von Diebitsch, the quartermaster general, who had made general in the recent campaign at the surprising age of twenty-seven. Clausewitz described him as "fiery, brave, and enterprising, decisive and bold, with great firmness and natural intelligence, somewhat brazen and imperious, a leader of men, and very ambitious."[17]

Wittgenstein advanced from the north with about 50,000 men, though 9,000 were militia. On October 16–18 his forces liberated Polotsk, giving them control of the bridge over the Dvina River. Wittgenstein then fought a nasty defensive battle against Marshal Claude Victor's troops near Smolyantsy on the Ulla River on November 13–14, stopping an effort ordered by Napoleon to try to push him away from the French line of retreat. Clausewitz joined Wittgenstein's force a few days after this fight. A day-and-a-half march to his south, on the road between Orsha and Borisov, lay Napoleon's route of retreat.[18]

Chichagov worried that Napoleon was making for Minsk, and many other Russian leaders shared his fear, or thought that he marched for Bobruisk. Napoleon had a bridge built at Ukholoda, south of Borisov, to leave this impression. Instead, he crossed north of Borisov at Studenka, marching for Vilna. Napoleon's forces swam the Berezina at Borisov on November 26, brushed aside the thin screen of defenders, and began laying two bridges. Napoleon then fought his way through Chichagov's main force, which appeared late on the 27th and lacked the strength to stop the retreating French.[19]

At the same time, Wittgenstein battled the French rearguard commanded by Victor on the Berezina's eastern shores. Wittgenstein now showed none of the aggressiveness that hard marked his generalship in the summer. On November 27 his troops reached Borisov, then turned and marched north to Studenka to halt the crossing. They hit the rearguard on the 28th, but stubborn French resistance, and the fact that Wittgenstein only committed 14,000 of his men to the fight, allowed the remains of the French force to escape across the Berezina. Clausewitz noted later that he had not been at the headquarters then, but instead was with a detachment that stayed back to protect the left flank, returning to Wittgenstein's army on the evening of November 28. He did nonetheless see the carnage of the debacle that was Napoleon's crossing of the Berezina in temperatures that had dropped to -20 Fahrenheit. A Russian observer described the scene: "The river was covered with ice which was as transparent as glass: there were many dead bodies visible beneath it across the whole width of the river. The enemy had abandoned huge numbers of guns and wagons. The treasures of ransacked Moscow had also not succeeded in getting across the river."[20]

The experience affected Clausewitz deeply. He wrote of it to Marie on November 29 from the ruins of Borisov on the Berezina's banks: "But what scenes I've seen here! If my feelings had not already been hardened, or rather jaded, I would not get a hold of myself for shuddering and disgust, and still after many years I will not be able to think about it without shuddering." Near the end of his letter, he wrote, mournfully, "I am writing you between corpses and the dying, among the smoking ruins, and thousands of ghost-like people file past and shout, and stand, and cry in vain for bread. God grant a quick change to these scenes!"[21]

Napoleon lost 25,000 to 40,000 troops crossing the Berezina, and nearly all of his artillery and baggage. As historian Dominic Lieven writes, "Had Napoleon held the bridge at Borisov or had the Berezina been firmly frozen, the great majority of these casualties would have been avoided." Yet three more weeks of miserable flight faced Napoleon and the remnants of his army, and, in a complete reversal from the previous month, December dawned bitterly cold even by Russian standards.[22]

Many believe he should not have escaped at all. Clausewitz was among them. "For ten or twelve days I have found myself once again in the midst of military action, namely in Wittgenstein's army," he wrote Marie, "where I arrived just at the moment of the loosening of one of the most crucial knots to have ever been released. The catastrophe is over; it could have been more decisive; however, we can be pleased with the entire campaign, which will be ended in four weeks at the latest."[23] In his later history of the 1812 invasion, Clausewitz spread the blame for not crushing Napoleon among the three Russian commanders, a criticism in line with the most recent scholarship. But Clausewitz also thought Alexander's plan to trap Napoleon in the retreat had been unrealistic and unworkable because of the conditions on the ground, and remarked that none of the prongs fulfilled its appointed task. He noted that Wittgenstein could have marched to Borisov and attacked the French. "He might have been beaten by Bonaparte, but he would certainly have delayed his passage by a day and might have made it impossible on the following day as well." This kind of sacrifice for the good of the whole, however, though it "sounds fine in books," Clausewitz wrote, was not something to count upon in the real world. Chichagov and Wittgenstein simply feared meeting Napoleon face to face, which was understandable considering his military reputation. Among the soldiers of Napoleon's army who escaped across the Berezina was Antoine-Henri Jomini, whose early works Clausewitz had read, and who would later be an intellectual rival.[24] This would not be the last time they stood on opposing sides, in war and out.

The war in Russia dragged on. Wittgenstein's army followed the path of the French retreat for three days before taking a different route. The Russian winter had descended in full fury. Frozen bodies of dead men and horses lined the icy roads of the French flight. Men's limbs turned to ice and broke off. Birds fell from the sky, completely frozen. "All its horrors were heaped up in almost unbelievable measure," Clausewitz wrote. "The sufferings of the French army have been described so often that the author considers it superfluous to add any new strokes to the picture." Often over-looked, however, are the simultaneous sufferings of the Russian forces. Clausewitz wrote that "the road taken by the advance guard was always marked by dead Russian soldiers who had succumbed to cold and fatigue. Wittgenstein also lost a good third of his troops in the last four weeks of the campaign, for he had above 40,000 men at Czaśniki and scarcely 30,000 at Vilna." Clausewitz himself suffered from frostbite, cold, and prolonged exposure to the elements. This permanently reddened his face, which led some to later accuse him of spending too much time with the bottle.[25]

They rested at Niemenczyn (about fifteen miles northeast of Vilna), leaving the town on December 17th. Clausewitz now served on the staff of the aforementioned General Diebitsch, who though Wittgenstein's quartermaster general, temporarily led part of their army's advance guard. On December 23 their 1,300-man force stood west of Telstch, two days' march from Diebitsch's objective: Memel (now Klaipėda, Lithuania). He had planned to take Memel, believing that the enemy corps of the French marshal MacDonald had already withdrawn through this Baltic coast city and across the sands of the Kurland Spit. But they received intelligence that MacDonald was actually approaching them from the east. Diebitsch turned his force around and marched eastward to the village of Wormi. Learning here that the French rearguard was southeast at Wengkowa, they headed due south, planning to ambush them on the 25th at Koltiniani, which lay on the French line of retreat. When they reached Koltiniani at about 10 the next morning, however, instead of the French rearguard they discovered sutlers—civilian merchants who supply armies in the field—who had been supporting the Prussian expeditionary force fighting with Napoleon. Although they learned from the sutlers that most of the enemy column had already marched by, Diebitsch decided to go after the rest of the rearguard.[26]

The approach of the rearguard caused Clausewitz grave distress: two of his older brothers served as officers in the Prussian force. "The older was a major and commanded its light infantry," Clausewitz wrote, and one "could assume with fair certainty, that, as a good outpost officer, he would be in command of the entire rear guard. The thought of perhaps seeing him here taken prisoner was even more painful than that of being opposed to him all day under fire." Information from captured stragglers relieved this fear, but created new ones. Coming at them was not the Prussian rearguard, but four infantry battalions, a pair of cavalry squadrons, and an artillery battery, all under the command of General Friedrich von Kleist. Diebitsch's men stood no chance against such a force.[27]

Diebitsch, living up to the description Clausewitz gave him, concocted a plan. He asked Clausewitz if he would take a flag of truce to Kleist and see if they could confer. Clausewitz said that as a Russian officer he would do whatever his superior wished, but advised Diebitsch to send someone else, as the appearance of a former Prussian officer—now wearing Russian green—would not be kindly received. Diebitsch agreed, and dispatched Major von Rönne, who told Kleist that Russian forces blocked his route but that they could reach an arrangement to prevent any pointless bloodletting. Kleist refused to talk because he wasn't in command, but noted that his superior, General Yorck, was expected that evening and that the matter could wait until then. This news shook Clausewitz and his Russian comrades. It meant that they had not cut off the rearguard, but actually faced the vanguard of the main Prussian force.[28]

The situation presented Diebitsch with both opportunity and danger. The Russians had periodically negotiated with Yorck; one of the activities of Clausewitz's unfortunate friend Tiedemann had been trying to convince the Prussians in Yorck's corps to switch allegiance and fight the French in the ranks of the Russo-German Legion. Yorck had rebuffed their efforts, but he had also informally offered himself as mediator between the crowns, and a message soon went via Yorck to Berlin. But the military situation had certainly changed since then. If Diebitsch could reach some kind of profitable understanding with Yorck, it would be a great coup for the Russians. This effort was naturally not without risks. Yorck had 14,000 men under his command. If he decided to simply crush Diebitsch and continue his march, the Russian general couldn't stop him.[29]

Clausewitz personally had mixed views of Yorck, all gleaned from lengthy experience working with him and other members of the Prussian elite: "General Yorck is an upright person," Clausewitz noted in his history of the 1812 campaign, "but he is morose, melancholic, and secretive and therefore a bad subordinate. Personal attachment is rather foreign to him; what he does, he does for the sake of his reputation and because he is naturally competent." Diebitsch decided to take his chances. Yorck arrived as expected and met Diebitsch at dusk on Christmas night. Diebitsch spoke frankly, admitting that he didn't think he had the forces to stop the Prussians, but that he would try his best to snare Yorck's baggage and guns if it came to a fight. The core of his argument was that Napoleon's army had been destroyed and Czar Alexander had ordered that the Prussians be treated as the old allies they were—and were expected to be again. Because of this, Diebitsch offered Yorck a neutrality agreement. Yorck, believing his military situation not so dire as to honorably take the course suggested, demurred. The two agreed to leave their men in place that night, and Yorck would march in the direction of Lawkowo the next day to meet with Diebitsch at Schelel. "You have quite a few former Prussians officers with you," Yorck said to Diebitsch at the end of their parley. "Do send one of them to me from now on; it will give me more confidence." Diebitsch asked a willing Clausewitz to take up the task and a string of talks followed.[30]

That night at their camp at Koltiniani, Clausewitz warned Diebitsch of Yorck's cunning streak and told him to keep alert. Later, Clausewitz recalled, he and the general "dismounted at a house, laid ourselves down on the straw fully clothed, and had scarcely closed our eyes when pistol shots were heard from the rear of the village. They were not single shots but a general fire, which lasted some minutes." Clausewitz thought it was Yorck. He and Diebitsch mounted their horses and discovered that a detachment of Prussian Dragoons had pushed some Cossacks back into the village, but not being strong enough to fight their way through, had retreated. Later, they learned the men were carrying a message to Yorck from Marshal MacDonald, his French superior. This would cause problems for Clausewitz.[31]

Diebitsch and Clausewitz went to meet York on the 26th as planned. When they arrived, Yorck refused to talk, and dressed down the officer who escorted Diebitsch and Clausewitz. Instead of appearing in person, Yorck sent Friedrich zu Dohna, Scharnhorst's son-in-law and an old friend of Clausewitz's with whom he had entered Russia in 1812. Dohna, now a lieutenant-colonel, was in the Russo-German Legion and had been sent to Yorck as a negotiator by another Russian general. Dohna made it clear that Yorck was sincere, but had to keep up appearances. The way to do this was for him to slowly move toward the Prussian border.[32]

Diebitsch still didn't trust Yorck, and continued to press him to make an agreement, while each day Yorck marched a little closer to Tilsit—and the Prussian frontier. Meanwhile, Yorck's French superior, MacDonald, moved farther to the west, drawing out the distance between the two forces and giving Yorck the ability to claim abandonment by his French ally. The talks also went on and Clausewitz and Yorck negotiated long into the night of December 28, Clausewitz failing to bring the general to a decision.[33]

Diebitsch's superiors, however, were losing patience with Yorck. At noon on December 29, carrying two letters from his superiors, Clausewitz was dispatched to yet another meeting. Clausewitz walked into Yorck's room. "Keep away from me," Yorck barked. "I want nothing more to do with you. Your damned Cossacks have let a messenger from Macdonald through, who brings me an order to march on Piktupöhnen and join him there.... Your troops do not advance, they are too weak, I must march, and I won't have any further negotiations, which would cost me my head." Clausewitz replied that he had some letters to lay before the general, and asked that he be allowed to carry out his mission. Yorck relented and summoned candles and Colonel Roeder, his chief of staff. The first note revealed that Wittgenstein's advance forces would be in striking distance of Yorck's army and line of retreat in two days and made it very clear that Yorck would be given no more time to vacillate. The second letter was a captured dispatch from Marshal MacDonald disparaging the leadership of the Prussian contingent. Yorck thought for a moment. "Clausewitz," he said, "you are a Prussian. Do you believe that General d'Auvray's letter is honest, and that Wittgenstein's troops will really reach the places named by the 31st? Can you give me your word of honor?" Clausewitz vouched for the honesty of the letter, but, he added, "whether these dispositions will really be achieved I can, of course, not guarantee, since Your Excellency knows that in war with the best will in the world one must often fall short of the line one has set oneself."[34]

Yorck asked Roeder his counsel. Roeder believed the matter too important for him and refused to comment, but he warned that the choice would be dangerous for Yorck personally. "What? My person?" scoffed Yorck. "For my king I would go the scaffold—I agree." Yorck turned to Clausewitz and thrust out his hand. "You have me," he said. He promised to bring other Prussian forces with him and summoned a cavalry officer from outside. "What say your regiments?" he asked. The horseman was enthusiastic about changing sides and insisted his men felt the same. "It's easy for you to talk, you young people," Yorck said, "but this old man's head is shaking on his shoulders."[35]

That night Dohna and Clausewitz brought Diebitsch the news. Diebitsch embraced Dohna and "shed tears of joy." The next morning at the mill in Poscherun the parties signed one of the pivotal agreements of the Napoleonic Era: the Convention of Tauroggen, which Clausewitz drafted. It rendered Yorck's army neutral for two months—and changed the nature of the war. As we will see, Yorck had made a monumental decision that utterly overturned Prussian policy and changed Prussian history.[36]

Even before the destruction of Napoleon's army, Clausewitz realized that he had been part of something momentous. He wrote Gneisenau on

Der Abschluß der Konvention von Tauroggen. Nach einer Originalskizze von M. Blanckarts auf Holz gezeichnet von H. Merté. (S. 466.)

Figure 6.1. The Conclusion of the Convention of Tauroggen.
Wood engraving by Heinrich Merté, after the drawing by Moritz Blanckarts. Published in "Das Buch für alle." Stuttgart, ca. 1880.

Figure 6.2. Clausewitz in His Russian Uniform. It is possible that Marie painted the now lost original.

November 7, bursting with pride: "We have, however, made a campaign that certainly ranks among the most original in the history of warfare, and which perhaps will be the most momentous in the annals of nations." The December 30, 1812, agreement at Tauroggen only solidified this assessment. Clausewitz wrote later of Yorck's decision—and its effects—in a very measured, understated tone: "It cannot be denied that the decision of this general had enormous consequences and in all likelihood very considerably speeded up the final outcome."[37] It meant this—and more.

The same day Clausewitz wrote Marie about the events there and his hopes for the immediate future, which seemed brighter because of Yorck's capitulation and Clausewitz's reunion with the Prussian forces. "Tomorrow fate divides us again, but at least now we don't stand opposite one another, and, if the monarch wills it, not again." He told her that he hoped to leave for the German Legion, which already boasted some 4,000 men, in four to eight weeks. "I am told that Gneisenau is on the way back and will probably be put at the head of the Legion; then I am happy!...I cannot write any more at this moment because time is too short. I hope to soon be in Königsberg."[38]

This letter marked a noticeable change in Clausewitz's attitude. Before Tauroggen, despite all he had seen and accomplished during his Russian sojourn—with the added bonus of having emerged alive when so many hundreds of thousands of others had not—Clausewitz remained profoundly disappointed with what the war had brought him. He had been in many battles, including Borodino, one of the biggest of the age, experiences he found "rich in instruction." But he had not earned any special distinction for himself, which, he confessed, had been one of his primary reasons for going. Clausewitz's inability to communicate with most Russian officers and men meant that the most practical postings for him were on staffs, but he felt strongly that one achieved glory leading men in action; not pushing a quill.[39] Though Clausewitz never seems to have admitted it, considering his training and experience, and the great shortage of men with such skills in the notoriously poorly educated Russian officer corps, the Russians had generally made the wisest disposition of the asset they possessed in him.

All of his youth Clausewitz dreamed of distinguishing himself on the battlefield in a manner that would set him apart from other men—a dream that never came true. The most important military achievement of his life was his action at Tauroggen, an action fought with words, not with his sword. And it is because of his words that we remember him today.

7

1813

War, Uprising, and Armistice

[I]t betrays a lack of historical knowledge or insight into human nature
when one expects anywhere perfection in practical matters.

The agreement at Tauroggen helped launch an uprising in Prussia. Yorck's
unprecedented step in going against the policy of King Frederick
William required an immense amount of moral courage as he risked not only
his own head but also the position and possessions of his family. Yorck and
the others who soon gathered around him did not see themselves as revolting
against their king, however. They insisted that they acted for their king. In
any event, their move proved popular among Prussian subjects. In his letter
to Frederick William explaining what he had done, Yorck asked whether or
not he "should now advance against the true enemy"—meaning of course
the French—"or whether political conditions demand that Your Majesty
condemn me." He would, he said, "swear to Your Majesty that I shall meet
the bullets as calmly at the place of execution as on the field of battle."[1]

Yorck reached Tilsit on January 1, 1813, and marched into Königsberg
on January 8, where he met with General Wittgenstein. Here, he received
the king's denunciation of the Convention of Tauroggen and the orders for
his relief, arrest, and court-martial. The denunciation changed his mind
about whether he should wait for the king's approval before fighting the
French. Yorck believed the people as well as the army wanted war against
Napoleon, even insisting the king did too, but his monarch's situation
didn't allow him to admit as much. Patriotism drove Yorck.[2]

The waves from Yorck's defection overturned the political and military
strategies of all the powers involved. Murat had inherited command of the

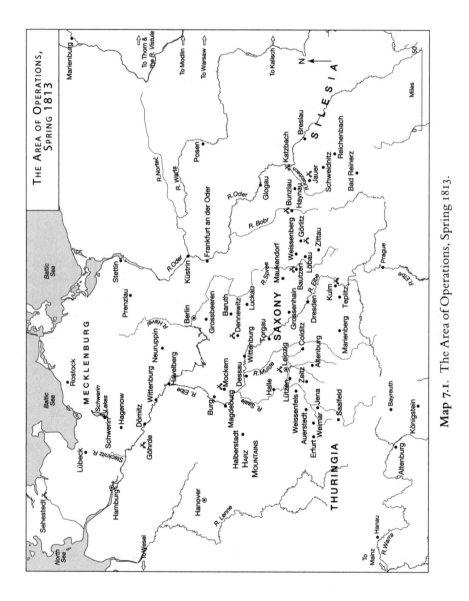

Map 7.1. The Area of Operations, Spring 1813.

French forces when Napoleon left for Paris on December 5. Yorck had made an already tenuous French position even more dangerous, and Murat withdrew French forces across the Vistula. In January 1813 he retreated to Posen, but left behind French garrisons to hold the fortresses of Danzig and Thorn. The three weeks following the crossing of the Berezina had seen further erosion of Napoleon's army. In 1804 Clausewitz had written in *Strategie* that "if Bonaparte should ever reach Poland, he would be easier to defeat than in Italy, and in Russia I would consider his defeat to be a foregone conclusion." His prediction had proven correct. When the last of Napoleon's forces crossed the Russian frontier, they numbered fewer than 20,000—although this included the bulk of his senior and experienced commanders and their staffs, as well as 2,500 officers of the Guard. They formed the core around which Napoleon would reconstitute his military strength to fight the campaign of 1813.[3]

Later, though he did criticize a number of Napoleon's decisions in 1812—particularly operational ones—Clausewitz mounted a defense of sorts of Napoleon's strategic approach. He "acted as he had always done. This is how he had come to dominate Europe, and this was the only way in which he could have done so. No one who admired Bonaparte as the greatest of commanders in his previous campaigns should feel superior to him with regard to this one." He also gives this evaluation of Napoleon's invasion: "This was not the kind of campaign that drags feebly on to its conclusion, but the first plan ever made by an attacker bent on the complete destruction of the adversary."[4]

Napoleon left Russia to raise a new army, envisioning putting an additional 656,000 men in the field. He could raise the infantry and artillery by tapping into the resources of both France and its empire but rebuilding his shattered cavalry force proved impossible; he simply lacked the horses. Napoleon now consistently suffered from a lack of intelligence on his enemy because of it. It also limited his ability to pursue a foe defeated on the battlefield, one of the cavalry's critical roles.[5]

In Prussia it was difficult for the ever-cautious Frederick William to break with France, and political forces at home pushed him both ways. The presence of a French garrison of 19,500 troops in Berlin, as well as the 25,000 they had in other Prussian cities and fortresses, discouraged him from aggressive action. Even after the debacle in Russia the French could still bring 150,000 men to bear against Prussia.[6]

The king fled Berlin on January 21, driven by rumors that the French would seize him. In Breslau, though unsure of what to do, he began preparing Prussia for war. In early February he summoned Scharnhorst back to the colors. On February 8 he issued a call for citizens to form volunteer companies of *Jägers* (Riflemen), and he made all male Prussians officially liable for military service, at least temporarily. But internal pressure mounted for the king to act and as February wore on he faced the real possibility of revolution against his rule.[7]

The Russians, meanwhile, continued their advance. At the beginning of the 1812 campaign, Alexander's objective had been survival; now, it became the overthrow of Napoleon and the liberation of Europe. Kutusov hoped to wait and rest his army, but Alexander wanted him to push on into Germany, taking as much ground as possible and bringing Prussia and Austria into the war against France. Alexander also realized that half-measures would not suffice: Russia—and its abundant resources—must be fully committed to the fight.[8] In this respect the campaign of 1813 inaugurated modern warfare.

The campaign had badly depleted the Russian armies. When Clausewitz left Kutusov's army at Taurutino in late September 1812, the Russian commander had 97,000 men. On December 19 Kutusov had 42,000; 48,000 men were in hospitals. Wittgenstein's army was in slightly better shape, though Chichagov's was not. Both officers and men often wore tattered rags. Boots—if they had them—were often falling apart. Disease, particularly typhus, which reached plague levels among the prisoners, also bit into the Russian army. The typhus epidemic affected the forming Russo-German Legion as well. It killed Chasot, Clausewitz's companion on his trek to St. Petersburg, and many of the unit's officers and men, drove others to their sickbeds, and generally kept the Russians from finding enough recruits to fill out its complement.[9] Nevertheless, a tough, experienced cadre had survived. This became the core around which the Russians rebuilt their forces for the next campaign.

Yorck, Stein, and the other exiles that returned in the train of the Russian army now led an uprising in East Prussia as Yorck convened its assembly, the Landtag, at Königsberg on February 5 and endeavored to launch a "People's War." Stein, Yorck, Ernst Moritz Arndt—the Prussian poet and nationalist—and Count Alexander zu Dohna worked to move the Landtag toward war with France. Yorck spoke to the convened delegates, declaring, "I hope to fight the French wherever I find them. I count on everyone's support; if their strength outweighs ours, we will know how to die with honor." That night Yorck and the seven members of the Estates Committee that ran the Landtag agreed to mobilize in their province a *Landwehr* (militia) of 20,000 active members, supported by a *Landsturm* (essentially a home guard) of another 10,000 in reserve. Except for certain professions, they imposed the requirement to serve on every male under forty-five, even Jews—yet another break from Prussia's past. The East Prussian leadership approved Yorck's program on February 9. By the end of the month, Frederick William had lost control of his East Prussian province, while simultaneously the Russians talked of seizing portions of East Prussia. The king now faced the choice of either an alliance with Russia and open war with Napoleon, which risked disaster just as in 1806, or watching his kingdom get torn apart by internal and external forces.[10]

Ernst Moritz Arndt believed the *Landwehr* was the quickest and most potent way to put Prussia back on its feet. Moreover, he saw Scharnhorst as the creator and founder of a modern Prussia, believing Scharnhorst's methods of thinking and forging officers and men had proven pivotal to building a new state. But he also thought others played key roles in 1813 to birth the new Prussia. Arndt placed Alexander von Dohna among the first rank of Prussia's deliverers, along with one of Scharnhorst's favorite pupils—Clausewitz. These three were pivotal players in the re-creation of Prussia through the *Landwehr*: Dohna provided the key leadership, Scharnhorst provided the intellectual foundation, and Clausewitz provided the practical plan. "With his energetic clarity," Arndt wrote in his memoirs, Clausewitz had already drawn up "a very nice paper" on creating a *Landwehr*. Clausewitz based this new proposal upon his "Political Declaration," composed before he departed for Russia. The Dohna brothers, Friedrich and Alexander, shaped and reworked Clausewitz's text into a legal form. All of the province's reserve officers, as well as those on half-pay, were summoned to help lead the new force via an announcement in the February 11, 1813, issue of the Königsberg newspaper. They were ordered to report to Clausewitz, who helped organize the force.[11]

Meanwhile, Frederick William continued trying to navigate the difficult political terrain. Rebuffed in his overtures to Austria, and failing to drag concessions from Napoleon, he turned to the Russians. Scharnhorst met with the Russians at Kalisch (now Kalisz, Poland, approximately 160 miles east of Warsaw) on the 27th, and signed a treaty with them the next day. The Prussian king told his advisors: "Well gentlemen, you force me on this course but remember, we must conquer or be annihilated." The terms of the treaty restored Prussia to a position of strength equivalent to what it possessed in 1806 through awarding it pieces of conquered German territory; they also committed to fielding 80,000 men. The Russians promised a 150,000-man force and would receive Prussian Poland. Both agreed to make no separate peace. The British now reestablished relations with Prussia and began supplying arms and ammunition. British gold followed. A previous treaty in August 1812 between Russia and Sweden brought another ally. Russia would get Finland, Sweden would get Norway. In exchange, Sweden would land 30,000 men in Germany and light fires in Napoleon's rear. The Sixth Coalition against Napoleon was now in the field.[12]

Having delayed to buy more time for mobilization, on March 16 Frederick William finally declared war on France. The next day he issued a proclamation, *An mein Volk* (To My People), calling upon the Prussian populace to fight against France. They would now create a *Landwehr* on a national scale. This was not the kind of "People's War" suggested by Clausewitz, Gneisenau, and others. Frederick William also signed another treaty with the Russians on March 19, the Treaty of Breslau, which firmed up the diplomatic alliance. A few weeks later, on April 21, the Prussians took their most radical step yet and created the *Landsturm* for the entire nation—volunteer local forces that elected their officers from among certain prescribed groups.[13]

Eugène de Beauharnais, Napoleon's stepson, had succeeded to the command of the eastern French forces on January 17, 1813. Napoleon gave his stepson the Herculean task of holding as much territory as possible to gain the emperor time to raise new troops, while holding key bridgeheads and fortresses. His area of responsibility essentially covered the North German plain from Hamburg to Posen, and up the Elbe River to Austria's frontier. He was quickly forced to abandon Posen for Frankfurt-am-Oder, where he scratched together a paltry 30,000 men to block the Allied advance.[14]

Wittgenstein restarted his westward march on January 13. He crossed the Vistula and used 20,000 men to pin the French forces in Danzig. Reinforced with both Prussian and Russian units, he pushed on, taking Posen on February 13. The same day, Russian general Ferdinand Wintzingerode, pushing through Poland with his Russian force, defeated the French VII Corps at Kalisch, seventy-five miles to the southeast.[15]

On February 20, before the Prussians entered the war, the Russians crossed the Oder and made a quick march to try to seize Berlin. Eugène abandoned the city, angering Napoleon, and retreated to Magdeburg on

March 5. Kutuzov smelled an opportunity and ordered all of his forces to strike for the Elbe. In the north, the army of Wittgenstein (with Yorck's and Bülow's corps) pushed westward. Blücher led a southern thrust from Silesia aimed at Dresden and Kutusov trailed behind with the remainder of the forces.[16]

Scharnhorst was brought back as army chief of staff, but struggled to coordinate with the Russians because of Kutusov's suspicions about the Prussian forces. The two new allies nonetheless decided upon a quick offensive against Eugène before Napoleon brought new forces to the theater. Wittgenstein would strike for the Elbe south of Magdeburg. Blücher's army, farther south in Silesia, would march to support him and, when he closed, the two forces would aim for Leipzig. The hope was that when Eugène discovered Wittgenstein's force on the Lower Saale River, and Blücher's army marching on the Pleisse River, he would be prevented from retaking Berlin. Meanwhile, Bulow's forces guarded the approaches to the Prussian capital. Eugène withdrew in the face of their advance, and then retreated across the Elbe.[17]

Wittgenstein's Russian army had entered Berlin on March 7. With him were Clausewitz (who was still on his staff) and Stein. The city threw a party to honor the Russians on March 13. Clausewitz had left Berlin almost exactly a year before. Reunited with Marie, he spent the next two weeks with her and her mother in Berlin.[18] He also began trying to get readmitted to the Prussian army.

On March 26 Barclay de Tolly wrote the orders detailing Clausewitz and his aide—Sub-Lt. Lukash—to Scharnhorst.[19] Clausewitz had already left for his new posting, arriving at Kalisch on March 25 on his way to Blücher's headquarters in Dresden. Officially, he had been assigned there but he preferred a posting with Scharnhorst, something his old teacher had wanted as well. "I have never undervalued your great worth," Scharnhorst had written Clausewitz a few days earlier. Clausewitz knew Scharnhorst wanted him back, the general having told Stein as much, but there was an obstacle to this: the king. Clausewitz's personal situation at court was made worse by the fact that it was filled by his and Scharnhorst's enemies. He remained uncertain where he would land, fearing that in the worst case he would remain with the German Legion, which would fight in Germany under Count Ludwig Georg von Wallmoden-Gimborn, whom he met in Kalisch. He still felt keenly that he had to prove himself. "In Russia, as I wrote you," he told Marie, "I could not distinguish myself; I must do it in

Germany." Though he remained pessimistic on the personal front, he felt good about the future. Political change was sweeping across Prussia. "The prospects seem to get better each day," he wrote his wife. The news from France was also generally good for them and the progress of Prussia's military preparations went well.[20]

Clausewitz reached Dresden on March 31. Though he did not meet Scharnhorst there, he did learn that his mentor had asked Frederick William to allow Clausewitz to rejoin the Prussian army. He was told the king replied: "Clausewitz—hm!—yes; I want to inquire if he has served well with the Russians." Friends wangled his appointment to Blücher's Silesian army, officially as a Russian liaison officer. Scharnhorst served as Blücher's chief of staff and Gneisenau as quartermaster. Scharnhorst and Gneisenau were of course among Clausewitz's closest friends and near-fathers, and he respected Blücher immensely. Considering the circumstances of his departure from Prussian service, Clausewitz could hardly have landed any better; he had what he had wished for so often in Russia—to serve in a German command. He wrote Marie about his new post: "Being with a very dear little army, which is headed by my friends, passing through beautiful country during the nice time of the year, for such a purpose, is pretty much the ideal of Earthly existence (that is if you think of this life as transient and leading to other existences). My friend G.[neisenau] looks like a god in his general's uniform. The troops are happy and sing 'Auf, auf, Kameraden!' and similar songs, others yodel to perfection. I see myself surrounded by friends and living again in the environment of my mother tongue. I even see my students again, I've never had so much fun as under these circumstances."[21]

But Clausewitz was not entirely carefree. The Prussian court still presented problems, and some of them marched with Blücher's army. His old superior Prince August had pled his case, as had Gneisenau and Hardenberg. "The Crown Prince," Clausewitz wrote of his former student, "has welcomed me with his customary awkwardness, and without any sign of goodwill and friendship, Prince Frederick is very cold, very ceremonious, Prince William was somewhat friendly, but not much, Prince August genuinely warm." The king, for his part, received him coldly and the youthful court grandees treated him contemptuously, turning their backs when he came in. In Breslau at the end of March, the younger of the princely brothers he had tutored (the future German emperor William, or Wilhelm I), spotted Clausewitz in the market buying clothes. He wrote to his older brother, the Crown Prince Frederick William, with a play on words comparing Clausewitz to lice: "Mr. Lausewitz!!! is coming from the Russian side into Blücher's headquarters. How will you meet him? I hope with rather distinct coldness. I have seen him from my window, but not greeted him.... I find it a little much that precisely this person is sent to headquarters." Their sister, Princess Charlotte (who married the future Czar Nicholas I and was the mother of Czar Alexander II), harbored similar feelings toward Clausewitz. She had read a pamphlet in which "fighting against one's own Fatherland is portrayed as the greatest virtue and Tiedemann, Clausewitz, and company are presented as the greatest men of honor and friends of the Fatherland. This, I confess, has disgusted me to my core." The work she refers to is likely Arndt's 1813 piece on the origins and purpose of the Russo-German Legion.[22]

In early April Clausewitz received the formal response to his request to reenter the Prussian army. "In consequence of your letter of the 11th," the king replied, "I have ordered your process quashed,"—meaning the legal proceedings against him were at an end. "But you can be readmitted to the service of the fatherland only when you have won the right for special consideration by particularly distinguishing yourself in the coming campaign." The ending of the legal action was good news, but the king's denial, which Clausewitz deemed constructed in a manner designed "to humble my pride, to offend my vanity," hurt and angered him, he wrote Marie. "It is my pride to serve the Fatherland, and my double pride to do so under humiliating conditions; I will satisfy these conditions the King has put out for me."[23]

Upon learning of the westward advance of Wittgenstein's army, Eugène marched to meet him. On the morning of April 5 Wittgenstein attacked Eugène's army at Möckern, about fifteen miles east of Magdeburg in central Germany. Both sides suffered light casualties, but the fight demonstrated the anti-French intensity in Prussian ranks, and delivered a profitable propaganda victory to the Allies. Eugène retreated back over the Elbe. This confirmed the value of the changes wrought in the Prussian army by Scharnhorst, Gneisenau, Clausewitz, and the other reformers. They had mastered the tactical innovations of the period: Prussian infantry could fight as skirmishers, maneuver on the field, and fight in line or in column. More importantly, the new Prussian army fought for its homeland; most of the rank and file, as well as the officers, possessed a patriotic and moral strength that had been lacking. The Prussian army of 1806 had some backward tactics and little depth of morale. Defeat in the field too often brought shock and surrender. In 1813, though the Prussians suffered defeats at Lützen and Bautzen, they did not see a lost battle as a lost war—indeed, the army hardly viewed these as defeats at all—and remained willing to fight again tomorrow. What Clausewitz later described in *On War* as the "moral forces" had finally been unleashed in Prussia.[24]

After Möckern, on April 27, 1813, the czar appointed Lieutenant General Prince Wittgenstein to replace the ailing Kutusov, who died the next day. Wittgenstein's position, however, was not as clear as it seems. He commanded the forces under Blücher and Wintzingerode, but two of the main elements of the Russian army answered to Alexander, who took upon himself the de facto position of Allied general in chief. Wittgenstein united his forces with Blücher's army in Silesia, then ordered an Allied concentration around Leipzig. He hoped to push the French out of Saxony (the southern German state south of Berlin between Prussia and Hapsburg Bohemia) and by doing so convince the Austrians the time had come to join the fight.[25]

By late April Clausewitz and the others in Blücher's army could sense the French forces amassing against them. Writing from Altenburg on April 25, however, Clausewitz was optimistic regarding their coming clash. He observed a palpable difference between 1813 and his experience fighting in this same region in the disastrous 1806 campaign. "Most people look forward to the events with great calm, as befits a manly way of thinking."[26]

Around this time, Napoleon developed what is sometimes referred to as his "Master Plan" for the 1813 campaign. He would cross the Elbe, seize Berlin to have a base for supplying his forces (and the area bordered by the Elbe and Oder Rivers), cross the Oder, then march to the Vistula River. This would also augment his army by freeing besieged French garrisons behind the Allied lines. He would then advance northward, to the Vistula, threatening the Russian communications and forcing them to retreat from Central Europe, bringing Prussia back under his thumb. He aimed via demonstrations—meaning, effectively, various shows of force—to convince the Allies he intended an invasion of Silesia and an attack on Dresden, but he would actually strike northward with 300,000 men, seizing Havelburg (southwest of Berlin), then reaching Stettin and Danzig within fifteen days. By day twenty Napoleon planned to take Marienburg (now Malbork, Poland, near the Baltic coast) and take control of the Vistula's lower bridges. Napoleon believed Berlin's capture would break Prussia's morale, and over the next few months he would make many efforts to seize it. In the end, however, Allied action consistently forced him to deal with numerous situations himself, which meant he could spare neither the troops nor the personal time to implement this plan. Instead, as we will see, he embarked upon derivatives of it.[27]

On April 30 Napoleon began to move. Launching from a base area near Erfurt (in central Germany), his 120,000-man army crossed the Saale River in three separate columns, marching westward on Leipzig, about eighty miles away. Wittgenstein was heading the same way from the area of Altenburg with a 75,000 man force that included two Prussian corps and a Russian corps that marched a little farther back as his reserve. The French crossed the river and marched toward Leipzig, not realizing that all of Wittgenstein's army was headed toward them. While two columns continued the advance, Marshal Michel Ney—one of the eighteen marshals of France that Napoleon had originally named—was ordered to halt to cover the French march on Leipzig, and with two of his divisions occupied four villages south of Lützen (Kaja, Rahna, Großgörschen, and Kleingörschen), then pressed his three other divisions on to Lützen. Allied reconnaissance picked up on Ney's tenuous possession of the hamlets and the fact that the French army was strung out, and Wittgenstein saw an opportunity to destroy the flank of Napoleon's army. Napoleon, like Ney, was not fully aware of the forces the enemy could bring to the fight.[28]

Clausewitz, who was with Blücher's forces, knew the history of this area well. The legendary Swedish general Gustavus Adolphus had fought and died at Lützen in 1632, and Clausewitz had written a history of his campaigns. The terrain was open, sloping farm country. Small villages dotted the plain, hamlets with stone cottages and walls and narrow cobblestone streets. A hedge-lined stream—the Flossgraben—twisted by the twin settlements of Klein and Großgörschen. About a mile southeast of Großgörschen, its banks grew to a small crest.

The first of Wittgenstein's troops topped this tiny outlook at about noon on May 2. Spread out before them were what they estimated to be 2,000 French infantry, cooking their lunch. Wittgenstein ordered a general attack and then sent in Blücher's cavalry, sure that they would quickly overrun the enemy. Blücher soon discovered that they faced two French infantry divisions. He thought better of the move, withdrew, and ordered up his artillery. Initially shocked by the assault, the French recovered, deployed in the villages of Großgörschen and nearby Starsiedel, and called

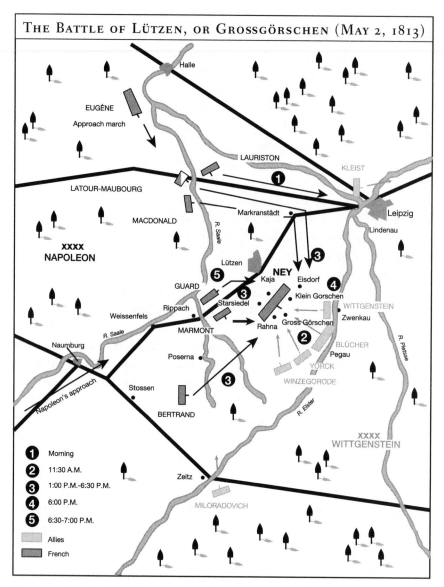

The Battle of Lützen, or Grossgörschen (May 2, 1813)

Halle

EUGÈNE
Approach march

LAURISTON

KLEIST

LATOUR-MAUBOURG

Leipzig

Markranstädt

Lindenau

MACDONALD

R. Saale

XXXX
NAPOLEON

Lützen

NEY

Kaja   Eisdorf

GUARD

Klein Gorschen

WITTGENSTEIN

Rippach   Starsiedel

Zwenkau

Weissenfels

Gross Görschen

R. Saale

MARMONT   Rahna

BLÜCHER

Naumburg

Pegau

Poserna

YORCK

R. Plesse

WINZEGORODE

Stossen

R. Elster

Napoleon's approach

BERTRAND

XXXX
WITTGENSTEIN

① Morning
② 11:30 A.M.
③ 1:00 P.M.–6:30 P.M.
④ 6:00 P.M.
⑤ 6:30–7:00 P.M.

Zeitz

Allies

MILORADOVICH

French

Map 7.2. The Battle of Lützen, or Großgörschen (May 2, 1813).

for the rest of Ney's corps. Prussian artillery forced the French out, but Ney arrived, reversed the retreat, and ordered a counterattack. The two armies became locked in a hand-to-hand brawl for control of Rahna and the twin Görschens.[29]

When Napoleon received word of the fighting, he ordered reinforcements for Ney, including the Guard, sending one corps to come against the Allied eastern flank and another to try to strike its west. He reached the battlefield himself at 2:30 p.m. The Prussians and Russians were mauling Ney's troops and had almost broken them. Napoleon, exposing himself often to enemy fire, pieced the situation back together.[30]

The bitter fighting continued and the Russian reserve corps had yet to appear. The reserves were delayed by Czar Alexander, who apparently wanted to lead them himself and deliver the final blow to the enemy. Wittgenstein's reserves arrived at around 4:00 p.m. and he launched a general assault, forcing the French out of the Görschens and pushing through almost to Kaja. Napoleon sent in a division of the Young Guard to throw back the assault. The Allied counterattack took the Görschens again as well as Rahna, while the two sides once more fought bitterly for the little hamlets.[31]

By 6:00 p.m. the situation had begun to shift against the Allies. Napoleon had put 110,000 men on the field against the 80,000 of Wittgenstein, and his flanking units had moved into position. Napoleon massed a seventy-gun battery near Kaja, pounded the Allied center, then sent in the Guard. The Allies began giving ground as Napoleon's northern flanking corps hit their right. They then started to retreat. This was no rout, however; it was rather an orderly, controlled withdrawal. The French lacked the cavalry to launch a proper pursuit, and the Allied rearguard had no difficulty keeping the French at bay.[32]

Clausewitz fought in this particularly bloody battle, and saw many of his friends and comrades killed and wounded. "General Blücher has a contusion," he wrote Marie, "General Scharnhorst has a wound in his leg, but it's not dangerous." His own danger was evident. "Since we were not able to exercise a decisive influence on the conduct of the battle," Clausewitz wrote of the staff officers, "we had no choice but to act with sword in fist." Gneisenau, Scharnhorst, Blücher, and Clausewitz all fought hand to hand. Clausewitz participated in at least one cavalry attack, probably against a French infantry square, and at one point found himself surrounded by French troops. "I am very well," he reassured Marie, "even though a little

Frenchman has hit me behind the right ear with a bayonet. The fighting was furious, and I was right in the middle among the enemy." At one
moment in the battle Clausewitz also ran across his brother Wilhelm and
they carried on a conversation, as he put it, "in the middle of withering rifle
fire." Scharnhorst asked Blücher to put Clausewitz in for a decoration. He
would be ineligible to receive the new Prussian decoration, the Iron Cross,
because he was technically a foreigner, but, he insisted afterward, this fight
would remain one of the most memorable events of his life.[33]

In his short work on 1813 Clausewitz discussed in detail the last Prussian
cavalry assault. Whether or not he participated in this is unknown, although
the detail he provides in his letter to Marie of cavalry fighting among the
bayonets of French infantry, as well as the head wound he received from a
French bayonet (perhaps early in the day), suggests a similar personal experience. "One more attempt was planned to see whether the cavalry aided
by good fortune and the sudden fall of darkness could achieve a great result.
The attack was made suddenly at 10 o'clock on the foremost enemy troops
by nine squadrons of the Prussian reserve cavalry that happened to be in the
vicinity, which had over the course of the eight hour battle lost one third of
its strength. Indeed they broke into them [the French infantry] and drove
them back in disorder." But nothing could come of this attack, given that
"the mass of enemy troops behind them was too large on the one hand, and
on the other was that the cavalry had broken apart because it had to pass
under darkness through a ravine at the fastest gallop speed."[34]

The battle cost the French 22,000 casualties, the Allies, 10,000. "These
animals have learned something," Napoleon said after the battle, in grudg-
ing admiration. The Allies retired in good order, and the scarcity of French
cavalry, as we've seen, weakened the pursuit. After the battle, Clausewitz
wrote to Scharnhorst (who had left for Vienna) about the new spirit ani-
mating the Prussian army.[35] Again, the force's actions and internal disposition after the battle demonstrated the success of the reformers in the years
since 1806. This was not the army of Jena and Auerstedt.

The Allies decided to leave Bülow's corps to shield Berlin while they
retreated to Bautzen and fortified the banks of the Spree River. They
marched back through Dresden on May 7 and 8. Napoleon continued
implementing his "Master Plan," though a modified version of it, as the
emperor did not command the northern thrust. He marched after the
retreating Allied army and sent Ney with 45,000 men along the Elbe
River to rescue the French garrisons besieged in Wittenberg and Torgau.

This move endangered Wittgenstein's right flank, and Napoleon hoped the threat would convince him to retreat from the line of the Elbe River. Wittgenstein continued his eastward retrograde, soon reaching the Spree River. Napoleon also hoped a threat to Berlin would draw the Prussian army away from their Russian ally, giving him a chance to destroy the Prussian force. If the Prussians didn't rise to the bait, he believed Ney could take Berlin.[36]

Napoleon now made Dresden his base for future operations in Germany. When he determined that the Allies stood at Bautzen, Napoleon sent Ney's corps on a swing around the northern flank to try to cut their communications and thus leave them only one withdrawal route—into Austrian territory. Meanwhile, Napoleon planned to pin them with his main force, delivering a decisive blow against the Allies. But Napoleon's instructions to Ney were not clear.[37]

Though some in the Allied high command wavered after Lützen, most of the leadership—especially Prussian—saw no reason to despair. "Now we have fallen back behind the Elbe," Clausewitz wrote Marie on May 8; "the enemy seems to be marching with his main force to Dresden and to be sending a corps from the lower Elbe against Berlin. What will happen next is not for me to say. We are hoping for a strong diversion by the Austrians, which was even announced to the army in a letter from the King. In no event must we despair." Like many of the Prussian leaders, Clausewitz had great faith in the chances of the Allies. Even should they suffer defeat, however, he told Marie he found no reason to lose hope: "Even if everything goes completely badly, and I have fulfilled my duty to the last moment, I will hasten to you and we will search for some corner of the earth which brings us peace and happiness—will we not?"[38]

On the night of May 14–15, 1813, Gneisenau and Clausewitz met with Theodor von Hippel, an assistant to the Austrian chancellor Hardenberg, in the attic of a farmhouse. Hippel brought with him detailed information on the Austrian army and its future participation in the campaign. He also inquired about the feelings in their army toward another battle. The two soldiers replied that not only was it possible to fight another battle, it was also advisable. On the 16th, Gneisenau—who had replaced Scharnhorst as Blücher's chief of staff—met with the chancellor to arrange this. Clausewitz remained on Blücher's staff as well with two other lieutenant colonels, Müffling and Rühle. An officer at one of the staff meetings with them during these days noted the justifiable seriousness of the men: the fate of Silesia, the army, and perhaps Prussia itself rode on their decisions. Clausewitz stayed in his post despite the reoccurrence of his past health problems. He wrote Marie from Bautzen on May 18: "I am well except for rather severe gout pain that afflicts me all night in my barn."[39]

Clausewitz wrote later about the importance of the moment. Doing battle would not have been a good idea, he said, "if it were not a part of the Allied plan to fight as much as possible for every bit of ground in order to show Europe that one had not suffered a defeat in the first battle and was not either morally nor physically unable to continue to defy the enemy." But he also believed it critical to prove to the Austrians that their potential allies were willing to sacrifice their own forces. Clausewitz also noted the importance of nurturing the army's spirit and believed withdrawing without a fight would have broken the spirits of the men and sapped their confidence in their leaders.[40]

Having determined their course, the Allies prepared to fight. "For eight days we have stood here awaiting the enemy, who has also stood opposite us for eight days, but until now has not yet attacked," Clausewitz wrote Marie on May 18. "Most likely in the morning, or perhaps the day after tomorrow, will be again the day of a great battle. Our troops are full of courage and we have received some, though not significant, reinforcements, so that we, after what the enemy has lost in battle and has detached after the battle, can hope to be equal to him."[41]

The area around Bautzen is cut by small rivers and the town itself sits on the Spree, whose banks are of varying height. There were a number of gentle areas an army could ford. Two miles eastward ran another rivulet, the Blossauer Wasser. Small ponds—often used for fish-farming—and marshy ground lay between them, providing nice defensive obstacles. North of Bautzen sat a clump of small hills, the Kreckwitz Heights, whose villages the Allies fortified. A thick wood and a pair of hamlets—Drohmberg and Schmortzberg—held the south flank. Bautzen itself boasted medieval fortifications, strengthened and modified by Russian engineers to create some nastier defensive positions. The Allies elected for a layered defense, with the initial first line at Bautzen itself on the Spree. The second and more critical defensive line they built along the Blossauer Wasser. Wittgenstein realized the danger they faced of being forced into Austria and destroyed, and believed that this meant a major French blow would come from the north. The czar, on the other hand, believed that Napoleon would instead hit the southern flank of their army and insisted upon the concentration of forces there, as well as the reserves. The czar's interference—and subsequent direction of the battle—reduced a frustrated Wittgenstein to taking a nap under a tree.[42]

On the night of May 19–20, the Allies launched an ultimately unsuccessful effort to destroy the French V Corps. The assault, however, convinced Ney to keep the III Corps north of Königswartha, a town about

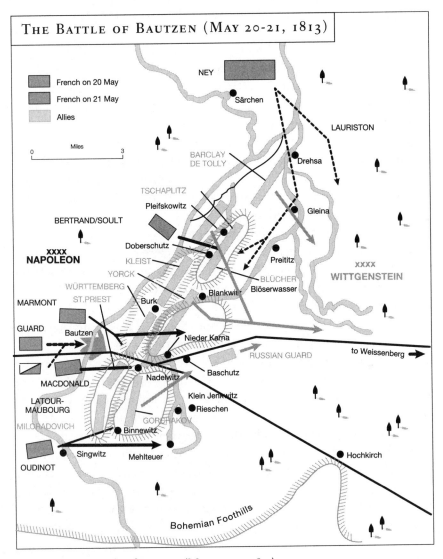

Map 7.3. The Battle of Bautzen (May 20–21, 1813).

eleven miles north of Bautzen; he also began to expect an Allied attack. The French commenced their bombardment at noon on May 20. Napoleon planned an attritional day as he waited for Ney to move into position. The attack began at 3:00 p.m. By 6:00, the French seized the town of Bautzen and pushed half a mile into the lines. The Allies also now realized Ney was approaching from the north, but did not grasp the immensity of the threat. The next day, as Napoleon continued grinding the Allies, Ney received orders at 4:00 a.m. to push southward to help surround the Allies and finish the job, and was told to be at Preititz by 11:00 a.m. Ney hit Barclay de Tolly's small corps, seizing Preititz at approximately 9:30. Taking the village would have flanked Blücher's position, forcing him to abandon his hilltop post. Blücher reinforced Barclay, and his Prussians threw back Ney and recaptured the village at roughly 1:00 p.m. The French then counterattacked with three divisions and threw the Prussians out at around 3:00 p.m. Ney again seized the village, despite the pleas of his chief of staff, Antoine-Henri Jomini, to simply mask Preititz and push on south, thus cutting the enemy's communications and completing Napoleon's grand flanking attack. Ney now turned his attention to the Kreckwitz Heights, where Clausewitz stood with Blücher and his staff.[43]

Meanwhile, the French units in the center, who were to deliver the blow when Ney struck, had spent most of the day before building a giant earthwork. On the 21st, the French massed 20,000 men and waited for Napoleon to order their advance. They attacked shortly after 2:30 p.m. By 3:00 they had pushed to the Kreckwitz Heights and Blücher's position now faced extreme pressure from both the north and the west. He retreated in time to prevent his encirclement. The French overran the empty heights.[44]

By this time, despite Wittgenstein's entreaties, the czar realized the danger. He agreed to a general retreat, which was ordered at 4:00 p.m. Clausewitz wrote later of the decision: "For political reasons, however, one of the main goals of the Allies was never to expose themselves to a decisive defeat, preferring to break off battles before their final conclusion." There was therefore no hope that Blücher would make an effort to recapture lost ground, particularly since there were "serious concerns" about the state of Blücher's corps. "It is for these very reasons," Clausewitz concluded, "that the army command decided to break off the battle at this point and order the withdrawal at approximately 3 and 4 o'clock in the afternoon." Both the Prussian and Russian forces retired in such good order that they left only nineteen spiked guns at Bautzen's blood-soaked ground. The French had suffered at least 20,000 casualties, the Allies 11,000. In *On War*, Clausewitz compared Bautzen to another fight in which he participated: The battle of Borodino, which also was "*never completely fought out. At Bautzen, the defeated party chose to leave the battlefield early.*" Clausewitz participated in Bautzen, but left no record of his service there. As he was on the staff of Blücher's corps, it is likely that he was upon the Kreckwitz Heights for the contest, again across the field from Jomini.[45]

A few months later Clausewitz offered his assessment of Napoleon's situation, which was that Lützen and Bautzen were not victories on which the emperor had counted. "He was," wrote Clausewitz, "used to inflicting decisive defeats on his opponents with relatively few losses in order to thereby conclude hasty peace treaties." Now, after Bonaparte's Russian debacle and its aftermath, he was in "twofold or three-fold need of splendid victories to suppress the awakened hopes of Europe and to frighten his new and arming enemies."[46]

As the Allies continued their retreat after Bautzen, bickering and internal division began to emerge. Wittgenstein resigned, frustrated by the czar's interference, and was replaced by Barclay de Tolly on May 26. Wittgenstein assumed command of the southern column, Blücher the other. Barclay wanted to retreat to Poland. Blücher and Gneisenau wanted another battle. They decided to retreat to the Silesian city of Schweidnitz in southern Germany (now Świdnica, Poland), which would allow them to maintain lines of communication with Austria and Poland, while also defending Prussian territory. When Barclay departed for a meeting with the czar, however, Blücher was left in command and immediately ordered the Prussian rearguard to ambush the French advance forces, pursuing them at Haynau on May 26. Clausewitz wrote an account of the action, but he doesn't relay any hint of his own participation—if any—though he was present and on Blücher's staff at the time.[47]

The same day, the Allied army crossed the Katzbach River and turned southeastward, taking up a position near Schweidnitz on May 29. Here, they found the fortifications—and thus the position—not as strong as they had hoped. Clausewitz nevertheless remained optimistic. "The army is in very good condition and probably already stronger than the enemy," he wrote Marie from Schweidnitz. "The enemy is desperate, and only the miserable faintheartedness of our leaders could see things differently. Later this will be clearly recognized and everyone will be indignant." Clausewitz thought their chances of victory better now than in the previous two contests, but also believed that even if defeated it would move the Allies closer to their goals. "The Emperor Napoleon has never played such a desperate game. Why should we burden ourselves with fear? That would be genuinely childish."[48]

Napoleon came on behind them, taking Breslau on June 1. The emperor had reached the Oder once again, putting himself into a position to cut the Allies' communications, and leaving them the choice between a forced march out of the pocket or fighting with their backs against the Austrian frontier. But the Allies kept retreating, and, by June 4th, had escaped. On June 7 the Danes had advanced on Hamburg, but then they changed sides—largely over the Allied agreement to hand Denmark's possession of Norway to Sweden—and helped the French drive out the small Russian force that had seized the port city. Clausewitz called the city's recapture "indisputably the most painful loss that the Allies had suffered up to that point."[49]

On June 4 Napoleon and the Allies signed a cease-fire, something Napoleon later regarded as an error as he believed that it had cost him his position in Germany. Clausewitz, disheartened, thought it a lost opportunity for the Allied coalition. From where he stood with the Allied army at Rothschloß in Silesia, he saw their forces collecting large numbers of French prisoners and deserters, while watching their own strength increase by 40,000, including 20,000 *Landwehr*. He wrote Marie: "If we are now afraid of Napoleon, then we deserve the rod."[50]

Napoleon's situation was far from ideal. His army was worn out, he had lost half his strength since April, and Cossacks constantly attacked his supply lines. As noted, he lacked the cavalry necessary to destroy a defeated enemy in a pursuit, and he was growing concerned about Vienna's plans, since they were at that moment massing 150,000 men in Bohemia. Despite the weakness of Napoleon's position, however, the Allies needed the armistice as much as he did. They were exhausted from the campaign and needed to rest and refit. When the Austrian chancellor Metternich proposed mediation and a cease-fire, both sides took him up on it, signing what became known as the Armistice of Pleiswitz on June 4; it eventually extended to August 10. Metternich viewed this as the first step toward getting a negotiated continental settlement, one that the British would then be forced to agree to. He wanted to preserve Napoleon, believing that deposing him would bring too much disorder to the continent.[51] His eventual overthrow would mark the start of one of Europe's more peaceful eras.

Unexpectedly, on June 28, Scharnhorst died from the wound he had received at Lützen. Clausewitz received word a few days later. It struck him hard. "The last news of Scharnhorst was that he was passing away," he wrote Marie. "You can imagine how sad I am. Whether he is equally indispensable for the army, for the state, and for Europe, I can barely think on all of this, and I'm losing at this moment only the dearest friend of my life, and no one can ever replace him, and who I will always miss.... Besides you there has never been a person who has shown me so much kindness and who has had such an influence on all the good fortune of my life." Together Clausewitz and Gneisenau wrote obituaries for Scharnhorst, but they had to fight the Prussian government and bureaucracy to get them published unaltered because the works were seen as portraying the state as insufficiently appreciative of what Scharnhorst had accomplished in its service. Clausewitz also penned a defense of the *Landsturm*.[52]

Clausewitz wrote a more substantial tribute to Scharnhorst in 1817, one originally intended for publication in Britain but which did not see print until it appeared in his collected works after his death. It reveals Clausewitz's deep affection for Scharnhorst, as well as indicating how the general had helped shape Clausewitz's thinking. He focused on two things in particular. The first was Scharnhorst's "absolute independence of judgment, unconstrained by any authority, be it that of a great name, of age, or of precedent," and the other "was his great preference and respect for the power of historical evidence in all matters that occupied him." These animated, indeed underpinned, the manner in which Clausewitz approached his own historical and analytical writings. "He hated men who served only for money," Clausewitz added, and, "kept his distance from men who sought distinction and honors above all, and scorned those who without higher ambition simply followed routine." Clausewitz concluded with a phrase that sums up so much of how he believed one should act if necessary, and how he undoubtedly viewed part of his own service to Prussia: "But men who *sacrificed* themselves for a noble goal immediately earned his affection and respect, whatever other qualities they might possess."[53]

A few weeks after the cease-fire, Clausewitz met Marie at the Silesian town of Bad Reinerz (now Duszniki-Zdrój, Poland), where Gneisenau also decided to go with his family. As always when he had a free moment, Clausewitz's pen was active. It was in Reinerz that Gneisenau asked him to write what turned out to be his most important piece of this period, and

one of only a few works Clausewitz published during his lifetime: a quick
study of the 1813 campaign. Beginning as the stirring propaganda piece
it was intended to be, the study praises Prussian bravery and honor, but it
then moves on to give some interesting operational and tactical dissection
and analysis. It is an overtly political document, whitewashing Frederick
William's resistance to Prussian entry into the war and his slowness in
reaching the decision to act, and the difficulties Clausewitz and the other
reformers had faced building the Prussian army. He was careful to note
that Prussia was still able to field 150,000 men who were at least partially
prepared for war in 1813. The army, as always to Clausewitz, was critical
to the state, and his view (and that of many of the reform party), was that
it had accomplished a great deal. "[It was] enlivened by a new spirit. It had
been brought closer to the people and one had reason to consider it as a
school for military training and education in the national spirit." He also
defended and lauded the most recent changes, ones that he, Gneisenau,
and others considered critical: "Onto this new creation was affixed in culmination of the state in arms, the idea of national defense by the *Landwehr*
and the *Landsturm*. By means of the first, the army itself could be possibly
doubled in wartime," which would greatly help a small state defend itself.[54]

The document is also sensitive to external political realities. Clausewitz
denounces the German states fighting alongside Napoleon, but treads
lightly on Austria. "Unfortunately," he notes, "Austria had not yet completed her preparations," and remarks that considerations of Austrian opinion influenced the decision to agree to the armistice. This was true, but
also politic, as was his take on the Allied defeat at Lützen, what some would
classify as a wonderful example of spin: "This all happened against an
enemy who was far superior and, therefore, this battle could be considered
a victory from the standpoint of a matter of honor, which had increased the
glory of Allied arms." As Peter Paret points out, this work is exceptional for
its time (and, one might add, even now) for its inclusion of the political and
strategic background, as well as operational and tactical detail, and topping
it off with cogent analysis.[55]

The Clausewitzs and Gneisenaus spent significant time together during the armistice. In the wake of Scharnhorst's death, Gneisenau became
the principal father-figure and mentor in Clausewitz's life. The feelings
between the two men were mutual; Gneisenau told a friend, "Clausewitz
is a man whose advice always pleased me, whose talent I rate about my
own."[56]

The armistice brought yet one more disappointment for Clausewitz. Shortly after its signing, the king appointed Gneisenau governor general of Silesia and the head of the Silesian *Landwehr*. Gneisenau asked the king whether Clausewitz could be brought back into the Prussian army to work for Gneisenau. The king refused. "I don't know yet what I will do," Clausewitz wrote Marie, "at the moment I've decided to return to Blücher's army." Gneisenau told him to wait. The king soon gave Gneisenau (who had also been made the new army chief of staff) instructions to name some officers to new posts. Gneisenau, hoping to bring Clausewitz back into Prussian service and make him the quartermaster general of the Silesian army, put his friend forward along with a pair of other officers. On June 10 Frederick William approved the latter two. "Lieutenant Colonel v. Clausewitz, however," he wrote, "I cannot assign to you since he is in the service of Imperial Russia."[57]

By the time the king's refusal had worked its way through the bureaucracy, the Russians had more firmly established the Russo-German Legion. Clausewitz was still designated as its quartermaster general and set his mind on returning there. He had to wait, however, for the czar's approval. On July 3, 1813, Clausewitz received word of his transfer. Meanwhile, Gneisenau, with Hardenberg's help, struggled in vain to keep Clausewitz with him. Gneisenau wrote in the middle of August that his headquarters staff had lost not only Clausewitz, but also Clausewitz's friend Grolman, "and these men are not easy to replace."[58]

8

1813

Leipzig, Göhrde, and the Stecknitz

Politics, moreover, is the womb in which war develops.

The fighting had ceased in the summer of 1813; the diplomacy had not. On June 8 at Reichenbach (now Dzierżoniów, Poland), the British entered into treaties with Prussia and Russia whereupon all agreed to no separate peace with Napoleon. British money began flowing to Berlin and St. Petersburg—Vienna later became party to both of these—and Spain and Portugal already fought beside Britain.[1]

Meanwhile, the Austrian chancellor Metternich pushed for peace, while also preparing to enter the war. He feared Russian domination of Europe as much as he did French hegemony, and worked to balance the influence of both, all for Austrian interests, of course. He also worried about the unleashing of German and Italian nationalism as a result of the French Revolution and Napoleon's conquests. This had already begun amongst the Prussians, who branded the struggle a "war of liberation."[2]

On June 27 Prussia, Austria, and Russia signed the Treaty of Reichenbach. This gave Metternich the freedom to attempt to convene a peace conference with Napoleon based upon minimal terms; Austria agreed to join the war if Napoleon refused (as was nearly certain). An alliance with Sweden followed on July 22. The Russians, Prussians, and British had wanted to offer Napoleon harsh terms, but Metternich had convinced them to issue lesser demands as the price for a peace conference. The Allies agreed that Metternich would present to Napoleon his proposal for a preliminary peace that did not firmly tie the Allies to specific future settlement terms. All believed Napoleon would never agree and that this

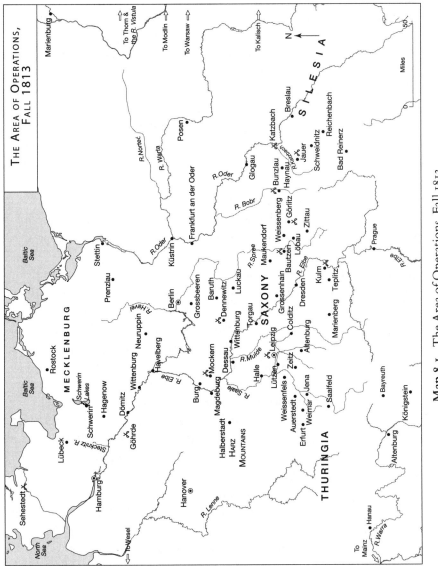

Map 8.1. The Area of Operations, Fall 1813.

diplomatic failure would demonstrate the hopelessness of achieving any settlement with France. With this established, Metternich could overcome his emperor's reluctance to fight and bring Austria into the struggle against Napoleon if necessary.[3]

Through all of this the Allies were willing to negotiate a fairly limited peace; Napoleon was not. He refused the Austrian offers but agreed to Vienna's mediation, and won an extension of the armistice to July 10. An early July conference in Prague followed, one Napoleon never took seriously. The French emperor's closest advisors pressed him to make peace, and Metternich made it clear that Austria would declare war on France on August 11 if they did not. Napoleon had just defeated the Allies at both Lützen and Bautzen and saw no reason to sign a peace in which he did not set the conditions. He also underestimated the possibility of Austria renewing its struggle against him.[4]

The armistice expired on August 10, 1813; Austria declared war the next day. In the words of historian Steve Ross, "for the first time in the history of the Revolutionary and Napoleonic Era *all* of Europe's major powers were ranged against France."[5]

This latest alliance against France—the Sixth Coalition—had an advantage in numbers. When hostilities recommenced in Central Europe, Napoleon faced an even more dangerous two-front war than that of 1812 (during which his forces were also fighting in Spain). Using conscription, the Prussians raised 272,000 men for the fall 1813 campaign, including 160,000 *Landwehr*. The Austrians had managed to raise a total of 479,000 men, 298,000 of them combat troops. The Swedes brought 35,000 men under their new crown prince, Bernadotte, a former French marshal. The Russian forces in Germany and Poland stood at 296,000. Between 1812 and 1814 the Russians conscripted more than 650,000 men. The Russian reserve army back in the home country had a paper strength of 325,000, but could hardly hope to put this number in the field.[6]

The coalition also had weaknesses. First among these was that in August 1813 the Allies lacked a unifying political objective. The Austrians (and this meant Metternich) wanted to contain Russia and prevent the outbreak of further revolutions and believed the best way to do this was not to depose Napoleon but to drive him back to France's supposed "natural frontiers." He also wanted the restoration of Austrian power to its 1805 level. Russia wanted control of Poland; Prussia wanted Saxony and other German lands (Russia and Prussia hewed to their previously mentioned February 1813 Kalisch agreement). Britain wanted the freedom to do as it wished in pretty much the rest of Europe's periphery, as well as on the high seas. Bernadotte brought Sweden into the coalition to obtain Norway from Denmark, not to defeat Napoleon. All agreed to the severing of French control over the various German states. The Allied powers fought for limited objectives and would have made peace if Napoleon had been interested in a lasting agreement. This produced the one thing that kept this group of determined, self-interested monarchs and would-be monarchs together: fear of Napoleon Bonaparte.[7]

Napoleon possessed great strength as well. He amassed 442,000 troops to face the coalition, including 40,000 cavalry. He personally commanded most of the French force: 314,000 men in encampments north of the Bohemian Mountains stretching from Dresden to the Silesian city of Liegnitz in what is now southern Germany. Marshal Oudinot led another 70,000 men camped in Saxony about midway between Leipzig and Frankfurt-am-Oder and due south of Berlin, which potentially threatened the Prussian capital. In northern Germany, Marshal Davout had a French-Danish force at Hamburg. Napoleon had 80,000 men garrisoning fortresses on the Elbe River and still besieged in key areas of Prussia and Poland, and 40,000 more men in reserve. Eugène built a 52,000-man army in Italy. New levies filled many of these units, but a strong leavening of experience made the force more formidable than most freshly raised armies.[8]

Since the Austrians contributed the most men to the coalition, they insisted upon naming the commander-in-chief of the Allied forces. They selected Austrian field marshal Prince Karl Philipp zu Schwarzenberg. Schwarzenberg was forty-two at the time, not especially ambitious, and possessed of more diplomatic than military skills. The historian Gordon Craig likens him to General Dwight David Eisenhower wrangling the Allied forces in Europe during the Second World War. The comparison is apt; Schwarzenberg, like Eisenhower, needed the skills to navigate the political machinations of the fourteen nations that eventually comprised the Allied coalition of 1813–1814. In addition to the French, the unfortunate Schwarzenberg had to deal constantly with King Frederick William, Czar Alexander (one of whose advisors now included Jomini, who had defected from the French), and their various chiefs of staff and hangers on, as well as his own emperor and the domineering Metternich. "It really is inhuman what I must tolerate," he wrote, "surrounded as I am by feeble-minded people, fools of every description, eccentric project makers, intriguers, asses, babblers." All of this did little to further Allied unity of action and purpose.[9]

The Allies' strategic plan for fighting the war is traditionally attributed to the chief of Schwarzenberg's general staff, Lieutenant Field Marshal Count Radetzky von Radetz, who would become famous for his campaign in Italy in 1848–1849. Historian Dominic Lieven gives the bulk of the credit for its composition to von Toll, Czar Alexander's chief quartermaster general. It undoubtedly had input from many fathers. Scharnhorst had wanted a multipronged advance whereupon the Allies would quickly concentrate for battle, but the Austrians, despite all the changes in warfare wrought by the French Revolution, still favored an eighteenth-century war of march and maneuver that did not emphasize battle. Radetzky, realizing that Austria would not stay out of the struggle, had submitted his plan in May 1813. In June he met with Toll at the czar's headquarters. In July the Allies (not including Austria, which had not yet joined) met at Trachenberg and agreed upon a plan proposed by Bernadotte and Toll similar to Radetzky's, but which was later altered to make it even more like the Austrian proposal. Toll, under whom Clausewitz had served in Russia, helped produce a compromise between competing programs. Bernadotte gave him a hand in this.[10]

The Allied strategy became known as the "Trachenberg Plan," after the castle of this name located not far from Breslau, where they made the agreement. It was essentially a strategy of attrition, designed to make Napoleon split his forces to counter Allied advances, and wear down his armies using superior numbers and resources. One could also describe it as "simultaneous pressure," meaning the Allies would press Napoleon at different points at the same time using their three armies. This would rob Napoleon of the advantage of interior lines. The constant pressure would also prevent him from concentrating his forces against one of the Allied armies and crushing it, thus enabling him then to defeat the Allies in detail.[11]

There was an important caveat to the Allied plan: They would attack only smaller elements of the French army—"the Austrian Army to be the pivot, while the Allies would form the swinging wings." If Napoleon gathered sufficient forces under his direct command to attack the Allies, they would withdraw to keep from becoming embroiled in a fight with a more numerous force. As Clausewitz noted, "The strategic [operational, in this instance, we would call it today] talent of Bonaparte could not be expected from any of his marshals. Therefore, the more he was obliged to place his forces into the hands of others, the better." Attack weakness, withdraw in the face of strength; this defined Allied strategy, and they hoped this would allow them to preserve sufficient power to later strike a decisive blow.[12] The difficulty for the Allies—obviously—became implementing their strategy.

To execute their plan, the Allies fielded four primary armies, three of which were multinational forces. They would not have used the modern term "burden sharing," but that is exactly what the coalition did. Each of these armies provided an operational prong of the strategy. Bernadotte commanded the 100,000-man Army of the North based at Berlin, a mixed force of Prussians, Swedes, and Russians. Blücher commanded the Silesian Army in the center, a Prussian-Russian force of 87,000. Austrian field marshal Schwarzenberg commanded the main force, the 252,000-man Army of Bohemia, the bulk of which camped south of the Erzgebirge Mountains in northern Bohemia northeast of Prague; Prussian and Russian units beefed up an Austrian core. The last force was Bennigsen's Russian Reserve Army of 60,000 in Poland.[13]

The generals implementing the Allied strategy had specific instructions for their operational prongs. The Allies believed Napoleon would aim his major blow at Schwarzenberg or Bernadotte and planned accordingly. Schwarzenberg planned to push into Saxony on the Elbe's left bank. Bernadotte was to advance southward. If Napoleon attacked him, or if he had to withdraw, Bernadotte was to hit the French flank. Bernadotte was also to use some of his forces (Wallmoden's corps) to pin Davout in Hamburg, while marching others toward Leipzig. If he faced attack, he was to retreat while the other Allies struck the French. Blücher—while covering Silesia and with the Russian general Bennigsen protecting the communications of the czarist forces—was to advance against the French to and over the Elbe, then link up with Bernadotte, without getting into a major clash unless it was one he was sure he could win. If Napoleon moved against him, he was to fall back and pull the French into Silesia. The problem—as well as benefit—of having Blücher in command was that he almost always thought he could win. Unlike many of the other Allied commanders, he had no fear of defeat. Indeed, it seems to have had essentially the same effect on his willingness to continue the war against Napoleon as victory. Bennigsen was ordered to march on Glogau (now Głogów in southwestern Poland), supporting any Allied attack and thwarting any French thrust into the Polish lands.[14]

The Russo-German Legion—where Clausewitz landed—formed an element in Wallmoden's corps of Bernadotte's Army of the North. A treaty was signed in July to take the Legion into British pay and increase its numbers to 10,000. Clausewitz, as we've seen, was still penciled in to serve as the unit's chief staff officer. "As much as I hate leaving Gneisenau," he told Marie, he thought his new posting a good one, "an appropriate sphere of action" for him. He also appreciated the salary: 2,500 talers a year, which meant he now made more than the famous professor Fichte.[15] But when he reached Berlin a few days later, he discovered that the Legion would probably be operating as a corps of observation against the French and Danish troops in Hamburg and Holstein, a role that put Clausewitz out of the primary theater of action, and of which he wrote Marie, "is not very welcome to me."[16]

Clausewitz joined the Legion at Schwerin in early August, where Wallmoden was reviewing it. He and Wallmoden knew one another, having become acquainted in Kalisch in the spring of that year. "He received me in his usual way," Clausewitz told Marie, "with neither honor nor repulse." A few days later Wallmoden surprised him by naming him quartermaster general of, he told Marie, "his not inconsiderable army." As Wallmoden's quartermaster general, Clausewitz was the chief planning and administrative officer. He plotted the route of march, managed the supplies, organized the movements, and guided and advised in the deployment of troops for combat. A rough modern equivalent might be the executive officer of a command, with the responsibilities of the supply or logistics head included. His training, education, and experience had prepared him for this. "I've been up to my ears in papers," he told Marie after taking up his new post, "because I'm still missing all of the assistants and overall the entire composition of the army is still very new." He believed this was the most important job he had yet been given, though he would have been even happier if their army had had a more important mission.[17]

Wallmoden's corps was a diverse bunch: Swedes, Mecklenburgers, Hanoverians, Hanseatic troops, the British King's German Legion, Cossacks, British hussars, a half battery of British rocket troops, a Prussian Freikorp unit, and the Russo-German Legion. The Legion had six battalions of infantry, eight hussar squadrons, and two batteries of horse artillery of eight guns each. Wallmoden had 22,729 men, 18–20,000 fewer than his primary opponent, Davout. The Legion had an authorized complement of 10,000, but at the beginning of August it only had 6,000 men, and was still being built up to its authorized strength. A British officer who inspected the Legion in mid-August judged it well-turned out and well-led, especially considering the newness of the force.[18] Serving alongside Clausewitz in the Legion's key positions were a number of other Prussians who had left their homeland to enter Russian service in 1812, including Lt. Colonel Alexander Wilhelm von der Goltz and Major Friedrich zu Dohna, who led the cavalry. To call it the "Russo-German" Legion was a misnomer. Though originally raised by the Russians among former Germans, its recruitment practices did not remain limited. For example, a roster of the nationalities of the members of the Legion's First Hussar Regiment included Germans from Prussia, Saxony, Hanover, and Bavaria, but it also included Poles, Russians, Danes, Dutch, Flemings, Swiss, and even a dozen Frenchmen among the unit's ranks. An infantry unit added Italians and Spaniards to the national mix, and even a couple of Americans.[19]

As Clausewitz and Wallmoden prepared their men, Napoleon concentrated the bulk of his army in the area of Bautzen and Dresden, in the homeland of his Saxon ally. He planned to initially sit on the defensive, allowing the Allies to come to him, whereupon he would concentrate and force a battle, hoping to do this very early in the campaign. He again aimed to make north Germany the theater of decision by seizing Berlin (and dispatched a force under Oudinot to do this), destroying Bernadotte's army, and then driving to Stettin on the Baltic coast. Oudinot would be supported by Davout's advance toward Berlin from his Hamburg base, with some other units reinforcing him and forming the link between Oudinot and Davout.[20]

Napoleon changed his plan on August 13. He had 300,000 men at Dresden, and created the 120,000-man "Army of the Bober" to protect Oudinot's right as the marshal marched against Berlin. Napoleon then moved the bulk of his forces in an effort to destroy Blücher's Army of Silesia. Marshal Marmont warned his emperor that he had divided his forces too much and that this could rob him of the strength necessary to win a decisive battlefield victory over the Allies. Napoleon replied that he had taken everything into account and that "the rest depends upon Fortune."[21]

The scale of warfare, however, had changed. Depending upon one battlefield victory—for either side—was not the sure route to success it had been even in 1809. The depths of the resources in manpower and equipment available to each side meant that tactical prowess, though indeed critical, was not the single key to success. Defeat in a single battle did not stand the same chance it once had of breaking the will of the opponent. Operational and strategic capability and execution mattered as well because even when one side won a battle, the enemy had armies in the field in other locations. Modern warfare had arrived.

Writing later, Clausewitz identified another problem facing Napoleon when the fighting began anew, one foreshadowing *On War*'s discussion of the "center of gravity" while also offering the Emperor an alternative approach. For Napoleon, there was "a lack of an object of strategic attack that would have had enough importance to decide the entire matter. No operation could be mounted to force any of the three Allies into a separate peace." Clausewitz argued that "the only option remaining open to Bonaparte, like Fredrick the Great in the Seven Years War and everyone else in a similar situation, was to remain in between his enemies and to grind them down little by little with individual victories, to divide them, and to discourage them." He believed Napoleon had to concentrate his main elements at Dresden because it gave him a strong position from which to strike at Brandenburg (which contained the Prussian capital of Berlin), Silesia, or even Austrian Bohemia.[22]

The French prong that Napoleon hoped to aim at Berlin faced Wallmoden and Clausewitz. The Crown Prince Bernadotte's general instructions to Wallmoden were to stop Marshal Davout where possible, especially by trying to pin his forces in their garrisons in Hamburg and the Baltic coast city of Lübeck. When the war began, Wallmoden was to secure the route between the Trave, which emptied into the Baltic northeast of Lübeck, and the Elbe to the south. If Davout advanced, and they were too strong for Wallmoden, he was to retire without fighting. He should hold along the Stecknitz if they could, but if they had to fall back farther, General Vegesack's divisions were to retreat along the coastline to Stralsund, which had a garrison of between 3,000 and 4,000 new English troops. If Wallmoden could not retreat there, he was to withdraw with the rest of his corps toward Berlin in order to protect the rear of the crown prince's army. Acting as a corps of observation against Davout—basing initially in Hagenow (about fifty-five miles east of Hamburg)—was not something that either Clausewitz or Wallmoden relished.[23] There was little fame or glory to be won here.

At an August 13 meeting with his Prussian subordinate commanders Bülow and Tauentzien, Bernadotte revealed his fear that his inexperienced army had to protect too much territory, while also facing dangers from Davout's forces in Hamburg, the French garrison holding Stettin in his rear, and those at Wittenberg, Magdeburg, and Torgau. He did not think the other Allied commanders could be relied upon to help, and feared Napoleon aimed at him—a former French marshal—as well as Berlin. Bernadotte, instead of following the Trachenberg Plan, wanted to do what he thought best for himself, Sweden, and his Army of North Germany: *nothing*. If pressed, he planned to abandon the defensive lines south of Berlin—and even the capital itself—without a fight. His Prussian commanders rebelled—especially Bülow (the brother of the military theorist whom Clausewitz criticized in his first published work)—and Bernadotte bent to their suggestions to put one corps south of Berlin, and most of the army north and east of the capital while masking Magdeburg with 5,000 *Landwehr* and protecting nearby Genthin and Burg. In general, the Prussians distrusted Bernadotte and doubted his willingness to fight against his former homeland.[24]

Hostilities began anew on the night of August 16–17. Blücher inaugurated the Allies' fall campaign. Basing in Silesia, he pushed westward with his force. Launching from Bohemia, Schwarzenberg advanced down the Elbe to Dresden, linking up with a Russian force. Bernadotte's main army advanced south of Berlin from Brandenburg.[25]

Napoleon had the central position and set about implementing his plan. He sent Oudinot against Berlin and went after Blücher to try to destroy the Army of Silesia. Attacked by Napoleon's forces on August 21, Blücher followed the Allied strategy and began to withdraw. Bülow, Bernadotte's subordinate, defeated Oudinot at Grossbeeren on August 23; Oudinot began retreating. Then Napoleon received word of Schwarzenberg's advance. He next turned west to stop Schwarzenberg, who was advancing on Dresden. He next sent a corps under Vandamme to try to hit the rear of Schwarzenberg's army. Napoleon could have had Vandamme reinforce Dresden while he struck the Allied army with his main force, but did not.[26]

Dresden, Saxony's capital, had 30,000 inhabitants, and straddled the Elbe. Napoleon used it as his base of operations in the region; it was part larder, part ammo dump, part hospital. When they reached the city, Allied hesitation about storming it gave Napoleon time to shift his forces and mount a savage attack against them on August 27. The Allies suffered 35,000 casualties. They withdrew from the wreckage of the battle during the night of the 27th into Bohemia along three routes, keeping Napoleon from landing the killing blow. Napoleon sent part of his forces after them, including a corps under Vandamme. The Allies saw a chance to redeem their situation and struck Vandamme at Kulm on August 29, destroying his corps.[27]

Napoleon now debated whether he should strike for Prague or Berlin. He chose the latter, which fit into his earlier Grand Plan. To Napoleon, Berlin still remained a decisive point. In reality, however, the Allied strength lay not in Berlin but in their armies—the biggest of which was Schwarzenberg's. Napoleon struck northward with his full fury. He sent Ney to make the attempt on Berlin, giving him Oudinot's old command, as well as objective, and decided to lead a supporting force himself against the Prussian capital.[28]

The Allied fortunes now changed quickly as Napoleon's plan unraveled. After dispatching Ney against Berlin, Napoleon had to abandon his plans because he needed to join MacDonald to reorganize this defeated army, which Blücher had crushed on August 26 (the same day as Dresden) on the Katzbach River in the midst of a downpour and was now pursuing it. Napoleon intended to smash Blücher, and did press him, but Blücher realized what was going on and again retreated in line with the Trachenberg Plan. Ney—who never received the news that Napoleon was no longer coming to support him—was defeated by Prussian forces under Bülow and Tauentzien at Dennewitz on September 6. The battle could have been even more lopsided but for Bernadotte's refusal to commit his Swedish battalions until after the contest had been decided. The defeat at Dennewitz sent ripples through Napoleon's German allies. Bavaria defected, joining the Allies on October 8. Other German states would follow.[29]

Emboldened by their series of victories, the Allies outlined their political objectives with the September 7 Treaty of Teplitz. Prussia, Russia, and Austria decided to partition the Duchy of Warsaw, restore both Prussia and Austria to their pre-1805 standings, end the independence of the smaller German states between the Austrian and Prussian frontiers and the Rhine, and reestablish the pre-1803 realms of the continent's northwest. Critically, they again agreed to make no separate peace with France.[30]

The Allies resumed their multipronged advance. Schwarzenberg pushed along the Elbe's eastern shore, hoping to unite with Blücher so they could together attack the French. Barclay de Tolly led the Russian and Prussian elements of Schwarzenberg's army along the western bank. Barclay's move was a ploy to draw Napoleon to Dresden, Schwarzenberg hoping that if the emperor took the bait, Schwarzenberg could link arms with Blücher to destroy MacDonald. Napoleon, who had arrived in Dresden on September 8, marched to meet Barclay at Teplitz, but the strong defensive terrain led only to a staring match. Next, basing from Bautzen, Napoleon struck out after Schwarzenberg, who withdrew when he identified his opponent. Blücher went after MacDonald, who escaped across the Elbe.[31]

Meanwhile, Napoleon's communications and rear units faced incessant attacks from Cossacks. He suffered constant "wastage" of men and material from this partisan war, as well as immense losses from desertion, battle, illness, and straggling, and had to use thousands of his scarce cavalry to secure his rear areas. Napoleon concluded that he had to retreat across the Elbe, hold the key bridgeheads, gather his forces (260,000 men), and wait for the Allies to give him an opportunity to use them properly instead of his having to chase them all over eastern Germany. He garrisoned Dresden, began his retreat across the Elbe on September 24, and massed his army at Leipzig. By the end of September, the Allies held the initiative.[32]

Though a part of Bernadotte's Army of the North, Wallmoden's corps (and Clausewitz with it) was far from the main theater of action in central Germany. Wallmoden initially deployed his units in a series of posts in a region of northwestern Germany dominated by the province of

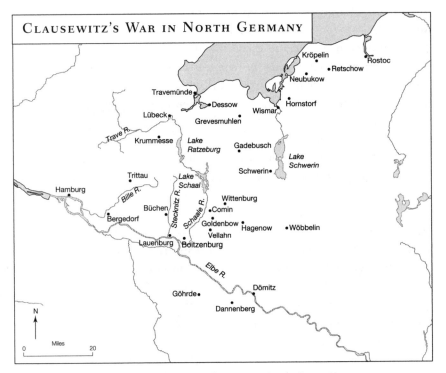

Map 8.2. Clausewitz's War in North Germany.

Mecklenburg over which their area of operations stretched in a rough tri-angle. Hamburg, on the north German coast, formed the tip. It opened to and along the Baltic coast in the north and up the Elbe River in the south. A crooked base stretched from the Baltic northeast of the Danish-held city of Lübeck, then south along the massive Lake Ratzeburg to Lauenberg where the Stecknitz River joins the Elbe. There were bridges across the Stecknitz, from north to south at Krummesse, Donnerschleuße, Mölln, Büchen, and Lauenberg. Only a few miles behind the Stecknitz lay a number of smaller lakes, and yet more sat north and east of Mölln, dotting the land all the way to the Elbe. A canal gave his forces communications with the Baltic via Travemünde, northeast of Lübeck.[33]

To prepare for the renewal of hostilities, Wallmoden anchored his lines in the north at Ratzenburger, on the lake. He spread his cavalry and some supporting units over the center region along the Stecknitz River at such hamlets as Mölln and Büchen and put the bulk of his infantry in the defenses of Lauenberg, south of Büchen. The Stecknitz formed his first line of defense, but troops held other cities, including Boitzenburg to the east of Lauenberg, Dömitz on the banks of the Elbe, Wittenburg, and Hangenow (where Wallmoden established his headquarters).[34]

Wallmoden had orders to go on the offensive when the war began, but the French didn't give him the chance. Napoleon had ordered Davout to march against Berlin in support of Oudinot's drive. Davout, with the Danes, had around 40,000 men. Wallmoden had roughly 22,000—spread over a large tract of northern Germany—when the campaign opened. On August 17 the Allies spotted a column advancing against the entrench-ments at Lauenberg. Davout hit the city hard the next day; it fell quickly. The same day—the 18th—Wallmoden's forces also abandoned Büchen under French pressure.[35]

"We didn't counterattack the post," Clausewitz wrote to Marie of Lauenberg a few days later, "because it is not our intention to fight on the Stecknitz." He also told her that they had captured a note from Napoleon to Davout in which Napoleon told his marshal to not let himself be deterred "by rabble like Wallmoden's Hanseatic troops." Clausewitz obviously thought more of their force, and had quickly grown to like the personality of his new commander. "Under the guise of a complete world-weariness glows a noble fire," he told Marie on August 20, and soon found their working relationship an enjoyable one, although he reserved judging Wallmoden's skills as a soldier until he had seen a bit more of him.[36]

They did not fight on the Stecknitz as Clausewitz told Marie, and Davout was not in the least deterred. After overrunning their posts on the Stecknitz, Davout jumped the river and advanced in three columns. His northern column (his left wing) took the road to Cammin on the Schaale River and Wittenburg, north of Goldenbow, the two others aimed at the area of Goldenbow-Vellahn. A few miles west of his base at Hagenow, at Cammin and on the heights stretching north-south from there to the hamlets of Goldenbow and Vellahn, Wallmoden placed the bulk of the Russo-German Legion and some other forces in support. His cavalry watched the plains, the woods and marshes of the Elbe anchored his southern flank. In all, he had about 9,000 men. Davout slammed into Wallmoden's men at around five in the afternoon of August 21 with 16,000–18,000 men. The Russo-German Legion and other units fought off the French at Vellahn until nightfall, then withdrew to the forests on the nearby rivulet of Schaal. Davout took Cammin at 9:00 p.m. Wallmoden withdrew to Hagenow on August 22.[37]

Davout kept up the pressure. On the afternoon of August 23 he marched northeastward from Wittenburg, seized Wismar on the Baltic coast, and then advanced along the Baltic to Rostock. Wallmoden massed his men between Wöbbelin and Lübelow, south of Lake Schwerin, and on the main road leading to Berlin, and held posts from Wismar on the Baltic to south on the lake. On the night of August 25, some of Wallmoden's detachments from Dömitz hit French posts on the left bank of the Elbe, pursued the enemy, and overran Dannenberg about eleven miles away. On August 26 Wallmoden received an order from Bernadotte to withdraw eastward to Brandenburg (Berlin's province), masking Davout. Wallmoden marched, but received orders on the 28th to go back westward to Wöbbelin.[38]

Amidst the back-and-forth marching, Clausewitz and his comrades fought. Some have branded the actions between the forces of Wallmoden and Davout a partisan war, but it more closely resembled an eighteenth-century "War of Posts," where each side fought for key positions. "We have had a few small, very insignificant skirmishes," Clausewitz wrote. "In one of them I wondered at General Wallmoden. I have hardly ever seen similar bravura. He rode three times down the front of an enemy battalion that was shooting at us at a distance of 80 paces . . . I will never forget the proud calm with which he faced the shower of bullets."[39]

Oudinot's August 23 defeat at Grossbeeren and retreat to the Elbe meant Davout couldn't link up with Oudinot, and he halted his advance at Schwerin. At the end of August, he began pulling back from some of his advanced positions—including Schwerin—and posted most of his troops along the Stecknitz from Travemünde on the Baltic, southward via Lübeck to Ratzeburg on the south shore of the lake of the same name, to Mölln near the headwaters of the Stecknitz, and to the Elbe at Lauenburg.[40]

Meanwhile, the Allies continued their multipronged offensive. Schwarzenberg received a Russian army under Bennigsen as reinforcement. They elected to swing south in an effort to get behind the French and cut their line of retreat at Leipzig. Blücher was to guard Silesia until Bennigsen passed, then march north, join with Bernadotte, move west, and cross the Elbe.[41]

Napoleon began moving on September 24. Blücher fought his way across the Elbe at Wartenberg on October 3. Bernadotte passed over the river to his northwest. Napoleon now believed the Allies had given him his opportunity. He left a force to block Schwarzenberg's advance, another to guard his base of Dresden, and then he marched north with 150,000 men. By doing so, Napoleon had violated the principle of concentration and, some argue, robbed himself of the ability to bring enough forces to bear against the Allies to inflict upon them a decisive defeat.[42]

Blücher now pushed his and Bernadotte's armies southward toward a junction with Schwarzenberg at Leipzig, though Bernadotte lagged several days behind. Murat, meanwhile, conducted a brilliant rearguard against Schwarzenberg, blocking the Allies' 240,000-man force with his 42,000. As Blücher and Bernadotte came south, Napoleon saw an opportunity to destroy them before the other Allied troops arrived. But the threat to Dresden from Bennigsen's army forced him to leave a garrison there, dissipating his strength. Bernadotte, for his part, wanted to withdraw back across the Elbe in the face of Napoleon's advance. Blücher and the Prussians refused. Instead, they marched westward, crossing the Saale on October 11. When Napoleon realized they had gotten away, and after reports of Schwarzenberg's advance and Bavaria's defection, on October 14, he ordered his forces to concentrate at Leipzig.[43]

Napoleon hoped to eliminate Schwarzenberg's army before Blücher and the lackadaisical Bernadotte arrived. He held Leipzig with 175,000 men. The Allies marched 345,000 against him. Unwilling to abandon Saxony, or to retreat, and also holding the central position, Napoleon sought to defeat the Allied forces in detail as they came on. On October 16 the Battle of Leipzig, also known as the Battle of Nations because of its diversity of combatants, commenced amongst the hamlets south of the city as Napoleon attacked the advancing Prussians. Both sides suffered heavy casualties, but the Allies gained little ground. The next day the armies glowered at one another as more Allied troops moved in. Bernadotte's army appeared in the north, and Austrians and Russians gathered to Leipzig's east. Outnumbered, Napoleon fought a defensive battle on October 18 as the Allies launched attacks around the French perimeter. Both sides bled copiously, but Allied numbers began squeezing the French into a smaller and smaller pocket. Napoleon decided he had to save his army and began to retreat on the 19th. He had abandoned Moscow exactly one year before.[44]

Though Allied troops arriving from the west threatened to block Napoleon's retreat, his army fought its way out of the pocket the way it had done at the Berezina. But they also suffered a disaster. Leipzig sat on the eastern shore of the Elster River, and the French now held only one crossing. Under pressure, the French blew the crowded bridge—too early. Twenty thousand of Napoleon's troops remained on the eastern shore and soon went into the Allied bag. While the Allies prevailed, both sides suffered immense losses. The Allies had 52,000 killed at Leipzig, Napoleon, 68,000. The difference was that the armies of the Sixth Coalition could better replace the losses. Napoleon had no choice but to abandon Germany and make for the Rhine. His forces crossed the river on October 31.[45]

The Allied strategy and operations—and hard fighting—had delivered results. In the first four weeks of the fall campaign season it had succeeded in liberating Germany by a series of victories over Napoleon's subordinate commanders: Bernadotte and Bülow defeated Oudinot at Grossbeeren; Blücher defeated MacDonald at the Katzbach; coalition forces scored a victory over Vandamme at Kulm; Bülow triumphed over Ney at Dennewitz. Finally, the Allies had tackled Napoleon himself at Leipzig in a three-day bloodletting that forced Napoleon's withdrawal across the Rhine. France now faced invasion. After Leipzig, Clausewitz noted later, "victory was no longer in doubt. A decisive victory brought the Allies to the Rhine and under the circumstances a bit further."[46]

Though he wrote about it later, Clausewitz was well aware at the time that what happened to their small army in Mecklenburg ultimately depended upon events farther south in Saxony, but he was also pleased with the actions of their small force. "We have not had a single decent fight," Clausewitz wrote Marie on September 1, from Wöbbelin, "and we had deliberately avoided one as we have found the means of bringing the enemy to a halt without, or at least attaching a lead weight to his designs." Clausewitz believed that the scant forces they could bring against their more powerful opponent left them little choice. He told Marie to not permit anyone to brand them inactive or indecisive, or lay the blame on Wallmoden. Their circumstances allowed them to act no differently, "and what has happened so far is definitely in line with my views, and for the most part done at my suggestion." If this is the case—and we have no reason to think otherwise because he served as the chief staff officer—we should look at Wallmoden's campaign as perhaps the best example we have of Clausewitz's possible skill as an operational commander.[47]

During this time, Clausewitz's health suffered. His gout flared up at the end of August, torturing him with "the most horrible cramps." The affliction hit him so hard that Dohna—who took care of him—thought he was going to die. A doctor gave him opium, temporarily relieving the pain.[48]

Wallmoden's men had marched to launch a September 2 strike on Davout's forces at Wismar on the Baltic coast when they received word of Davout's retreat. This surprised Clausewitz and he suspected (incorrectly) that Davout would now cross the Elbe to try to reinforce Napoleon's forces in Saxony. Clausewitz and Wallmoden began preparing for their crossing of the Elbe. Bernadotte also sent them some *Landwehr*. Wallmoden's force remained outnumbered and since he had such a large command area, Clausewitz believed they could never hope to concentrate more than 14,000–15,000 men in one place. Davout, Clausewitz believed, had 33,000 infantry, as well as 1,000–4,000 cavalry with which to oppose them. But when looked at in a broader context, Clausewitz thought reinforcing Wallmoden "folly," because "it lies in the nature of our role that we can never be important." This frustrated Clausewitz, and the fact that they had marched back to Dömitz, one of their old positions, and descended into a short period of inactivity, fed these feelings.[49]

At Dömitz, Wallmoden began making preparations to cross the Elbe in force, though this did not prevent a march to the Stecknitz, and the movement of the headquarters yet again to Hagenow on September 10. "For the last two days we have been back at the same spot where the campaign was opened," Clausewitz wrote Marie on September 12, "and in about the same conditions," though the coalition forces had won four battles on the Elbe. Davout's actions baffled Clausewitz, as he expected him to march to Napoleon's aide. He wrote of the Allied cause: "God grant us only a single victory over Napoleon himself!"[50]

On September 12 a patrol captured an artillery officer with a letter regarding the movement of the French 50th Division under the command of General Marc Nicolas Louis Pécheux on the left bank of the Elbe. Wallmoden immediately decided to seize the opportunity. He marched from his headquarters at Hagenow on September 12 and at midnight on the 14th crossed the Elbe at Dömitz on "a pontoon bridge as stately as the Pont Neuf in Paris," Clausewitz said, one they had thrown up in only three days. They marched to Dannenberg, then early on the 16th to the hunting lodge at Göhrde, where they hid their troops in the valley. Pécheux crossed the Elbe at Dahlenberg and took up a position near Göhrde on the evening of the 15th. On the morning of the 16th, Pécheux pushed back some of the Cossacks that Wallmoden was using to screen his movements, but he didn't continue his advance as Wallmoden hoped. At the urging of his staff, Wallmoden decided to attack before the opportunity slipped away.[51]

The area around Göhrde was heath and hills with groves of oaks. The French occupied the heights of Göhrde on the road to Dannenberg, but their main force was a half hour behind Göhrde between Oldendorf and Eischdorf. With Tettenborn's Cossacks as a vanguard, Daniel von

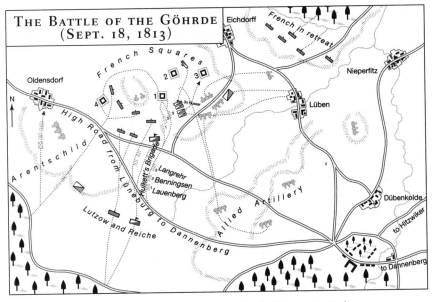

Map 8.3. The Battle of the Göhrde (Sept. 18, 1813).

Arentschildt and the Russo-German Legion were sent through the Göhrde forest to the left flank, and Wilhelm von Dörnberg with two hussar regiments from the King's German Legion and Hannover, respectively, a horse artillery battery, and the half rocket battery were sent on the right flank against Dubbelwald. Arentschildt's men jumped off first, at noon, with the rest marching an hour later. At four in the afternoon, both columns emerged from the forest, the enemy artillery replied weakly, and surprised by the appearance of the strong body of infantry, the French made preparations to retire. Wallmoden sent the Hanoverian infantry and two artillery batteries to attack the enemy in front of the main road to the hunting lodge. Right after Wallmoden's advanced troops made first contact with the enemy, the sound of cannon fire drifted over the Elbe from the direction of Boitzenburg, indicating a French attack there. Wallmoden refused to be distracted and pushed his men forward. The advance revealed the enemy aligned on some high ground behind the villages of Lüben and Oldendorf. Their artillery opened on the Allies, whose guns in turn began pouring fire into the French.[52]

When the Russo-German Legion came out of the forest they opened up with their guns on the French left. Pécheux's left flank began to give way, while his right stood in a three-battalion column on the heights to cover the retreat. At 5:30 p.m., Wallmoden's infantry attacked two of these columns on all sides. Arentschildt's men mounted a bayonet charge against the French position, seizing the villages of Oldendorf and Eichdorf as Dörnberg's cavalry hit the other French flank. The French formed four squares against the cavalry and began to retreat. They fought fiercely, inflicting over 100 casualties on the Legion. Wallmoden's troops hit them with cannon and rocket fire, but the squares held. The hussars of the King's German Legion were ordered to charge, but the broken ground prevented it from going home. Three squadrons tried again and went around the French left flank; their attacks broke three of the enemy squares, as the original square collapsed under an infantry assault. The French still tried to keep their ranks, but the pressure from Wallmoden's forces simply overwhelmed them. "After several hours of very violent fighting," Clausewitz wrote after the battle, the French force "was shattered and retreating in all directions." The pursuit began. It continued until nightfall and was then given over to the Cossacks.[53]

Wallmoden estimated that the French lost 100 officers and 1,800–1,900 men captured, 700–800 wounded, and 400–500 dead. Wallmoden suffered

550 officers and men killed and wounded. Because they lacked wagons, many of the wounded spent the night on the field, pounded by a heavy rain. Going into the fight Clausewitz and Wallmoden thought they faced 9,000 to 10,000 men. At the time Clausewitz believed they brought about 10,000 men to the contest (various sources say 12,000–13,000). Pécheux's force was actually much smaller than what they had expected, perhaps no more than 3,000 men.[54]

Clausewitz, though proud of their success, thought the victory somewhat hollow, as they lacked the forces to capitalize upon the value of any territory they seized south of the Elbe. He wrote a few days after the battle that "had my dispositions been entirely accepted"—though he doesn't tell us what these were—"nothing, absolutely nothing of the enemy corps would have escaped. Also, we would have even gotten the division general himself, Pécheux, and taken 800–1,000 more prisoners, if the Count [Wallmoden] would have been persuaded to let the cavalry continue pursuing for another hour; it was still not completely dark." Something, perhaps Wallmoden's lack of aggressiveness at the end of the fight, dampened his enthusiasm for his new boss. "Just between us," he wrote Marie, "the Count is not enterprising, not fiery enough in battle, otherwise, excellent." Wallmoden, on the other hand, remained happy with Clausewitz. In an official report he praised his quartermaster general as well as others.[55]

Clausewitz's later remarks on the situation bear special mention: "In line with the usual criterion of the Russians, I would be made a colonel for this affair; what the count will do for me, I don't know; according to his way of being and thinking, I suspect not much. Probably I will be fobbed off with the order of St. Anne, which would anger me very much." There is a hint of bitterness here, but also the ever-present desire to succeed: "To become colonel is a great object of my ambition." One wonders if his bitterness here was fed by his being in constant pain. "The gout torments me again," he told Marie, so much so that he had to take opium every evening to rest. He could not seek the aid of their doctor, Kohlrausch, as he "is so busy with amputations."[56]

At the end of September, Wallmoden received orders from Bernadotte to attack Davout, or at least the Danes. He had received similar orders before but had managed to resist doing so because he felt his force too numerically inferior against the French, about which he was entirely correct. A British officer with Wallmoden's army noted the unlikelihood of refraining this time; nevertheless, Wallmoden told his superiors it was too dangerous. Together, the Danes and French possessed superior numbers, and attacking only the Danes wasn't practical because they weren't isolated. Davout's forces also held good positions along the Stecknitz River. Clausewitz agreed wholeheartedly with his commander. They could bring 14,000 infantry to bear against Davout's Stecknitz forces, but they assessed the enemy's strength at 22,000. The terrain in the area, cut as it was by ditches, hedges, and twisting rivulets, was not suited for cavalry, and the greater part of Davout's forces—18,000 men—were massed close together between Ratzenburg and Mölln. "I view our enterprise as highly risky under these circumstances," he wrote Gneisenau, "and believe it is very possible that we come back beaten and then have to vacate Mecklenburg." But he did see some chance of success, be it ever so slight. What angered him far more was that they would not hold any area they took and already had orders to withdraw and cross back over the Elbe in a few days. "Even if we were able to stay," he continued to Gneisenau, "it would still be nothing, we would be in front of Hamburg with a gaping mouth, and that's that. Instead of this senseless, purposeless operation, and not without danger; we could be ten times more useful on the left bank of the Elbe. But it is a political whim of the Crown Prince that we should defeat the Danes. You must admit that it is very hard that for nothing we must jeopardize the welfare and existence of the corps, and"—Clausewitz added—"our reputation." Clausewitz's disillusionment with Bernadotte is clear—he remarked to the general that he was happy to hear that Gneisenau's army operated on the basis of a plan because it was clear to Clausewitz that Bernadotte's did not—but the pressing desire to make a name for himself, or perhaps win his way back into the Prussian army, also shines through. Clausewitz asked Gneisenau to remember Bernadotte's army, and thus Clausewitz, in his future planning because they could prove helpful.[57]

9

Clausewitz and the Fall of Napoleon (1813–1814)

The destruction of military forces is therefore the immediate aim of warfare, and in every case the shortest path there amounts to the law of art.

Clausewitz, in his history of the 1814 campaign in France—one most likely written in the early 1820s—said he believed it provided great examples to illustrate strategic thinking (again bearing in mind that his definition of strategy encompasses what today we would call operations—campaigns—as well as strategy). He appreciated the manner in which diplomatic and political machinations affected the strategy and operations of both sides, even acting as brakes upon them and contributing to the "complete manifestation of the nature and purpose" of the war. He saw as important the large number of troops involved, and how the "great results" came in a short time in a small arena. Clausewitz also found lessons in the distinct offensive and defensive phases, the circumstances that created opportunities for operational maneuver, the importance of mass mobilization, bases of operation, and lines of communication, and lastly, the impact of "moral factors" arising from the familiarity of the commanders and their troops with one another.[1] Regarding all of these, as we will see, he was quite correct.

Napoleon's defeat at Leipzig shattered his military forces and cost him control of Germany. He had no choice but to withdraw back over the Rhine. When he crossed the river he had perhaps 70,000 men, and an outbreak of typhus soon killed thousands of these. His strategic situation worsened in November, when the Dutch rose against the French and declared independence. This opened the way for Allied troops to press into the country. The emperor needed time to rebuild his forces as he had done

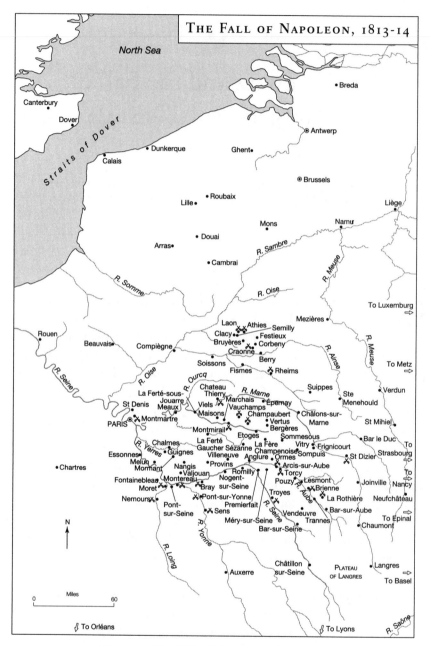

Map 9.1. The Fall of Napoleon, 1813–1814.

after the debacle of his Russian invasion. He thought he found it in an Allied proposal to negotiate a peace.[2]

At Teplitz in September 1813, the Allies had agreed to a political objective of liberating Germany. This had been accomplished. Now they faced the task of deciding what to do next: agree upon new objectives or make peace. One of the great difficulties in opting for either of these—and a characteristic of coalitions in general—was that national interests drove the various powers; only a fear of Napoleon kept them together. As previously mentioned, the Allies also had factions within their own camps that disagreed over whether the Allies should depose Napoleon and whether or not their armies should cross the Rhine.[3]

November saw the Allies gathered at Frankfurt-am-Main, not far from the banks of the Rhine, to discuss the war's next stage. Metternich insisted upon negotiating with Napoleon. He and Alexander agreed to the terms on October 29 and handed them to Napoleon's representative on November 9. The Allies offered peace based upon France's "natural frontiers," meaning the Pyrenees, Savoy in the south, Belgium, the Rhine, and the Alps. They watered down the offer later, but Alexander and Metternich never expected Napoleon to take the terms anyway. Alexander firmly believed that peace would only come with Napoleon's removal. Frederick William felt the same, but the Austrians had to overcome their own fears of Russian domination to be dragged to this conclusion.[4]

Napoleon responded by proposing a conference. Metternich insisted that Napoleon first accept their Frankfurt Proposals; Napoleon stalled. The Allies then tried to split the French people from Napoleon by publishing a manifesto based on their proposals, making it very clear that they fought only against Napoleon, and scoring a stunning propaganda blow against their opponent. Napoleon eventually bent to Metternich's requirement in early December, but by then it was too late. Both Metternich and the czar concluded he was not serious about peace and merely wanted time to prepare for the next round. Meanwhile, Napoleon made a failed bid to end his war with Spain and issued numerous calls for additional troops, seeking to raise approximately 500,000 more soldiers—all French.[5]

Meanwhile, the Allies argued over what to do. Blücher, always aggressive, believed they should press Napoleon by immediately crossing the Rhine. He saw this as the way to a quick peace. Bernadotte wanted to campaign in Denmark to achieve his goal of seizing Norway (a Danish possession). He believed that marching into France itself carried too much risk and might cost the Alliance its hard-won gains, feelings shared by the influential advisor to the Habsburg emperor Francis, General Count Ferdinand Bubna von Littitz. Bubna also worried that invading France would provoke a general French uprising against the invaders. Czar Alexander pushed for an invasion, though he temporized occasionally.[6]

The Allies at this point took what today we might term a "strategic pause" of about six weeks before they jumped the Rhine and began the 1814 campaign against France. The Allies certainly believed this was necessary, and many modern historians agree. Dominic Lieven clearly demonstrates that the Allied forces, particularly the Russian ones, were a wreck from a very bloody and costly campaign. During the pause, the Russians received substantial reinforcements and Wittgenstein alone received 25,000 men. Another Russian commander saw his force double from 30,000 to 60,000 in this short time. The six weeks allowed them to launch the new campaign in an even stronger position in relation to their opponent. The pause also gave them time to make up equipment shortfalls.[7]

Clausewitz, in his study of 1814, was very much in agreement with Blücher, believing the Allies had made a mistake. He thought the Allies could still have had an active field army of 150,000 to oppose the 60,000–70,000 that Napoleon could bring against them. Even if he drew men from Spain and Italy, Clausewitz believed Napoleon would have had no more than 80,000 men in his field force. By continuing their offensive the Allies could have made Napoleon choose to either fight a critical battle for Paris or be forced to give up the city. He also argued that the reinforcements the Allies had coming in meant they could reach Paris with 150,000 men. In his discussion of the situation after Leipzig and the opportunity facing the Allies, Clausewitz argued that the Allies possessed such a preponderance of numerical strength that they could capitalize upon the momentum won by their victory to keep the pressure upon France—without incurring fatal risks—and force another critical battle or seize the French capital of Paris. Here, Clausewitz engages with an idea he will develop in *On War* (which he was writing at the same time)—the culminating point of victory: "A possible reversal of the equilibrium or the culmination point of victory lay deep in France. Until this point was achieved, there were a number of possible avenues to this splendid success, and that even having arrived at this point of culmination, the arrival of reserves always insured against great disasters."[8]

The Allies eventually agreed upon a plan for fighting the war, with pressure from the czar proving critical. They developed a multipronged offensive not unlike the Trachenberg Plan and had 1,099,000 troops—of all types—under arms in January 1814. Strategically, one could describe their strategy as simultaneous pressure. Operationally, some familiar faces commanded the offensive arms. Schwarzenberg again swung the main blow. He would lead his 155,000 men through pro-French Switzerland, cross France's eastern frontier into the Franche-Comté, and from there enter the Langres plain east of Dijon, all the while intending to sever Napoleon's lines of communication. He would then attempt to join forces with Wellington's army advancing into France from Spain, or march on Paris (he seems not to have decided which beforehand). Supporting them was a 68,000-strong Austrian army pushing across northern Italy and into southern France. Blücher would lead his 50,000 men (though detachments soon reduced this to 27,000) through the Palatinate (north of Strasbourg through what is now southern Germany), cross the Rhine, aim at the eastern French city of Metz, then cross the Marne River, in an effort to draw the attention of the main French field army. To his north, troops under Bülow (with some British support) would invade the Netherlands, taking advantage of the rebellion there, and then sweep into Belgium. A new force under the Bavarian general, Karl Philipp von Wrede, marched between Schwarzenberg and Blücher, guarding both the Middle Rhine and Germany (until it was absorbed by Schwarzenberg). Bennigsen's Army of Poland would reduce the remaining French fortresses in the Allied rear areas and then join Bernadotte, who was given the task of liberating the Netherlands. The Austrians wanted to avoid bloody battles while putting enough pressure on Napoleon to force him to negotiate.[9]

Clausewitz disagreed with not only the pause, but also the guts of the Allied strategy. In his analysis of 1814 he gave his view that the Allies could defeat Napoleon by destroying his armed forces and seizing Paris. "As one can only become the master of large and broad countries by means of internal divisions, this was especially the case in France. The capital city is as a rule the root of these disputes, and Paris is more so than any other. Therefore, it had to be the object of the strategic attack: a complete defeat of the enemy military power and the conquering of the capital city. Neither one alone would suffice." He developed these ideas further in *On War* in his "center of gravity" discussion.[10]

Clausewitz—following his own advice that one should not condemn a plan without offering an alternative—proposed a different approach. He favored a single drive on Paris and the forcing of a decisive battle against Napoleon's army. He also believed the various secondary operations often needlessly weakened the Allies. Instead of sending the main army via Switzerland, it should have simply crossed the Rhine and marched on Paris. "Wisdom," he said, "dictated advancing relentlessly."[11]

Clausewitz did not ignore the advantages that Napoleon possessed by being on the defensive. He believed Napoleon's best hope for survival and regenerating his hold on his empire was to place himself at the head of a powerful army and win victories over the Allies. The defensive gave him "powerful means" for this. "It weakened the armies of his enemies, unified his troops, established the equilibrium at this point, and gave his talent as a commander its old room to maneuver."[12]

Meanwhile, Wallmoden waged an unsuccessful campaign against Bernadotte's insistence that they attack the superior French and Danish forces opposing them. But he was fortunate enough to receive an October 4 order to act as he saw fit. To appease Bernadotte and keep Davout occupied, Wallmoden launched a heavy reconnaissance against several points. On October 6 his men hit Büchen, on the Stecknitz north of Lauenberg, the nearby hamlet of Kogel on the 8th, and probed Davout's Ratzenburger camps. Wallmoden's corps suffered between 400 and 500 casualties doing so. They moved back to their positions on October 10 and he then sent a detachment of between 1,800 and 1,900 troops under Tettenborn to seize Bremen and cut Davout's communications on the Weser River, which they did on October 15. But now Wallmoden had to control a line from Lübeck on the Baltic stretching in a half-circle to Bremen, southwest of Hamburg, with 20,000 men. The French force in Hamburg alone outnumbered his. He put the bulk of his men in the area between Wittenburg and Boitzenburg, northeast of the Elbe.[13]

Napoleon's defeat at Leipzig on October 16–19 had profoundly affected the military situation everywhere. The coalition forces had pushed to the Rhine. The French garrisons in the rear of Wallmoden's and Bernadotte's armies surrendered, and Wallmoden's forces took Hanover and Brunswick. Clausewitz and Wallmoden also saw an opportunity and approached Gneisenau about having Wallmoden's corps transferred from what Clausewitz branded "this unfortunate war of observation against Holstein." Clausewitz also sent along a copy of Wallmoden's request to Bernadotte, asking that they be sent to Hanover or Holland.[14]

Meanwhile, Wallmoden's army returned once again to Dömitz. Before the end of October, to protect the pontoon bridge they had built in the town, they improved Dömitz's ancient fortifications and added some redoubts and fleches at spots Clausewitz selected. He also helped a British officer draw a map of the positions (Map. 9.2) that is published here for the first time.[15]

Back in their Dömitz laager, Clausewitz wrote a letter to Gneisenau that reveals elements of the theoretical approach that made him famous, and

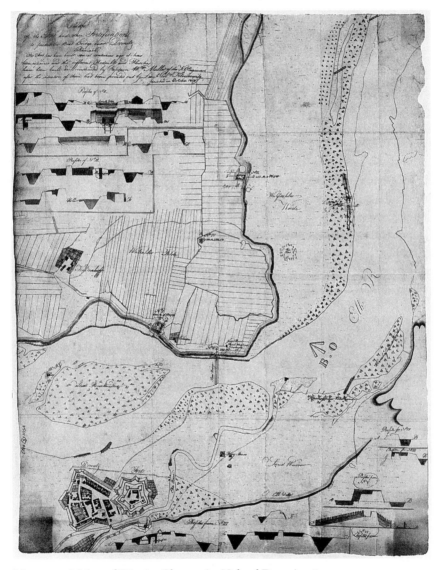

Map 9.2. A Map of Dömitz Clausewitz Helped Draw in 1813.
Courtesy British National Archives/Public Record Office

his view of what the Allies should do to defeat Napoleon. "I am in great suspense over the operations that will soon occur at the Rhine; I do not doubt that Napoleon will withdraw across this river. The operations on the other side of the Rhine will be so difficult and under such different circumstance that I am almost convinced that one is stronger in the defensive than in the offensive. Nevertheless," Clausewitz went on, "I hold it as completely decisive that one must cross the Rhine and continue the operations without delay until the peace, going all the way to Paris," striking what he would later term a "center of gravity." Napoleon's army had been nearly destroyed, and Clausewitz believed the emperor had no more than 80,000–100,000 men he could put in the field against an Allied force two or three times as large. "Leave him no time to form a new army, or to make an orderly halt until he reaches Paris." In other words, keep him under pressure, something he later wrote about in *On War* that others sometimes refer to as "the Principle of Continuity." "A conspiracy in Paris, a revolt by the army, rebellion in the provinces will meet us halfway and one will easily have the two cornerstones of a durable peace with the liberation of Holland and Switzerland." The Allies would score not just military victories by doing this, but achieve a sound political aftermath.[16]

When he was writing this in November 1813, Clausewitz very much feared a winter pause on the Rhine. This would, he insisted, give Napoleon time to rebuild his army and then oppose them in the spring with 200,000–300,000 men. Considering Napoleon's ability to replace his losses after 1812, this was a rational fear. He had another concern as well: "Although the Allies no doubt will be in a position to place twice the manpower against these forces, it is to be feared very much that the usual dissension will have time to produce an awful rupture. These thoughts haunt me day and night, ten times more than our situation here." Clausewitz understood the additional political risks of waiting, and correctly foresaw the difficulties of keeping the Allied coalition together and on course. He counted upon Gneisenau to get the Allies over the Rhine.[17]

In early November, Bernadotte sent an aide to try to convince the Allied high command that attacking Davout and the Danes was not only necessary defensively, but would also hurry the conquest of the French possession of Holland. Czar Alexander replied with the plan that the Austrians and Prussians had devised: the Allies would move on Paris in several prongs. Wellington would push from Spain, Austria from Italy, Blücher across the Rhine, Bernadotte via Holland. Bernadotte wasn't happy with this, as it didn't mention Denmark and Norway, and argued that it was inexpedient to invade Holland without first dealing with the Danes and what he estimated would be about 130,000 French troops in the rear of his advance.[18]

By November 5 Clausewitz, as Wallmoden's quartermaster general, was preparing his subordinates for the next phase of the war. Bernadotte had sent his Russian corps commanded by Pavel Aleksandrovich Stroganov to the Duke of Brunswick (the son of the famous Duke of Brunswick killed in 1806) into Holland. Prussian forces under Bülow also pushed into the Low Countries while the crown prince himself marched to Hanover with his Swedish contingent. "The intention shall be to cut off Marshal Davout from Holland and, in case he doesn't go over the Elbe," Clausewitz wrote, "to attack him in Holstein, from which it then would follow that the Crown Prince must cross the Elbe here at Dömitz." Wallmoden planned to push the various units of his own corps into the area bordering Hamburg on the south, as well as along the routes from Hamburg to Bremen. Bernadotte soon changed Wallmoden's and Clausewitz's plans. "Just now the Crown Prince has ordered that we should take our position between Wittenberg and Hagenau in order to await further orders," Clausewitz wrote two days later, though a number of Wallmoden's units still moved against the environs of Hamburg from the south and along the Elbe.[19]

Some of Clausewitz's professional correspondence during this period is marked with amused disillusion at the actions of his superiors. An example: "The corps remains here today and probably tomorrow as well. We go back again to the beloved Stecknitz, I presume supported with Vorontsov, the Crown Prince is coming to Lüneberg and wants to cross there, or he will finally pursue his favorite plan on the right bank. Tettenborn should, however, observe Harburg and Zollenspieker—now Winzingerode [sic] and Bülow are also there on the Weser, 80,000 men against the movement that four weeks ago I was supposed to defeat with 18,000. I have asked for permission to go to headquarters for 12 hours; this time, I want to get my bearings myself."[20]

During their long stay at Dömitz, Marie found the time to visit. She later revealed to Gneisenau Clausewitz's deep dissatisfaction with his position and the difficulties Wallmoden faced as a commander. Her remarks also leave no doubts about Clausewitz's view of Bernadotte, as well as her husband's frustration. "When I left him," Clausewitz "believed that he, with the Crown Prince's help, could come up with something serious against Davout, and I stayed here in order to be closer to the reports, but everything seems still the same, and the Crown Prince still occupied with resting."[21]

On November 12 Davout abandoned his advance post at Ratzeburg and withdrew behind the Stecknitz. Soon, all his forces lay behind the much abused river. Four days later, Bernadotte sent his army toward Denmark and went to lead it himself. The Allies gave him his string and the crown prince's envoys eventually got the Allies to agree to Bernadotte's course. "Events here on the Stecknitz are not as we have believed," Clausewitz wrote Marie the same day. "Up to now the French have only left the camp at Ratzeburg as well as the city, but have remained behind the Stecknitz from Lübeck to Lauenberg. We have therefore done nothing other than advance a little the outposts of our right wing and move our headquarters to here [Dammerow], where I am in a room with six officers."[22]

In late November Clausewitz, while still at Dammerow, and working as does any good staff officer, prepared for the British a detailed paper on the pay and organization of forces based upon Prussia's 1807 practices. This was undoubtedly related to Allied organizational changes. Beginning in December 1813, the various German units raised in Russia and Germany came—technically—under the control of Hanover, but the British paid Hanover £600,000 annually in exchange for keeping 15,000 men in the field, which the British set about raising.[23]

Bernadotte marched north with 60,000 men to join those already there. Mikhail Vorontsov's division crossed the Elbe at Boitzenburg. Others closely blockaded Hapt and Harburg near Hamburg. Part of his reason for taking such a significant force northward were the repeated warnings from Wallmoden that his lone corps had no hope of taking Hamburg or decisively dealing with Davout.[24]

Clausewitz and Wallmoden also finally received word from Gneisenau that it was impossible for him to move them to another command. "There are big problems here," Gneisenau told them, and inflicted upon them the reality that alliance politics necessitated using a Russian corps for the invasion of Holland. Gneisenau also revealed that the primary Allied army would operate out of Switzerland, which Clausewitz believed wasted time.[25]

Davout had been planning to stay on the river until it froze and ceased to serve as an effective obstacle. On December 2, after the temperature fell, Davout suddenly abandoned the Stecknitz, pulled his troops from all of his posts between Mölln and Lauenburg, and retreated thirty miles westward to his Hamburg defenses. The same day the Swedish army concentrated at Mölln and Boitzenburg under Bernadotte, while Wallmoden

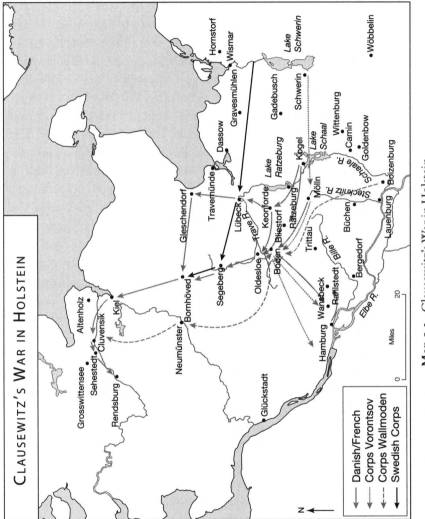

Map 9.3. Clausewitz's War in Holstein.

concentrated at Ratzeburg. Bernadotte arrived at Lübeck on December 3 and told Wallmoden that he planned to invade Holstein and force a peace on Denmark. The next day Wallmoden's corps crossed the Stecknitz and the entire Swedish army—20,000 men—aimed at Lübeck on December 4. Bernadotte pinned Davout in Hamburg with a Russian corps and launched a two-pronged invasion of Holstein.[26]

Wallmoden's corps (which had 15,000–16,000 men in November) formed the left wing of the invasion; Bernadotte led the right. The crown prince took Lübeck's surrender on December 5, having allowed the garrison twenty-four hours to march away. Wallmoden's advance guard under Dörnberg fought a small action at Siebenbäumen on the 4th. "We (Wallmoden) march against Oldesloe in order to expel the Danes from the Trave; but they will probably not wait," Clausewitz wrote Marie. "Finally we break free from the damned Stecknitz." Clausewitz proved correct. Wallmoden's advance forces reached an empty Oldesloe on December 6. They pushed on—north-eastward—deeper into Holstein. Wallmoden's force camped at Neumünster on December 7, as Bernadotte's troops turned north and made a parallel advance upon Kiel. Bernadotte ordered Wallmoden on to Rendsburg. Wallmoden reached the Eider River on December 8 and crossed an advance guard while putting out flank detachments to watch Kiel on his right and Rendsburg on his left. He sent artillery to begin shelling the Rendsburg fortress, and seized the bridge at Cluvensik. Clausewitz noted that only the "unending efforts of the troops" marching through often brutal terrain allowed Dörnberg's advance force to reach the banks of the Eider on the 9th. Dörnberg then pushed northward to Eckernförde, and got himself entangled with a Danish baggage train, which his men set about vigorously looting. Wallmoden and Clausewitz were now without the reconnaissance information that Dörnberg was supposed to provide.[27]

What had sent Dörnberg north was a captured letter, one Wallmoden received on the evening of December 9 as his army camped at the Cluvensik bridge. The note revealed that the Danish forces in Kiel had marched out of the city at 7:00 a.m. that morning, heading north for Eckernförde. The next morning, Wallmoden's advanced force crossed the Cluvensik bridge, marched through Osterrade, crossed the bridge over the tiny Alte Eider, and passed through the village of Sehestedt on their way to Eckernförde to the north. Sehestedt sat astride the road running from Rendsburg in the west to Kiel in the east. The Alte Eider bordered its right. A few miles north were the village of Holtsee, and to the northeast, Lake Witten. Eight and a half miles from this lay Eckernförde. At eight o'clock, 9,000 Danish troops marched directly at Sehestedt from the north, arrayed for battle. "All reports say that the Danes are going to Eckernförde and Schleswig," Clausewitz wrote Gneisenau afterward.[28]

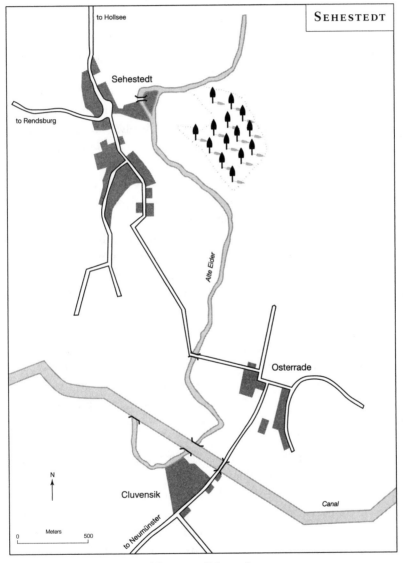

Map 9.4. Sehestedt.

The Danes had left Kiel on the 9th, but headed west for Rendsburg, not north to Eckernförde. They camped that night at Gettorf, halfway between Kiel and Rendsburg. The next day they marched for Sehestedt. Leading the Danes was Prince Frederick of Hessen. Unlike Clausewitz and Wallmoden, he had excellent intelligence regarding his enemy's situation. He was also desperate. A British deserter from one of Wallmoden's hussar units revealed that Wallmoden had left Nordtoff on the morning of the 8th. By the 9th, the Danes knew the enemy was in Eckernförde and Cluvensik, that some of Dörnberg's men were at Groß-Wittensee northwest of Sehestedt, and that Wallmoden was in Sehestedt itself, cutting the road to Rendsburg. Feeding the Danes' desperation was the presence of the Swedish army at Kiel behind them. Hessen knew they were cut off from all sides, and that his men were exhausted from their retreat from the Stecknitz; he feared his units would simply dissolve. He also decided that it was in the best interest of Denmark for him to reinforce the important fortress of Rendsburg, then held by only four weak battalions, something the enemy knew. He resolved to march to Rendsburg and destroy anything blocking his way. He had fourteen battalions and twelve squadrons of cavalry, a little more than 9,000 combatants.[29]

The Danes overran some of Dörnberg's troops at Holtsee, about three miles north of Sehestedt, at roughly 7:30 on the morning of December 10. Hessen sent some units to keep Dörnberg off his back, and deployed his forces to attack Sehestedt. He moved in with a dispersed light infantry brigade in a skirmish line in his fore, supported by its battery, which was covered by an infantry battalion. The skirmishers anchored their left on the Alte Eider and their right on the Habyer Moor. They slowly advanced against Sehestedt, supported by artillery on the left and right of the road. Behind them came the rest of the infantry of the first brigade in a tight attack column. Another brigade simultaneously came up the road, also in column. Hessen used his Lancers to protect his route of retreat, just in case things went wrong.[30]

Wallmoden stood outside of Sehestedt with some of his adjutants, a half-hour march from the Cluvensik bridge, when the Danes appeared. Though surprised, he sent word for Dörnberg to return—quickly. "In haste," Clausewitz noted, they put a battalion into the village, but the bulk of their troops could not begin to arrive before noon. About 2,200 paces north of Sehestedt the Danes hit some infantry and artillery that Wallmoden had on a low height, and also began taking fire from one of

Wallmoden's Jäger battalions in the woods to Sehestedt's right across the Alte Eider. Hessen pushed both units back and drove on to Sehestedt.[31]

As the Danes began their attack against the enemy in the village, Wallmoden's men could see that he was getting stronger by bringing in and deploying more battalions north of the town, and Wallmoden's lines soon stretched from the Alte Eider to the Hohenfelde road. The Danes began shelling Sehestedt, then mounted an attack with an infantry column as Wallmoden's troops poured artillery fire into them. Hessen himself led a brigade into the maelstrom. The Allied forces to the left and west of Sehestedt were thrown into confusion. The Danish light infantry that had been supporting the attack now poured into Sehestedt.[32]

Since most of Wallmoden's troops were strung out in march column when the attack began, they were slow to come up. The Danes, who had been in a denser formation—and ready for a fight when they came down the road—were able to more quickly throw troops into the town. By 10:00 a.m., they had pushed out Wallmoden's forces and captured two guns and a number of prisoners. The fighting stopped southeast of the village and a number of Wallmoden's battalions formed up here.[33]

Clausewitz, hoping that Dörnberg would soon arrive to attack from the other side, and that the Swedish advance guard that he thought was following the Danes would strike even more terror into them, proposed a counterattack with the few battalions they had managed to bring across the Eider by noon. But, as Clausewitz also pointed out, an attacker faced problems. Once across the Eider, the road to Sehestedt became a long bottleneck. Earthen walls and thorny hedges six to eight feet high bordered the 100–200 paces-wide path, making the use of cavalry and artillery impossible, and preventing any rapid infantry advance. Wallmoden didn't want to use artillery and cavalry in this unfavorable terrain until he was convinced that Dörnberg was coming back. He sent one battalion up the road and one on each side of it, but ditches and hedges broke up the terrain beside the track, and the flanking forces dissolved almost completely into skirmishers.[34]

The moment the Danes reached Sehestedt's southern end, a battalion of the Russo-German Legion commanded by Lieutenant Colonel Goltz slammed into them from the south, pushed the Danes back, and seized a gun, but the terrain kept Goltz's men from taking away their prize. The Danes brought more and more infantry against them, pushed around Goltz's left flank, and sprayed the Legion battalion with heavy grapeshot.[35]

Hessen then committed his dragoons. They galloped out of the village and stormed down the narrow road straight at the attacking battalion. Goltz's men panicked, throwing themselves into ditches and hedges—where cavalry couldn't reach—and flinging away their guns. Despite the efforts of the Legion's officers, the Danes captured or killed the entire battalion, took Goltz, 200 prisoners, and two guns, and recaptured the one they had lost. They advanced as far as Osterade, even reaching Wallmoden's reserves at the Cluvensik bridge.[36]

Wallmoden responded with a charge of his own, dispatching the Legion's hussars. The Danish dragoons retreated with their prisoners and cannon as the hussars—supported by infantry—fought their way back into Sehestedt. "Little by little we brought some four battalions and two guns into the fight to retake the village," Clausewitz said. The terrain, however, gave the Danes a superior position and made it impossible for Wallmoden and Clausewitz to use their cavalry as they wished, or to make any quick advance with their infantry. The Danes hit back with their dragoons and some hussars. The horsemen made little headway, but the Danish infantry supporting them pushed Wallmoden's men out of Sehestedt.[37]

Wallmoden replied with another counterattack, this time with his 120-man strong Mecklenburg Horse Jägers. This proved disastrous. A Danish infantry battalion occupied the ditches on each side of the road, and an artilleryman had bored a hole through an earth wall: he fired two rounds of grape into the attacking horsemen. The unit broke against the Danes, and Prince Gustav of Mecklenburg, the unit's commander, was wounded and captured. Hessen said that only six of the Mecklenburgers escaped the fire of the Danish infantry. Clausewitz wrote of the cavalry action: "The Danish cavalry (Holstein Dragoons) fought very bravely; with one squadron in a very narrow path they made a brilliant charge through the middle of our infantry. One squadron of the 1st Hussar Regiment of the German Legion and one from the Mecklenburg Horse Jägers did the same against the Danes so that the path, the only terrain in which the cavalry could ride, is littered with the people and horses of both sides and presented a horrific scene."[38]

Wallmoden pulled back behind the Eider to Osterrade, and for a time the sides exchanged some light cannon fire. The Danes thought Wallmoden had withdrawn. But then two enemy battalions came down the footpath of the canal in what the Danes saw as an attempt to take their position in the rear. More Danish troops arrived and pushed them back in a half-hour of fighting. Hessen also sent two squadrons to attack an enemy party still north of the Eider. They threw them back over the bridge. One of the cavalrymen claimed that he came close to capturing General Wallmoden, so close that he actually grabbed him, but the general's horse saved him and the Danish trooper got only the general's coat. Hessen wrote that the enemy now withdrew "in great haste and disorder" over the canal. They exchanged artillery fire, but the battle was over and the Danes had achieved their objective of opening the road to Rendsburg. Hessen marched away at 4:30 in the afternoon, very much aware that Vegesack's division had now arrived to reinforce Wallmoden.[39]

It had been a bloody action for both sides, though the sources very much disagree on the losses. Wallmoden's corps, on the low side, lost perhaps 500–600 prisoners and 400–500 killed and wounded; Clausewitz said it cost them 600–800 men and two cannon. Another source puts their casualties at forty-two officers and 1,129 men, including more than 600 prisoners. The Danes had 800–900 killed, wounded, and captured (Hessen gave his losses as 548 killed and wounded. The Russo-German Legion's losses are estimated at 800 men, including 600 captured).[40]

The outcome of the engagement caused Clausewitz much bitterness. "Our infantry is fighting badly, Dörnberg does not attack, the Swedes do not come; and we have to let the Danes, who even take two cannon and a few hundred prisoners from us, pass by." The result, he told Gneisenau, had not left him "in the best mood." He saw in the incident a missed opportunity. "I could despair when I think what a brilliant battle was denied us," he wrote Marie. He believed if they had reached the Cluvensik bridge only six hours earlier, they would have had all their forces north of Sehestedt in advantageous terrain—and closer to Dörnberg—thus allowing them to strike the Danes united. This would have forced the Danes back to Kiel where the Swedes waited, Clausewitz believed, and resulted in the destruction of Hessen's force—although this seems somewhat optimistic. He went on: "It is a revolting feeling to have been so near to such a splendid success and to have fallen short of it. Although the Crown Prince heaped praise upon us, but what is that for a substitute!" He believed Bernadotte had failed them, making them wait a day for Vegesack's unit or march without them (they marched); ordering the Swedish advance guard that followed the Danes from Kiel to stop at the Eider River, which meant Wallmoden received no support from the Swedes; and finally, generally not supporting Wallmoden. He also thought Bernadotte had mismanaged the invasion itself, particularly missing an opportunity to simply trap all the Danes in Lübeck at the beginning of the offensive and march to Rendsburg.[41]

But is all of this merely the protest of a young officer, one intensely concerned with reputation and prestige, who has just suffered a defeat? One can certainly hang upon Bernadotte the failure to support Wallmoden and to keep contact with the retreating Danes. Also, Dörnberg's forces did not sufficiently communicate with Wallmoden and provide the intelligence they were supposed to. But one also has to credit Hessen for being smart enough to pin Dörnberg's forces and keep him out of the fight. Hessen demonstrated solid tactical acumen. He executed a very textbook Napoleonic action, did it superbly, and chose *exactly* the right moment to commit his cavalry reserve. In the defense of Clausewitz and Wallmoden one must point out that they could only bring to the fight 4,000 men against Hessen's 9,000. But one must critique Clausewitz for assuming too much on the part of Wallmoden's subordinates and the Swedes. The attack Clausewitz urged Wallmoden to make was based upon the assumption that Dörnberg would arrive to assist and that the Swedes were pursuing the enemy as Napoleonic doctrine dictated. These are very big assumptions on which to base one's planning. The more mature Clausewitz would recognize this as well. As he later noted in *On War,* "In war more than anywhere else things do not turn out as we expect."[42]

Clausewitz would later sometimes discuss intelligence (or reports about the enemy) in cynical terms. Quoted earlier is Clausewitz's remark after the battle of Sehestedt that their information had the Danes marching to Eckernförde and Schleswig—not at them. It would be a great example of overreach to argue that it is from this experience that he derived the skepticism about intelligence that occasionally emerges in *On War,* but it is certainly an example of why a healthy suspicion of any information obtained under the pressures of war should receive a cynical eye. Considering the vast number of military actions in which Clausewitz was involved, it is probably not too presumptuous to say that this part of his experience at Sehestedt was not unique.[43]

The Allied offensive began anew four days before Christmas, 1813, when Schwarzenberg's men crossed into Switzerland. Troops entered rebellious Holland the next day. Blücher crossed the Rhine on New Year's Day. Their armies now pressed France from every direction—simultaneously. Wellington's army crossed the Pyrenees and invaded southern France while Austrian forces cleared the French from Illyria and Venetia. Stiffening the

Allies were various German states that had changed sides. The Allies forced them to provide the same numbers of troops as had Napoleon, as well as matching numbers of *Landwehr*, and much money.[44]

The Allies faced the challenge of mounting a winter campaign. This increased the difficulty of supplying their armies, which meant they risked relying more upon levies from the local population. This in turn increased the risk of provoking the French populace into rising against the invader, something the Allies feared. They also faced geographical obstacles: the Rhine, Moselle, Meuse, and Marne Rivers slowed any invasion from the east, as did the Vosges Mountains in the south. Eastern France was also studded with the world's most extensive network of fortresses, all placed to thwart the invader.[45]

Napoleon had to defend France on many fronts while maintaining the support of the French people and keeping the supporters of France's former Bourbon rulers in check. In November 1813, Napoleon divided the French frontier from the North Sea to Switzerland into three defensive zones—a 400-mile front—each commanded by a marshal. He planned to hold the Rhine, using it as a barrier behind which to mobilize new forces, as well as a propaganda tool for convincing the French people that he was defending the homeland's "natural frontiers." Within three weeks he was also reinforcing the Netherlands. He also began building a reserve based upon a rejuvenated Imperial Guard. In December though, he had only 103,600 men to guard this extended frontier. He did not fortify Paris because he feared that being seen doing so would undermine the faith of the populace in his military abilities. Military skill and success had won his throne; this remained its foundation. The Allies attempted to split the French people from their emperor by issuing pamphlets declaring that they fought against Napoleon, not the French, but there was little immediate chance of a popular revolt in France. The reverse of this coin was the aforementioned Allied fear of an uprising of the people against the invader. The Allies encountered some of this, but it never grew beyond a nuisance. Clausewitz wrote later that the Allies had little chance of facing "a significant uprising of the people, because such a buildup of pressure among the masses is never the result of a few weeks, but of months and in most cases it takes years before it becomes a reality."[46]

The Allied advance continued. Wellington pushed against Soult in southern France. Blücher's army captured a Marne bridgehead on January 23, 1814, and continued its westward march. Schwarzenberg's army aimed at Troyes, south of Paris, along the main road. Murat, the king of Naples (and Napoleon's brother-in-law), changed sides on January 11 so as to keep his throne. By January 27, Allied forces had overrun a third of France and freed much of the Low Countries.[47]

But the coalition began to suffer from strains fed by the delays in executing the campaign. Alexander viewed Schwarzenberg's advance as dilatory, which invoked the czar's suspicions of Austrian motives. He was right: the slow Austrian drive was in part a result of Metternich's goal of having France beaten but not broken, and Austria not paying too high a price for such an outcome. In mid-January 1814, the Allies reached Basel, Switzerland. Here, Alexander refused any further negotiations and declared he would accept nothing less than Napoleon's abdication, and suggested Bernadotte as a successor. On January 16 Metternich responded by ordering a halt to Austrian military operations (Schwarzenberg had reached Langres) and encouraged Frederick William to do the same with Prussian forces. He insisted the Allies agree upon their political goals before taking one step farther westward.[48]

After much bluster, threats, and bitter negotiations, on January 29–30 the Allies agreed to resume the offensive, with Schwarzenberg still prosecuting the campaign as he wished. Simultaneously, they agreed to open negotiations with Napoleon in the hopes of convincing him to accept peace terms based upon keeping France's 1792 borders. Gneisenau had proposed a more aggressive approach: an immediate march upon Paris with their forces on the Rhine. "We have fourteen marches to Paris, eighteen days will suffice to complete these marches, deliver a battle, and dictate an armistice. In order to secure victory, why should we not move concentrically on Paris with everything that we have on the Rhine?" The Allied leaders—Schwarzenberg among them—believed this too risky, and Gneisenau and his boss Blücher then and after have been criticized for taking too many unnecessary risks while not paying sufficient attention to the protection of their own forces. Clausewitz and the Prussians certainly disagreed. In *On War*, Clausewitz described Schwarzenberg's staff as "timid and irresolute."[49]

The Langres Conference began on January 25. The Allies agreed to seek a peace based upon France's pre-Revolutionary War borders. The Austrians and Russians resolved their differences by compromising; Metternich agreed to make Paris the Allies' objective if Alexander would agree to negotiations with France. Talks with Napoleon at Lusigny and Châtillon followed. Those at Lusigny revolved around a potential armistice, while the discussants at Châtillon tried to negotiate a basis for a peace. When the Châtillon Conference opened February 5, the Allied terms had become less generous: they offered the frontiers of 1792. The French representative, Caulaincourt, thought France should agree, but he would not sign without first asking his emperor. Meanwhile, influenced by Napoleon's defeat at La Rothière, Alexander had concluded that removing Napoleon—something eminently desirable in the czar's mind—was now also very practicable. Austria, Britain, and eventually even Prussia lined up against the czar in insisting that the terms offered to Caulaincourt were perfectly acceptable.[50]

The war went on during all of this. The interest of each side in an armistice swayed with the results on the battlefield, which remained fluid as each combatant scored victories and neither was serious about negotiating a peace.[51]

Like the other rulers, Bernadotte was negotiating, and his talks with the Danes directly affected Clausewitz and Wallmoden. They began on December 12, and on the 15th a fourteen-day cease-fire was concluded. In mid-December, during the armistice, Clausewitz again approached Gneisenau to deliver him, Wallmoden, and the Russo-German Legion. The unit's original political purpose had long since disappeared, something Clausewitz and the other Prussians serving in its ranks well understood. Clausewitz feared for their future, especially as they entered into British pay, and believed that the most the British would do would be to build a formation around it from men in their province of Hanover, something that the Legion's members did not want. Wallmoden wondered whether the Russo-German unit could become the basis for a truly German Legion, or perhaps be rolled into a similar Austrian organization. "If you take up this matter," Clausewitz told Gneisenau, "you would do a very charitable deed for orphaned children who no longer have a homeland." Colonel Stülpnagel, another former Prussian officer who served in the Legion, expressed to Gneisenau similar concerns about their fate. Clausewitz's desire was for their force to serve under Gneisenau in the next campaign. "I am fed up with the Crown Prince," he wrote, and told Gneisenau he would find in Wallmoden a solid advance force commander. "What is lacking in enterprising spirit, you can easily compensate with pressure from behind."[52]

Gneisenau replied in January, and he did not send good news: he could do nothing either for the Legion or Wallmoden's army. And it got worse: "In regard to your person, you were destined to become the Chief of Staff of a German corps. The king himself had recommended you to the Duke of Coburg. The emperor of Russia, however, declined it, saying that you were indispensable in your present post. So once again one of my plans has failed.'[53]

The tortuous negotiations between Sweden and Denmark continued, but they resolved nothing and the fighting resumed on January 6, 1814. Wallmoden's troops were put to blockading Rendsburg, although the snow made it difficult to do much of anything. Bernadotte's forces pushed into Denmark. On January 7 Denmark sued for peace. Another cease-fire occurred on January 9 and a peace was signed on the 16th.[54]

The peace with Denmark delivered Bernadotte's primary objective for entering the war: securing Norway for Sweden. But the war with France went on. Earlier, Bernadotte had had no desire to invade the country of his birth. After Leipzig, he had opposed the Allied plans for invasion, fearing that such a move too early could provoke a rising of the French people. But by the end of November 1813, fueled by ambitions for the French crown, he began preparing for this very thing.[55]

For Clausewitz and his comrades, the war now moved south. Wallmoden's corps camped in the area around Neumünster, south of Kiel, until January 17, 1814. On the 18th one column marched via Bramsädt-Webel-Barschudt, crossing the frozen Elbe on the 21st at Blankenese. The other column went to the left via Elmshorn to Zollenspieker, crossing the Elbe at the latter town and marching to Winsen, then Buxtehude, where the units reunited and cantoned not far from Hamburg. The English-German Legion, and some artillery, departed to go to General Graham in Holland. Wallmoden left Stroganov's corps to blockade Harburg on January 26, and the rest of his army made for the Rhine.[56]

On January 25 Napoleon marched from Paris. Using the advantage of his central position, he attempted to seize victory as he had always done: by inflicting stunning defeats on his foes. He blocked Schwarzenberg's advancing force and went after Blücher's army. Napoleon, with around 30,000 men, drove Blücher—who had similar numbers—out of Brienne on January 29. The French pushed the Allies back to Trannes, but part of Schwarzenberg's army united with Blücher, giving him 100,000 men to bring against Napoleon. Blücher defeated Napoleon at the previously mentioned battle of La Rothière on February 1, a contest fought in a driving snowstorm. For the first time, Napoleon had lost a battle on French soil, feeding desertion in the French ranks. The emperor withdrew, and rejoined his other forces in Troyes.[57]

The Allied offensive had also begun producing results. By the end of January they controlled large parts of eastern France. This made it difficult for Napoleon to raise, equip, feed, and supply new forces. Also, the French conscription system was beginning to break down and simply could not deliver the men Napoleon wanted—and needed.[58]

Napoleon, however, still relied on his sword. The Allied armies had separated and Blücher marched for Paris via the Marne. Schwarzenberg aimed at the same objective along the Seine route. Napoleon once again masked Schwarzenberg's force and marched against Blücher, this time with 70,000 men. In *On War*, Clausewitz lauded this move, believing it more important for Napoleon to strike Blücher because of "his enterprising spirit," and because "the center of gravity lay with him, and he pulled the other forces in his direction."[59]

Napoleon hit an element of the Prussian force—which was strung-out over more than forty miles—at Champaubert on February 10, and then at Montmirail the next day. Blücher retreated, but when he learned Schwarzenberg was on the move, he reversed course and again marched to the west. Napoleon stung him again not far from Vauxchamps on February 14. The emperor had inflicted 15,000 casualties on Blücher's army in five days, fully a third of Blücher's force. Again, Blücher retreated. Napoleon turned south against Schwarzenberg, who was within forty miles of Paris, marched his army thirty-six miles in forty-seven hours, and slammed into an element of Schwarzenberg's army at Montereau on February 18. Beaten, Schwarzenberg withdrew. The falling temperature froze the ground, easing Schwarzenberg's retreat. Schwarzenberg had 6,000 casualties to add to Blücher's, but the Allies possessed such wells of strength that they made up the losses within ten days.[60] Attrition would play to the Allies' favor.

Later, Clausewitz said of Blücher's detachment from the main army: "we cannot disguise that we regard the departure of Blücher as being rash and therefore, a mistake. The catastrophe that Blücher experienced on the Marne was, admittedly, not an unavoidable result of his departure, but one of them nevertheless. The main reason why we consider every unnecessary division to be a mistake is that one cannot be sure whether the enemy is also dividing himself in the same fashion as we are." This gave Napoleon an opportunity he would not otherwise have had, allowing him

to mask Schwarzenberg while concentrating his field force against Blücher.
Clausewitz also argued that "Napoleon's move against Blücher was "the
best of the entire war." He said this because Blücher, being more aggressive, would not allow himself to be so easily contained as Schwarzenberg.
Blücher was also weaker and thus Napoleon had a better chance of scoring a
victory over him. A French force already pursued Blücher, and Napoleon's
timing—attacking right after he had suffered a defeat and the Allies
believed him "crippled"—was, Clausewitz wrote, "a great surprise. This
was akin to an ambush, and it had its full impact."[61]

One minor piece of popular Napoleonic conventional wisdom is that
as Napoleon grew older he became less capable on the battlefield. In *On
War* Clausewitz offers an assessment of Napoleon's actions in February 1814
that shatters this, while also providing an interesting counterfactual line of
thought:

> The world was filled with admiration when Bonaparte, in February
> 1814, turned from Blücher after beating him at Etoges, Champ-Aubert,
> Montmirail, and elsewhere, to fall on Schwarzenberg, and beat him at
> Montereau and Mormont. By rapidly moving his main force back and forth,
> Bonaparte brilliantly exploited the allies' mistake of advancing with divided
> forces. If, people thought, these superb strokes in all directions failed to save
> him, at least it was not his fault. No one has yet asked what would have hap-
> pened if, instead of turning away from Blücher, and back to Schwarzenberg,
> he had gone on hammering Blücher and had pursued him back to the Rhine.
> We are convinced that the complexion of the whole campaign would have
> been changed and that, instead of marching on Paris, the allied armies would
> have withdrawn across the Rhine.[62]

On the French side, as historian Steve Ross put it, Napoleon's victories
were tactical, not strategic, but they did impact the Allies in several ways.
The mood in the Allied camp quickly changed as Alexander now talked not
of marching on Paris but of an armistice. Many of the leaders of the smaller
German states also began to panic. Napoleon essentially frightened the
Allies into establishing clear—and unified—policy objectives. Metternich
seized the opportunity to weld a tighter alliance and to get Alexander to
agree to the possibility of a peace with Napoleon if Bonaparte would accept
the 1792 frontier, or his removal if he would not, with Louis XVIII replac-
ing him. In Metternich's eyes, these conditions would allow the balance
of power to be maintained in Europe, meaning that the Russians would
not dominate the continent. The agreement of February 15 was made a

formal alliance by the March 1, 1814, Treaty of Chaumont. They agreed to no separate peace, and signed a twenty-year alliance to resist any French aggression. Holland, Switzerland, and Italy would be freed from France, the Bourbons would return to Spain, and a German federation would be established.[63]

Schwarzenberg, after his defeat at Montereau, retreated to Troyes. He and Blücher planned to unite their forces at Méry-sur-Seine, which sits astride the river's banks, twenty-five miles northwest of Troyes and roughly eighty-five miles southeast of Paris. Schwarzenberg could then add Blücher's 50,000 men to his own 90,000. Schwarzenberg deployed his army at Troyes on February 22, but didn't like his position and retreated eastward to Bar-sur-Aube the next day. This further fed Russian suspicions of Austria, and the strains in the coalition intensified. The czar declared on February 22 that he would make no peace that left Napoleon on the throne. A particularly bitter conference ensued at Bar-sur-Aube on February 25.[64]

Schwarzenberg, fearing for his logistical situation, wanted to retreat to Langres, where they had been a week before. Alexander stood against this and threatened to take his army, combine it with Blücher's, and march on Paris. Frederick William stood with him. Schwarzenberg believed he couldn't fight a battle against Napoleon. He thought his supply situation was inadequate and believed the area between the Seine and Marne Rivers had been too marched and fought over to provide for his massive army. Clausewitz argued later that instead of Schwarzenberg retreating, he and Blücher should have joined their armies, fought a decisive battle (they could bring 150,000 troops against what Clausewitz estimated would at best be 60,000 under Napoleon), and then taken Paris.[65]

The Allies eventually agreed to a new operational plan. Schwarzenberg's retreat would go on, to Langres if need be, where he would be reinforced by new Austrian forces. If Napoleon pursued, Schwarzenberg would fight. Blücher would march on Paris, hopefully drawing Napoleon to him and away from Schwarzenberg. If Napoleon went after Blücher, Schwarzenberg would then march on Paris. Supporting these operations was the advance of the corps of Wintzingerode and Bülow. They had been taken from Bernadotte's command and transferred to Blücher, and were near Soissons on the banks of the Aisne River, sixty-five miles northeast of Paris. These two corps, added to Blücher's forces, gave the marshal 100,000 men. His force alone outnumbered Napoleon's field army. An army built around a Saxon corps controlled much of the Low Countries.[66]

Bernadotte's army would remain in the Netherlands, part of it blockading Antwerp; he was also to support Blücher if needed. The Allies created a new army under Prince Hesse-Homburg—the Army of the South—to protect Schwarzenberg's line of communications and supply through Switzerland, which were threatened by a French force under Marshal Pierre Augereau. This proved less a danger than the Allies feared. Augereau missed a chance to capture Geneva at the end of February and by March 9 he was pinned up in Lyon and couldn't threaten Schwarzenberg's rear as Napoleon had hoped.[67]

The Allied offensive now resumed, though Clausewitz insisted later that the Allies had simply wasted too much time marching with no purpose. At the time, however, he believed the Allies should concentrate at Troyes and then take the offensive. In line with his orders to first unite all the forces under his command, Blücher marched away from Schwarzenberg's army, moving north to link up with Wintzingerode's and Bülow's 30,000 men advancing from the Low Countries. Blücher expected Napoleon to either strike him or cut his communications, and knew his move would threaten Paris while taking pressure off Schwarzenberg.[68]

Napoleon had little choice but to go after Blücher. He had pursued Schwarzenberg, entering the town on February 24, and then sent troops after the Allies when they marched to Bar-sur-Aube. He blocked Schwarzenberg with troops under Oudinot and MacDonald and set out from Troyes on February 27 to destroy Blücher's Army of Silesia. Napoleon, when going after Blücher, planned also to roll eastward into Lorraine and bulk up his army with units holding his fortresses. He instructed the commanders of the bastions in Alsace, Lorraine, Luxembourg, and Belgium to leave minimal troops in their defenses and move every available man to Nancy. General Nicolas Joseph Maison, the French commander in Holland, was ordered to do the same in Antwerp, Bergen-op-Zoom, Gorcum, Lille, and Ostend. Napoleon hoped to gather 55,000–60,000 men this way, which, combined with his own forces, would give him 100,000. With these he planned to move behind Schwarzenberg, cut his communications, make him retreat, and force him to fight a battle in a hostile country against equal forces commanded by Napoleon himself. But to make this plan work, the French emperor had to first destroy Blücher's army.[69]

When Napoleon set off after Blücher, he believed the Prussian commander only had 70,000 men. Blücher linked up with Wintzingerode and Bülow at Soissons and then withdrew twenty-five miles to Craonne in the face of Napoleon's advance. Here, Blücher fought. His plan to envelope

Napoleon's left flank misfired, and one of his Russian corps fought elements of Napoleon's army through most of March 7, until Blücher ordered a withdrawal to Laon, about ninety miles northeast of Paris. Napoleon pursued, although by now he had given up on his plan to gather troops from his eastern fortresses and only sought to keep Blücher out of Paris. He called for a rising of the French people against the invader on March 5 and hit Blücher again on March 9 at Laon; he had only 37,000 men against Blücher's 100,000. Ten thousand more French troops reached the battlefield during the fight, but this only increased the death toll of the stalemated bloodletting. Clausewitz wrote later that because of the great disparity in numbers, Napoleon had no hope of victory at Laon and "had to count himself lucky that he was not completely ruined there." Blücher counterattacked that night, and physically collapsed from exhaustion. After much contentious egomaniacal activity on the part of the various Russian and Prussian generals in the corps, Gneisenau took command. But he worried about Prussia being betrayed by its allies and spent more than a week doing nothing but foraging. Clausewitz contributed what became essentially two weeks of inactivity by the Army of Silesia to the suspicions of its leaders that they were carrying the burden while Schwarzenberg did nothing, and the leadership vacuum resulting from the breakdown of Blücher's health.[70]

Clausewitz commended Blücher's detachment from Schwarzenberg's army in this instance. "Nothing deserves more praise than in the midst of such conditions to take the decision to depart once again," he wrote in his study of 1814. "Thus, the retreat was inoculated by a new, although weak, principle of the advance. It had an immediate result. Bonaparte felt it, and he pulled back his arm ready to strike in order to parry. Hereupon, the main army stopped." As Clausewitz wrote—and in accordance with their agreed upon plan—when the Allies became aware that Napoleon had left the front of Schwarzenberg's army, they gave up the idea of falling back and went on the offensive. Frederick William proved instrumental in getting Schwarzenberg to act. They attacked and defeated the French forces at Bar-sur-Aube on February 27. Schwarzenberg—on tenterhooks—followed the retreating French. He took Troyes (again) on March 5. His army now stood approximately 100 miles southeast of Paris and about 120 miles south of Blücher's force.[71]

In late February, while the armies of Schwarzenberg and Blücher fought Napoleon, Wallmoden was called to Hanover (which kept Clausewitz

Map 9.5. The Belgian and Dutch Theater.

busy) to help organize the new Hanoverian troops. His force was also reduced. His Russian detachments under Benningsen, as well as some other units, went to cut Hamburg's southern communications.[72] The Legion reunited on February 25, 1814, at Bremen. It was allowed a complement of 7,400 men, but only had 5,508. They then continued their march to the Rhine. Wallmoden also put Clausewitz's name forward for promotion to colonel during this time (March 14). Their corps crossed the Rhine at Düsseldorf on February 14–17. Ten days before, Wallmoden had received orders from Bernadotte to go to Venlo and Maastricht on the Dutch border to observe the fortresses there.[73]

By March 19 most of Wallmoden's forces cantoned at Masseik, Belgium, on the left bank of the Meuse, south of Roermonde. Because of detachments and casualties, Wallmoden's entire corps now only numbered roughly 7,400 men. Some of Clausewitz's letters to Marie during this period almost give one the sense that he has become part of a heavily armed tour group. He remarks upon the beauty of the Dutch and Belgian villages, comments upon the furniture in the rooms where he stays, and says of the French food that "what should have been sweet was sour, and what should be neither was both at the same time." Clausewitz was always a determined observer. The area also reminded him of his time in France as a prisoner. "I am an odd person with respect to the past," he told Marie. "I love dwelling on it, even if it wasn't good for much."[74]

Clausewitz's letters also express disappointment with the success of the campaign, his as well as that of the Allies. "We could have helped Blücher so much more," he told Marie. Except for Antwerp and some of the forts, the greater part of what is now Belgium and the Netherlands was already in Allied hands. Moreover, they were about to march to help the British besiege Antwerp. A larger issue worried him as well: he had heard that the Austrians would not agree to Napoleon being deposed. He branded this an "unfortunate weakness," believing the war had no hope of an end otherwise.[75]

He lamented that Blücher's victory over Napoleon at Laon on March 9 had produced no great result, though he thought they had little to fear because they kept winning, they were consuming the enemy's resources, and Napoleon had little hope of pushing more forces to the theater than the Allies. Clausewitz also noted that Bernadotte was angry because the Allies had taken some forces from him, and threatened to leave the alliance. Clausewitz realized the Allies' success did not depend upon Bernadotte, but he feared that if Bernadotte followed through on his threat people would read it as the first step in the dissolution of the coalition. "So I can write to you of nothing but trouble, poor Marie," he concluded the letter, though he added that "it would be foolish to hold all of the apprehensions of our anxious minds as sureties. How rare it is that things turn out in the world as one imagines."[76]

Wallmoden's corps was ordered to join General Graham at Mechlen. They marched from Masseik on March 23, arriving at Louvain on the 27th. Here they received an urgent call to rush to Brussels to defend it and its 1,500-man garrison against a detachment of what was believed to be 8,000 men under the very experienced French general Maison. When the call for reinforcements arrived at Wallmoden's headquarters, the general was not there. Clausewitz took it upon himself to order up the support. "Fortunately," he wrote later, "Count Wallmoden arrived on the day of departure and authorized everything." Wallmoden reported the events to Field Marshal Curt von Stedingk in Bernadotte's headquarters in Liège. Bernadotte wasn't there as he had gone to the Allied headquarters. Stedingk, realizing the impression that would be conveyed if Brussels fell while 25,000 Swedish troops sat in their camp, moved a division to Louvain to support Brussels. Bernadotte, when he returned, sent his entire army on the march to the city.[77]

Maison had marched from Lille on March 24 with a little more than 5,000 men. Despite what the Allies thought, Maison had no intention of taking Brussels. He masked Alost with a demonstration, and on the 30th made a quick march to Courtrai (Kortrijk), drove the small Prussian detachment from the city, temporarily took Oudenarde, and took Ghent on March 26. He was then able to link up with a division that sortied from Antwerp on the 28th, adding 4,500 men to his strength. Johann Adolf von Thielmann was dispatched to follow him. Thielmann seized upon the apparent immobility of Maison on 28 and 29 March to suggest he move to attack Maison in the rear while Wallmoden moved to hit his front. Wallmoden rejected the plan, and Saxe-Weimar (with whom Goethe observed the siege of Mainz in 1793), Thielmann's commander, vetoed it because it was too risky and told him to stay in Oudenarde. Thielmann obeyed, but still sent an officer to Wallmoden at Aalst on the afternoon of March 29 to try to win his assistance for the move. Wallmoden suggested they instead unite their forces at Oudenarde on the 30th and act against Maison together the next day. Thielmann said the roads were too bad and insisted upon his idea.[78]

Maison left Ghent on the morning of March 30 in two columns, pushing aside outposts of enemy forces they met along the way, and put his divisions in Courtrai and Harlebeke. Wallmoden told Thielmann on the 30th that he was leaving Alost that evening to join with him at Oudenarde (Audenarde) so they could link up and fight Maison together, and that he would arrive at Oudenarde early on the 31st at 10 or 11. Thielmann worried that the lag time would allow Maison's escape. The French had marched from Ghent to Courtrai and could be under the guns of their fortresses in two marches. Thielmann refused to wait. He departed Oudenarde on the evening of the 30th and unsuccessfully attacked Maison the next morning at Courtrai. Thielmann suffered heavily, with more than 250 killed, approximately 450 wounded, and nearly 1,200 prisoners or missing.[79]

Clausewitz considered Thielmann's attack "reckless." Thielmann only had 6,000 men to face what the Allies thought were 8,000 French (Maison actually had closer to 9,500), and even wondered if it was not an act of vanity on Thielmann's part. "The troops mostly fought very poorly," Clausewitz wrote of Thielmann's men. They retreated back to Oudenarde—pursued by Maison—at the same time as Wallmoden's units arrived. "We just had time to draw up our troops on the other side of the city to cover his retreat through the city.... Fortunately," Clausewitz continued, "General Maison only pursued about half way and then turned against Tournai." Wallmoden's corps had only reached the area with six battalions and Clausewitz believed the sight of Thielmann's defeated force would potentially have had a very bad effect on their men. Maison pursued Thielmann to Tournai, then retreated to Lille, having successfully collected a division from Antwerp, as well as allowing another from the garrison of Avelghem to reach Lille unmolested.[80]

What worried Clausewitz the most about the entire situation with Maison was the potential impact upon the reputation of Wallmoden's force, and thus himself. They had feared a fight against Maison, whom Clausewitz believed at the time had 12,000 men, with their much reduced force, one that they believed must inevitably end in defeat. "It would have been said once again," he wrote Marie, "'Wallmoden's corps has lost a battle.'"[81] Sehestedt was the only battle they had lost, but this weighed heavily on Clausewitz's mind.

As Clausewitz waited for others to decide his future, Napoleon—as always—remained determined to create his own. The Emperor withdrew from Laon on March 10, but on March 13 surprised and successfully attacked an isolated Russian-Prussian division at Reims. The victory stunned the Allies. Blücher abandoned his advance and retreated back to Laon. Schwarzenberg, who was crossing the Seine, stopped. Napoleon left 20,000 men to guard Blücher's 100,000. A French force of 20,000 blocked the advance against Paris of Schwarzenberg's now 122,000-man force to the capital's south. Napoleon, with only a little more than 20,000 men, marched south to try to strike Schwarzenberg's communications. Schwarzenberg's army fell back toward Troyes, but his forces were strung out over eighty miles. Clausewitz later criticized Napoleon's course of action, particularly the fact that it did not protect Paris. "This move was, therefore, a mistake, as is everything one does without a definite plan."[82]

Napoleon's forces met Schwarzenberg's at Arcis-sur-Aube (about 100 miles east of Paris) on March 20. Napoleon, though he had intended to cut the communications of both Schwarzenberg and Blücher, instead found himself entangled with Schwarzenberg's main force because Schwarzenberg had unexpectedly reversed his withdrawal southward to Troyes, turned north, and attacked the advancing French. A two-day action around nearby Torcy followed. Napoleon eventually brought 28,000 men to fight against the 80,000 Schwarzenberg brought to the field. Heavily outnumbered, and aware that his expected reinforcements would never arrive, Napoleon retreated.[83]

Clausewitz argued that Schwarzenberg's decision to attack the French at Arcis on March 20, 1814, was "indisputably . . . the best and most audacious thing that Schwarzenberg did during the entire campaign." He believed this because the information the Allies possessed stated that Napoleon had perhaps between 50,000 and 60,000 men, which the Allies could oppose with at a minimum of 80,000. "Such a narrow superiority was until then unheard of." Despite the boldness of Schwarzenberg's move, however, "this battle also turned out to be inconclusive."[84]

On the evening of March 22, some Cossacks in Blücher's army captured a note revealing Napoleon's plans to attack Schwarzenberg's lines of communication. Since they knew they could not turn the army around quickly enough to stop Napoleon from getting into their rear, they kept to their plan: uniting Blücher's and Schwarzenberg's armies and attacking Napoleon. On March 24, after reading some other captured dispatches about the poor morale of Napoleon's army and Paris's empty arsenals and depots, Alexander met with three of his generals and asked whether they should attack Paris or chase Napoleon. General Toll, Clausewitz's old superior, advised taking the city. This was probably what Alexander wanted to hear. Alexander convinced Frederick William and Schwarzenberg. They would send the main force against Paris, while screening Napoleon with a substantial cavalry force, a decision Clausewitz, in his history of the campaign, deemed "splendid."[85]

On March 25 Alexander ordered an advance on Paris, regardless of the risk. Schwarzenberg pushed aside the French forces blocking their advance, and pushed on to Paris's outskirts. Blücher also marched on the French capital. Napoleon did not discover until the 27th that the Allies had fooled him. On March 29 the order went out to the Allied forces to be prepared to assault Paris the next day. Not all went as planned, and the initial assault lacked the strength the Allies intended. Only at 3:00 p.m. were all the units aligned; the full-scale attack began. Paris's commander, Marshal Marmont, saw the pointlessness of continued resistance. In the pre-dawn hours of

March 31, 1814, Marmont concluded an armistice with the Allies and marched his troops out of the French capital.[86]

"This march into the blue," Clausewitz wrote of Napoleon's attempt to cut up Schwarzenberg's lines of communication, "was indisputably the worst thing that Bonaparte did in the war, and its consequences have indeed shown this. The Allies marched unified on Paris, and Bonaparte's circumvention showed its ridiculousness in that he immediately turned towards there, marched day and night, and still arrived around 24 hours too late."[87]

On the same day the Allies attacked Paris—March 30—Wallmoden's men reached Brussels. They moved on to Leuze and Ath in April to observe Condé. Near Ath, Clausewitz learned that Paris had fallen, and was convinced that the war would soon end. Always ambitious, and still anxious about the fate of the Legion, he had investigated entering Dutch service, but found the Prince of Orange insufficiently anti-French. The czar had promised in mid-March that the Legion would remain in Russian service until the end of the war. Afterward they could enter the service of any German prince, which gave him some confidence in the future. He had also heard from Stein that Prussia would likely take the Legion, but he had no surety of this. "Despite all the difficulties associated with it," he wrote Marie in early April 1814, "I would still like to re-enter the Prussian service again, I still cannot do it without having offered the king the free choice of my service or dismissal. And thereupon the latter can easily result." Despite this uncertainly, he wrote, "I am still not concerned for my future; I know not whether it is recklessness or reason, but it is the proud knowledge to have something to do with the fact that I have still not merited being cast out and rejected by all armies."[88]

On April 4, 1814, Napoleon abdicated the throne. Clausewitz wrote to Marie of his dissatisfaction with how the war had ended. "Bonaparte is as tough as a Jew and just as shameless. But in general it is surely an injustice to not have given him personally the final blow." He also received word that the Legion would enter Prussian service, though the arrangements were not final. This presented a personal issue for Clausewitz: the king was accepting the entire Legion into Prussian service, but Clausewitz wanted something more specific in regard to his own fate. He sent Marie a copy of the letter on this he intended for the sovereign. He mentioned the good fortune of the Legion to be taken into the king's service, but he recalled Frederick William's verdict of the year before to not take him back and believed it his duty to ask for a special decision regarding his own reentry into Prussian service. "It is against my sentiments to sneak back into your Majesty's army with an entire corps," he wrote. And if he was not fortunate enough to be considered worthy of serving the king on his own merits, he had no choice but to endure the "unavoidable evil" of resigning from the Legion. If Frederick William did not take him back, Clausewitz insisted he would find another position, possibly in Holland. "'The race is not to the swift,' the Bible says," Gneisenau wrote in a letter to Marie. The general believed the Legion would enter Prussian service and the only issue would be what rank Clausewitz received. "His talents will sooner or later carry him to his deserved rank," he said.[89]

After the surrender of the French positions in Belgium and the Netherlands, the Russo-German Legion marched to a cantonment on the Rhine. On July 19, 1814, the Legion was sent to Liège and became part of Thielmann's 3rd Corps of the Prussian army. Clausewitz, now a colonel, commanded the 2nd Brigade. He was thirty-four years old. On July 22, 1814, King Frederick William officially took the Legion into Prussian service as part of the 3rd Corps of the Prussian army. Clausewitz once again served under the Prussian flag.[90]

10

1815

The Waterloo Campaign

In analyzing strategy the main thing is always to put yourself precisely into the position of the individual who had to take action.

Late October 1814 found Clausewitz on the Rhine at Königswinter, south of Bonn, still with the Legion, and still worried about its fate—and his own—enough so to ask Hermann von Boyen, the Minister of War, to leave them on the Rhine and not allow them to be put under the command of Yorck or Bülow because both of these officers had in the past spoken ill of the Legion. In December Gneisenau told Clausewitz that they faced many difficulties in the postwar reorganization of the army and sought to reassure his younger friend by telling him: "the Minister of War has plans that he has not yet brought forth, but that he is thinking of pushing through despite the difficulties facing you. From what I know of your wishes, these should correspond quite similarly."[1]

But the uncertainty of his position frustrated Clausewitz. By late December he was calling himself "the provisional commander of what is itself a provisional Legion," having become commander of its two brigades sometime in October. With Marie he took the waters at Aachen, a common practice when his health troubled him, as it did much of that winter of 1814–1815. His visits to other places included Mainz, where he had fought as a child. At Aachen he learned from Boyen that there had been no movement in Berlin regarding his fate. "I see quite clearly that the king's grudge against me has not lessened," he told Gneisenau, and hoped Boyen found him a not too unpleasant post. The combination of health problems and the future of his career weighed upon him. He found his situation "insipid."

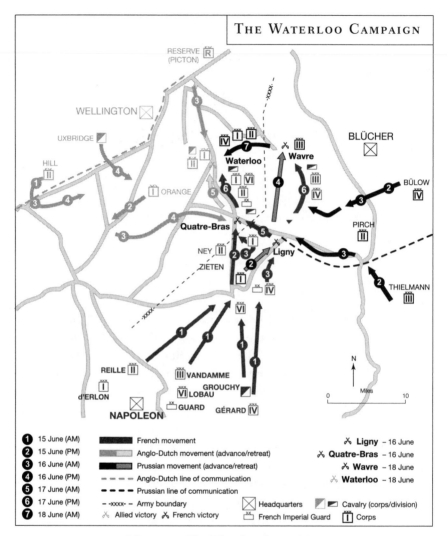

Map 10.1. The Waterloo Campaign.

The joy of his life with Marie made all else bearable, but he confessed to
Gneisenau in February 1815 to being "pretty gloomy" and "quite anxious
for my future, when I consider that a military reputation for me shall no
longer bloom, and no such sphere of activity shall arise from which any such
creation could arise, that in the direction in which the light of the Prussian
state is cast, I will stand there as a figure without light and shadow."[2]

Napoleon, however, was about to give him one more chance. In
February 1815, as Clausewitz cooled his heels at Aachen, representatives

of all the powers met in Vienna to remake the Europe that the French Revolutionary and Napoleonic Wars had created. The events of early March shocked the Allies from their victorious reverie: The "Corsican Ogre" had escaped from exile in Elba. On March 1, 1815, Napoleon landed in southern France. The troops sent to arrest him instead rallied to his banner. Napoleon marched north. Other army units defected. The frightened Bourbon king, Louis XVIII, fled Paris. By March 20 Napoleon once again ruled France.[3]

Napoleon's new regime had no hope of survival unless the other Great Powers agreed to let him rule, but they feared and distrusted him far too much to simply watch him ride back into Paris. Napoleon also immediately antagonized his former enemies. He publicly claimed he only wanted peace, but immediately prepared for war. He called on the French people to follow him once more to glory, tried to rally former Allies to his banner, and pled for soldiers who had served under him—even those now in other lands—to march in his regiments once again. He even planned an uprising in France to throw off foreign and Bourbon shackles.[4]

The Allies quickly moved against their old nemesis. On March 13 they declared him an outlaw. Twelve days later they renewed the alliance of the year before and determined to overthrow him. The British agreed to foot much of the financial bill for the war and the armies began their march against France. The diplomats in Vienna went back to work and concluded the conference before their troops entered combat against Napoleon's forces in June.[5]

Napoleon built a new army of 284,000 men, with a field force of 128,000. He tried to break up the coalition by revealing to the czar a copy of a secret January 1815 Allied-Bourbon agreement to counter the czar's sway over Poland. But Alexander feared Napoleon more, and the coalition remained firm.[6]

The numbers were against Napoleon from the start. The Allies had the potential to raise nearly a million men to fight France. They quickly assembled an English, German, Dutch army of 92,000 under Wellington near Brussels. A Prussian army of 121,000 under Blücher stood not far away around Namur. Schwarzenberg marched via Alsace with 225,000 men, 168,000 Russians trailing behind him. In Italy, Murat had changed sides yet again. The Austrians sent 25,000 men to face him, and another 60,000 to invade the south of France. The Spanish and Portuguese prepared to cross the Pyrenees to add their numbers to the troops already on the move. The Allies intended to first defeat Napoleon's army in Belgium; then the forces of Wellington, Blücher, and Schwarzenberg would drive on Paris. Barclay de Tolly's Russians would follow up the main push, while another force aimed at Lyon.[7]

Nonetheless, much of this was theory. Only Blücher's and Wellington's armies were in the field in late May 1815. The Austrians could not reach the Rhine until July and the Russians would take even longer. Blücher and Wellington met at Tirlemont (today Tienen, Belgium, about thirty miles east of Brussels) on May 3 and decided to unite their armies along the line from Quatre-Bras eastward to Sombreffe, with Wellington anchoring the west. This would block Napoleon's route into Brussels and toward the Rhine. The Prussians also planned to defend the Sambre River crossing north of Charleroi, forward of Quatre Bras, and had troops in the area to do so. If they could not defend the crossings, they were to retreat eastward to Gosselies.[8]

Napoleon had two choices in how to conduct the war. He could stay on the defensive, buying time to raise more troops, while the Allied forces did the same. Or he could strike at the two armies already in the field, hoping successful blows here would produce political results, or at least further military opportunities. Napoleon, of course, chose the latter. One factor feeding this decision was the discovery by French intelligence of the tensions between the British and Prussians. Their differences had resulted in each army having a distinct line of communication. That of Wellington's army stretched from Brussels, to Ostend, then across the English Channel to home. Blücher's ran from Liège, eastward into central Germany. Napoleon saw in this an opportunity. If he moved quickly enough, and struck before the enemy united their forces, he could defeat one foe and then turn on the other, using his central position to defeat them in detail. Napoleon launched into Belgium, hoping to quickly smash Wellington and Blücher, conscious of the psychological effect a victory would have on both the Allies and the French populace.[9]

By mid-March, soon after Napoleon's escape from Elba, Clausewitz had already begun commenting to Gneisenau upon the French emperor's options and analyzing his actions. He believed a route open to Napoleon was a quick march into the Rhineland to reawaken the allure of conquest. He thought the Allies should act immediately, concentrating all the troops in Belgium and the Rhine on the French border and immediately marching for Paris. He believed 80,000 men could decide now what could later demand a year of the nation's effort. He also asked Gneisenau not to leave him behind to prepare the Legion, which needed another 3,000 men to be useful. Far more important to Clausewitz was fighting this new war wearing Prussian blue. His situation stung his pride. "I must also ask about a definite place in the army and a uniform. To participate in the campaign as a Prussian officer in a Russian uniform," he wrote his old friend, "would have the appearance that the king could not overcome his reluctance to see me in his army; it would throw a ridiculous, disdainful light on me to which I would not expose myself under any circumstance." His fate depended upon Gneisenau, and he told him so. On March 30, 1815, Clausewitz was reinstated in the Prussian army as a General Staff colonel.[10]

Clausewitz remained on the staff of the 3rd Corps as the Prussian army mobilized for yet another war against Napoleon. Despite his pleas to be done with the Legion, which was part of the 3rd Corps, Gneisenau ordered him to form a regiment from its men. Part of Clausewitz's discontent with the unit resulted from the Saxons who now primarily filled the Legion's ranks. Prussia had occupied and then acquired much of Saxony in the peace, and Clausewitz had written to Gneisenau in December about their near rebellion. They remained troublesome, so much so that Clausewitz reported to Gneisenau that he feared swearing them in would cause more difficulty than they needed, so he had decided to forgo their oaths until he received further orders. Clausewitz was right to worry: some of Blücher's Saxon troops rebelled in May.[11]

Clausewitz now asked Frederick William to assign him to a line infantry unit. The king refused Clausewitz's specific request on May 15, but he also remarked that he had confidence that Clausewitz would serve well in the post he would give him.[12]

When Frederick William's official ruling came down, Clausewitz was already in Bastogne, in what is now Belgium (and later, of course, the epicenter of the German Ardennes offensive at the end of 1944). Because of Boyen's intervention, he found himself chief of staff to Lieutenant-General Johann Adolf von Thielmann, the commander of the Prussian 3rd Corps. Clausewitz enjoyed his new appointment. "General Thielmann is exceptionally kind to me," he wrote Marie. He found the others in the headquarters interesting and clever, "so we laugh a lot and are tolerably cheerful."[13]

Thielmann, like many of the senior officers of the Napoleonic era, had fought both for and against the French. He began his career in his native Saxon army as a cadet in 1780, and his many combat actions included fighting at Jena in 1806 against the French as an ally of Prussia. He led a Saxon cavalry brigade in the French army at Borodino in 1812, and in 1813, he commanded the fortress of Torgau. When his king ordered him to turn it over to French control, he obeyed, resigned, and then took service under the Russian flag and fought in the 1813 and 1814 campaigns, eventually commanding the 3rd German Corps in the Low Countries, where Clausewitz encountered him in 1814. Prussia annexed about half of Saxony, and he moved to the Prussian army in March 1815. The Saxon revolt of May placed him—temporarily—in a quite uncomfortable position. When the campaign began, Thielmann's corps had 24,143 men.

They soon moved into quarters near Namur, and Clausewitz wrote Marie from there on the 17th. He was fortunate enough to see his brother Wilhelm, who was also in the field. Clausewitz's gout (or arthritis, or possibly Lyme disease) plagued him solely in the mornings, and he had only once had to resort to opium to deal with the pain. His aversion to the drug pleased him immensely. What amazed him even more was the state of the army in which he now served. "When one now sees the Prussian army, one cannot get over the surprise at its change since 1794. When I think back to those camps, and recall again all the camp ceremonies, which I have not seen for 21 years, I am glad to see now realized in the army what was then the subject of my youthful plans and wishes." The impressive changes Clausewitz witnessed in the army made him think of Scharnhorst, who had worked so hard for military reforms: "I don't know how far we would have come in all of these things without Scharnhorst, but one can't see all of this and not continually think of him." He also wrote to Marie that, among other changes, "now regular morning and evening prayers are held, which are very solemn and not an empty ceremony. If I should praise something like this, it must have deep meaning."[14]

On June 15 Clausewitz wrote Marie from their camp at Ciney, a few miles southwest of Namur and about fifty-five miles southeast of Brussels, where they had been for a month. "During the night we received a rather sure report of Bonaparte's arrival in Mauberge on the evening of the 9th. These give the reports of an approaching offensive some likelihood."[15] Clausewitz was about to fight his last campaign.

Napoleon had concentrated his forces in the area around Beaumont in what is now Belgium, about fifty miles south of Brussels. Through tight security measures and good staff work, the French did this quickly and without their enemy being fully aware.[16] The Allies had two armies to face the French: the Anglo-Dutch force commanded by Sir Arthur Wellesley, Duke of Wellington, and Blücher's Prussians.

Napoleon roused his troops at 2:00 a.m. on June 15 and began marching toward Brussels. He had decided to first hit the Prussians because he believed Blücher would advance faster than Wellington. Napoleon hoped to attack before the enemy could concentrate their dispersed forces, though the details of his plan would change with the circumstances. His reserve was at Charleroi, and the two columns of his army aimed at Frasnes-lez-Gosselies and Fleurus, respectively northeast and northwest of Charleroi. The opening blows of the 1815 campaign landed in the small area between Charleroi and Brussels.[17]

The Prussians had had reports of campfires around Beaumont, but Napoleon still managed to catch both Wellington and Blücher off guard. The Prussian advance forces were commanded by Lieutenant-General Hans von Zieten. "Thus," Clausewitz wrote in *On War*, "the first Prussian Corps, under General Zieten, numbering about 30,000 men, faced Bonaparte with 120,000 men; yet, on the short stretch from Charleroi to Ligny—a bare ten miles—it was able to gain more than twenty-four hours for the concentration of the main Prussian army. General Zieten was first attacked about nine in the morning of 15 June, and the battle of Ligny did not begin until about two in the afternoon on the sixteenth. General Zieten admittedly did suffer heavy casualties.—5,000 or 6,000 men killed, wounded and taken prisoner." Napoleon pushed away the Prussian screen as he advanced, and the enemy began to react as Clausewitz said. Wellington and Blücher had agreed to concentrate three Prussian corps at Sombreffe, and by late on the 15th, Blücher began implementing the Allied plan. This put Blücher at risk, as he was concentrating in the face of an aggressive and powerful foe, but Blücher never feared risk. "We quick-marched to Namur," Clausewitz wrote Marie, "arriving in the night. Two hours later, we broke camp and proceeded to Sombreffe," barely a mile northeast of the village of Ligny.[18]

Wellington did not react as quickly as Blücher. He spent most of the 13th at a cricket match with a lady friend. He heard rumors on June 14, and received firm reports of Napoleon being on the march at 3:00 p.m. the next day. Wellington sent a screen of forces west to Oudenarde to protect his lines of communication, fanned out several divisions running eastward from there, gave orders to concentrate two corps at Nivelle, south and west of Brussels, and ordered his cavalry reserve to Brussels. However, he was placing his forces west of Brussels while the Prussians were concentrating to its southeast. Wellington, by increasing the distance between his army and that of his ally, was not following the previously agreed-to plan. A dispatch from Blücher that Wellington received at 10:00 p.m. revealing the Prussian concentration at Sombreffe did not see Wellington alter his orders.[19]

On the 15th Napoleon sent the left column of his army, now commanded by Ney, north toward Brussels. He sent the right column, under Grouchy, down the Fleurus road to take Sombreffe, but Grouchy moved so slowly that Napoleon rode to his camp to push him along. Ney cleared Gosselies, but halted to wait for some other units instead of pushing north to Frasnes. By 8:00 p.m., he had camped for the night and Grouchy's forces soon did the same.[20]

The same day units under the Prince of Orange, one of Wellington's subordinates, occupied the key crossroad of Quatre-Bras. His chief of staff, Baron Jen de Constant Rebeque, possessing a better picture of the situation facing the Allies, then ignored Wellington's order to concentrate at Nivelle. It is fortunate for the Allies that he did. The plan Wellington and Blücher had originally constructed had been destroyed by events unknown to Wellington as the Prussians had been pushed back and Charleroi had already fallen. Executing Wellington's orders exactly would have meant the abandonment of the important Quatre-Bras crossroads. Its possession blocked the French advance and made it impossible for Ney to seize it and then use the road to attack Blücher the next day.[21]

That evening Wellington received more news from Quatre-Bras and Blücher, and deduced what was going on. He also realized Napoleon had stolen a march on him. He ordered a concentration at Quatre-Bras, but knew he could not stop Napoleon there. He chose a fallback position for a second fight—Waterloo.[22]

Napoleon thought that both Wellington and Blücher would retreat in the face of his advance. He now decided to try to strike Wellington first, to—at a minimum—push him away from Blücher. But he needed to keep Blücher out of the way as well. He decided that Grouchy needed to quickly take Gembloux and Sombreffe to cut the line of communications between the two enemy armies. He was to attack any Allied forces encountered, but also stand ready to assist Ney against Wellington. Ney would advance on Brussels once the reserve joined him. Until then, he was to push a division five miles to the northwest of Quatre Bras, put six other divisions in the town, and send another eastward to Marbais to establish communications with Grouchy. But after sending out these orders, Napoleon received word that Blücher was approaching in force and decided to attack him first instead of Wellington. Initially, however, Napoleon had not believed the reports and delayed his concentration against Blücher.[23]

Between 1:00 and 2:00 p.m. on June 16, Blücher and Wellington conferred near the Brye Mill not far from Ligny, Wellington having ridden over from Quatre Bras. Wellington committed to supporting Blücher at Ligny—but with an important caveat: that he himself was not attacked. Blücher expected 20,000 reinforcements from Wellington. In his history of the 1815 campaign, Clausewitz insisted it was risky for Blücher to bet on Wellington's arrival, especially since it hinged on such a dangerous "if." Clausewitz found it "unreasonable to suppose that the duke could arrive in a few hours with his whole army." But he also believed that it was better for Blücher to fight than withdraw because a retreat would have simply put him in a worse position vis-à-vis Wellington while also making "a bad impression on the troops."[24]

Blücher also had one fewer corps than he had planned to have at Ligny. Confusion over the order (and not a little professional vanity) meant Bülow's 4th Corps was not in support. In *On War* Clausewitz criticized Bülow's response: "Blücher, it is true, got news of the enemy's advance and began to concentrate his troops on the night of the fourteenth of June—that is, twelve hours before Zieten was actually attacked. But by nine the following morning Zieten was under fire, and it was not until that very hour that Thielmann at Ciney received orders to move toward Namur. He thus had to assemble his troops into divisions, and then march thirty-two miles to Sombreffe, which he did in twenty-four hours. General Bülow could have been there at the same time if he had been properly impressed by the order." Blücher resolved to fight anyway.[25]

The Prussians deployed in a seven-mile line along the rivulet of Ligny's marshy banks. Zeiten's Corps arrived first, with 32,000 men. Pirch brought about the same number. Thielmann's Corps (with Clausewitz as chief of staff) arrived last, at Sombreffe, around 10:00 a.m. They took up a strong position behind the Ligny, stretching southeastward from Sombreffe, north of Ligny village, where the battlefield hooked eastward along the stream's banks. Colonel von Borcke's 9th Brigade anchored Thielmann's right at Sombreffe and linked with Pirch's Corps. Thielmann put two brigades on the heights of Le Point du Jour, where the highway turned sharply northeast toward Gembloux, as a reserve. Colonel von Kemphen's 10th Brigade

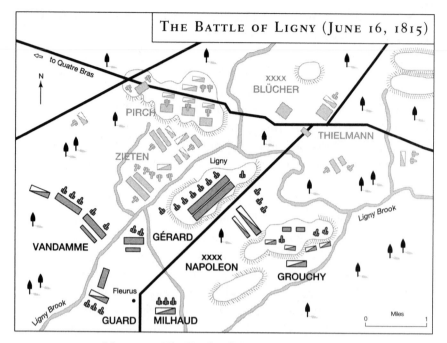

Map 10.2. The Battle of Ligny (June 16, 1815).

held the left wing, with Hobe's cavalry nearby. Thielmann's force raised the Prussian strength to 84,000, including 8,000 cavalry and 224 guns. It was a large front for them as the doctrine of the day prescribed 20,000 men per mile. The Prussians strengthened the position by incorporating at least ten villages into their works.[26]

When he first encountered Blücher's forces, Napoleon thought he faced only a single Prussian corps of about 40,000. His view changed as the day lengthened. Napoleon could tell from Blücher's deployments that the Prussians expected Wellington to arrive on the Prussian right. He thus planned to pin the Prussian left with cavalry, while Vandamme and Gérard hit the center and right, respectively, to try to push the Prussians farther from their allies. Napoleon, like the Prussians, also had some false assumptions built into his tactical plan: Ney would have seized the crossroads at Quatre Bras and would be marching around to attack the right and rear of the Prussian force by six in the evening. He would then destroy perhaps two-thirds of Blücher's army, force the survivors to retreat away from the British, and then turn against Wellington.[27]

At 2:30 the battle began. Grouchy's cavalry moved against the Prussian left (the French right) and Vandamme attacked the center. Vandamme concentrated upon seizing two hamlets, St. Amand and Ligny. This would pin Blücher's forces and force him to use up his reserves to replace his casualties. French artillery tore gaps in the Prussian lines amid brutal fighting for the villages. Ligny hamlet finally fell to the French after their fifth assault.[28]

Napoleon sent two messages to Ney to march to his support, but Ney was entangled with Wellington at Quatre Bras, and at around 3:30 Napoleon received word of this. Also, Napoleon finally remembered that he had a division near Charleroi in reserve and ordered it up. He then probably dispatched another note, ordering Ney to send D'Erlon's Corps. Historians don't agree upon what happened in regard to D'Erlon, but the result was that his troops wandered around between the two battles when their presence could have proven decisive at either.[29]

It was comparatively quiet on Thielmann and Clausewitz's side of the battlefield for much of the day. At 3:00 p.m. Blücher took a brigade of their cavalry, and an hour later a brigade of infantry. But around 4:00 p.m. Napoleon's forces began pushing against the villages of Tongrinne and Boignée that formed the center of Thielmann's line. Later, Gneisenau, who was Blücher's chief of staff, pulled away another brigade to reinforce Sombreffe, where the Prussians repulsed four enemy attacks.[30]

Napoleon had the Guard in position to finish the job at 6:00 p.m., but then he received word of the approach of 20,000 unknown troops on his left. Napoleon paused, waiting until he received solid information on the new force. Blücher, meanwhile, had realized he could expect no help. He plugged holes and stiffened his lines, hoping to hang on grimly until nightfall gave him a chance to withdraw.[31]

By 6:30 Napoleon knew the mystery force was D'Erlon, though he had not received the standard warning of their approach. It turned out to be only a single division of D'Erlon's Corps, however, as the rest of his force had headed back to Quatre Bras. Blücher then counterattacked. Leading the six-battalion assault in person, the seventy-two-year old field marshal retook part of St. Amand from the surprised French, only to then be pushed out by the Young Guard.[32]

Napoleon now committed the Old Guard, one column against each side of Ligny, with sixty artillery pieces in support. By 8:00 p.m. they had broken into Ligny. Gneisenau decided to try to hold the village for another half hour and pushed every man he could find into Ligny. Blücher, mistaking some movement for a French retreat, led a second counterattack, this time at the head of cavalry. At the same time, unknown to Blücher, the French had broken through in Ligny and French cuirassiers, dragoons, and a mounted Guard Grenadier Regiment rode through the gap. The French threw back the Prussian assault. Blücher's horse was killed under him and the injured field marshal was only saved from capture by the loyal exertions of Karl von Nostitz, one of his aides.[33]

At about the same time, around 8:00 p.m., Thielmann believed he could see the French horsemen before him withdrawing and thought they were pulling back. He pushed his remaining cavalry and a horse battery down the road. Thielmann soon discovered he had erred. Some hedges prevented Thielmann's cavalry from forming up, and "Scarcely had these units approached the nearby heights," Clausewitz wrote in his history of the campaign, "when some enemy regiments threw themselves on the two squadrons and took five guns from the horse artillery battery, which had attempted to unlimber its guns instead of turning back. The remaining three guns had time to save themselves." The French attack threw back Thielmann's cavalry. Fortunately for the Prussians, their infantry opened up on the French, allowing the Prussian horsemen to withdraw. Half an hour later the French launched another attack on Thielmann's men that was repulsed by Captain Pochhammer's *Landwehr* battalion.[34]

After Blücher's incapacitation, Gneisenau took command and organized the Prussian withdrawal. Knowing Blücher's desire to maintain his communications with Wellington, Gneisenau sent the army north. Napoleon had destroyed the center of the Prussian army, but the left and right wings held together and the darkness gave them a chance to withdraw. Between the battle and desertions during the night, the Prussian army lost 25,000 men. The French probably had between 8,000 and 12,000 killed and wounded. Napoleon did not order the customary pursuit; he did not know the whereabouts of Bülow's Corps, nor did he have news from Ney. He also assumed the Prussian force no longer posed a significant threat. But this was not the Prussian army of 1806; this was Scharnhorst's new machine. Napoleon also did not count upon Blücher's tenacity; he should have recalled his experience with the Prussian commander the previous year.[35]

In his history of the 1815 campaign, Clausewitz criticized the use of Thielmann's Corps in the battle. He believed that one of the reasons for Napoleon's continual victories was the emperor's habitually judicious use of his reserves, which meant he had troops ready to commit at the decisive

moment. Other than draw away a few of Thielmann's units, Blücher generally ignored Thielmann's 3rd Corps during the battle when, Clausewitz
argued, he could have used it as his reserve. But as is typical with Clausewitz's
analysis, he also saw the other side, arguing that there were advantages in
preserving Thielmann's 3rd Corps. Committing it might have simply used
it up as well. Moreover, the Prussians really needed the added weight of
Bülow's Corps to ensure a victory—and he wasn't coming.[36]

The performance of Thielmann's Corps at Ligny is a point of minor
controversy.[37] Herman von Petersdorff, Thielmann's biographer, is critical
of his subject, and blames Clausewitz: "Nevertheless, the leadership betrays
a certain timidity and great caution. There is nothing directly it can be
criticized for; it was, however, lacking in true command boldness. One
would not be remiss, if one were here to see the influence of the delib-
erate Clausewitz on the usually not-so-timid Thielmann."[38] Petersdorff
offers a caricature of Clausewitz as the methodical, theoretical soldier, a
picture of Clausewitz also painted by the British novelist C. S. Forester
in his *Commodore Hornblower*. As detailed in the last chapter, Clausewitz
was indeed critical of Thielmann's performance in Holland in 1814, but he
simply believed Thielmann assumed too much risk. Petersdorff also forgets
that Blücher was in command, not Thielmann, and thus Clausewitz and
Thielmann did not have the freedom to act with the "audacity" Petersdorff
believed necessary.

As the Prussians and French tore into one another at Ligny, about seven
miles away, Wellington fought Ney. On the morning of June 16 Ney was
south of Quatre Bras at Gosselies. He took his time, issuing his first orders
at 11:00 a.m. His troops did not begin marching until 11:45. He essentially
wasted six hours of daylight, which the Allies used to reinforce Quatre
Bras. The French opened a cautious attack a little after 2:00 p.m. against an
Allied force of about 8,000 with roughly 23,000 men.[39]

What followed was a day-long slugfest as both sides continually brought
up troops and Ney tried desperately to fulfill Napoleon's command to seize
the key crossroads. A vicious back-and-forth ensued. At 5:00 p.m. a desperate charge by French cavalry succeeded in breaking through the British
lines and reaching the crossroads, but Ney did not support them and they
were thrown back. By 6:30, Wellington outnumbered Ney and began taking back most of the ground he had lost during the day. By 9:00 p.m. the
battle had burned itself out. The drawn fight cost the French 4,000 killed
and wounded. Wellington's losses were 4,800.[40]

As for Thielmann's men at Ligny, "Our participation was limited," Clausewitz wrote Marie, "but in the evening, after Thiele [a Colonel on Gneisenau's staff] brought the news that we had been ordered to retreat, and that the retreat was to be toward Wavre—not toward the Meuse but toward Brussels—we found ourselves in a dismal situation. We were cut off from the Field Marshal [Blücher] and had to make our own way. Our fire-fight ended with an unfortunate cavalry affair." He noted that he managed to escape the French cuirassiers "only with great difficulty." In another letter he added: "I and all near acquaintances are well, dearest Marie. For us the battle was the least violent, but Stülpnagel has alone lost 1,200 men of his brigade. The battle is not completely decisive, I hope it comes yet at a happier [moment]—but I am for many reasons very sad."[41]

Many of the men in Blücher's army endured the same confusion mixed with terror as they embarked upon their nighttime retreat. Gneisenau, as Blücher's chief of staff, tried to rally their forces at the miniscule hamlet of Tilly near the Ligny battlefield, but the Prussian army had been too shattered by its defeat to make this possible. When Gneisenau discovered that Blücher had been brought to Mellery, five miles north of Ligny, he joined his master, the headquarters gathered there, and Gneisenau began reassembling the army. He ordered the various corps to bivouac around Wavre, including Bülow's wandering horde, and ordered Thielmann's Corps to Bawette, twenty miles north of Ligny and a mile north of Wavre.[42]

The night of June 16 was harrowing for Clausewitz and his comrades. They marched along a secondary road to Namur, spread among the "countless wagons" of the other retreating corps, in darkness so intense they couldn't use couriers. "I believe my hair turned gray that night," he wrote Marie, "and, apart from the few moments it took to write my report to the Field Marshal, I did not dismount my horse. As always in such cases, the worst did not happen, and before daylight we were able to gather the small band of troops that remained and march to Gembloux. The enemy's pursuit was weak."[43]

By 6:00 a.m. on June 17, Blücher had established his new headquarters in Wavre. At 4:00 or 5:00 a.m. the same day, Thielmann's corps marched from Sombreffe for Gembloux. "At noon on the 17th," Clausewitz wrote Marie, "the weary troops arrived at Gembloux in driving rain after having had to wade through a defile for half an hour in water above their ankles. The only food we had to eat for the next 24 hours was that which a small town of 2,000 inhabitants can give to a corps of 20,000 men."[44]

Clausewitz soon left Gembloux. "At two o'clock we again departed and marched toward Wavre via a detour, because we had to rejoin the Field Marshal's army. Once again a horrible downpour, once again a defile where the tired soldiers had to march along a slippery sunken road in an unceasing struggle." By 8:00 p.m. Thielmann's forces began to reach Wavre, and parts of Bülow's Corps had arrived nearby. "Half of the corps went through the small town of Wavre," Clausewitz recalled, "and arrived in their positions at 1 am. The other half remained on the road in front of the town because the column was constantly bogging down; heavy rain continued the whole night. It was only in the morning that the last of the infantry passed through; the cavalry did so only shortly before the beginning of the battle." The morning of the 18th found Clausewitz in better shape, though not necessarily his men. "The troops had no rations other than meat, yet hardly any time to butcher and cook it. Think what it is like to have to walk for a mile to get wood and water and then be your own cook."[45]

Napoleon took an unhurried approach to the dawning of June 17. But while he enjoyed his breakfast he received news that the Prussians were retreating toward Liège (which was false) and that Wellington still stood at Quatre Bras. Napoleon saw an opportunity to strike Wellington. He sent an order to Ney indicating that he should pin Wellington there until Napoleon brought his forces to Quatre Bras. Napoleon ordered Grouchy's Corps (33,000) to follow Blücher and keep him away from Wellington. He would set off for Quatre Bras himself with 69,000 men. But Napoleon waited until he received Ney's report at 11:00 a.m. before he moved and spent the morning towing Grouchy around the Ligny battlefield.[46]

Ney spent the morning of the 17th in a manner even more relaxed than his emperor. Napoleon arrived at Ney's camp at 1:00 p.m. to find the troops having a leisurely lunch. In an explosive rage Napoleon put Ney's force on the march by 2:00 p.m. and sent D'Erlon's cavalry in pursuit of Wellington. A massive thunderstorm then broke over both armies, inundating the countryside and making it impossible to pursue Wellington cross-country. This enabled Wellington's force to escape and emplace itself over the ridge lying north of Mont-St.-Jean. Napoleon reached nearby La Belle Alliance that night.[47]

When Wellington learned of Blücher's defeat and retreat to Wavre, he decided he had to also fall back. He sent word to Blücher that he would make a stand at Mont St. Jean (directly south of Waterloo)—if he had the promise of the support of two of Blücher's Corps.[48]

Napoleon later received a report of Prussian troops moving on Wavre, but he believed Grouchy would keep the Prussians occupied. He also had a note from Grouchy, alerting him that the Prussians were retreating to Wavre. Grouchy intended to pursue and keep them from Brussels and Wellington. Marshal Soult suggested they order Grouchy to join them. Napoleon dismissed this while also ignoring a report that the two Allied armies planned to unite. He told Grouchy to reach Wavre as soon as possible, driving any Prussians before him, while also extending his communications to make contact with Napoleon's army.[49]

That same morning (June 17), Grouchy's forces were just to Clausewitz's south in Gembloux. The rain that allowed Wellington to slip away after Quatre Bras the day before also impeded Grouchy's efforts to catch the fleeing Prussians. Moreover, Grouchy did not begin his pursuit of the Prussians until 2:00 p.m. on the 17th, as Napoleon kept him busy going around the Ligny battlefield. Grouchy's patrols alerted him to the presence of Prussian units in Gembloux, and to Namur's abandonment, and he pushed Vandamme's Corps northward. His troops entered Gembloux at 7:00 p.m. and Gérard reached the city at 10:00 p.m., but Thielmann's Corps had left five hours before. By this time Grouchy's intelligence had the Prussians retreating to Namur and Wavre, and he sent word of this to Napoleon. He decided he would advance to Sart-à-Walhain on the morning of the 18th and then determine whether to take the road to Namur or Wavre. This put him in a position that made it impossible to stop the Prussians from reinforcing Wellington.[50]

During the night of June 17–18, Gneisenau wrestled with a different quandary. He knew the location of two of his corps, but had no contact with Thielmann and no confirmation that Bülow had received his orders. Wellington had requested two Prussian corps to support him at Waterloo on the 18th, promising to fight if they could join him. If not, Wellington planned to retreat to the Antwerp fortress. Gneisenau was also missing his army's ammunition wagons, which reached Wavre at five in the evening on the 18th. Shortly before midnight, Gneisenau received another note about Wellington's decision to fight at Waterloo. Blücher and Gneisenau discussed this for an hour and over Gneisenau's objections Blücher promised to send three corps. Wellington had word of this by 2:00 a.m. As Clausewitz wrote later, "This decision by Blücher is unquestionably worthy of the highest praise. Ignoring all the false courses of action that traditional practices and misplaced prudence might have suggested in such a case, he followed his common sense and decided to turn toward Wellington

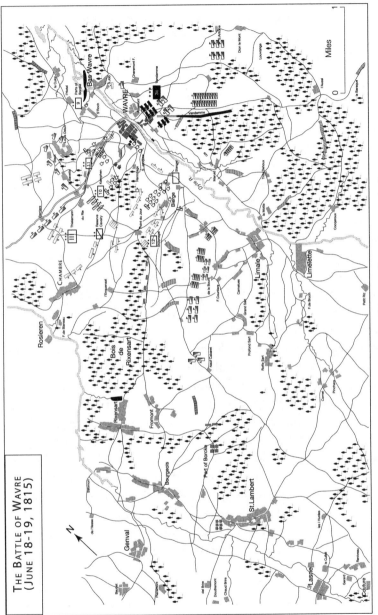

Map 10.3. The Battle of Wavre (June 18–19, 1815).

on the 18th, preferring to abandon his own line of communications rather than adopt half-measures."[51]

At 6:00 a.m. on the morning of June 18, Grouchy sent a note to Napoleon saying that the Prussians were either retreating to Brussels (due north of Waterloo) or marching to Wellington's side. Napoleon probably received this note by 10:00 a.m., revealing the likelihood of having to face the Prussians that day. When Grouchy reached Sart-à-Walhain, he sent another note that the emperor probably received by 2:00 p.m. indicating that four Prussian corps were marching toward Brussels and relaying a gathered account of a conversation from Prussian officers about their joining Wellington. Grouchy intended to have his troops assembled at Wavre by evening.[52]

At 11:30, as he was having breakfast, Grouchy and his staff heard cannon fire in the west. General Gérard wanted to march to the sound. Grouchy brushed him off, announcing they would follow the emperor's orders. This has long been considered one of the most controversial of the French decisions made during the Waterloo campaign. Grouchy is often vilified for not doing what many critics of the battle insist was obvious. Historian Peter Hofschröer, however, argues that the topography facing the French marshal, particularly the flooded Dyle and the muddy roads, made it very unlikely that Grouchy could have arrived in time to help Napoleon. Clausewitz defended Grouchy's decision by deeming the principle that "the commander of a detached column should always head in the direction where heavy firing signifies the crisis of a decisive battle...hastily fabricated." He believed it only applicable if the commander of the detached column had no clear task and would otherwise be merely marching around purposelessly. "But to demand of Marshal Grouchy that he should have taken no further notice of Blücher, but instead should have marched to where another part of the army was fighting a battle against a different enemy, would have been contrary to all theory and experience.... he who does not bear the responsibility for a decision should not be too emphatic in formulating it."[53]

At 7:00 a.m. on June 18, Bülow's Corps began marching through Wavre on the way to Waterloo. They had missed Ligny and were in the best shape of the Prussian units, thus Gneisenau selected them to lead the Prussian advance. Pirch's Corps followed, then Zieten's. Initially, Thielmann received orders to wait for further instructions, but Clausewitz learned from a conversation with his old friend Grolman, now a general, that they would be ordered to either defend Wavre or serve as the rearguard. Thielmann's Corps, because it was in the second-best condition, was designated the rearguard and told to stop any French force that appeared. If one did not, they were to march to Placenoit after the rest of Blücher's army. "Our corps remained behind to observe the position at Wavre," Clausewitz wrote Marie, "in other words to defend the Dyle, thereby covering the road to Louvain, along which the Prussian army would retreat in the event of a defeat. Initially, there was little activity near Wavre, and we had begun our march toward the main body of the army to serve as a reserve force. However, the appearance of a strong enemy formation near Wavre forced us to turn back." Elements of their 9th Brigade and the 2nd Corps's 8th Brigade, who were on the Dyle's left bank, were in what Clausewitz termed "a lively engagement." Thielmann decided to fight the French at the Dyle crossings and sent word of this to Blücher.[54]

The "turning back" Clausewitz mentioned led to an event that left him puzzled at the time, as well as in his later history of the campaign. Before Thielmann reversed course to stop the advancing French, he had told Borcke, the commander of their 9th Brigade, to station two of his battalions in Wavre as the rearguard and then follow Thielmann's Corps with the rest of his troops. Borcke had Colonel Zepelin protect the bridges with two battalions, one *Landwehr*, that were then reinforced with some skirmishers. Borcke then sent two more battalions (including one with Clausewitz's comrades from the Legion) and some cavalry into southern Wavre via Bas-Wavre because the town was jammed with troops. When Thielmann turned around to defend the town, he gave the order to pull back to the northern bank of the Dyle, but Borcke never received word of this. Borcke, later seeing a column departing Wavre, mistook it for Thielmann's Corps (it was actually from the 2nd Corps), and with the honest intention of obeying his orders, marched off behind it with the rest of his brigade. This was a substantial force: five and a half infantry battalions, a cavalry squadron, and an artillery battery. Neither Thielmann nor Clausewitz, who were watching the French deploy, saw Borcke leave.[55]

Seeing the French build up across the Dyle, Thielmann deployed his men to fight a rearguard action to protect Blücher's advance, something with which Clausewitz had acquired an immense amount of experience in 1806 as well as in Russia. Thielmann, reinforced by some detachments left behind by the 1st Corps, had about 14,000 men. He put the 10th Brigade on the heights northwest of Wavre (his cavalry reserve behind them), the 11th behind the town, blocking the road leading north to Brussels, the 12th southwest of Wavre on the heights near the Bierges mill, and spread the artillery in support. He ranged his skirmishers from Bas-Wavre in the northeast, along the banks of the Dyle southwestward to Bierges. Zepelin

posted two *Landwehr* companies to hold the Bas-Wavre bridge and another
company guarded the bridge at Bierges, its skirmishers out. The troops in
houses cut loopholes in the walls. Clausewitz said that Thielmann intended
these dispositions to maximize the use of his artillery and use as little infantry as possible in the firefight. Also, by keeping his infantry back and in
column, if the French tried to batter their way through, he could hit them
with a massed attack. Thielmann intended his reserve for use against any
flank attack the French mounted.[56]

"Misfortune caused one of these arrangements to fail," Clausewitz wrote
later. As we've seen, much of Borcke's Brigade, which Thielmann intended
to use as his reserve, was gone. "It was not until about 7 p.m., when it was
realized that the reserve might be needed, and a preparatory order was
sent, that it was discovered that General Borcke had marched away instead
of remaining with the Reserve Cavalry." They tried—in vain—to find
Borcke nearby. "General Thielmann let the matter rest," Clausewitz said.
They could hear a deep cannonade in the distance and Thielmann concluded that since the greater issues would be decided under those guns, it
was better for Blücher to have the other brigade.[57]

Clausewitz wrote that Borcke's departure meant Thielmann now faced
Grouchy with only 15,000 men (other sources say 14,000). The French had
33,000. Grouchy also had five times as much cavalry, though he probably
only used 10,000–12,000 men on the 18th. Thielmann sent word to Blücher
that he could not possibly hold against such numbers. He received a reply
from Gneisenau telling him to fight the enemy for every step; the losses to
his corps would be made up by the victory over Napoleon.[58]

The Dyle River cut through the center of Wavre. Two stone bridges in the
center of town—one narrow, the other wide—linked the main part of the
village on the north bank of the river with the suburbs to the south. There
were other bridges—wooden ones—southwest at Limal and Limelette, and
at Bierges just southwest of Wavre where a stone mill bordering the town's
southern edge became a strongpoint for Thielmann's defense. Hills lined
both sides of the river—giving the Prussians excellent sites for their guns—
but those on the French side were even higher. Marshy flat meadows sat
between the hills and stretched south from the town and the Dyle. The
road running south from Brussels to Namur was paved and passed through
Wavre by way of the larger of the stone bridges. The heavy rains and the
river's steep banks made it impassable except by the few bridges.[59]

Thielmann's forces had hardly deployed when Vandamme's men
approached around 4:00 p.m. They immediately began shelling the town,

pushed the Prussian skirmishers out of the suburbs south of the Dyle, and forced their way over the stone bridge against the inferior numbers of Prussian troops. A bloody house-to-house street fight emerged in Wavre as Thielmann fed in more and more men and eventually pushed the French back over the river. The French counterattacked, recaptured the bridge, and fought their way up the main street into the center of Wavre. The Prussians pounded them from the side streets and then drove them back over the bridge with a bayonet attack. Thielmann fed in yet more troops.[60]

Grouchy arrived, spurred by an order to storm the town. He added simultaneous attacks to the north and south of Wavre to Vandamme's assault. The dragoons of Rémi Joseph Exelmans rode to Bas-Wavre in the north, some infantry following. Until 2:00 a.m. they fought with some Prussian militia who were trying to destroy the bridge while the French tried to take it. The Prussian infantry holding the Bierges mill at the south end of Wavre repulsed Étienne Maurice Gérard's attack, badly wounding the general.[61]

Between 6:00 and 7:00 p.m., Grouchy received his orders to march to Napoleon. He sent Claude-Pierre Pajol southwest of Wavre to Limal. They reached it as night descended and found the town and river crossing undefended. Grouchy threw troops over the river, turned them north, and drove them against Thielmann's flank up to the village of Delburg. Clausewitz says they learned of Grouchy's move at around 10:00 p.m. The bridge had been guarded by a battalion of the 2nd Corps, Clausewitz wrote Marie, but it had moved off with its unit and hadn't told them. Thielmann thought Grouchy's attack was merely a detached column, sent Stülpnagel there to block the advance with every unit he could find, and rode to the point of contact himself. "Stülpnagel and his brigade charged with a 'hurrah,'" Clausewitz recalled. A confusing night action now developed, one fought amongst head-high cornfields, deep ditches, and sunken roads. "The enemy held firm and we fell into disarray . . . we had great difficulty in restoring order. This continued until midnight." Thielmann decided there was no point in pushing forward. He pulled his forces back and formed a line stretching from the Bierges mill to the Rixensart Forest. As the night lengthened, the fighting died down.[62]

As Thielmann and Clausewitz stood against Grouchy's push, about twelve miles away the French and Allied armies fought the Battle of Waterloo. The armies drew up on opposing ridges about 1,500 yards apart along 5,000 yards of frontage in an area of only three square miles.

Wellington's troops were arrayed along the ridge road, the village of Mont St. Jean to the rear of his center, La Haye Sainte his most forward post; his left rested on Château Hougomont (which also marked the battlefield's west as tiny Papelotte did its east). Wellington protected his men behind the slope, which meant they suffered less from French artillery and musket fire. The French forces stood on the opposite ridge, with their left across from Hougomont and its orchard, and their right on the village of Frichermont. Napoleon's center rested on the village of La Belle Alliance. His 72,000 Frenchmen faced Wellington's Anglo-Dutch army of 68,000. Together, the two forces brought more than 400 cannon to the fight.[63]

The position Wellington had chosen was in front of the Soignies Forest. He put most of his troops on the reverse slope, as was his practice, placing more of his strength on his right, betting that Blücher would arrive in time to support his left flank. Napoleon intended to break Wellington's center and then build upon his success, but decided to delay his primary attack until 1:00 p.m., after his artillery commander suggested they let the ground dry to get proper ricochet and follow through from solid shot.[64]

Napoleon opened the battle at 11:30 with an intense preparatory artillery bombardment of Wellington's center with eighty massed guns. His main attack on the center was to be supported by a demonstration on his left against Hougomont. Instead of this attack drawing in the British, the French found themselves consumed with taking the position.[65]

Napoleon prepared to launch his attack on Wellington's center when word arrived that the distant mass on the horizon was Bülow's corps marching to Waterloo. Napoleon believed he could break Wellington before the Prussians arrived and set about trying to do so. Wellington's men stopped the assault in the center, however, and replied with a cavalry charge that pushed the French back down the hillside, and then charged the French positions. They met French artillery and cavalry, which drove them back to their lines and cost them a third of their men.[66]

Napoleon ordered Ney to seize La Haye Sainte in Wellington's center. The assault failed, but Ney observed some British artillery wagons leaving the battlefield. He believed this meant a British retreat and ordered his cavalry to attack. Five thousand French horsemen rode into the teeth of the British. The infantry formed squares and the artillery pounded them with canister. They passed through the British lines and the British attacked with their own cavalry, pushing them back to where they had come. The aggressive spirit seemed to grip the rest of Napoleon's cavalry, which launched a second largely unsupported and ultimately futile charge, many of the units doing so without the emperor's orders. Ney eventually followed up with his infantry at 6:00 p.m., but they were bloodily repulsed. He did afterward finally succeed in taking La Haye Sainte, however. His forces gained a toehold on the Wavre road and Ney asked Napoleon for reinforcements.[67]

Bülow, meanwhile, drew up on Napoleon's right, forcing the emperor to commit infantry to slow the Prussians. Bülow pushed the French back to Placenoit, around which a nasty see-saw fight developed that required Napoleon to commit some of the Young Guard.[68]

After Ney's attack, Wellington's center was so thin that he personally took the Brunswick troops there as reinforcements. Napoleon brought up eight battalions of the Middle and Old Guard, and gave them to Ney. But Zieten's Prussian Corps had arrived on Wellington's left, allowing him to reinforce his center. The Guard attacked Wellington's center, unsupported by cavalry, and was rebuffed. Zieten, who now formed a line tying Bülow with Wellington's army, attacked, drove back the French forces before him, and seized the hamlets of La Haye and Papelotte. Wellington ordered a general attack, and the French army simply disintegrated. Clausewitz later wrote of the closing stage of the contest, and particularly the commitment of the Guard, "We can therefore see that Blücher's arrival did not just snatch victory out of Bonaparte's hands, which would have also been the case had Turenne, Frederick the Great, or any other great commander been placed in the same situation. It also provoked the emperor into hurling his forces in helpless rage against Wellington's rocklike stand, shattering them, and thereby placing them in a state of complete disintegration as this remarkable day ended."[69]

The arrival of June 19 found Thielmann's men in a tough spot. Grouchy had four infantry divisions, plus cavalry—twice Thielmann's strength. Grouchy wasted no time using what he had. "The first cannon shots began at dawn," Clausewitz noted later. The French hammered the Prussians with artillery, disabling five Prussian guns. Grouchy then attacked the Prussian right in the Rixenart Forest, where the fighting had stopped the night before. He threw in three infantry divisions supported by cavalry in an effort to push Thielmann eastward and seize the road to Waterloo. "I hurried over," Clausewitz recalled, "collecting as many troops as could be spared. All at once the firefight became very intense, and it lasted until about eleven o'clock in the morning." Stülpnagel's unfortunate men were only 500 paces from their French attackers. "A violent struggle now commenced," according to Clausewitz, "during which the French methodically pushed their four divisions forward under the protection of a large line of skirmishers."[70]

In the midst of this—at 10:00 a.m.—Clausewitz and Thielmann received a message from General Pirch that the Allies had defeated Napoleon at Waterloo. The general perception is that the Allied victory at Waterloo brought the war to an immediate end; it did not. And Clausewitz and Thielmann, though informed that the victory was "brilliant," could not know for sure its scale. Nevertheless, Thielmann cleverly took advantage of what he did know. "He had his troops shout loud hurrahs and show signs of rejoicing," Clausewitz noted, in order to convince the French that if they continued to push they risked being cut off. It didn't work. Thielmann then counterattacked, recapturing the Rixenart Forest on his right, but Grouchy hit them again, throwing them back and also taking Bierges. Pirch also told his comrades that he planned to cut off Grouchy's Corps. "However," Clausewitz recalled, "the locations where he intended to cut them off were so far removed from us that the action promised us no relief. Cut off as we were from the main body of our army as a result of the enemy's flanking maneuver, we were left to our own resources with Vandamme and Grouchy's superior force of 45,000 men against us [there were actually around 33,000]. We expected to be able to hold out for only another hour, and still no General Pirch."[71]

French pressure became so intense that at one point Clausewitz ordered the commander of a *Landwehr* regiment "to defend his position to the last man, and to counterattack the advancing enemy." "In these circumstances," Thielmann wrote in his report, "I decided to quit Wavre and fall back on the main road to Louvain. The Reserve Cavalry covered this maneuver and the corps fell back, without any more losses than the many already dead and wounded, towards St. Agatha-Rode, two hours from Wavre in the direction of Louvain. Here, we took up positions on the left bank of the Dyle with our outposts in Ottenburg. The enemy did not push any further, but deployed...parallel to the Brussels road." The fighting had lasted four hours.[72] Afterward, Gneisenau was satisfied with the performance of Thielmann's Corps and could think of nothing more important for the 3rd Corps to have done. "Without its defense of the Dyle," Gneisenau wrote Clausewitz, "it would have been even worse for us."[73]

By noon on June 19, Clausewitz and his comrades stopped in the vicinity of Achtenrode (St. Agatha-Rode). Clausewitz described their men as "utterly exhausted" and Thielmann refused to push them after Grouchy until they had rested. They also believed Grouchy's rearguard would not pull back until night, "making it impossible," Clausewitz argued in his history of the 1815 campaign, for any pursuit they made to achieve anything significant. Thielmann concentrated his forces at Ottenbourg, and his cavalry vanguard left from there in the direction of Gembloux at 5:00 a.m. on June 20. They arose that morning with the intention of attacking Grouchy's forces before them, but discovered the French gone. Grouchy, after learning of Napoleon's defeat at Waterloo, decided to withdraw to France via Namur. Thielmann pursued, his cavalry taking the lead. They reached Namur within five or six hours, where they attacked some French forces and chased them into the town. Grouchy retreated through Dinant on June 21, pursued now by both Thielmann's and Pirch's Corps.[74]

Clausewitz and Thielmann are sometimes criticized for losing contact with Grouchy's force during their retreat from Wavre, thus making it easier for the French to escape. Whether it was due to the rough terrain, incompetence, or a lack of aggressiveness has never been agreed upon.[75] Colonel Friedrich von der Marwitz, who commanded Thielmann's rearguard on June 19, and was also Clausewitz's brother-in-law, said Clausewitz recommended their retreat from Wavre down the Louvain road, arguing that the more Grouchy followed, the more likely his destruction; they also planned to turn back against the French the moment the enemy stopped. In his memoirs Prussian veteran Ludwig von Reiche recorded a conversation with Thielmann in which the general "pushed most of the blame onto his then chief of staff," Clausewitz. Thielmann said that Clausewitz, who the general insisted always saw things in the blackest light, did not intend for them to stop until they had found a solid position to take up and wait for the enemy's advance. Clausewitz himself, however, makes no mention of any this.[76]

Marwitz, who echoed Thielmann's aforementioned remarks about the troops being fatigued, also introduced a forgotten factor into this argument: the actions of the enemy. Rather than blame the Prussians for failure, Marwitz credits Grouchy for success, noting the French general's superb use of skirmishers—fine enough that he so thoroughly hid the French withdrawal that the Prussians only caught on at dawn the next day, sixteen hours after it had begun.[77]

What we do know—from Clausewitz's aforementioned writing—is that they believed Grouchy had 45,000 men. The morning of Wavre, Thielmann and Clausewitz had about 14,000. They then suffered 2,500 casualties over the next two days and were already short much of Borcke's brigade. From their saddles it looked as though they faced an opponent outnumbering them perhaps four to one, and whose infantry units were regular line regiments, not the *Landwehr* that filled out Thielmann's Corps. One could also certainly insist that it was their duty to keep contact with the enemy; Clausewitz castigated Bernadotte in the wake of the Battle of Sehestedt for acting similarly. The historian Christopher Bassford, however, identifies what really seems to matter in all of this: "It was Clausewitz's corps which—outnumbered two-to-one—held Grouchy's forces at Wavre, contributing decisively to Napoleon's defeat at Waterloo."[78] Clausewitz's actions during the 1813 Battle of the Göhrde and the 1814 Battle of Sehestedt present better—and somewhat clearer—lenses through which to evaluate him as a battlefield commander, or rather as the close advisor to one.

Marie revealed after Clausewitz's death that her husband considered the night of their retreat from Wavre the worst of his entire life. "He lived through great, glorious years," she wrote, "but never had the good fortune of fighting in a victorious battle. The night from the 18th to the 19th June 1815, which the field marshal [Blücher], who spent it pursuing Napoleon, used to call the most beautiful of his life, was among the most terrible for him, after the battle of Wavre."[79] At first this might seem surprising when one recalls Clausewitz's nerve-shattering retreat after Auerstedt in 1806, or the laundry list of horrors he experienced during the 1812 campaign: Borodino, the burning of Moscow, the crossing of the Berezina. But even as a child Clausewitz had been driven by the desire for military success—military glory—and he realized after Wavre that his ambition would never be achieved.

There is perhaps also something else that made this night unbearable for Clausewitz: the shame of defeat and the potential impact of this upon his reputation. We see in his letters after the defeat at Sehestedt that he constructed what one could deem very elaborate reasoning for why they should have been victorious but were not. He blamed the intelligence and of course had told Gneisenau that "Our infantry is fighting badly, Dörnberg does not attack, the Swedes do not come." In late March 1814, during their dance of maneuver with the French general Maison in Belgium, Clausewitz had worried they would be forced to fight Maison's larger force, and that this would result in a lost battle and another injury to the reputation of the corps in which he served. After Wavre he reacted as he did in the wake of Sehestedt: he looked for someone to blame. In a July 15, 1815, letter to Marie—almost a full month after the fact—he says that when General Pirch sent word of the victory over Napoleon at Waterloo he also told them he would come to their support and try to cut off Grouchy, but that Pirch's poorly chosen locations gave them no help and they had to withdraw. In September he sent Gneisenau a copy of Grouchy's after-action report. He pointed out the great number of French forces arrayed against them, but put the blame for Grouchy's ability to cross the Dyle River at Limal (and thus to turn Thielmann's flank) on the shoulders of Lieutenant-Colonel Stengel of the 1st Prussian Corps, and criticized Stengel for not occupying the village and having his forces too far behind it.[80]

The night after Wavre, Clausewitz wasn't concerned with losing contact with Grouchy's force. Instead, he was concerned with why they lost and what it meant for his future, his reputation, and the possibility of fulfilling his deepest ambitions. These things were what truly mattered to him.

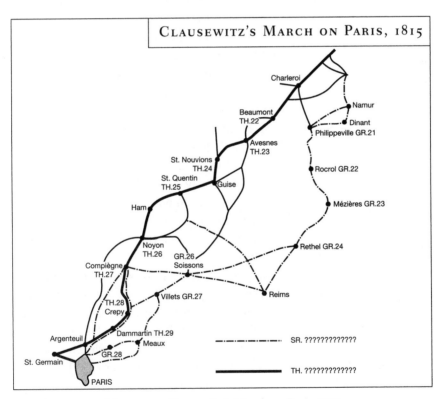

Map 10.4. Clausewitz's March on Paris, 1815

Clausewitz and his comrades now embarked upon a bloody, muddy, and hungry advance into France. After Waterloo, Napoleon sent orders on the night of June 18 for troops from Alsace and the Vendée to mass at Paris. The remnants of the defeated French force at Waterloo began assembling at Philippeville and Beaumont, and then pulled back to Avesnes, which became a rally point.[81]

Blücher and Wellington, meeting after the battle, decided the Prussians would take charge of the pursuit. Gneisenau sent orders on the morning of June 19 to seize a number of key river crossings to try to block the French retreat from Belgium. They also decided upon a combined march on Paris, but Wellington and Blücher adopted different operational approaches to the invasion of France. Wellington waited, considering what course he should follow next, and moved with his supply trains, but Blücher, bent on revenge against France, simply refused to wait. He leapt into France at the head of his army, pushing his men hard, his eyes fixed on Paris. Three Prussian corps led the charge. Two marched on Paris in columns on parallel roads. Thielmann's Corps came behind as the reserve.[82]

Meanwhile, Soult and Grouchy put together an army of 55,000 at Philippeville and by the end of June the French had a field force of 117,000 men in the north. They also had thousands of men in fortresses and 170,000 conscripts being trained. Because they needed to pin the French fortress troops, Wellington's army was soon reduced to only 52,000 men and Blücher's to 66,000. Moreover, French forces scored a victory over the vanguard of the combined Allied army when the Austrians tried to cross the Rhine, and had another success in Piedmont in northern Italy. Napoleon, who had resolved to continue the fight with any forces he could gather, had reached Paris on June 21. But the French political leadership no longer supported him and he abdicated the next day. The provisional government that followed the emperor begged for peace, but the Allies, refusing to take half measures, insisted upon taking Paris.[83]

On June 23 Thielmann resupplied his corps at Avesnes. Two days before, General Zieten's Corps had been shelling the town, a key depot and supply center for the French, when at around 10:00 p.m. they hit the main powder magazine. The explosion wrecked much of the city and the garrison surrendered the next day. Clausewitz witnessed the aftermath. He saw mass burial pits and found "scarcely a window in the entire city." "The explosion was so enormous that two-thirds of the city lay in ruins," he recalled. "I have never seen a picture of such destruction in my entire life.... Entire streets were full of rubble and impassable; in other streets all the roofs were gone. The scene was highly depressing, and I will never forget the impression made on me by a young child, who was looking out the window of such a shattered house and rejoiced at the sight of our troops marching by." Nevertheless, Clausewitz noted that the troops benefited from arriving in this devastated spot. "We have found lots of food, which we have lacked since the beginning of the war."[84]

On June 27 Clausewitz's corps entered Soissons, the city where he had been sent with Prince August after their surrender in 1806. The rapid pace of the Prussian advance into France had such an adverse effect on Thielmann's Corps that Clausewitz began to worry about its coherence and effectiveness. "Since the 20th we have marched 50 miles," he wrote Marie on July 3, plagued by a "complete lack of bread, continual bivouacking, and incessant rain... Our exertions were so taxing that several men shot themselves out of despair; others dropped dead."[85]

Clausewitz continued to write Marie frequently during their march to Paris, always looking forward to their reunion and trying—unsuccessfully—to anticipate when and where they might meet, a hope fueled by expectations of a quicker end to the war than what actually occurred, as Napoleon's defeat at Waterloo and subsequent abdication had not ended the struggle. As is typical in his letters, he often described the beautiful surroundings of their route. From his window at his billet in Dammartin on the outskirts of Paris, he could see "the golden pinnacle of les Invalides," but his gout had flared up, forcing him to take opium to be able to sleep, and none of the beauty he observed kept him from being "gripped by melancholy." "Farewell, dearest soul mate!" he closed one letter. "Hopefully we shall be together again soon.... I feel inexpressibly fortunate, even after such epoch-making events, that I possess something more valuable to me than any triumph, and I eagerly anticipate a moment that will exceed any other. I never love you more than in moments of great fortune or great misfortune. You are worth more to me than any manifestation of the former, and this overshadows any impact that the latter could have on my fate."[86]

On June 28, as the Prussians neared Paris, the Chamber of Deputies—now governing France—declared the capital to be under siege and summoned all former soldiers back to the colors. Other French units were also marching into the city. The Prussians reached Paris the next day. Wellington suggested the Prussians wait for him to move into position, but Blücher had already made his initial moves against the city by capturing the Seine Bridge at St.

Denis. Blücher realized the French had mounted their strongest defense on Paris's north rim, so on June 30 he decided to simply screen the north, march westward, and attack Paris's unprotected southern underbelly.[87]

Clausewitz's corps left Dammartin on June 30 at 5:00 a.m. and pushed on around the French capital. They reached St. Germain in the south at 3:00 a.m., "having covered thirty-two miles in less than twenty-four hours." By July 1 Blücher had concentrated his forces at St. Germain. The next day they marched north. Clausewitz's unit, he wrote later, "advanced through Versailles as far as Plessis-Piquet without encountering a significant enemy force." Wellington arrived on July 2, as Bülow shifted his forces and the ring began to tighten around Paris. The French resisted the moves and Thielmann's men had several firefights before they could take Châtillon. The French requested a cease-fire. Blücher refused; he was not yet in Paris.[88]

Vandamme made an attack against Zieten's Corps on July 3, but the same day saw the signing of the Convention of Paris. Zieten's men paraded through Paris on July 7 and the next day Louis XVIII returned with the Prussian and British armies.[89]

Even after the fall of the capital, fighting for control of various fortresses in northern France continued. Prince August, now a general, had the responsibility for reducing those in the Prussian area of operations. The last, Givet-Charlemont, did not surrender until November 30—ten days after the peace treaty ending the war had been signed.[90]

With France's surrender Clausewitz soon found himself quartered at Fontainbleau as part of the occupation force involved in what today would be termed a "post-hostility operation." He quickly became disenchanted with Prussian policy, or more accurately, the lack of one. As they camped around Paris in the second week of July, Clausewitz could not decipher exactly what it was that the Prussian leaders wanted out of the war. The contempt and bitterness in the manner of the Prussian treatment of the returned Bourbons, as well as the French themselves, struck him as foolish. He believed the Prussians were doing everything possible to make themselves unpopular in the eyes of the French, unlike the English, who "surreptitiously favored the entry of the king, stay in camp, don't impose contributions, and don't plunder." The Prussians also tried unsuccessfully to blow up the Jena Bridge in Paris. "This tragedy became a farce," Clausewitz wrote. He found infinitely distasteful "the position of having a foot on the neck of another" and judged the behavior of the British more noble because they were not driven by retribution and revenge. Simply put, the Prussians were bad winners.[91]

In late July Clausewitz's unit left Fontainebleau to make way for the Austrian occupation troops and marched to Estampes, which lies on the Paris road to Orleans. He found the town of 8,000 a boring place and feared having to spend the entire summer there. He also remarked upon the gullibility of Frenchmen, using the example of the inhabitants of Estampes, who didn't believe Napoleon had actually been imprisoned (he would sail to exile on St. Helena in August). He described them as unbowed, possessed of "a cold pride," and "characterized by a carelessly concealed malice" toward their occupiers. The orders from Clausewitz's superiors made things even less enjoyable. The Prussians were extracting compensation from France for the costs of the war by "squeezing contributions of boots, cloth, etc." from the population. At the end of July they were sent to LeMans.[92] Clausewitz would never have another opportunity to achieve the military glory he had sought so intensely.

II

The Sum of It All (1815–1831)

I think the course of my life will rise once more, a culminating point shall come...

Clausewitz may not have been satisfied with the effects of the 1815 campaign on his career, but his performance as the 3rd Corps's chief of staff during the campaign satisfied General Thielmann. "He fills his post with distinction," Thielmann wrote on the Napoleonic-era equivalent of a modern "fitness report," adding that Clausewitz was "a man of just as much intellectual as moral value and on the general staff is fully in his element." Deep into the autumn of 1815 Clausewitz went to serve as General Gneisenau's chief of staff—a posting that pleased him immensely—and he and Marie, reunited after their long separation, set up in Coblenz, where some of their close acquaintances in the army also landed. In the expanded and reorganized postwar Prussia, Gneisenau commanded the Rhine military district, one of seven in the realm. Clausewitz was a full colonel at the relatively young age of thirty-five, and in August 1816 the government credited to him as time in service the period he wore Russian green.[1]

Clausewitz performed a variety of normal staff duties such as planning and training, but also took up political tasks, traveling, for example, in January 1816 to advise Prussian officials conducting border negotiations with the Dutch. His time with Gneisenau proved short, however. A combination of Gneisenau's petulance and exhaustion, Prussian bureaucratic confusion, and the mistaken belief that the general's past and continued desire for reform betrayed revolutionary tendencies (a broad-stroke brush of a charge that simultaneously colored Clausewitz and others of a reformist bent), led to Gneisenau's July 13, 1816, departure and his replacement by

Figure 11.1. Clausewitz at Age Fifty.
Wilhelm Wach, 1830. Courtesy www.clausewitz.com.

General Albrecht Georg von Hake. This upset Clausewitz and Marie, both of whom enjoyed close relationships with Gneisenau and his wife.[2]

Under Hake's tenure Clausewitz considered himself no better than "a trained poodle," and Marie branded the general as a pedant, and in 1817 Clausewitz told Gneisenau that in Coblenz he and Marie "led a quiet but somewhat insipid life." Hake was very much cut from the pre-reform school of Prussian officers who valued mastery of military minutiae over more substantive activities, and thus not in the camp of the reformers. Arguably, however, one of Hake's biggest sins in the eyes of the Clausewitzes was that he was simply not Gneisenau. Nevertheless, Hake was not without intelligence, as well as an ability to assess those under his command, some-thing made clear by the fitness report he wrote on Clausewitz in 1816. "He expresses himself little," Hake wrote. "I consider him to be a good person. He has a great sense of truth and justice, is generous, full of a sense of honor, perhaps vain, hence, he likes to assert his views. However, he possesses also no negligible amount of military knowledge and was beneficial as a teacher of young officers. His mind especially seeks after ideas." Hake also noted that although Clausewitz's manner was sometimes "a bit rigid, he expects, nevertheless, to be treated with tact. If this is shown to him, then it is easy to get along with him. I have up until now only had cause to be satisfied with him and consider him to be a good general staff officer."[3]

When the administrative director of the Prussian War College in Berlin died in September 1817, Gneisenau put forward Clausewitz as the replace-ment. Clausewitz, however, preferred an appointment as inspector of the *Landwehr* because this would allow him to protect it against its reaction-ary enemies. The king's unwarranted fears that Clausewitz might possess sympathies that leaned too far toward republicanism slowed the standard investigation into the candidate's moral and political character. Many of the Prussian elite still viewed any desire for political, military, or social reform as possible stalking horses for republican government, and those promoting the ideas as bald-faced revolutionaries of the French mode.[4]

Despite his hesitations, on May 9, 1818, the king appointed Clausewitz director of the War College, a change for which he was grateful to both the minister of war and the king. After a short time as commandant of Aachen (Aix la Chapelle), supervising the Congress of the various pow-ers that began there on September 30, Clausewitz returned to where he had taught under Scharnhorst. With the appointment came a promotion to *Generalmajor* (the equivalent to a modern American brigadier general), made official on September 19; this would be his final rank. He and Marie moved to Berlin shortly before Christmas 1818.[5]

The course for War College students had by now been expanded to three years. Clausewitz immediately set about evaluating the curriculum, con-cluding that the coursework too closely resembled that of a civilian uni-versity and thus did not meet the army's needs. Three months later he had readied a reform proposal.[6]

Clausewitz realized that students attending a university had been pre-pared to do so; those coming to the War College had not. He also observed that the university student paid his own tuition and wanted to acquire the skills for a profession; because of this he studied hard. But the military student already had a career and the government was bearing the cost of his education. Because of this the instruction at the War College needed not only to be more rigorous, but also more practical. Clausewitz wanted to narrow the number and variety of classes, decrease the focus on mathematics, and change the manner of instruction away from lectures to classes in which students were forced to react to ideas and concepts, to discuss, think, and function on a practical level useful to the army.[7]

Clausewitz's post made him merely the chief administrator, however; it did not give him the authority to alter the curriculum. And the climate for reform was not conducive. On March 23, 1819, a member of a radical student group murdered a playwright known for his conservative politics. The assassination sparked a reactionary fever in Prussia, one eventually leading to the dismissal of Clausewitz's political patron and ally, Boyen, from his post as minister of war. Reaction, not reform, became the rule.[8]

Whereas the Clausewitz of 1812 would have persevered and challenged the authorities, the Clausewitz of 1819 simply shrugged and walked away. Whether this was from exhaustion, complacency, or perhaps simply the realization that fighting against the entrenched, closed-mindedness of the Prussian bureaucracy was ultimately futile—or some combination—isn't clear. Only the catastrophe of 1806 had made any change possible. Now, Prussia saw no profit in reform. When changes in the curriculum eventually occurred, in 1826, many along the lines Clausewitz had proposed six years earlier, he stayed out of the process.[9]

In any event, there were other compensations. Clausewitz received a number of decorations in the years after Waterloo. On October 2, 1815, he had been awarded the Iron Cross, 2nd Class. The Prussian crown also gave him the Order of the Red Eagle, 3rd Class—a fairly standard decoration—in 1822, and the more prestigious 2nd Class stamp of the same award six years later. Also in 1822, the Russians named him a Knight of the Order of St. Anne, 2nd Class, backdating the award to the summer of 1813. The Russians had also previously awarded him—in December 1816—the Order of St. George, 4th Class, for bravery. Because of these distinctions, as well as, undoubtedly, the distinguished service of his two older brothers in the Prussian army—both ended their careers as general officers—the Clausewitz claim to nobility was confirmed in 1827.[10]

Clausewitz also made a concerted effort to enter the diplomatic service. On May 12, 1819, Gneisenau put forward Clausewitz's name for the position of ambassador to London. Clausewitz had taken a trip to London the year before, possibly laying the groundwork for this effort. For a time it looked as though this would succeed, but a long, drawn-out, multinational affair ensued. The debate over the future of the *Landwehr*—which the reformers lost—did not help Clausewitz's cause. Some of the resistance to Clausewitz on the British side came from the Duke of Cumberland (a son of King George III and the future king of Hanover), who saw Clausewitz as a radical. Sir George Henry Rose, the British ambassador to Berlin, supported the duke. Clausewitz's critics viewed him as having too much sympathy for the forces of democracy and he was suspected (wrongly) of being a member of a secret reform-era subversive group. When he became aware of the difficulties surrounding his appointment, Clausewitz made a verbal offer to withdraw, but it wasn't accepted. Nonetheless, all of this conspired to kill Clausewitz's appointment. Clausewitz's friend, Prussian foreign minister Christian Günther von Bernstorff, also put forward Clausewitz's name as ambassador to Bavaria, but the king refused to endorse the appointment.[11]

Many of the health problems he had suffered for years continued to afflict him. In 1818 one associate wrote: "Clausewitz, one of the most excellent, brightest, and most honest men in the army—drags around a cheerful and courageous spirit in a still gouty body." On June 3, 1822, he suffered a temporary paralysis of his right arm as the result of something similar to a stroke. In 1817, 1825, and 1826 he went on extended leave (including at least one two-month period) to take the waters at Wiesbaden, Marienbad, as well as Ems. The following year he became so ill he thought death imminent.[12]

Moreover, as he had throughout his career, Clausewitz battled melancholy in addition to his poor health. On a May 1821 trip to Potsdam, frustrations with his position, as well as Prussia's political atmosphere, mixed with the uneasy memories of his father depositing him into the arms of the Prussian army, cast him into a particularly morbid spirit of mind. "How many decisive moments have I experienced with you," he wrote Marie, "how many difficult days and worrying nights have I lived and stayed awake through! And of it all I have hardly even any faded memories! Now, it is going slowly and gently downhill, and the grave, which may still be very far away, therefore, seems closer to me because nothing seems to separate me from it. That, however, does not want to enter my head; I think the course of my life will rise once more, a culminating point shall come, and even if it were only so that you could say 'a beautiful death honours the whole life,' in short, I have not worked enough to be able to rest, and I do not feel tired enough to go to sleep."[13]

Clausewitz's literary output in the decade and a half after 1815 can only be viewed as astounding. His job made this possible. He lived on the War College campus, and his duties proved not particularly demanding. He could easily handle the necessary administrative tasks early in the morning, freeing the rest of his day for other pursuits. He worked on his manuscripts in Marie's drawing room in their apartment. A contemporary noted that Marie assisted him closely. The college's 15,000-volume library undoubtedly proved infinitely useful.[14]

One can divide Clausewitz's works after 1815 into four rough—often overlapping—groups: professional, political, historical, and *On War* itself. The professional includes the aforementioned reevaluation of the War College's curriculum. In that class we could also lump an essay he wrote on Scharnhorst, one that he intended to publish until Gneisenau convinced him to wait. His Scharnhorst study broke with the practices of the day in that it examined his mentor's character. "He hated men who served only for money, kept his distance from men who sought distinction and honors above all, and scorned those who without higher ambition simply followed routine." Such an approach fit the portrait of an artist or intellectual; Clausewitz's innovation was applying it to a soldier. His admiration for Scharnhorst and his mentor's accomplishments are clear in the text. While still in Coblenz, Clausewitz also completed military studies in relation to his job, such as a plan for the defense of the Rhineland, as well as an evaluation of a proposed territorial swap to solidify the fragmented Prussian domains.[15]

Among his professional writings are his responses to two training exercises assigned to Major von Roeder of the General Staff. Roeder had served with Clausewitz in the 3rd Corps during the Waterloo campaign and wanted his superior's opinion. When he received Roeder's note, Clausewitz had just come to his conclusions about the necessity of revising *On War* (which he began writing in 1816) to further develop his concept that all wars were fought either for regime change or something less, as well as his theory on the ways politics permeated war. Clausewitz told Roeder that the problem with evaluating their proposed plans for a defensive war against Austria and Saxony was that there was no political context. Similarly, in February 1815, when mentioning a campaign plan that Gneisenau sent him (one now lost), Clausewitz said he didn't like to "break his head on such work, because without any solid data" one would simply be acting on assumptions and get lost in "boring musings."[16]

By 1827 he had solidified his reasons for viewing matters this way. "War is not an independent phenomenon," he wrote Roeder, "but the continuation of politics by different means. Consequently, the main lines of every major strategic plan are *largely political in nature*, and their political character increases the more the plan encompasses the entire war and the entire state." Because of this, Clausewitz believed "there can be no question of a *purely military* evaluation of a great strategic issue, nor of a purely military scheme to solve it." This letter has his clearest expression of what would become the core of his intellectual approach in *On War*.[17]

His political writings included a trio of works defending the *Landwehr*, which, given that they deal with the army, are also professional. Clausewitz and the other reformers struggled to preserve the *Landwehr*, as we've seen, which came under attack on military and political fronts. He insisted the organization strengthened Prussia's defenses as well as the connections between the crown and its subjects, going so far as to recommend arming the populace. He also made the impolitic suggestion that Prussia consider moving to a government built along British parliamentary lines. The king ignored the pleas of the reformers and placed the *Landwehr* under the army's control in December 1819.[18] These papers also include a short 1818 study on the organization of a German army drawn from the states of the German Federation, the post-Napoleonic-era replacement for the Holy Roman Empire.[19]

Also among the political works is a piece known as "Agitation," which Clausewitz penned sometime between 1820 and 1823, for reasons unknown. In the piece Clausewitz backpedaled from his support for a Prussian parliamentary government, and denounced the more radical student agitators then stirring Prussia's political landscape. When considering why and when this piece was written, one clue can be found in the work's sweeping study of the political evolution of Europe, where Clausewitz writes on the demise of the feudal knight: "Since the noble knew no other means of supporting himself except by the sword, the moment when there was nothing more to be gained by it was the true culminating point of his existence."[20]

Clausewitz's historical works are by far his most numerous. He always had a sense of history and an awareness of epoch-marking moments. For example, he asked for permission to join the Prussian parade through Paris in 1815 "because last year I missed the similar fun and would not like to do without the sight of such a remarkable age and historical period as it culminates in this last act." Clausewitz's historical work is also differentiated from others by its immersive, exhaustive quality. He examined perhaps 130 past battles, giving him a foundation for development and testing of his theoretical ideas.[21] In *Campaign of 1814* (probably completed after 1819) we get a sense of his use of history. He begins the analysis section with some theory, then poses some questions and analyzes the historical facts based upon these questions. Theory is only useful "to educate the practical person and develop his judgment rather than to be of direct assistance in the course of his business." In *On War* he writes that "the primary purpose of any theory is to clarify concepts and ideas that have become confused and entangled."[22] *Observations on Prussia in Her Great Catastrophe*, written between 1823 and 1825, is a historical examination of his homeland's disastrous 1806 war with France. His criticism of Prussia and its leaders made it too hot politically to include in his collected works and it languished in the Prussian archives until 1888. In July 1825 he also wrote a smaller piece that discusses aspects of the 1806 campaign, particularly the battles of Jena and Auerstedt.[23] Although the bitter tone of his younger years faded somewhat as he aged, the work is still a biting critique of the Prussian state and lacks the objectivity of his other historical works. He had intended it to be a larger study but never completed it. He also asserts in this text the primacy of political policy that he develops in *On War*, writing "we are convinced that Prussia's desperate position in 1806 was due entirely to her own poor policies. Even the most effective policies might not have prevented her collapse, but defeat would have been accompanied with more honor, respect, and sympathy."[24]

In 1814 he had begun his study of the 1812 campaign. He probably intended two versions, a campaign account and a personal memoir, but combined them into one manuscript during 1823–1825. Here he lays the groundwork for some of the concepts he would develop in *On War*, such as friction, the culminating point, and the center of gravity, which emerges in his assessment of Napoleon's strategic and operational approach for his invasion of Russia. "To defeat the enemy's army, to destroy it, to occupy his capital, to drive the government to the farthest corner of the country, and then in the chaos that followed to win the peace—that until now had been the operational plan of all of [Napoleon's] wars. In Russia he had the vastness of the country against him and the disadvantage of two widely separate capitals. These circumstances would diminish the *psychological* effects of his victories." Clausewitz also offers some advice on how the soldier should prepare for war: "The man who means to move in such a medium as the element of war, should bring with him nothing from books but the general education of his understanding." To bring "ideas cut and dried," rather than "derived from the impulse of the moment," Clausewitz believed, was folly, as the events of war would only "dash his structure to the ground before it is finished." Such a man could never be a leader, nor would he inspire confidence in others.[25]

Clausewitz composed his study of the 1815 campaign sometime between July 1827 and the spring of 1830. The manuscript was probably never intended for publication and he believed readers would have no interest in it. Yet some point out—correctly—that Clausewitz's history of 1815 may have been his most sophisticated in its connection to his theory. None of Clausewitz's other historical studies utilize so many tools that later appear in *On War*, including the center of gravity, military genius, rational calculation, chance, and luck, as well as Clausewitz's approach of combining history, theory, and critical analysis to objectively evaluate the combatants and their decisions.[26]

Also in the early 1820s, Clausewitz examined Frederick the Great's wars.[27] In 1826, or perhaps after, he composed a short commentary on the War of Spanish Succession after reading a recently published set of letters.[28] Between 1827 and 1830, he wrote studies of the 1796 campaign in Italy and the 1799 campaign in Italy and Switzerland, as well as a brief examination of John III Sobiesky's wars with the Turks, and probably his study of Prussia's Duke of Brunswick-led 1787 war in Holland, though the date of this work is disputed.[29] His other short historical pieces include a study of the uprising in the Vendée in 1793 and an examination of the Russo-Turkish War of 1736–1739.[30] That, roughly, is a round-up of Clausewitz's professional, political, and historical works.

And then comes the work that combines elements of all he had written before—*On War*. So many factors influenced its creation, some of which we have already touched upon: extensive military experience; his study of history; and his reading of the works of Machiavelli, Bülow, Jomini, and many others. If any single event exerted the greatest influence, it was the French Revolution and the harnessing of the population to war.[31]

As we have seen, Clausewitz acquired some of his method of analysis from the philosophy of Immanuel Kant in 1804 or 1805 via the Berlin lectures of Johann Gottfried Kiesewetter. The emphasis on comparative inquiry rooted Clausewitz's thought in the preceding historical, theoretical, and philosophical works, but he also delved into art and literature, borrowing ideas and concepts from these fields. Many find in Clausewitz's approach Hegel's dialectic—the use of thesis-antithesis-synthesis—and even terms taken from the famous philosopher, while others see his methodology as more reflective of the Greek philosophers due to his use of opposites. Another source of inspiration was undoubtedly Scharnhorst, who, Marie wrote, put Clausewitz on the path to *On War*. Clausewitz credited Scharnhorst for giving him the intellectual confidence he needed.[32]

Scharnhorst himself was influenced by the writing of the Welsh military historian and theorist Henry Lloyd (1718?–1783), who stressed practical training and development of the mind, and also utilized the concept of "genius" in his work. Another source was George Heinrich von Berenhorst, a veteran of Frederick the Great's army, who published *Reflections on the Art of War* beginning in 1796. Berenhorst discussed the psychological forces involved in war, as well as genius and chance. Bülow, Jomini, and Lloyd all touched on the use of war as a state political tool. Clausewitz was familiar with Montesquieu's *The Spirit of Laws*, partially due to Scharnhorst, and Montesquieu's examination of the motivations of a nation's people may have influenced his thinking.[33]

As mentioned earlier, Clausewitz took up the writing of *On War* at Coblenz in 1816, but his work on it intensified when he assumed his post at the War College in 1818. He labored over the manuscript for the next dozen years. In the spring of 1830 Marie wrote, "He arranged his papers, sealed and labeled the individual packages, and sadly bade farewell to an activity that had come to mean so much to him." They remained untouched until his death.[34]

Clausewitz began his magnum opus with the intent of writing a small text, but—as he put it—his tendency to "develop and systematize" led him to expand it. "It was my ambition," Clausewitz noted, "to write a book that would not be forgotten after two or three years, and that possibly might be picked up more than once by those who are interested in the subject." Existing military theory was "unscientific," and he intended to build his work "on the secure foundation either of experience or the nature of war as such." Nonetheless, he had no illusions that he had written the final word on the subject, and adds a note of modesty: "Perhaps a greater mind will soon appear to replace these individual nuggets with a single whole, cast of solid metal free from all impurities."[35]

In a note of July 10, 1827—one generally published with *On War*—Clausewitz writes that he intended to revise it in light of his idea that

wars are either fought for regime change or something less. He had
by that point composed no fewer than six books and planned to write
eight—the "individual nuggets" had grown exponentially since 1816. "I
regard the first six books," he wrote in the note, "which are already in
a clean copy, merely as a rather formless mass that must be thoroughly
reworked." He planned to next revise Book 7 in light of the aforementioned, as well as Book 8, which was little more than a rough draft
and also needed to be subjected to his new ideas. His desire for revision is confirmed in another note, traditionally dated to 1830, in which
Clausewitz writes, "The manuscript on the conduct of major operations
that will be found after my death can, in its present state, be regarded as
nothing but a collection of materials from which a theory of war was to
have been distilled." He further adds: "The first chapter of Book One
alone I regard as finished."[36]

Thus arises the question as to how complete *On War* was when Clausewitz
died. Some believe that at the time of Clausewitz's death, the tome still had
a long way to go. Others, historian Jon Sumida being among the idea's
most recent proponents, view the text as more complete. This argument
partly hinges on the accuracy of the date of Clausewitz's 1830 note, which
some contend was written before his July 1827 missive. Earlier dating, it
is argued, implies Clausewitz had time to make the changes he insists he
intended, and to believe otherwise would be to assert the near-stagnation
of Clausewitz's work between 1827 and 1830.[37] In reality, we simply don't
know how complete *On War* truly is, and this is a question that cannot be
definitively answered because we know that Clausewitz never finished the
book.

Clausewitz's 1827 note also forecast one of the problems *On War*
would encounter: "If an early death should terminate my work," wrote
Clausewitz, "what I have written so far would, of course only deserve to
be called a shapeless mass of ideas. Being liable to endless misinterpretation
it would be the target of much half-baked criticism, for in matters of this
kind everyone feels he is justified in writing and publishing the first thing
that comes into his head when he picks up a pen, and thinks his own ideas as
axiomatic as the fact that two and two make four." Despite his reservation,
Clausewitz still believed the manuscript made significant contributions to
military theory. Even in their incomplete state, he wrote, in the first six
books the reader "may even find they contain the basic ideas that might
bring about a revolution in the theory of war."[38]

Clausewitz proved right on both counts (though the latter took a while), and largely has himself to blame for the first. Much of the misreading and criticism of Clausewitz's text has to do with his putting forward the concept of "absolute war."[39] Clausewitz writes that "war can be thought of in two different ways—its absolute form or one of the variant forms that it actually takes," meaning that war has an "absolute," "pure," or theoretical state, as opposed to war in reality, which is fought either for the overthrow of the enemy government or something less than this. "In the absolute form of war, where everything results from necessary causes and one action rapidly affects another, there is, if we may use the phrase, no intervening neutral void." Or, in other words, in "absolute war," nothing inhibits the struggle. But in reality, many things do.[40]

Clausewitz clouds the picture further by using the term "total war" (*ganz Krieg*) as a synonym for "absolute war" (*absoluter Krieg*), and he does not use "total war" in the modern sense where it generally conveys the scale of the conflict (the American Civil War or the First World War—with much debate—usually being deemed the first examples): "This conception would be ineluctable even if war were total war, the pure element of enmity unleashed." The equality of "absolute" and "total war" is further demonstrated by the discussion in the rest of this chapter and is an example of Clausewitz's tendency to use different terms for the same concept—something that Peter Paret has noted is not unusual in Clausewitz's writings. Some authors argue that the concept of "absolute war" derives in at least some manner from Kant, who established the idea of "pure reason," and from this derived a "practical reason" fit for the everyday. Others, such as Michael Handel, suggest the influence of Sir Isaac Newton and his discussion of a "frictionless world."[41]

In *On War*, Clausewitz presents his theory of absolute war while emphasizing the need to keep the political nature of all aspects of war "in mind when studying actual practice." He continues, "We will then find that war does not advance relentlessly toward the absolute, as theory would demand. Being incomplete and self-contradictory, it cannot follow its own laws, but has to be treated as a part of some other whole; the name of which is policy."[42]

Clausewitz then makes his own position difficult by contradicting himself (not unsurprising in an unfinished work). On the one hand, "absolute war" is a theoretical concept, and on the other it is something that Clausewitz said he had himself observed. "After the short prelude of the

French Revolution, Bonaparte brought it [war] swiftly and ruthlessly to that point... Surely it is both natural and inescapable that this phenomenon should cause us to turn again to the pure concept of war with all its rigorous implications." He continues in this vein, arguing that "we must... develop our concept of war as it ought to be fought, not on the basis of its pure definition," while leaving "room for every sort of extraneous matter." "We must allow for natural inertia, for all the friction of its parts, for all the inconsistency, imprecision, and timidity of man; and finally we must face the fact that war and its forms result from ideas, emotions, and conditions prevailing at the time—and to be quite honest we must admit that this was the case even when war assumed its absolute state under Bonaparte." Two pages later he writes that "absolute war has never in fact been achieved." "Absolute war" was a point of reference, not a reality.[43]

In 1827 Clausewitz embarked upon a considerable revision of *On War*.[44] There is voluminous literature dedicated to interpreting his ideas in *On War* and no arguments will be settled here. Those who make use of Clausewitz's work are typically the least interested in these matters, and perhaps for good reason. The primary students of Clausewitz's *On War* are serving military officers exposed to it during some segment of their education, and usually for no more than one or two weeks. Those among them who are truly interested in Clausewitz's theories often want to know how Clausewitz says one should fight a war, or, more specifically, what Clausewitz tells us about how to *win* a war. In fact, Clausewitz teaches us that though his work will not tell them how to win a generic war (which Clausewitz would say doesn't exist), it does do something perhaps more important: teach them how to *think* about waging war.

Significantly, Clausewitz's work reminds such soldiers just what they were getting themselves into: "War is an act of force to compel our enemy to do our will." He calls it a "duel on a larger scale" and notes that "kind-hearted people might of course think there was some ingenious way to disarm or defeat an enemy without too much bloodshed, and might imagine this is the true goal of the art of war. Pleasant as it sounds, it is a fallacy."[45] Clausewitz had stood on too many battlefields and seen too many of his friends killed and wounded to have any delusions about what was involved.

If war's outcome cannot be controlled, its purpose can be guided. To Clausewitz, the establishment of the political objective is of supreme importance. "When whole communities go to war—whole peoples, and especially *civilized* peoples—the reason always lies in some political situation, and the occasion is always due to some political object. War, therefore, is an act of policy." The goal being sought by the combatant drives what they are willing to do to get it, and for how long. When the "value of the object" has exceeded what one is willing to pay, "the object must be renounced and peace must follow." But one must also remember that the political objective can change, being driven by events and their effects. Where Clausewitz stands apart from other theorists is not the fact that he identifies war as a political instrument, but in insisting that political goals affect every level of military activity." "The political object is the goal," Clausewitz writes; "war is the means of reaching it, and means can never be considered in isolation from their purpose."[46]

From the aforementioned Clausewitz points us to the next step: consideration of the means required to achieve the political objective. But how does one determine this? Clausewitz recommends doing what in today's defense parlance would be part of an assessment. First, consider each side's political aim; then evaluate the strength of the enemy and compare the character and abilities of its government and people against one's own; and finally, examine the political inclinations of other states and the effect of the struggle upon them. Clausewitz is keenly aware of the challenge faced by those saddled with the task of determining the resources to be mobilized for war: "To assess these things in all their ramifications and diversity," he writes, "is plainly a colossal task."[47]

Paramount to the assembly of a proper assessment, Clausewitz believes, is to gain an understanding of the nature of the war being fought. This, in his mind, is the most important task of the political and military leaders, and "the first of all strategic questions." While Jomini provides a laundry list of types of wars ("Wars of Expediency" and "Wars of Intervention," for example), Clausewitz boils war down to the two types mentioned herein, evoked most fully in his July 10, 1827, note: "War can be of two kinds, in the sense that either the objective is to *overthrow the enemy* to render him politically helpless or militarily impotent, thus forcing him to sign whatever peace we please; or *merely to occupy some of his frontier-districts* so that we can annex them or use them for bargaining at the peace negotiations." Later, he breaks these down further, arguing that there are two types of limited wars, an "offensive war with a limited aim" and a "defensive war."[48]

Given Clausewitz's core belief in the political nature of war, we might again ask how it connects to "absolute war." As noted earlier, some say

Clausewitz argues that war *should* be waged so. Actually, however, it is all but *impossible* for this to happen. War cannot reach this absolute (though it dearly wants to) because of various factors acting upon it to restrain the forces unleashed by the conflict. Key among these—again—is politics itself. Clausewitz writes that "we also want to make it clear that war in itself does not suspend political intercourse or change it into something entirely different." Political direction places limits on the war, be these geographical, related to resources and manpower, or any number of other factors. Human nature—or moral forces—are also counted among these chains. Clausewitz writes that "since the moral elements are among the most important in war," they "constitute the spirit that permeates war as a whole, and at an early stage they establish a close affinity with the will that moves and leads the whole mass of force." The difficulty with such forces, Clausewitz notes, is that they "will not yield to academic wisdom. They cannot be classified or counted. They have to be seen or felt." Such "Principal Moral Elements" include *the skill of the commander, the experience and courage of the troops, and their patriotic spirit.*[49]

War may be driven by the logic of internal politics, but it is susceptible to contingencies, external factors of which the greatest is perhaps chance. "No other human activity is so continuously or universally bound up with chance" as war—an unpredictable experience that "most closely resembles a game of cards." And through chance, he notes, "guesswork and luck come to play a great part in war." Uncertainty, incomplete information, circumstances—all these influence how the war is fought. These are all part of war's "human factor." For this reason, "a sensitive and discriminating judgment is called for; a skilled intelligence to scent out the truth."[50]

Indeed, "intelligence" of a different sort is a significant factor in Clausewitz's discussion of uncertainty. "By "intelligence," he means "every sort of information about the enemy and his country—the basis, in short, of our own plans and operations." But such intelligence is not easy to come by. Clausewitz advises skepticism here, arguably cynicism. Most of the information those fighting wars receive is, he insists, "unreliable and transient," making war "a flimsy structure that can easily collapse and bury us in ruins." "Many intelligence reports in war are contradictory; even more are false, and most are uncertain . . . and the effect is to multiply lies and inaccuracies." The "general unreliability of all information" thus adds to the uncertainty constantly present in war. "All action takes place, so to speak, in a kind of twilight, which like fog or moonlight, often tends to make things seem grotesque and larger than they really are."[51]

Such views have produced the accusation that Clausewitz did not value intelligence. As noted earlier, it would be presumptuous to draw a straight line from Clausewitz's experience at the battle of Sehestedt in 1814—when all of his unit's information incorrectly said the Danes had taken a different route—to his doubts here, but considering Clausewitz's background as a staff officer handling the material coming in, it is probably safe to say that his Sehestedt experience was not his only such contact with an intelligence failure. While such experiences undoubtedly colored his view of tactical intelligence during wartime, it is obvious from other parts of the text that Clausewitz values information on the enemy and his intentions. He is insistent upon calculating whether or not one has available the military means for achieving their political ends. How can one deduce this other than by gathering intelligence—or information—on the enemy? In 1804, in his unpublished *Strategie*, Clausewitz wrote: "Good intelligence is indispensable, in order to know the enemy disposition in general."[52]

How is a soldier (or the reader of *On War*) to make sense of the crucial importance of intelligence as well as its potential unreliability? Clausewitz offers advice in two places. First, he suggests one should be "guided by the laws of probability." Second, he writes, one has to be either naturally talented or willing to gamble. "Whatever is hidden from full view in this feeble light has to be guessed at by talent, or simply left to chance. So once again for lack of objective knowledge one has to trust to talent or to luck."[53]

Along with "chance" and "intelligence," another factor that makes absolute war an impossibility is "friction," which has come up earlier. Friction is "the force that makes the apparently easy so difficult." In other words, friction is essentially any difficulty that can arise. Clausewitz insists that it cannot "be reduced to a few points," and that it "brings about effects that cannot be measured, just because they are largely due to chance." The weather provides an example: fog can prevent an enemy from being seen, the effects of which then ripple over the combatants. Fear is also a form of friction. When someone is trying to kill you, it can affect the efficient performance of the task at hand.[54]

What can overcome all of the problems of friction? To Clausewitz there is only one thing: "combat experience." "If one has never experienced war," he writes, "one cannot understand in what the difficulties constantly mentioned really consist, nor why a commander should need any brilliance and exceptional ability. Everything looks simple." And indeed, he cautions, "Everything in war is very simple, but the simplest thing is difficult."[55]

Also important in his enumeration of external forces is interaction with the enemy. To Clausewitz, war was an interactive process, and fighting something alive, organic. This is one of the contentions distinguishing his thought from many other military theorists. He points out that the enemy will not be static; they will react. This reaction will then cause a counteraction. Rather than being an "exercise of the will directed at inanimate matter," the will in war is directed at "an animate object that *reacts*." The results of this can also sometimes push the combatants to extremes.[56] How does one deal with these forces? Clausewitz emphasizes good staff work, experience, and, as we shall see, genius.

Another tool of assessment that Clausewitz offers is his "paradoxical" or "wondrous trinity" (*eine wunderliche Dreifaltigkeit*). There is much argument over translations of the passage in which this "trinity" arises, as well as what Clausewitz actually means by it, and even the name itself. Christopher Bassford has constructed an effective composite depiction, one based upon the various English translations of the original text and discussions with scholars. It reads so: "War is thus more than a mere chameleon, because it changes its nature to some extent in each concrete case. It is also, however, when it is regarded as a whole and in relation to the tendencies that dominate within it, a fascinating trinity—composed of: (1) primordial violence, hatred, enmity, which are to be regarded as a blind natural force; (2) the play of chance and probability, within which the creative spirit is free to roam; and (3) its element of subordination, as an instrument of policy, which makes it subject to pure reason."[57]

Every war is based upon the interaction of these three forces, which generally manifest in a specific way. Passion arises from the people, the general and his troops address the challenge of chance, and the government decides the political aims. Clausewitz doesn't believe that the waging of a war requires the balancing of these forces, as some insist. What he has done is develop a theoretical approach that maintains "a balance between these three tendencies, like an object suspended between three magnets." In other words, his work will show their relationships.[58]

As always with Clausewitz, however, there are exceptions to his analytical method ("*there is an exception to every rule*," he emphasizes in another place): the elements do not always behave as they should. For example, governments can go to war for passionate reasons, or a people behave rationally instead of with passion. This is what makes Clausewitz's "trinity" a "paradox." The stress in Clausewitz's work here is on the forces themselves, not where they are more likely to manifest.[59]

After one assesses the resources necessary for war, how should one prosecute it? How do we go about achieving our political end? Clausewitz has a single answer: combat. There is no other way. To Clausewitz, the conduct of war is made up of both planning and fighting, though "if fighting consisted of a single act, no further subdivision would be needed." Critically, one must keep in mind the following: "No one starts a war—or rather, no one in his senses ought to—without first being clear in his mind what he intends to achieve by that war and how he intends to conduct it." Clausewitz defines these two concepts as political purpose and operational objective. Together, they provide the "governing principle" that sets the course of the war and decides what means and exertions are demanded, "down to the smallest operational detail."[60]

Politicians—those acting on behalf of the polity—define the objective, which in turn determines the required means, indicating to the military leadership whether they must fight a defensive or an offensive war. This leads us to another traditional point of controversy: Clausewitz's insistence that defense was superior to offense. Defense "consists of two different elements—the *decision* and the *period of waiting*." The object of defense, Clausewitz writes, is preservation. "It is easier to hold ground than take it. It follows that defense is easier than attack, assuming both sides have equal means. Just what is it that makes preservation and protection so much easier? It is the fact that time which is allowed to pass unused, accumulates to the credit of the defender. He reaps where he did not sow." Letting pass an opportunity to "attack—whether from bad judgment, fear, or indolence—accrues to the defenders' benefit."[61]

Though passive by definition, defense must still have an active purpose, "both in strategy and in tactics." Clausewitz insisted "that within the limits of his strength a defender must always seek to change over to the attack as soon as he has gained the benefit of the defense." Defense is not permanent: "If defense is the stronger form of war, yet has a negative object, it follows that it should be used only so long as weakness compels, and be abandoned as soon as we are strong enough to pursue a positive object."[62]

Clausewitz's conclusion here is certainly based upon much study and analysis, but did his abundant combat experience also influence this conclusion? In 1812, for example, Clausewitz participated in an extensive defensive campaign that then switched to the offensive after the strength of Napoleon's army was spent and the Russians could gain nothing else from the defensive. Clausewitz also explored this concept in his study of the 1812 campaign, noting that "whoever investigates the subject will say to himself that the offensive form is the weaker, and the defensive the stronger, in war; but the results of the first, when successful, are positive, therefore the greater and more decisive; of the later only negative, by which the equilibrium is restored, and one may be advocated as well as the other."[63]

Whether on the defense or offense, one must decide where to direct the effort against the enemy (or where the enemy might direct theirs against us). To determine this, Clausewitz offers one of his most famous concepts in *On War*, and one alluded to a number of times: the center of gravity (*Schwerpunkt*). "One must keep the dominant characteristics of both belligerents in mind. Out of these characteristics a certain center of gravity develops, the hub of all power and movement, on which everything depends. That is the point against which all our energies should be directed," he writes. The key, therefore, is determining what an enemy's center of gravity is. It is often the army, but this is not true in every case. For small dependent states, it is generally their ally's army. In alliances, the center of gravity is found in "the community of interests," and in popular revolts it will be found in public opinion and the temperament of the leadership. In states subject to "domestic strife," Clausewitz notes, "the center of gravity is generally the capital." When this center is determined, Clausewitz writes, it is "the point on which your efforts must converge." As always, however, Clausewitz offers an exception: "The principle of aiming everything at the enemy's center of gravity admits of only one exception, that is, when secondary operations look exceptionally rewarding. But we repeat that only decisive superiority can justify diverting strength without risking too much in the principal theater." The difficulty, of course, lies in identifying these various centers and their relative importance. Clausewitz brands this "a major act of strategic judgment."[64]

One point of contention around Clausewitz's concept of the "center of gravity" is whether or not he means it to apply to what today we term the strategic level or the operational (i.e., campaign) level of war. This in turn raises the larger question of what, exactly, Clausewitz meant by "strategy" (*Strategie*). As we've seen, Clausewitz separated the levels of conflict into the political, strategic, and tactical. This is clear from nearly all of his writings, and from his continuing efforts throughout his life to clarify what they meant. Today, we insert the operational level between the strategic and the tactical and this most closely corresponds to the execution of a campaign. As we have discussed, Clausewitz's definition of strategy (and Jomini's as well) encompasses our strategic and operational levels of war, something that no doubt feeds some of the confusion surrounding the text. Clausewitz's mention of public opinion and leaders implies the strategic realm. His other centers can also be strategic in nature. It is undoubtedly applicable to both.[65]

Generally, however, in *On War*, Clausewitz defines tactics (*Taktik*) and strategy (*Strategie*) in relation to each other: "tactics teaches *the use of armed forces in the engagement;* strategy, *the use of engagements for the object of the war.*" "Tactics," he said, "are chiefly based on fire power." Clausewitz believes that strategy is harder than tactics because you have more time to act and thus more time to doubt. Also, in tactics you can see what is going on, in strategy you have to guess. "The best strategy," Clausewitz argues," is always *to be very strong;* first in general, and then at the decisive point. Apart from the effort needed to create military strength, which does not always emanate from the general, there is no higher and simpler law of strategy than that of *keeping one's forces concentrated.* No force, for example, should ever be detached from the main body unless the need is definite and *urgent.*" He also writes that "strategy is the use of the engagement for the purpose of the war. The strategist must therefore define an aim for the entire operational side of the war that will be in accordance with its purpose. In other words, he will draft the plan of the war... shape the individual campaigns and, within these, decide on the individual engagements."[66]

In any case, both strategy and operations are tied to the "center of gravity" that comes up in Book 8, a volume entitled "War Plans," which provides guidance on how to defeat the enemy. As always, Clausewitz begins with the political, and also addresses matters that today we would classify as strategic, but the bulk of the book is concerned with what we would today deem "operational" matters. After one has defined the enemy's center of gravity, Clausewitz tells us how to proceed: "The first principle is that the ultimate substance of enemy strength must be traced back to the fewest possible sources, and ideally to one alone." From here, "the attack on these sources must be compressed into the fewest possible actions—again, ideally, into one. Finally, all minor actions must be subordinated as much as possible. In short the first principle is: act with the utmost concentration." After concentration, Clausewitz suggests the second most important principle is speed. "No halt or detour must be permitted without good cause," he writes. In both cases, "the grand objective of all military action is to over-throw the enemy—which means destroying his armed forces...destruc-tion of the enemy is what always matters most."[67]

When on the offensive (perhaps trying to destroy that center of gravity), Clausewitz argues for constant pressure upon the enemy: "If the enemy is thrown off balance, he must not be given time to recover. Blow after blow must be aimed in the same direction: the victor, in other words, must strike with all his strength and not just against a fraction of the enemy's. Not by taking things the easy way—using superior strength to filch some province, preferring the security of this minor conquest to great success" (some label this "The Principle of Continuity"). Although Clausewitz emphasizes the need to strike decisively and with all of one's strength, he is also aware that it is not always possible. Interruptions—"necessary evils"—he terms them, will occur, but they need to be minimized at all costs.[68]

When fighting a war, Clausewitz writes, one must also be sure to keep one's forces concentrated. Operationally, he saw the most important fac-tor as "the possession of strength at the really vital point." Having strength at this "decisive point" is contingent on an army's strength and the skill of its employment. "The first rule, therefore, should be: put the largest possible army into the field. This may sound a platitude, but in reality it is not." Not only must the largest possible force be employed, but all available forces should be utilized *simultaneously*. "This application will be so much the more complete the more everything is compressed into one act and into one moment." And of course, as is so often the case in Clausewitz's theory, obeying the "rules" does not mean one will succeed: "Superior numbers, far from contributing everything, or even a substantial part, to victory, may actually be contributing very little, depending upon the circumstances."[69]

Another approach that Clausewitz offers for fighting the enemy is what he calls "The People in Arms," the first time this type of analysis appears in military literature. It is also the closest that Clausewitz comes to writing about the modern conception of guerrilla warfare. It is obviously influ-enced by his pre-1812 plans for how Prussia could resist Napoleon, as well as his study of the revolts in Spain, the Tyrol, and the Vendée. To Clausewitz, "The People in Arms" was "a general insurrection as simply another means of war," and when used intelligently it offered "some superiority over those who disdain its use." Clausewitz's theory is set apart from what is so often voiced as the modern, conventional vision of guerrilla war in its view of an uprising of the people as part of a larger war plan, rather than as a primary means of resistance. Those doing the fighting, "militia and bands of armed civilians," Clausewitz wrote, "cannot and should not be employed against the main enemy force—or indeed against any sizeable enemy force. They are not supposed to pulverize the core but to nibble at the shell and around the edges. They are meant to operate in areas just outside the theater of war—where the invader will not appear in strength—in order to deny him these areas altogether."[70] Clausewitz as a theorist is sometimes accused of being irrelevant to discussions of guerrilla and irregular forms of warfare. This section—as well as his extensive lectures on "Little War"—argue otherwise.

For Clausewitz, the general with the misfortune of having to weigh all of these factors under the eyes of his political masters, while, incidentally, leading an army or perhaps running an entire war, should ideally possess extraordinary aptitude for this task. Clausewitz titles his chapter devoted to the preferred type of leader, "On Military Genius" (*Der kriegerische Genius*). Some argue that this would be better translated as "The Genius for War," and it appears this way in older English-language translations. Regardless, Clausewitz's section on military genius should be read not just for his exegesis of genius, but also for his examination of personality types, one written before the advent of modern psychological methods. Here again, Clausewitz possibly took some of his inspiration for this discussion from Kant, who noted that "Genius is a talent for producing that for which no definite rule can be given," a sentiment similarly expressed in some of Clausewitz's remarks. For example, he notes that genius "*rises above all rules*," and later writes that "what genius does is the best rule, and theory can do no better than show how and why this should be the case."[71]

To Clausewitz, war was the realm of chance, violence, chaos, "the realm of physical exertion and suffering." Operating at a high level of command in such an environment demanded certain skills. "If the mind is to emerge unscathed from this relentless struggle with the unforeseen," he wrote, "two qualities are indispensable: *first, an intellect that, even in the darkest hour, retains some glimmerings of the inner light which leads to truth; and second, the courage to follow this faint light wherever it may lead.* The first of these qualities is described by the French term, *coup d'oeil*; the second is *determination*." *Coup d'oeil* (which Clausewitz readily admits he is not the first to use, and can be translated as "glance") "merely refers to the quick recognition of a truth that the mind would ordinarily miss or would perceive only after long study and reflection." It is this ability to grasp things simply, "to identify the whole business of war completely with himself," that Clausewitz sees as the soul of good command. "Only if the mind works in this comprehensive fashion can it achieve the freedom it needs to dominate events and not be dominated by them."[72]

The successful military commander has other characteristics as well. One is courage, both in regard to facing physical danger, as well as the moral courage needed to make decisions and assume responsibility for them. Clausewitz also lists additional desired attributes for his military genius: ambition, "presence of mind," "strength of mind," energy, self-control, an understanding of terrain, imagination, and others.[73]

Even with a military genius in charge, there is, of course, no assurance of success. War is the most complicated of human activities. All we can do is balance its elements. "We would emphasize the essential and general; leave scope for the individual and accidental; but remove everything *arbitrary, unsubstantiated, trivial, far-fetched,* or *supersubtle.* If we have accomplished that we regard our task as fulfilled."[74]

When the general is fighting the war, particularly when they are commanding an offensive, one of the things they must keep in mind is what Clausewitz terms "the Culminating Point of the Attack." One author argues that "the pre-history of the concept of culmination" originates in astrology and astronomy and is fed by Machiavelli's writings, particularly his views on victory. Whatever the case, Clausewitz warns that when on the offensive one must be very clear about the objective sought, the strength available, and the all-important actions of the enemy. He believes that the majority of strategic attacks do not end the war, but "only lead up to the point where their remaining strength is just enough to maintain a defense and wait for peace. Beyond that point the scale turns and the reaction follows with a force that is usually much stronger than that of the original attack." Clausewitz also explains that since the attacker is trying to seize enemy land, he will continue to press until he no longer has the supremacy to do so. But herein lies a danger: this desire for territory can drive an attacker past his goal. "What matters therefore is to detect the culminating point [*Kulminationspunkt*] with discriminative judgment."[75]

But one must also be able to tell how far this has taken them on the road to achieving their political objective. To aide our thinking on this, he offers a related concept: the Culminating Point of Victory. "The end is either to bring the enemy to his knees or at least to deprive him of some of his territory—the point in that case being *not to improve the current military position* but to improve one's general prospects in the war and in the peace negotiations." In working "to destroy the enemy completely," he notes, it is possible that "every step gained may weaken one's superiority." Because of this risk, "one must know the point to which it can be carried in order not to overshoot the target; otherwise instead of gaining new advantages, one will disgrace oneself." It is extremely difficult to deduce this turning point, however, requiring a commander to guess the effects of his operations upon the enemy, which creates a new set of problems. Clausewitz notes that for this reason, "the great majority of generals will prefer to stop well short of their objective rather than risk approaching it too closely," and those who are courageous and enterprising "will often overshoot it and so fail to attain their purpose."[76]

At some point, of course, the war must come to an end, and when it does, only one thing is of supreme importance: "*final victory*. Until then, nothing is decided, nothing won, and nothing lost." Clausewitz reiterates this point: "Victory alone is not everything—but is it not, after all, what really counts?" Clausewitz does not mean, however, that a peace settlement is always war's true final act. "The defeated state often considers the outcome merely a transitory evil, for which a remedy may still be found in political conditions at some later date." Knowledge of this means that individuals sometimes will not push as hard as they should.[77] Like wars themselves, discussion of *On War*, and just what the text means, will undoubtedly never end.

As 1829 reached its end, Clausewitz's long dormant military ambition reawakened. He wanted to make *Generalleutnant*, and believing his path blocked to becoming chief of the general staff (which carried this rank), he concluded that he had to take a different path. On December 27, Clausewitz petitioned the king for an active command. Frederick William agreed and sent Clausewitz to the artillery, which had three brigade commands. The intercession of Prince August, who led the Prussian artillery, enabled Clausewitz's appointment. To familiarize himself with his new duties (something Clausewitz found a bit demeaning for a man of 50 who had been a general for 12 years), he was temporarily attached to Berlin's 1st Artillery Inspection on March 9, 1830 (while keeping his War College job), and then given command of the 2nd Artillery Inspection in Breslau on August 19, 1830. His time there was short. In December he was ordered back to Berlin to become chief of staff to Gneisenau, a post he officially assumed on March 6, 1831.[78]

As we have seen, 1830 was a year of revolution in Europe. Early in autumn of that year Prussia's Rhineland provinces beheld scenes of both urban and rural riot and uprising. These disturbances, and the Warsaw revolt of the Poles against the Russians, sparked fear in Berlin that Prussia's own subject Poles might become a problem. The situation in Poland concerned Clausewitz deeply because he saw in Polish independence an existential threat to Prussia and other German states. In 1831 he wrote three pieces—at least they are the only ones known to survive—dealing with the issue of Poland in relation to Prussian security. In "Europe since the Polish Partition," Clausewitz essentially denounced support of Polish independence as moral posturing, arguing that Poland was no better or worse off than had been the other nations absorbed throughout human history. Prussian and Austrian security could not afford an independent Poland. It would cost them too much in population and strategic position, and would weaken them vis-à-vis Poland's natural ally—France.[79]

Clausewitz also wrote "On the Basic Question of Germany's Existence." Here he comments on the revolutions in Belgium, Italy, and Poland—especially Poland—asserting that what matters most is the preservation of German (not merely Prussian) independence. The independence of Poland was the worst evil because of the traditional antagonism between Prussia and the Poles (he mentions the fact that East Prussia was once a Polish vassal), and, again, the more dangerous fact that Poland was a natural ally of France.[80]

Clausewitz tried unsuccessfully to publish this in the Augsburg, Bavaria, newspaper, *Allgemeine Zeitung*; it remained unpublished until 1878. Also related to the Polish revolt was a letter Clausewitz published anonymously in July 1831, first in the *Zeitung des Grossherzogtums Posen*, and then in other newspapers. Here Clausewitz defended his nation against Polish criticism of Prussia selling supplies to the Russian forces fighting in Poland. King Frederick William dispatched a note praising it, which both pleased and surprised Clausewitz. It was undoubtedly the king's only endorsement of anything Clausewitz ever wrote.[81] His fear of a future war between France and Prussia, one undoubtedly fed by the July 1830 revolution in France that brought Louis-Philippe to power, drove him to considering various alternatives to such an event.[82]

In March 1831 Clausewitz followed Gneisenau to Posen (now Poznań, Poland) as chief of staff for the army of observation Prussia had assembled. Before they left he had taken the time to study the Polish campaigns of 1793 and 1794. Though he enjoyed Gneisenau's company, he became increasingly exasperated with an apparent lack of decision in the Prussian leadership and his old melancholy returned. His letters to Marie sometimes turn to talk of his death. In Posen, there was little work for Clausewitz and his colleagues. General Carl von Grolman, the chief of the General Staff and Clausewitz's old friend, wrote to his wife in March 1831 that the only thing agreeable in his journey to the area was that he has seen Clausewitz and Gneisenau, but what the three of them mostly did was to wait and drink tea. Grolman also noted that the weather was so bad and the roads such a disaster that they couldn't move anyway and so resting was good.[83]Clausewitz did though keep a very close watch on military events in Poland (and in other parts of Europe). Generally, he had little complimentary to say about Russia's operations, which were commanded by his old superior Diebitsch. Clausewitz's opinion of Diebitsch had soured before the war because of what he judged as Diebitsch's poor performance in the Russo-Turkish War of 1828–29. Major Heinrich von Brandt worked almost daily with Clausewitz while they observed the Russians and Poles. He noted Clausewitz's uncomfortableness with the troops, but praised Clausewitz's other skills. Brandt was particularly taken by Clausewitz's powers of observation when examining the movements and operations of the warring forces, and his ability to forecast the point when their marches would produce a decision point. Brandt thought it unfortunate that Clausewitz never had the chance to prove himself in a position of high command and professed a firm conviction that as a strategist Clausewitz would have been "extraordinary." But Brandt also had the equally strong feeling that Clausewitz lacked the personality traits necessary to command and lead men in battle.[84]

By the summer, however, things had changed. By May the cholera epidemic became a concern and Clausewitz began making preparations to deal with the disease. In June Diebitsch, the commander of the Russian forces in Poland, died from the malady. This upset Clausewitz because he considered him a good man, but he also remarked to Marie—somewhat coldly—that he did not pity Diebitsch because he believed the general's reputation gone and that he was walking on the edge of disgrace because of his conduct of the war in Poland. Reputation still ranked high in Clausewitz's mind. By July the cholera had jumped the frontier into Prussia and killed the first soldier in Clausewitz's command. On August 22 it struck Gneisenau. His old friend and mentor died the next day. The loss dealt him a particularly heavy blow.[85]

In October 1831, even though the war in Poland was winding down, Berlin dispatched a replacement for Gneisenau, Karl Friedrich von dem Knesebeck. Clausewitz, who had been the de facto army chief, found this offensive. His over-sensitivity got the better of him and he was unjustifiably angry about what was a perfectly normal Prussian army response. Clausewitz and Knesebeck, though, came to work well together.[86]

The Russians soon finished crushing the Poles and by November 7 Clausewitz was happily back in Breslau with Marie and corresponding with his old superior, Prince August. On November 16 the cholera struck him. Caroline von Rochow, a friend of both Clausewitz and Marie, noted that Clausewitz got up that morning fine, gave an artillery lecture from 9:00 to 11:00, then began feeling unwell. Marie insisted he go to bed while she sent for the doctor. By noon Clausewitz displayed the symptoms of cholera, which at first the doctor's treatment seemed to be addressing. But later he was wracked by convulsions. The disease moved with deadly rapidity, and, at nine o'clock in the evening, Clausewitz died, possibly from a heart attack brought on by the disease.[87]

Caroline noted how heavy the blow fell upon Marie. "His poor wife loses just about everything with him because she has never for a moment lost the feelings she had for him as a bride." Marie wrote of his death: "It is a great comfort to me that at least his final moments were calm and painless, and yet the expression and tone with which he expelled his last sigh were heartrending; it was as though he pushed life away like a heavy burden. Soon afterwards his features became calm and peaceful; an hour later, when I saw him for the last time, they again expressed the deepest pain."[88]

Marie felt the anguish of her husband—the man with whom she had been "profoundly happy" for twenty-one years—having never achieved the glory he longed for, or the honors she felt he deserved, despite his remarkable life. "Life for him had consisted of an almost unbroken chain of effort, sorrow, and vexation. Certainly, on the whole he had achieved much more than he could have hoped for at the outset; he felt this deeply and acknowledged it with a grateful heart. But he never did scale the highest peak, and every pleasure that he experienced contained a flaw that clouded his enjoyment." What her husband had enjoyed was the friendship of "the most noble men of his time," and while he never received the honors he deserved, those friendships were perhaps more valuable. "And how did he not suffer with and for his friends!"[89]

Because of the cholera epidemic Clausewitz was interred with no ceremony in the military cemetery in Breslau. This also meant no one was allowed to be at the burial, though Marie's brother greased the palms of the gravediggers to get in. King Frederick William sent a letter remarking that his passing "is as unexpected as it is painful. The army has suffered a loss which will be difficult to remedy, which greatly saddens me." Clausewitz's remains were reinterred in his birthplace of Burg in 1971. A monument marks the grave.[90]

Marie soon took up the task of publishing Clausewitz's works, most importantly *On War*. Clausewitz had not, as we've seen, intended it to see print in his lifetime. "When I would try to dissuade him from this decision," Marie wrote, "he often responded, half-jokingly, but perhaps also with a presentiment of this early death: 'You shall publish it.' " Marie did, and despite her half-protestation otherwise, was the "true editor" of the text. Indeed, no one else was better qualified to take the job. She had worked closely with Clausewitz as he wrote it; no one had greater familiarity with his ideas or intentions. She had help assembling the text from her brother, the Prussian general Friedrich Wilhelm von Brühl, as well as Major Franz August O'Etzel, an instructor at the War College, who also saw to the maps.[91]

On War appeared as the first three volumes of his works (1832–1834). These eventually ran to ten volumes, the last appearing in 1837, a year after Marie's death. Brühl helped publish a new edition from 1853–1857 that corrected some errors in the first. We will never know exactly what changes he made (if any) from the now-lost original text and the first edition of *On War*. Brühl, however, did make alterations of his own to the first edition, such as placing the military commander-in-chief in the cabinet in Book 8.[92]

Incomplete, unfinished, sprawling, sometimes contradictory, and often as frustrating as it is endlessly rewarding, *On War* nonetheless assured Clausewitz of a form of the immortality that he had sought. Its incisive methodology, fed by a drive to clarify and define, both unshackled from dogmatism while grounded in experience and history, are just some of the qualities that make it the greatest monument to military thinking yet constructed.

Conclusion

Clausewitz's Legacy

[I]t is the weak, those likely to need defense, who should always be armed in order to not be overwhelmed. Thus decrees the art of war.

In 1965 the distinguished historian and Clausewitz scholar Peter Paret wrote, "It is not too much to expect that Clausewitz will come to assume a position in the study of war that is similar—not only in reputation but in substance—to the one now held by Tocqueville in the study of democratic societies." Paret's words have proven prophetic, though it would not have appeared so at the time, and even less so the century before. When Clausewitz's works initially appeared between 1832 and 1834, they were hardly bestsellers. The run of the first edition was only 1,500 copies and had not sold out when the second edition began appearing in 1857. The initial reaction of German-language reviewers to *On War* was generally enthusiastic, but there were also complaints about the text being difficult—that *On War* was a book to be studied, not read.[1]

An early French review in 1838 was dismissive, though we know that at least one veteran of the French armies read *On War*: Baron Antoine-Henri Jomini. Clausewitz had read at least some of Jomini's works, particularly the early texts dealing with tactics, and Jomini likewise studied Clausewitz's writings after their publication. He integrated into his *Summary of the Art of War* some of *On War*'s concepts, including the inherent political nature of warfare and the necessity of military leaders to be in line with their political overlords as to a conflict's aims. Jomini did not absorb Clausewitz's theory whole cloth, and described *On War* as overly complicated and too dismissive of other works of military theory (meaning, of course, Jomini's).[2]

The first complete French-language translation was finished in 1851 by a Belgian citizen, but the French only began reading Clausewitz after their defeat in the Franco-Prussian War (1870–1871). Prussia's military victories in the Wars of German Unification (1866–1871) led to *On War* becoming more widely known outside his homeland, though Clausewitz's writings had nothing directly to do with them. The first English translation appeared in 1873, by Britain's J. J. Graham, though his is not considered the most reliable rendering.[3]

Britain's preeminent naval theorist, Sir Julian Corbett, borrowed some of Clausewitz's ideas and applied them to naval warfare in his 1911 *Some Principles of Maritime Strategy*. Corbett discusses the importance of theory, the superiority of the defensive, and military genius, which he describes as "executive ability." Corbett also seizes upon Clausewitz's idea of limited war, and expands upon it.[4]

Although Clausewitz appears as a minor character in Leo Tolstoy's *War and Peace*, first published in 1869, the first Russian translation of *On War* only appeared in 1905. Lenin's interest in Clausewitz's teachings led them to be introduced into Soviet thought, particularly the political nature of war. Other Russian translations followed in 1932 and 1941, but Clausewitz fell out of fashion in Soviet military circles when Stalin decided *On War* was obsolete, a relic of a different age that no longer applied in the "machine age."[5]

The first Chinese version of *On War* appeared in 1910, actually a translation of a Japanese edition—which emerged in 1903, though Japanese officers had been exposed to some of Clausewitz's ideas via German instructors—therefore, problematically, a translation of a translation. Mao Zedong taught seminars on it to his Communist brethren after he first read it in 1938. The first Italian translation appeared in 1942.[6]

The greatest interest in *On War* was, of course, in Germany. Yet while *On War* was often quoted by soldiers as well as statesmen, it was rarely studied. After World War II, German general Gunther Blumentritt remarked that giving the military *On War* was akin to "allowing a child to play with a razor blade."[7]

In 1873 the J. J. Graham translation of *On War* reached the US, but with no fanfare. The first American edition wasn't published until 1943, in the middle of the Second World War, undertaken by O. J. Matthijs Jolles. Initially, Americans rarely studied *On War*, but in the 1950s and 1960s this began to change. Strategic thinker Bernard Brodie was among the first to promote its lessons.[8]

In 1962 retired Air Force colonel Edward M. Collins published *War, Politics, and Power,* "a translated and distilled" version of Clausewitz's *On War.* After the beginning of the 1968 Tet Offensive in South Vietnam, Lieutenant-Colonel David MacIsaac, an instructor at the Air Force Academy, had Collins's version of *On War* made part of the curriculum for the 1968–1969 academic year. In 1975 MacIsaac went to the Strategy Department of the Naval War College in Newport, Rhode Island, where he helped lead a renewal in the study of theory and succeeded in having Collins's Clausewitz text introduced into the curriculum. Four years later, MacIsaac was sent to the Air University at Maxwell Air Force Base in Alabama. His influence led to *On War*'s becoming part of its curriculum in 1978. The Army War College at Carlisle Barracks, Pennsylvania, began teaching *On War* in 1981, a decision partially driven by faculty conversations with MacIsaac.[9]

Colonel Harry Summers's *On Strategy: A Critical Analysis of the Vietnam War,* first published in 1981, began life as an Army War College study. Summers's text used Clausewitz's teachings (or at least a form of them) to analyze how and why the war was fought. Summers had gotten the idea for using Clausewitz's theories as "a unifying theme for analysis" from David MacIsaac. Indeed, a search for explanations for the debacle of the Vietnam War sparked intense American interest in *On War.* Historian Christopher Bassford observes that American military leaders found in Clausewitz's depiction of the "trinity," particularly the manifestation of the political in the realm of reason, as well as his discussions of civilian-military relations, elements of an explanation for the defeat. Summers's work in particular became very influential in shaping the views of American political and military leaders.[10]

Others also began drawing upon *On War.* The US Marine Corps's 1989 manual *Warfighting,* is, as Bassford points out, "essentially a distillation" of *On War.* This post-Vietnam intellectual quest, combined with the 1976 appearance of a fine English-language translation of *On War* by Michael Howard and Peter Paret, helped establish Clausewitz as one of the greatest analysts of war.[11]

Secretary of Defense Caspar Weinberger's "Weinberger Doctrine"—set out in November 1984—was very "Clausewitzian" in the sense that he argued, among other things, that the US should only use combat troops when there was obvious national interest, a clear objective, and a willingness to contribute sufficient means. It includes a quotation from *On War* about leaders first understanding what they want from the war and how they're going to get it before getting involved.[12]

While the success of *On War* has established Clausewitz's place in military theory, one unfortunate result has been that his other works—in particular his histories—have been overlooked. Paret and Daniel Moran are among those who have made an effort to acquaint a broader audience with these works. As we have seen, Clausewitz went beyond simply retelling events, mixing in cogent analysis of the motives of the combatants, military theory, and often penetrating portraits. In the nineteenth century Clausewitz was generally viewed as a historian, not a theorist, partially because seven of the ten volumes of his collected works contain historical treatises. *On War* occupies only the first three volumes. Today, this view is reversed.

But it is inescapable that Clausewitz's greatest legacy lies in military theory, and "Despite its rhetorical difficulty," Moran writes, "*On War* remains the greatest work on its subject yet written." Importantly, Moran notes that, "Its subject, however, is war, not strategy as such."[13] This is a critical distinction to make. Clausewitz's work is often cherry-picked to teach strategy, but Clausewitz intended it to do far more than that.

Clausewitz brought the study of war to a new intellectual level, turning it into a genuine discipline, placing it alongside other fields of study such as art, engineering, or philosophy. Philosophy professor W. B. Gallie writes: "If, as has been said, the idea of a literate general defeats the Anglo-Saxon imagination, what can we hope to make of the Prussian officer who was to become the world's first—and, as it may turn out, also its last—philosopher of war?" Paret writes that, "by taking war out of its military isolation and embedding it in society and politics, [Clausewitz] made possible the kind of broad analysis that alone, he thought, might lead to truth."[14]

There are many who think *On War* obsolete, believing, like Stalin, that history has simply passed it by. There is certainly reason to agree with this: its incompleteness, its lack of discussion of naval warfare, and the fact that so many of its teachings—particularly of the tactical kind—are derived from the experience of the Napoleonic Wars, the methods of which more recent technology has superseded. Books 4 and 5 (especially Book 5) are designed to equip the reader with the intellectual tools for being a good Napoleonic staff officer (which indeed Clausewitz was), while Books 1 and 8 are generally considered the most useful to the modern reader. But *all* of the text can be read with benefit. Even sections dedicated largely to the

Napoleonic method of warfare often include interesting and thought provoking insights relevant to the twenty-first-century reader. For example,
in Book 4 we find the following: "The probability of direct confrontation
increases with the aggressiveness of the enemy. So, rather than try to outbid
the enemy with complicated schemes, one should, on the contrary, try to
outdo him in simplicity."[15]

Some believe the advent of atomic and then hydrogen weaponry not
only ushered in Clausewitz's "absolute war," but simultaneously made him
irrelevant.[16] The problem with this argument relates to the continual misreading of Clausewitz's theory related to "absolute war." Friction—in all its
types—makes "absolute war" unattainable, as we have seen. The development of atomic and nuclear weaponry is a vast intensification of the means
of waging war, one that certainly shapes the political decision to go to war
in the first place. However, when we consider the number of wars that have
been fought since the bombings of Hiroshima and Nagasaki, we can safely
assert that Clausewitz's ideas retain their relevance.

Some have argued that Clausewitz's work has been made obsolete in a
post-modern world where national states no longer exercise a monopoly on
military violence. How can Clausewitz help us in the age of transnational
jihad and home-grown terrorists? The discovery of a copy of Clausewitz's
On War in one of al-Qaeda's safehouses in Afghanistan, one in which the
passages discussing courage bore its reader's marks, demonstrates the global
interest that exists in the text.[17] Although groups like al-Qaeda use religion as
a tool, they still have political goals. Terrorist groups still have leaders, allies,
and supporters that are subject to the same forces—physical and moral—as
during the Napoleonic era. Human nature hasn't changed, and in the end,
while Clausewitz's masterwork is dismissed as merely a guide about how to
wage war, it is in fact a book that shows us how to *think* about war.[18]

What, in the end, do we make of *On War*? Clausewitz's own assessment, one echoed previously, is perhaps the best: "It is not *what* we have
thought, but rather *how* we have thought it, that we consider to be our
greatest contribution to theory." No one before or since Clausewitz has
used both history and analysis to study war and the forces affecting its conduct so deeply.[19]

In discussing Clausewitz's legacy as a theorist, we cannot forget what
was most important to him: achieving renown as a soldier. Clausewitz
certainly spilled his share of ink, but he also spilled blood—his as well as
that of the enemy. He experienced the warfare of his age at its most intense

Figure 12.1. Clausewitz's Gravesite in Burg.
Courtesy Vanya Eftimova Bellinger.

and visceral. He knew what it was like to be wounded, to be a prisoner, to have friends killed and wounded, to suffer hunger and thirst, and to have the heat and cold try to kill you after the enemy's best efforts have failed. Success on the field of battle—success meaning victory, and distinguishing oneself among one's comrades, who are also often brave and daring men—drove Clausewitz. Yet this is not the Clausewitz most know.

And in the end he did achieve the renown he so desired. No one remembers Frederick William III, the king he served for most of his life. Only historians and specialists remember his mentors and friends Scharnhorst and Gneisenau. The fame Clausewitz hoped to win for himself—with sword in hand—he won with his pen.

Appendix
Clausewitz's Battles

A critical element of Clausewitz's development—and an enormous part of his life—was his combat experience, something that many previous biographies touch upon but do not thoroughly explore. Below is a list of the combat actions at which Clausewitz was present. Determining all of those in which he was under fire is impossible from the currently known records. There are at least thirty-six incidents of Clausewitz, or the force he is part of, being under fire. His only known combat wound is noted.

1793

Feb. 2	Ginsheim
March 23–July 22	Siege of Mainz
June 6	Storming of Zahlbach Trenches (Mainz)
July 7	Storming of Zahlbach Heights (Mainz)
★Aug. 17	Kettrich Heights
★Aug. 20	Kettrich Heights
★Sept. 14	Pirmasens
★Dec. 22	Lembach

1794

★May 23	Kaiserslautern
★May 23	Trippstadt
★July 2–3	Two actions: Käshofen, Trippstadt, Johanniskreuz
★July 7	Leimen (Near Heidelberg)
★July 12–13	Schänzel
★July 13	Johanniskreuz
★The month of July	Probably eight actions total

1806

October 14	Auerstedt
October 16	Greußen—Rearguard
October 17	Nordhausen—Rearguard
October 28	Prenzlau—Captured

1812

July 19, and three weeks after	Russia—Rearguard: "several skirmishes"

July 27	Vitebsk
*Aug. 15-16	Smolensk
Sept. 7	Borodino
*Sept. 8	Mozhaisk
Sept. 10	Krymskoye. His horse was wounded.

After Borodino, until the Russians marched through Moscow on September 14, Clausewitz likely endured daily combat as he served in the rearguard blocking Napoleon's advance on Moscow.

1813

May 2	Lützen (Großgörschen)—Bayonet wound on head.
May 20–21	Bautzen
*May 26	Haynau
Aug. 21–Dec. 1	Stecknitz-Mecklenburg Campaign—Several skirmishes
Sept. 18	The Göhrde
Dec. 10	Sehestedt

1815

June 16	Ligny
June 18-19	Wavre
*July 2	Châtillon area, Paris—Several firefights

*Present, but whether he saw action is unknown.

Notes

INTRODUCTION

1. Clausewitz to Marie, July 29, 1831, quoted in Tiha von Ghyczy, Bolko von Oetinger, and Christopher Bassford, eds., *Clausewitz on Strategy: Inspiration and Insight from a Master Strategist* (New York: Wiley, 2001), 8–9. This book has a wonderful depiction of Clausewitz as a spy at Tauroggen in 1812, xi–xii.
2. Beatrice Heuser, *Reading Clausewitz* (London: Pimlico, 2002), 3; "By Marie von Clausewitz, Preface to the Posthumous Edition of Her Husband's Works, Including *On War*," in Carl von Clausewitz, *On War*, Michael Howard and Peter Paret, ed. and trans. (Princeton: Princeton University Press, 1984) (hereafter *OW*), 66.
3. "Preface," *OW*, 66–67; Hew Strachan, *Clausewitz's On War* (New York: Atlantic Monthly, 2007), 69.
4. Quoted in Tiha, et al., ed., *Clausewitz on Strategy*, 10; Heuser, *Reading Clausewitz*, 12–13; Antoine-Henri Jomini, *Summary of the Art of War*, O. F. Winslip and E. E. McLean, trans. (New York: Putnam, 1854), 14–15.
5. Quoted in Christopher Bassford, *Clausewitz in English: The Reception of Clausewitz in Britain and America, 1815–1945* (Oxford: Oxford University Press, 1994), 129–30; Carl von Clausewitz, "On the Genesis of His Early Manuscript on the Theory of War, Written around 1818," and "Note of 10 July 1827," in *OW*, 63, 70.

CHAPTER I

1. Clausewitz to Marie, Dec. 13, 1806, May 18, 1821, Karl Schwartz, *Leben des Generals Carl von Clausewitz und der Frau Marie von Clausewitz* (Berlin: Dümmlers, 1878) (hereafter *Leben*), 1:229–33, 2:252–54; Marie von Clausewitz, "Erinnerung an den General Clausewitz und sein Verhältniss zu Scharnhorst," in Leopold Ranke, ed., *Historisch-politische Zeitschrift* (Hamburg: Friedrich Perthes, 1832), 1:214–14. The dates of all documents have been translated into English.
2. Clausewitz to Marie, May 18, 1821, *Leben*, 2:252–54.
3. *Leben*, 1:20–26.
4. *Leben*, 1:13; Clausewitz to Marie, June 2, 1807, and Marie to Clausewitz, June 2, 1809, *Leben*, 1:272, 399–401; Peter Paret, *Clausewitz and the State*

(Princeton: Princeton University Press, 1985, 2007), vii; Klaus Hilbert, "Ergänzungen zum Lebensbild des Generals Carl von Clausewitz," *Militärgeschichte* 20 (1981), 208, 210.

5. Hans Rothfels, *Carl von Clausewitz: Politik und Krieg* (Berlin: Dümmlers, 1920), 4; Paret, *Clausewitz*, viii, 14–15.

6. Clausewitz to Marie, Dec. 13, 1806, Carl and Marie von Clausewitz, *Karl und Marie von Clausewitz: Ein Lebensbild in Briefen und Tagebuchblättern*, Karl Linnebach, ed. (Berlin: Warneck, 1916) (hereafter *Karl und Marie*), 70–75.

7. Clausewitz to Marie, Jan. 28, 1807, *Karl und Marie*, 82–85; *Leben*, 1:32, 66, 240–43.

8. Clausewitz to Marie, Jan. 28, 1807, *Karl und Marie*, 82–85; *Leben*, 1:240–43; Paret, *Clausewitz*, 18; Carl von Clausewitz, "From 'Observations on Prussia in Her Great Catastrophe,'" [hereafter Clausewitz, "Observations"] in Peter Paret and Daniel Moran, ed. and trans., *Historical and Political Writings* (hereafter *HPW*) (Princeton: Princeton University Press, 1992), 40.

9. Christopher Clark, *Iron Kingdom: The Rise and Downfall of Prussia, 1600–1947* (Cambridge: Belknap Press of Harvard, 2006), 190–96.

10. Ibid., 197–206.

11. Gordon Craig, *The Politics of the Prussian Army, 1640–1945* (London: Oxford University Press, 1964), 22–24.

12. Craig, *Politics*, 25–29; Clausewitz, "Observations," *HPW*, 36–37.

13. *Leben*, 1:33–34.

14. Clausewitz to Marie, Apr. 9, 1807, *Leben*, 1:265–67.

15. Clark, *Iron Kingdom*, 285; Michael V. Leggiere, *Blücher: Scourge of Napoleon* (Norman: Oklahoma University Press, 2014), 32.

16. Clark, *Iron Kingldom*, 285–87; Leggiere, *Blücher*, 32–33.

17. T. C. W. Blanning, *The French Revolutionary Wars, 1787–1802* (London: Arnold, 1996), 57–59; Clark, *Iron Kingdom*, 287.

18. Blanning, *Wars*, 72–73.

19. Gunther E. Rothenberg, *The Art of Warfare in the Age of Napoleon* (Bloomington: Indiana University Press, 1980), 12; Blanning, *Wars*, 63, 73–78; Carl von Clausewitz, "Der Feldzug des Herzogs von Braunschweig gegen die Holländer 1787," *Hinterlassene Werke des Generals Carl von Clausewitz über Krieg und Kriegführung* (hereafter *HW*) (Berlin: Dümmler, 1863), 10:217–71; *OW*, 518.

20. Blanning, *Wars*, 78–81, 131–35.

21. Quoted in, ibid., 79–82.

22. Ibid., 88–89, 91, 94–95; Hajo Holborn, *A History of Modern Germany, 1648–1840* (Princeton: Princeton University Press, 1982), 358.

23. Paret, *Clausewitz*, 19, 29; Steven T. Ross, *European Diplomatic History, 1789–1815: France against Europe* (Malabar, FL: Krieger, Reprint, 1981), 68; Günther Gieraths, *Die Kampfhandlungen der Brandenburgisch-Preussichen Armee, 1626–1807: Ein Quellenhandbuch* (Berlin: Walter de Gruyter, 1964), 113; *OW*, 113.

24. Ross, *European*, 68; Antoine-Henri Jomini, *Histoire Critique et Militaire des Guerres de la Révolution*, Vol. 3, *Campagne de 1793* (Paris: Magimel, Anselin et Pochard, 1819), 206; Leggiere, *Blücher*, 37; Jomini, *1793*, 202; Gieraths, *Die Kampfhandlungen*, 113.

25. Jomini, *1793*, 210–12.

26. F. Taeglichsbeck, *Das Füsilier-Regiment Prinz Heinrich von Preußen (Nr. 35), 1740–1806* (Berlin: Ernst Siegfried, 1891), 169; A. Wagner, *Der Feldzug der K. Preussichen Armee am Rhein im Jahre 1793* (Berlin: G. Reimer, 1831), 12; Jomini, *1793*, 206, 209, 211, 218–19, 221–22.

27. Gieraths, *Die Kampfhandlungen*, 113; Curt Jany, *Der Geschichte der Königlich Preußischen Armee bis zum Jahre 1807*, Vol. 3, *1763 bis 1807* (Berlin: Karl Siegismund, 1929), 3:266–67.

28. Jomini, *1793*, 231; Jany, *Geschichte*, 3:266; Johann Wolfgang von Goethe, *From My Life: Poetry and Truth*, Vol. 4, *Campaign in France, 1792/Siege of Mainz*, Thomas P. Saine, trans., and Thomas P. Saine and Jeffrey L. Sammons, eds. (Princeton: Princeton University Press, 1987), 756. Goethe gives the date as June 16. Wagner says June 18, Wagner, *Feldzug*, 31.

29. Goethe, *Campaign/Siege*, 610, 755–60.

30. Ibid., 757–60.

31. Jany, *Geschichte*, 3:266; Jomini, *1793*, 235–36; Gieraths, *Die Kampfhandlungen*, 113.

32. Jany, *Geschichte*, 3:267; http://www.meltonpriorinstitut.org/pages/textarchive .php5?view=text8ID=868language=English; Clausewitz to Marie, Jan. 28, 1807, *Leben*, 1:240–43.

33. *OW*, 113.

34. Goethe, *Campaign/Siege*, 762; *Leben*, 1:36; Kurt von Preisdorff, ed., *Soldatisches Führertum*, Part 8, *Die preußischen Generale von 1820 bis 1840* (Hamburg: Hanseatisches Verlaganstalt, [1937]), 65.

35. *Leben*, 1:35–36; Jany, *Geschichte*, 3:267.

36. Jany, *Geschichte*, 3:269; Theodore Fontane, *Wanderung durch die Mark Brandenburg: Die Grafschaft Ruppin*, Vol. 1 (Stuttgart: J.G. Cotta'sche, 1905), 1:208; Carl von Clausewitz, "Journal eine Reise von Soissons über Dijon nach Genf," *Leben*, 1:90–91.

37. Paret, *Clausewitz*, 30; Wagner, *Feldzug*, xix–xx.

38. Hew Strachan, *Clausewitz's On War* (New York: Atlantic Monthly Press, 2007), 185–86. For the lectures, see Carl von Clausewitz, "Meine Vorlesungen über den kleinen Krieg, gehalten auf der Kriegschule, 1810–1811," in *Schriften—Aufsätze—Studien—Briefe*, 3 vols. in 2 (hereafter *Schriften*) Werner Hahlweg, ed. (Göttingen: Vandenhoeck & Ruprecht, 1966–1990), 1:228–588, espec. Hahlweg's notes, 212, and Clausewitz's, 239.

39. Blanning, *Wars*, 96, 100–101.

40. Rothenberg, *Art of Warfare*, 12–14.

41. Ibid., 11–13.

42. *OW*, 591–93; Daniel Moran, "Clausewitz and the Revolution," *Central European History*, Vol. 22, No. 2 (June 1989), 183.

43. *OW*, 312, 319–21.

44. Rothenberg, *Art of Warfare*, 67.

45. Jany, *Geschichte*, 3:269–270; August Lufft, *Der Feldzug am Mittelrhein von Mitte August bis Ende Dezember 1793* (Freiburg: J. C. B. Mohr, 1881), 5 and fn. 1, 6; Gieraths, *Die Kampfhandlungen*, 113; Taeglischsbeck, *Das Füsilier-Regiment*, 170–71.

46. Blanning, *Wars*, 111; Wagner, *Feldzug*, 108; Jany, *Geschichte*, 3:271–72; Gieraths, *Die Kampfhandlungen*, 113; Leggiere, *Blücher*, 41. Jany does not include Clausewitz's regiment among those that fought in the September 14, 1793, battle, 273 fn. 61.

47. Leggiere, *Blücher*, 41, 43–45; Jany, *Geschichte*, 3:275, 277; Blanning, *Wars*, 111–12; Gieraths, *Die Kampfhandlungen*, 113.

48. Rothfels, *Clausewitz*, 5 and fn. 9; Clausewitz, "Journal eine Reise von Soissons über Dijon nach Genf," *Leben*, 1:90–91.

49. Gieraths, *Die Kampfhandlungen*, 113.

50. Fontane, *Wanderung*, 208; Gieraths, *Die Kampfhandlungen*, 113; Clausewitz to Marie, June 2, 1807, *Leben*, 1:272–74.

51. Blanning, *Wars*, 116; Leggiere, *Blücher*, 66–67; Clausewitz, "Observations," *HPW*, 57; *OW*, 518; Strachan, *Clausewitz's On War*, 37–38.

52. Blanning, *Wars*, 127.

53. Ibid., 131–35; Jany, *Geschichte*, 3:273.

54. Clausewitz, "Observations," *HPW*, 64.

CHAPTER 2

1. Clausewitz to Marie, Apr. 9, July 3, 1807, *Leben*, 1:265–67, 281–84; Paret, *Clausewitz*, 39.

2. Preisdorff, ed., *Soldatisches*, 65–66; Fontane, *Wanderung*, 209–10; Rothfels, *Clausewitz*, 10 and fn. 19; Clausewitz to Marie, July 3, 1807, *Leben*, 1:281–84; Paret, *Clausewitz*, 41–43, 46.

3. Paret, *Clausewitz*, 44–45; Clausewitz, "Observations," 40–41.

4. "Nachricht von den Industrieschulen des Regiments Prinz Ferdinand von Preußen zu Neuruppin," in Nicolai von Biester, ed., *Neue Berlinische Monatsschrift* 3 (June 1800), 407–08; Paret, *Clausewitz*, 45, 52–55; *OW*, 141, 158.

5. Preisdorff, ed., *Soldatisches*, 66.

6. Clausewitz to Marie, Jan. 28, 1807, *Karl und Marie*, 82–85; *Leben*, 1:38.

7. Charles Edward White, *The Enlightened Soldier: Scharnhorst and the Militärische Gesellschaft in Berlin, 1801–1805* (Westport, CT: Praeger, 1989), 2–6.

8. Ibid., 7–14.

9. Ibid., 15–18.

10. Ibid., 19–21.

11. Ibid., 87–90.

12. Paret, *Clausewitz*, 69–70.

13. Ibid., 74; Strachan, *Clausewitz's On War*, 41; Marie von Clausewitz, "Erinnerung," 214; Rothfels, *Clausewitz*, 12 fn. 26.

14. Clausewitz to Marie, Apr. 9, 1807, *Leben*, 1:265–67; Marie von Clausewitz, "Erinnerung," 214–15; *Leben*, 1:41; Strachan, *Clausewitz's On War*, 41; Paret, *Clausewitz*, 74.

15. Max Lehmann, *Scharnhorst* (Leipzig: Hirzel, 1886), 1:525; Scharnhorst quoted in Paret, *Clausewitz*, 76.

16. White, *Scharnhorst*, xiii, 205; "Auflösung der 26ten Aufgabe," Dec. 3, 1803, *Schriften*, 1:57–58; Paret, *Clausewitz*, 78 fn., 79 fn. 1. For the remaining fragments of these notebooks: Rothfels, *Clausewitz*, 197–220, Carl von Clausewitz, *Politische Schriften und Briefe*, Hans Rothfels, ed. (Munich: Drei Masten Verlag, 1922), 1–5, and Carl von Clausewitz, *Geist and Tat*, W. M. Schering, ed. (Stuttgart: Alfred Kröner, 1941), 7–10, 12–15, 17–19. Paret and Moran provide a translation and reconstruction of the surviving parts: Carl von Clausewitz, "Notes on History and Politics," and in *HPW*, 239–49, 264–68. See also their very useful editor and translator notes, ibid., 237–39, 264–64.

17. Clausewitz, "Notes on History and Politics," *HPW*, 241–42.

18. Ibid., 242–43; Rothfels, *Clausewitz*, 29–30 and fn. 5.

19. Carl von Clausewitz, *Strategie: aus dem Jahr 1804, mit Zusätzen von 1808 und 1809*, Eberhard Kessel, ed. (Hamburg: Hanseatische Verlagsanstalt, 1937), 37–82. I have generally relied upon a translation: Carl von Clausewitz, *Strategie: From the year 1804, with addenda from 1808 and 1809*, Marc Guarin, trans. (Unpublished manuscript, 2012), 1–46, (hereafter: Clausewitz, *Strategie*).

20. Clausewitz, *Strategie*, 10–12, 14–15.

21. Ibid., 17, 19, 22; Clausewitz, *Strategie*, Kessel, ed., 49–50.

22. Clausewitz, *Strategie*, 25; *OW*, 128.

23. Clausewitz, *Strategie*, 18–19, 24; Jomini, *The Art of War*, 59–62.

24. Clausewitz, *Strategie*, 17.

25. Ibid., 25.

26. Carl von Clausewitz, "Considérations sur la manière de faire la guerre à la France," *Schriften*, 1:58–63, 58 fn. 1.

27. Rothfels, *Clausewitz*, 30; [Carl von Clausewitz], "Bemerkungen über die reine und angewandte Strategie des Herrn von Bulow; oder Kritik der darin enthaltenen Ansichten," *Neue Bellona*, IX, No. 3 (1805), 252–53.

28. Clausewitz, "Bemerkungen," 255, 261, 266–67, 271, 273; *OW*, 128.

29. Clausewitz, "On the Life and Character of Scharnhorst," *HPW*, 103; Heuser, *Reading Clausewitz*, 9; Clausewitz, "Bemerkungen," 284; Rothfels, *Clausewitz*, 55.

30. Clausewitz, "Bemerkungen," 275.

31. Rothfels, *Clausewitz*, 57; Paret, *Clausewitz*, 93–94.

32. Rothfels, *Clausewitz*, 61; Carl von Clausewitz, "Strategische Beleuchtung mehrerer Feldzüge von Gustav Adolph," *HW* (1862), 9:1–90; "Historische Materialen zur Strategie," 91–128, "Turenne," 129–193, "Luxemburg," 195–230; "Der Briefe der Madame de Maintenon an die Prinzessin des Ursins," 231–35, all in *HW* (1862), volume 9.

33. Priesdorff, ed., *Soldatisches*, 65, 67; Paret, *Clausewitz*, 75–76, 109; Rothfels, *Clausewitz*, 25.

CHAPTER 3

1. Clausewitz to Marie, Sept. 18 [1806], *Karl und Marie*, 57–60; *Leben*, 1:217–20.

2. Clark, *Iron Kingdom*, 303–04; Walter Goerlitz, *History of the German General Staff, 1657–1945*, Brian Battershaw, trans. (New York: Praeger, 1959), 25.

3. Clausewitz, "Observations," 34.

4. Ibid., 34–35.

5. Michael V. Leggiere, *Napoleon and Berlin: The Franco-Prussian War in North Germany, 1813* (Norman: University of Oklahoma Press, 2002), 3–5.

6. Quoted in Leggiere, *Napoleon and Berlin*, 5–6; Paul W. Schroeder, *The Transformation of European Politics, 1763–1848* (Oxford: Oxford University Press, 1994), 254.

7. Leggiere, *Napoleon and Berlin*, 5–6.

8. Ibid., 6.

9. Ibid.; David G. Chandler, *The Campaigns of Napoleon* (New York: Scribner, 1966), 444.

10. Chandler, *Campaigns*, 443–44; Clausewitz, "Observations," 58–59, 65–67.

11. Leggiere, *Napoleon and Berlin*, 6–7; Clausewitz, "Observations," 68.

12. Leggiere, *Napoleon and Berlin*, 6–7.

13. Ibid., 7–9; Clark, *Iron Kingdom*, 304.

14. Clausewitz, "1806," 530–31.

15. Leggiere, *Napoleon and Berlin*, 9–10; Chandler, *Campaigns*, 466–67; Clark, *Iron Kingdom*, 305.

16. Leggiere, *Napoleon and Berlin*, 16; Clausewitz, "Observations," 42–44; Leggiere, *Blücher*, 98.

17. *OW*, 494; Clausewitz, "1806," 533, 536.

18. Clausewitz, "1806," 533–34; *OW*, 494.

19. Leggiere, *Napoleon and Berlin*, 16–17; Clausewitz, "1806," 534.

20. Clausewitz, "1806," 532–36, 541–45.

21. Chandler, *Campaigns*, 465, 467–68.

22. Ibid.; Ross, *European*, 258; [Carl von Clausewitz] to the editor, Feb. 19, 1807, in "Historische Briefe über die großen Kriegs-Ereignisse im October 1806," *Minerva*, No. 4 (Apr. 1807), 4–5. Clausewitz gives the distances in German miles, one of which is the equivalent of 4.7 current U.S. miles. I have converted

the numbers that he gave, which are as follows: seven or eight [German] miles; four [German] miles; 30 [German] miles.

23. Clausewitz to the editors of *Allgemeinen Jenaischen Literature-Zeitung,* May 23, 1806, in Werner Hahlweg, "Clausewitz bei Liddell Hart," *Archiv für Kulturgeschichte* XLI, No. 1 (1959), 100–05.

24. Clausewitz, "1806," 520–21; *OW,* 211–12.

25. Paret, *Clausewitz,* 98–99; Clausewitz to Marie, Sept. 11, Dec., 1, 1806, *Karl und Marie,* 54–57, 64–70; *Leben,* 1:214–17, 226–29; Marie von Clausewitz, "Aufzeichnungen der Frau von Clausewitz über ihr Jugendleben," *Leben,* 1:181–82. For their early relationship see Marie von Clausewitz, "Aufzeichnungen der Frau von Clausewitz über die Zeit der ersten Bekanntschaft mit ihrem Gatten," *Leben,* 1:183–95.

26. Paret, *Clausewitz,* 99–102, 109, 102 fn. 8; Clausewitz to Marie, Sept. 11, 1806, *Karl und Marie,* 54–57; Marie von Clausewitz, "Aufzeichnungen der Frau von Clausewitz über ihr Jugendleben," *Leben,* 1:175.

27. Clausewitz to Marie, Aug. 30, Sept. 18, 20, 26, 1806, *Karl und Marie,* 52–53, 57–60, 60–64; *Leben,* 1:212–14, 220–23.

28. Clausewitz to Marie, Sept. 29, 1806, *Karl und Marie,* 64–66; *Leben,* 1:223–26; Echevarria, *Clausewitz and Contemporary War,* 103.

29. Clausewitz to Marie, Sept. 29, 1806, *Karl und Marie,* 64–66; *Leben,* 1:223–26.

30. Chandler, *Campaigns,* 470–71; Ross, *European,* 258; Clark, *Iron Kingdom,* 305–06.

31. Clausewitz to Marie, Oct. 12, 1806, *Karl und Marie,* 67; *Leben,* 1:226; Chandler, *Campaigns,* 471–72; Ross, *European,* 258; [Carl von Clausewitz] to the editor [part 2], Dec. 19, 1806, in "Historische Briefe über die großen Kriegs-Ereignisse im October 1806," *Minerva,* No. 2 (Feb.1807), 194–95; August von Preußen, "Aus dem kriegsgeschichtlichen Nachlasse Seiner Königlichen Hoheit des Prinzen August von Preußen: Feldzug 1806," in *Kriegsgeschichtliche Einzelschriften,* Großen Generalstabe, ed. (Berlin: Mittler, 1883), 2:10 and 11 notes.

32. Ross, *European,* 258; Chandler, *Campaigns,* 479, 488.

33. Chandler, *Campaigns,* 479, 489; Ross, *European,* 258.

34. Clausewitz, "1806," 539; [Carl von Clausewitz] to the editor [part 2], Dec. 19, 1806, in "Historische Briefe über die großen Kriegs-Ereignisse im October 1806," *Minerva,* No. 2 (Feb. 1807), 193–209. The other two letters are: [Carl von Clausewitz] to the editor [part 1], Dec. 19, 1806, in "Historische Briefe über die großen Kriegs-Ereignisse im October 1806," *Minerva,* No. 1 (Jan. 1807), 2–21; [Carl von Clausewitz] to the editor [part 1], Feb. 19, 1807, in "Historische Briefe über die großen Kriegs-Ereignisse im October 1806," *Minerva,* No. 4 (Apr. 1807), 3–26.

35. Chandler, *Campaigns,* 490–91; Clausewitz, "Observations," 44.

36. Chandler, *Campaigns,* 492–95; Peter Paret, *The Cognitive Challenge of War: Prussia 1806* (Princeton: Princeton University Press, 2009), 25; Oscar von Lettow-Vorbeck, *Der Krieg von 1806 und 1807,* Vol. 1, *Jena und Auerstedt* (Berlin: Ernst Siegfried Mittler und Sohn, 1891), 1:392.

37. *OW*, 494.

38. Preußen, "Feldzug 1806," 2:11 and notes, 2:12; F. Lorraine Petre, *Napoleon's Conquest of Prussia—1806* (London: John Lane, 1914), 162; Clausewitz, "1806," 574–75; *OW*, 240.

39. Preußen, "Feldzug 1806," 2:13–14 and notes; Lettow-Vorbeck, *Der Krieg*, 392; Paret, *Cognitive*, 25–26; P. Roques, *Le Général de Clausewitz: Sa Vie et sa Théorie de la Guerre* (Paris: Berger-Levrault, 1912), 13.

40. Preußen, "Feldzug 1806," 2:14 and note; Lettow-Vorbeck, *Der Krieg*, 1:392; Paret, *Cognitive*, 26; Roques, *Le Général de Clausewitz*, 13.

41. Preußen, "Feldzug 1806," 2:14–15.

42. Ibid., 2:15.

43. Lettow-Vorbeck, *Der Krieg*, 1:392–93; Petre, *Napoleon's Conquest*, 162–63; Preußen, "Feldzug 1806," 2:15 notes; Paret, *Clausewitz*, 125; Prince August to the king, Feb. 16, 1809, *Leben*, 1:126–27.

44. Petre, *Napoleon's Conquest*, 162–63.

45. *OW*, 254–55.

46. Lettow-Vorbeck, *Der Krieg*, 392–93; Preußen, "Feldzug 1806," 2:15–18; Clausewitz, "1806," 599 note.

47. Preußen, "Feldzug 1806," 2:18.

48. Ibid., 2:18–19; Clausewitz, *1806*, 596–97.

49. Preußen, "Feldzug 1806," 2:20; M. A. Thiers, *History of the Consulate and Empire of France under Napoleon*, D. Forbes Campbell, trans. (London: Henry Colburn, 1847), 7:86.

50. Preußen, "Feldzug 1806," 2:22; Clausewitz, "1806," 599 note.

51. Preußen, "Feldzug 1806," 2:22; Thiers, *Consulate*, 7:86; Gieraths, *Kampfhandlungen*, 6, 49.

52. Preußen, "Feldzug 1806," 2:22.

53. Ibid., 2:22.

54. Ibid., 2:22.

55. Ibid., 2:22.

56. Ibid., 2:23.

57. Ibid., 2:23.

58. Ibid., 2:23; *Leben*, 1:50.

59. Preußen, "Feldzug 1806," 2:23–25 note, 26 note.

60. Ibid., 2:26.

61. Clausewitz, "1806," 604; Preußen, "Feldzug 1806," 2:27.

62. Clausewitz, "1806," 604; Preußen, "Feldzug 1806," 2:27–28.

63. Preußen, "Feldzug 1806," 2:28; Clausewitz, "1806," 604.

64. Preußen, "Feldzug 1806," 2:28; Clausewitz, "1806," 604–05.

65. Preußen, "Feldzug 1806," 2:28; Clausewitz, "1806," 605.

66. [Clausewitz] to the editor, Feb. 19, 1807, "Historische Briefe," 20–21; Preußen, "Feldzug 1806," 2:28; Clausewitz, "1806," 605–06.

67. Preußen, "Feldzug 1806," 2:28; Clausewitz, "1806," 606.

68. Clausewitz, "1806," 606–07.

69. Ibid., 607, 610; Preußen, "Feldzug 1806," 2:30.

70. Clausewitz, "1806," 595, 610–11.

71. Preußen, "Feldzug 1806," 2:30; [Clausewitz] to the editor, Feb, 19, 1807, "Historische Briefe," 20–01.

72. Clausewitz, "1806," 607–08; Preußen, "Feldzug 1806," 2:30.

73. Clausewitz, "1806," 608; Preußen, "Feldzug 1806," 2:31.

74. Clausewitz, "1806," 608–10; Preußen, "Feldzug 1806," 2:31; Clausewitz to Marie, Dec. 1, 1806, *Karl und Marie*, 67–70; *Leben*, 1:226–29. Clausewitz does not make absolutely clear in this letter that he is describing the events around Prenzlau, but it seems to fit as he gives the same duration for the fight in this letter—three hours—as he gives in his history of the campaign.

75. Clausewitz, "1806," 609–10; Chandler, *Campaigns*, 501.

76. Clausewitz, "1806," 609–10; Preußen, "Feldzug 1806," 2:31, 32 notes.

77. Chandler, *Campaigns*, 501–02.

78. Ibid., 502.

CHAPTER 4

1. Charles Esdaile, *Napoleon's Wars: An International History, 1803–1815* (New York: Viking, 2008), 274–76, 277, 282–84; Clausewitz, "1806," 603.

2. Ross, *European*, 260–63; Schroeder, *Transformation*, 319–20.

3. Ross, *European*, 263–64; Craig, *Politics*, 35; Leggiere, *Napoleon and Berlin*, 22–23; Janet M. Hartley, *Alexander I* (London: Longman, 1994), 78–79.

4. Roques, *Le Général de Clausewitz*, 14; [Clausewitz] to the editor, Feb. 19, 1807, "Historische Briefe," 20.

5. Clausewitz to Marie, Dec. 1, 1806, *Leben*, 1:226–29. During this time he also penned three unsigned letters about the 1806 campaign that were published in the journal *Minerva* in early 1807.

6. Clausewitz, "Mein Reisejournal," Jan. 9, 16, 18, 28, 1807, *Leben*, 1:237–40; Clausewitz to Marie, Jan. 3, 1807, *Leben*, 1:234–35.

7. Clausewitz to Marie, Jan. 23, 28, Feb. 4, 28, Apr. 9, 1807, *Leben*, 1:239–43, 245–51, 265–67; Ch. de Reitzenstein, "Journal d'un officier prussien prissonier de guerre à Nancy (1806–1808)," Alfred Martin, trans., *Le Pays Lorrain et le Pays Messin*, No. 11 (1910), 684; Eve Haas and Herzeleide Henning, *Prinz August von Preußen* (Berlin: Stapp Verlag, 1988), 57.

8. Clausewitz to Marie, Feb. 28, 1807, *Leben*, 1:246–51.

9. Clausewitz to Marie, Mar. 17, 28, 1807, *Leben*, 1: 246–51, 253–55, and 1:64; Reitzenstein, "Journal d'un officier prussien prissonier de guerre à Nancy," 688; Haas and Henning, *Prinz August*, 57–58.

10. Clausewitz to Marie, Mar. 16, 17, Oct. 5, 1807, *Leben*, 1:251–55, 293–300; Roques, *Le Général de Clausewitz*, 7; Clausewitz, "Notes on History and Politics," *HPW*, 265.

11. Clausewitz to Marie, Mar. 29, Apr. 2, 1807, *Leben*, 1:255–62, Apr. 2, Niels Nielsen, trans; Haas and Henning, *Prinz August*, 57.

12. Clausewitz to Marie, June 15, 25, 28, July 3, 1807, *Leben*, 1:275–84.

13. Clausewitz to Marie, Aug. 16, 1807, *Leben*, 1:285–87, and 1:64.

14. Clausewitz to Marie, Aug. 16, Sept. 1, 1807, *Leben*, 1:285–89. For a view of the relationship between August and Madame Recamier, see Roger Parkinson, *Clausewitz: A Biography* (New York: Stein and Day, 1971), 90–93.

15. "Pestalozzi," *Leben*, 1:110–15; Clausewitz to Marie, Apr. 5, Aug. 16, Sept. 15, 1807, *Leben*, 1: 262–64, 285–87, 289–91, and 64–65; Paul Saettler, *The Evolution of American Educational Technology* (Charlotte, NC: Information Age Publishing, 2004), 39.

16. *Leben*, 1:66; Alexandra Richie, *Faust's Metropolis: A History of Berlin* (New York: Carroll & Graf, 1998), 97–110.

17. Clausewitz, "Observations," 40.

18. Paret, *Cognitive*, 77; Craig, *Politics*, 38–39.

19. Quoted in Craig, *Politics*, 39–40.

20. Ibid., 40–41.

21. Peter Paret, *Yorck and the Era of Prussian Reform, 1807–1815* (Princeton: Princeton University Press, 1966), 122, 125–26; Craig, *Politics*, 38–39.

22. Craig, *Politics*, 37–38; Clausewitz, "Observations," 76.

23. Quoted in White, *Scharnhorst*, 131; Clausewitz, "Scharnhorst," *HPW*, 100–01.

24. Quoted in Craig, *Politics*, 42–44.

25. Paret, *Yorck*, 126 and fn. 27, 127; Haas and Henning, *Prinz August*, 60; Craig, *Politics*, 45, 48.

26. Paret, *Yorck*, 133–35.

27. Ibid., 135; Craig, *Politics*, 46–50.

28. Craig, *Politics*, 50; Paret, *Yorck*, 167–68, 179–80.

29. Craig, *Politics*, 51–52.

30. Ibid., 45.

31. *Leben*, 1:114; Scharnhorst to Clausewitz, Nov. 27, Dec. 17, 1807, Gerhard von Scharnhorst, *Scharnhorsts Briefe: Privatbriefe*, Karl Linnebach, ed. (Munich: G. Mueller, 1914), 1:333–38.

32. Clausewitz to Marie, Sept. 1, 1807, *Leben*, 1:287–89, and 121–22.

33. Clark, *Iron Kingdom*, 325; Hahlweg notes, *Schriften*, 1:613; Marie von Clausewitz, "Erinnerung," 1:216.

34. *Leben*, 1:122.

35. Clausewitz to Marie, Aug. 5, 1808, *Leben*, 1:309–11, and 1:141, 173 and notes.

36. Clausewitz to Marie, Aug. 22, 1808, *Leben*, 1:316; Marie to Clausewitz, Aug. 25, 28, 1808, *Leben*, 1:376–77.

37. Clausewitz to Marie, Aug. 10, 1808, *Leben*, 1:312–14.

38. Clark, *Iron Kingdom*, 326.

39. Clausewitz to Marie, Aug. 10, 1808, *Leben*, 1:312–14.

40. Preisdorff, ed., *Soldatisches*, 67; Clausewitz to Marie, Aug. 17, 1808, *Leben*, 1:314–16.

41. Clausewitz to Marie, Sept. 4, Dec. 4, 1808, *Leben*, 1:316–17, 324–26; Strachan, *Clausewitz's On War*, 48. Paret identifies the regulations originally published in Scharnhorst's name: [Carl von Clausewitz], "Kriegsartikel für die Unter-Officiere und gemeinen Söldaten (der königl. preussischen Armee)....Verordnung wegen der Militär-Strafen. Verordnung wegen Bestrafung der Officiere....Reglement über die Besetzung der Stellen der Port-epée Fähnriche und über die Wahl zum Officier...." *Jenaische Allgemeine Literatur-Zeitung*, No. 238 (Oct. 11, 1808), 65–68. It was reprinted in a slightly altered form in *Jenaische Allgemeine Literatur-Zeitung*, No. 238 (Nov. 2, 1808), see Paret, *Clausewitz*, 139–40 and fn. 8.

42. Marie to Clausewitz, Oct. 4, 1808, *Leben*, 1:377–79.

43. Schroeder, *Transformation*, 347–48; Clausewitz to Marie, Oct. 20, Nov. 27, 1808, *Leben*, 1:318–19, 323–24.

44. Marie to Clausewitz, Dec. 8, 1808, *Leben*, 1:385–86; Clausewitz to Marie, Dec. 4, 1808, Jan. 23, Feb. 23, 1809, *Leben*, 1:324–26, 335–35, 338–40; Priesdorff, *Soldatisches*, 67. Clausewitz also remarked that he also had some additional income that might raise his salary to between 1,300 and 1,500 thalers a year, but he does not specify what he meant by this. He is possibly referring to housing and mess allowances.

45. Leggiere, *Napoleon and Berlin*, 23–24; Frederick William III quoted in Clark, *Iron Kingdom*, 346.

46. White, *Scharnhorst*, 155–56; Craig, *Politics*, 54–53, 53 fn. 4.

47. Clausewitz to Marie, Apr. 23, 1809, *Leben*, 1:344–48; Marie to Clausewitz, May 8, 1809, *Leben*, 1:397–98.

48. Clausewitz to Gneisenau, Apr. 12, 1809, *Schriften*, 1:617–19, and Hahlweg notes, 1:44; Clausewitz to Marie, Apr. 23, May 10, 1809, *Leben*, 1:344–50; Clark, *Iron Kingdom*, 345; "Bedingungen, welche dem Oestreichischen Kriegs Ministerio vorzuschlagen wären," [Frühjahr 1809] and "Beförderungs Modus in der *Legion*," [Frühjahr 1809], *Schriften*, 1:671–76.

49. Clausewitz to Marie, June 19, July 20, 31, 1809, *Leben*, 1:358–64.

50. Clausewitz to Marie, May 16, Aug. 8, 1809, *Leben*, 1:352, 364–65; Leggiere, *Napoleon and Berlin*, 24.

51. Clausewitz to Marie, Jan. 2, 9, June 26, Oct. 9, 18, 1809, *Leben*, 1:330–34, 360–61, 370–72, and 142; Scharnhorst to Prinz August, Oct. 20, 1809, *Scharnhorsts Briefe*, 1:378–79.

52. Craig, *Politics*, 49, 55; Strachan, *Clausewitz's On War*, 48.

53. Clausewitz to Gneisenau, Feb. 8, 1810, *Schriften*, 1:619–23; Gneisenau to his wife, June [?] 1810, *Leben*, 1:147; G. H. Pertz and Hans Delbrück, *Das Leben des Feldmarschalls Grafen Neidhardt von Gneisenau* (Berlin: Reimer, 1864–80) (hereafter, Pertz-Delbrück, *Gneisenau*), 1:608–09.

54. Clausewitz to Gneisenau, June 24, Aug. 17, 1810, *Schriften*, 1:627–31; Paret, *Clausewitz*, 209.

55. For Clausewitz's, surviving service-related correspondence from Oct. 16, 1810–Mar. 25, 1812, see the letters and logs in *Schriften*, 1:106–208; Marie von Clausewitz, "Erinnerung," 1:215.

56. Paret, *Yorck*, 170; Peter Paret, 'Clausewitz: "Half against my will, I have become a Professor,"' *Journal of Military History* 75 (Apr. 2011), 592; Clausewitz to Gneisenau, June 24, 1810, *Schriften*, 1:627–29.

57. *Leben*, 1:152 and notes; Paret, *Cognitive*, 97; Paret, '"Half against my will,"' 593–600; Paret, *Yorck*, 176–78. Clausewitz's lectures: "Meine Vorlesungen über den kleinen Krieg, gehalten auf der Kriegschule, 1810–1811," *Schriften*, 1:228–588. See p. 321 for "Wassington."

58. Clausewitz to Gneisenau, Oct. 20, 1810, *Schriften*, 1:632–35; *Leben*, 1:149; Paret, *Clausewitz*, 194–95, and fn. 61; Hahlweg notes, *Schriften*, 2/1:102. For the surviving material related to Clausewitz's instruction of the princes see "Entwurf der dem Herrn General Guadi," *HW* (1857), 3:173–78.

59. Preisdorff, ed., *Soldatisches*, 65; Clausewitz to Marie, Apr. 9, 1807, *Leben*, 1:265–67, and 1:156, 172, 174.

60. Paret, *Clausewitz*, 211.

61. Ibid., and quoted in, 210–11.

62. Clausewitz to Gneisenau, Jan. 29, 1811, *Schriften*, 1:637–40.

63. Clausewitz to Gneisenau, Sept. 2, 13, 1811, *Schriften*, 1:661–63, 656–58; Clausewitz, "Mein Vertheidigungs-Plan für Schlesien," Sept. 13, 1811, ibid., 1:663–66; "Gneisenau's Plan einer deutschen Legion, Nov. 1811, von Clausewitz's Hand," Pertz-Delbrück, *Gneisenau*, 2:685–88, and 2:158–59.

64. Paret, *Yorck*, 155–56; Strachan, *Clausewitz's On War*, 50; Gneisenau, "Plan zur Vorbereitung eines Volksaufstands," Pertz-Delbrück, *Gneisenau*, 2:112–42; Clark, *Iron Kingdom*, 345, 350; Gneisenau quoted in Craig, *Politics*, 56–57.

65. Clausewitz, "Notes on History and Politics," *HPW*, 247 fn. 8, 249.

66. Clausewitz, "The Germans and the French," *HPW*, and Paret and Moran notes, 250–62. The original: Clausewitz, "Die Deutschen und die Franzosen," *Leben*, 1:73–88.

67. Clausewitz, "Notes on History and Politics," and "Letter to Fichte," *HPW*, 274, 280–84; Niccolò Machiavelli, *The Discourses*, Leslie J. Walker, trans. (London: Penguin, 1970), especially 436–37; Clausewitz to Marie, Apr. 15, 1808, *Leben*, 1:305–6; Clausewitz, "Ein kunsttheoretisches Fragment Warhscheinlich zwischen 1809 und 1812," *Verstreute kleine Schriften*, Werner Hahlweg, ed. (Osnabrück: Biblio, 1979), 147–56. The original letter to Fichte: [Clausewitz] to Fichte, June 11, 1809, Clausewitz, *Verstreute kleine Schriften*, 157–66. Paret notes that Clausewitz wrote a number of pieces on art theory that survive in various forms, but that the dating of each piece is a problem, Paret, *Clausewitz*, 163 fn. 31. The pieces (sometimes duplicated) can be found in Clausewitz, *Verstreute kleine Schriften*, 147–56; Schering, *Geist und Tat*, 153–78; Hans Rothfels, "Ein kunsttheoretisches Fragment von General von Clausewitz," *Deutsche Rundschau*, CLXXIII, No. 3 (1917): 373–82.

68. Clausewitz, "Ueber die Künftigen Kriegs-Operationen Preußens gegen Frankreich," *Schriften*, 1:66–90, 66 fn. 1, especially 80–81, 83, 85, 90.

69. Clausewitz, *Strategie*, 30, 38, 40–41; Richie, *Faust's Metropolis*, 100–02; Paret, *Clausewitz*, 99.

70. Clausewitz, *Strategie*, 39–41; Jomini, *Art of War*, 11, 59–62. On the links between "Little War" and *On War*, see Hahlweg notes, *Schriften*, 1:644 fn. 11.

71. Clausewitz to Gneisenau, June 17, 1811, *Schriften*, 1:640–48, Niels Nielsen, trans.

72. Clausewitz, [Bekenntnisdenkschrift], [Feb. 1812], *Schriften*, 1:742–43.

73. Hahlweg notes, *Schriften*, 2/1:17, 19–20; *Schriften*, 2/1:62, Niels Nielsen, trans., 2/1:78; Karl von Clausewitz, *On War*, O. J. Matthijs Jolles, trans. (Washington: Combat Forces Press, 1943), xxix, 3.

74. *Schriften*, 2/1:22–69, espec. 22, 44. Hahlweg points out that some of this material was published previously in Clausewitz, *Geist und Tat*, 52–60.

75. Paret, *Cognitive*, 140; Echevarria, *Clausewitz and Contemporary War*, 3–4, 22–25.

76. Paret, *Yorck*, 157.

CHAPTER 5

1. Leggiere, *Napoleon and Berlin*, 24.

2. Dierk Walter, "Meeting the French Challenge: Conscription in Prussia, 1807–1815," in *Conscription in the Napoleonic Era: A Revolution in Military Affairs?* Donald Stoker, Frederick C. Schneid, and Harold Blanton, eds. (London: Routledge, 2009), 32; Paret, *Clausewitz*, 140–41; Leggiere, *Blücher*, 172–73, 183–84.

3. Quoted in Leggiere, *Napoleon and Berlin*, 24–25; Paret, *Yorck*, 171 fn. 47.

4. Clausewitz quoted in Craig, *Politics*, 57–58; Carl von Clausewitz, *The Campaign of 1812 in Russia*, (hereafter Clausewitz, *1812*), foreword by Sir Michael Howard (New York: Da Capo, 1995), 1; Clausewitz to Marie, Apr. 23, 1809, *Leben*, 1:344–48.

5. Paret and Moran notes, *HPW*, 285–86; Paret and Moran provide a partial English translation, Carl von Clausewitz, "From the 'Political Declaration,'" *HPW*, 287–312. See especially, 289, 293, 295–96, 300. The complete original text: Carl von Clausewitz, [Bekenntnisdenkschrift], [Feb. 1812], *Schriften*, 1:678–750.

6. Clausewitz, "Political Declaration," *HPW*, 296; Clausewitz, [Bekenntnisdenkschrift], [Feb. 1812], *Schriften*, 1:713–14, 716–27, 734, 747 and fn. 190.

7. Clausewitz, [Bekenntnisdenkschrift], [Feb. 1812], *Schriften*, 1:742.

8. *OW*, 480.

9. Paret and Moran notes, *HPW*, 286; Clausewitz, "Political Declaration," *HPW*, 291.

10. Scharnhorst to Major v. Thile, May 17, 1812, *Scharnhorsts Briefe*, 1:433–34; Clausewitz to Gneisenau, [Beginning 1812], *Schriften*, 1:670–71; Clausewitz to Friedrich Wilhelm [Frederick William], Mar. 29, 1812, *Verstreute kleine*

Schriften, 169–71; Clausewitz to Marie, Apr. 12, 13, 1812, *Leben*, 1:508–10; *Leben*, 1:483 and notes.

11. Clausewitz to Marie, Apr. 2, 3, 4, 1812, *Leben*, 1:505–08; *Leben*, 1:483–84.

12. Clausewitz to Marie, Apr. 12, 13, 18, 28, 1812, *Leben*, 1:508–14, 516–17; Clausewitz to Friedrich Wilhelm [Frederick William], Mar. 29, 1812, *Verstreute kleine Schriften*, 169–71.

13. Carl von Clausewitz, *Principles of War*, Hans W. Gatzke ed. and trans. (Harrisburg, PA: Stackpole, 1960) (the original: "Die wichtigsten Grundsätze des Kriegsführens zur Ergänzung meine Unterrichts bei Sr. Königlichsten Hoheit dem Kronprinzen," *HW* (1857), 3:179–223); Paret, *Clausewitz*, 194 and fn. 62; Hahlweg notes, *Schriften*, 2/1:102–03.

14. Clausewitz, *Principles*, 11–12, 14; Paret, *Clausewitz*, 195–96, fn. 65; *OW*, 141.

15. Clausewitz, *Principles*, 15, 19, 26–27.

16. Ibid., 45–47.

17. Ibid., 50–51, 53, 57–58.

18. Ibid., 60–69.

19. Ibid., 67–68.

20. Ibid., 47–48, 57.

21. Ibid., 13, 45.

22. *Leben*, 1:484; Clausewitz to Marie, Apr. 20, 21, 1812, *Leben*, 1:514–15; Clausewitz, "1812," *HPW*, 128.

23. Clausewitz to Marie, Apr. 28, 1812, *Leben*, 1:516–17.

24. Clausewitz to Marie, May 5, 1812, *Leben*, 1:517–18.

25. Clausewitz to Marie, May 8, 1812, *Leben*, 1:518–20.

26. Clausewitz to Marie, May 15, 1812, *Leben*, 1:521–22.

27. Ibid.

28. Paret, *Clausewitz*, 212–13, 212 fn. 16.

29. Clausewitz, *1812*, 3; Clausewitz to Marie, May 23, 1812, *Leben*, 1:522–23; *Leben*, 1:485.

30. Clausewitz to Marie, May 10, 1812, *Leben*, 1:520; Gneisenau to Alexander I, May 20, 1812, Pertz-Delbrück, *Gneisenau*, 2:285.

31. Clausewitz to Marie, May 28, 1812, *Leben*, 1:523; Dominic Lieven, *Russia against Napoleon: The True Story of the Campaigns of War and Peace* (New York: Penguin, 2009), 137.

32. Lieven, *Russia*, 132, 289; William C. Fuller, *Strategy and Power in Russia: 1600–1914* (New York: Free Press, 1992), 198–99.

33. Alexander Mikaberidze, *The Battle of Borodino: Napoleon against Kutusov* (Barnsley: Pen & Sword, 2007), 3–5; Lieven, *Russia*, 58–59, 148.

34. Lieven, *Russia*, 120–24; Mikaberidze, *Borodino*, 6, 9.

35. Quoted in Lieven, *Russia*, 84–85.

36. Lieven, *Russia*, 92–93, 124.

37. Ibid., 124–25.

38. Quoted in Lieven, *Russia*, 130–31; Mikaberidze, *Borodino*, 7.

39. Mikaberidze, *Borodino*, 7–9; Clausewitz, *1812*, 15, 17; Lieven, *Russia*, 130; *OW*, 559, 583.

40. Clausewitz, *1812*, 14–17, 15n.; Mikaberidze, Borodino, 9–10.

41. Roques, *Le Général de Clausewitz*, 57; Clausewitz to Marie, June 6, 20, 1812, *Leben*, 1:523–24; Clausewitz to Gneisenau, June 15/27, 1812, *Schriften*, 2/1:129–31; Clausewitz, *1812*, 4–8.

42. Clausewitz, *1812*, 21–22.

43. Ibid., 17–25.

44. Pertz-Delbrück, *Gneisenau*, 2:336–37; Clausewitz to Tiedemann, June 28, 1812, *Verstreute kleine Schriften*, 175–76.

45. Clausewitz, *1812*, 25–26.

46. Ibid., 26–27.

47. Ibid., 28–29.

48. Ibid., 29–31.

49. Ibid., 31.

50. Ibid., 31–33.

51. Ibid., 33–34; Lieven, *Russia*, 150.

52. Clausewitz, *1812*, 33, 35.

53. Lieven, *Russia*, 150–51; Clausewitz, *1812*, 36–37; Mikaberidze, *Borodino*, 10. The czar's and Bagration's quotes are in Lieven.

54. Clausewitz to Marie, July 6/18, 1812, *Leben*, 1:525–27.

55. Ibid.; Clausewitz, *1812*, 42–43; Ludwig Freiherrn von Wolzogen, *Memoiren des königlich preußlichen Generals der Infanterie Ludwig Freiherrn von Wolzogen* (Leipzig: Otto Wigand, 1851), 96–97; Clausewitz to Marie, Aug. 12/24, 1812, *Leben*, 1:527–30.

56. Clausewitz to Marie, July 6/18, 1812, *Leben*, 1:525–27; Clausewitz, *1812*, 43–44.

57. Lieven, *Russia*, 154, 156–57.

58. Clausewitz, *1812*, 104–05.

59. Lieven, *Russia*, 157; Clausewitz, *1812*, 105–06; Edward Foord, *Napoleon's Russian Campaign of 1812* (New York: Little Brown, 1915), 223.

60. Clausewitz to Marie, Aug. 12/24, 1812, *Leben*, 1:527–30. He was designated to receive the award on October 4, 1812. It is also called "Knight of the Order of St. Vladimir." The award was reaffirmed in 1818, Petersburg, Feb. 28, 1818, *Leben*, 2:63–64.

61. Clausewitz, *1812*, 107–08.

62. Ibid., 106–07; Lieven, *Russia*, 157.

63. Clausewitz to Marie, Aug. 12/24, 1812, *Leben*, 1:527–30.

64. Mikaberidze, *Borodino*, 10–11; Clausewitz, *1812*, 100.

65. Mikaberidze, *Borodino*, 14.

66. Ibid., 16–17.

67. Clausewitz to Gneisenau, Oct. 26/Nov. 7, 1812, *Schriften*, 2/1:131–38; Mikaberidze, *Borodino*, 17; Clausewitz, *1812*, 131.

68. Clausewitz to Marie, Aug. 12/24, 1812, *Leben*, 1:527–30.

69. Ibid.
70. Ibid.
71. Clausewitz to Gneisenau, June 15/27, 1812, *Schriften*, 2/1:129–31; John Robert Seeley, *Life and Times of Stein, or, Germany and Prussia in the Napoleonic Age* (Cambridge: Cambridge University Press, 1878), 2:137–39; Goltz to Gneisenau, Oct. 28, 1812, and Chasot to Gneisenau, Oct. [?], 1812, Pertz-Delbrück, *Gneisenau*, 2:380–87; Clausewitz to Marie, Oct. 23/Nov. 4, 1812, *Leben*, 1:533–35.
72. Mikaberidze, *Borodino*, 18–21; Lieven, *Russia*, 189–91.
73. Clausewitz, "1812," *HPW*, 137; Mikaberidze, *Borodino*, 23–24; Clausewitz to Gneisenau, Oct. 26/Nov. 7, 1812, *Schriften*, 2/1:131–38. It is clear from the casualty numbers given in the letter that Clausewitz means what we now call Borodino and not Mozhaisk.
74. Mikaberidze, *Borodino*, xviii, 26–28; Lieven, *Russia*, 192; Chandler, *Campaigns*, 795.
75. Mikaberidze, *Borodino*, 27; Clausewitz, "1812," *HPW*, 145–50.
76. Lieven, *Russia*, 194, 198; Mikaberidze, *Borodino*, 68; Chandler, *Campaigns*, 798–99.
77. Chandler, *Campaigns*, 799–804.
78. Clausewitz to Marie, Oct. 23/Nov. 4, 1812, *Leben*, 1:533–35; Clausewitz, "1812," *HPW*, 149.
79. Clausewitz, "1812," *HPW*, 149–52.
80. Ibid., 152–53.
81. Mikaberidze, *Borodino*, 144; Clausewitz, "1812," *HPW*, 153.
82. Mikaberidze, *Borodino*, 145–46.
83. Clausewitz, "1812," *HPW*, 153–54. Clausewitz says Italians, but he is wrong about the nationality of their opponents; see Mikaberidze, *Borodino*, 148.
84. Clausewitz, "1812," *HPW*, 154; Mikaberidze, *Borodino*, 144–49.
85. Clausewitz, "1812," *HPW*, 154–55.
86. Ibid., 155; Mikaberidze, *Borodino*, 152–53.
87. Mikaberidze, *Borodino*, 150, 152.
88. Clausewitz, "1812," *HPW*, 157; Mikaberidze, *Borodino*, 201.
89. Mikaberidze, *Borodino*, 203–07, 217–18.
90. OW, 266–67.
91. Mikaberidze, *Borodino*, 202, 219; Petersburg, Aug. 10, 1819, *Leben*, 2:64–65.
92. Clausewitz, "1812," *HPW*, 159; Clausewitz to Gneisenau, Oct. 26/Nov. 7, 1812, *Schriften*, 2/1:131–38; Mikaberidze, *Borodino*, 203, 220–21; Foord, *Napoleon's Russian Campaign*, 223.
93. Clausewitz, "1812," *HPW*, 159–60; Foord, *Napoleon's Russian Campaign*, 224.
94. Clausewitz, "1812," *HPW*, 159–60.
95. Clausewitz to Marie, Oct. 23/Nov. 4, 1812, *Leben*, 1:533–35.

96. Clausewitz, "1812," *HPW*, 162–63; Clausewitz to Gneisenau, Oct. 26/Nov. 7, 1812, *Schriften*, 2/1:131–38.

97. Clausewitz, "1812," *HPW*, 161; Clausewitz to Gneisenau, Oct. 26/Nov. 7, 1812, *Schriften*, 2/1:131–38.

98. Clausewitz, "1812," *HPW*, 160–61, 163.

99. Mikaberidze, *Borodino*, 221–22; Clausewitz to Gneisenau, Oct. 26/Nov. 7, 1812, *Schriften*, 2/1:131–38.

CHAPTER 6

1. Clausewitz, "1812," *HPW*, 161, 163, and notes 20, 21.

2. Ibid., 164; Clausewitz to Marie, Oct. 23/Nov. 4, 1812, *Leben*, 1:533–35; Mikaberidze, *Borodino*, 222.

3. Clausewitz, "1812," *HPW*, 164–65.

4. Ibid., 165–66; *OW*, 114–15, 119–20.

5. Clausewitz, "1812," *HPW*, 169–70; *OW*, 467, 478, 528; Mikaberidze, *Borodino*, 222.

6. Clausewitz, "1812," *HPW*, 171; Clausewitz to Marie, Sept. 18/30, Oct. 23/Nov. 4, 1812, *Leben*, 1:530–31, 533–35.

7. Clausewitz, "1812," *HPW*, 171–72; Chasot to Gneisenau, Oct. [?], 1812, Pertz-Delbrück, *Gneisenau*, 2:384–87.

8. Hermann von Boyen, *Denkwürdigkeiten und Errinerungen, 1771–1813* (Stuttgart: Robert Lutz, 1899), 2:158–59; Wolzogen, *Memoiren*, 163; Marie von Clausewitz, "Erinnerung," 1:216.

9. Clausewitz to Marie, Oct. 15/27, Oct. 29/Nov. 10, 1812, *Leben*, 1:531–33, 535–36.

10. Clausewitz to Marie, Oct. 23/Nov. 4, 1812, *Leben*, 1:533–35; Clausewitz to Gneisenau, Oct. 26/Nov. 7, 1812, *Schriften*, 2/1:131–38.

11. Clausewitz, "1812," *HPW*, 173–74; Clausewitz to Marie, Oct. 23/Nov. 4, Oct. 31/Nov. 12, 1812, *Leben*, 1:533–37; Clausewitz, *1812*, 38.

12. Lieven, *Russia*, quote on 241, 242–46; Alexander Mikaberidze, *The Battle of the Berezina: Napoleon's Great Escape* (Barnsley: Pen & Sword, 2010), 33–36.

13. Lieven, *Russia*, 250–52.

14. Ibid., 265–66.

15. Ibid., 266–69.

16. Ibid., 269–74.

17. Clausewitz, "1812," *HPW*, 174–75.

18. Lieven, *Russia*, 274–75; Clausewitz, "1812," *HPW*, 174.

19. Lieven, *Russia*, 278–80; Mikaberidze, *Berezina*, 140.

20. Lieven, *Russia*, 280–81; Mikaberidze, *Berezina*, 149, 180; Clausewitz, "1812," *HPW*, 178.

21. Clausewitz to Marie, Nov. 17/29, 1812, *Leben*, 1:537–39.

22. Lieven, *Russia*, 281–82.

23. Clausewitz to Marie, Nov. 17/29, 1812, *Leben*, 1:537–39.

24. Clausewitz, "1812," *HPW*, 170, 178–81; Mikaberidze, *Berezina*, 160, 228–30; Christopher Bassford, "Jomini and Clausewitz: Their Interaction," an edited version of a paper presented to the 23rd Meeting of the Consortium on Revolutionary Europe at Georgia State University, Feb. 26, 1993, www.clausewitz.com, 5.

25. Mikaberidze, *Berezina*, 220–22; Clausewitz, "1812," *HPW*, 181; Schering, *Geist und Tat*, 151–52; [Steinman von Friderici], *Was sich die Offiziere im Bureau erzählten: Mittheilungen eine alten Registrators* (Mittler: Berlin, 1853), 36; Heuser, *Reading Clausewitz*, 4; Michael Howard, foreword, in Clausewitz, *1812*, xi.

26. Clausewitz, "1812," *HPW*, 182–84.

27. Ibid., 184.

28. Ibid., 184–85.

29. Paret, *Yorck*, 172, 192; Clausewitz, "1812," *HPW*, 188.

30. Clausewitz, "1812," *HPW*, 186–87, 189, 191.

31. Ibid., 189–190.

32. Ibid., 191.

33. Paret, *Yorck*, 192; Clausewitz, "1812," *HPW*, 191–92; Bruno von Treuenfeld, *Das Jahre 1813: Bis zur Schlacht von Groß-Görschen* (Leipzig: Zuckschwerdt, 1901), 185–86. For the text of the agreement see Maxim Blumenthal, *Die Konvention von Tauroggen* (Berlin: Richard Schroeder, 1901), 55–56.

34. Quotes and material, Clausewitz, "1812," *HPW*, 194.

35. Quoted and material, "1812," *HPW*, 194–95; Dohna in *Leben*, 1:503.

36. Dohna in *Leben*, 1:503; Clausewitz, "1812," *HPW*, 191; Paret, *Yorck*, 192; Paret, *Clausewitz*, 230 fn. 21.

37. Clausewitz to Gneisenau, Oct. 26/Nov. 7, 1812, *Schriften*, 2/1:131–38; Clausewitz, "1812," *HPW*, 199.

38. Clausewitz to Marie, Dec. 18/30, 1812, *Leben*, 1:539.

39. Clausewitz to Marie, Sept. 18/30, Oct. 15/27, 1812, *Leben*, 1:530–33.

CHAPTER 7

1. Quoted in Clark, *Iron Kingdom*, 359.

2. Paret, *Yorck*, 192; Leggiere, *Napoleon and Berlin*, 36–37.

3. Clausewitz, *Strategie*, 11; Mikaberidze, *Berezina*, 223; Lieven, *Russia*, 282–83, 292, 296; Leggiere, *Napoleon and Berlin*, 30–31; Lorraine F. Petre, *Napoleon's Last Campaign in Germany, 1813* (London: John Lane, 1912), 32.

4. *OW*, 559–60; 627.

5. Michael V. Leggiere, *Napoleon and the Struggle for Germany: The Franco-Prussian War of 1813*. Vol. 1: *The War of Liberation, Spring 1813* (Cambridge: Cambridge University Press, 2014, unpublished manuscript), chapter 2; Lieven, *Russia*, 306–08; Esdaile, *Napoleon's Wars*, 494.

6. Leggiere, *Napoleon and Berlin*, 29–30, 33.

7. Clark, *Iron Kingdom*, 362; Leggiere, *Napoleon and Berlin*, 39.

8. Lieven, *Russia*, 287, 289.

9. Ibid.; Pierre Holstein to Alexander, Jan. 13/15, 1813, Fond 846, Opis' 16, Delo 3591, Roll 53, Rossiinskii Gusudarstvennyi Voenno-Istoricheskii (RGVIA), *The Napoleonic Wars, 1805–1815, Military Science Archive at the Russian State Military History Archive* (Woodbridge, CT: Primary Source Microfilm, 2002).

10. Clark, *Iron Kingdom*, 360–61; Leggiere, *Napoleon and Berlin*, 38.

11. Ernst Moritz Arndt, *Erinnerungen aus dem außeren Leben* (Leipzig: Weidmann'sche, 1840), 184–85; Alexander zu Dohna to Schön, Feb. 20, 1820, Einem Ostpreußen [?], *Zu Schutz und Trutz am Grabe Schön's: Bilder aus der Zeit der Schmach und der Erhebung Preußens* (Berlin: Franz Duncker, 1876), 554–55; Paret, *Yorck*, 192; Paret, *Clausewitz*, 231, 231 fn. 23. For Clausewitz's text see, "Das Wesentliche in der Organisation eines Landsturms und einer Miliz," in Treuenfeld, *Das Jahre 1813*, in "Beilage," 139–42.

12. Leggiere, *Napoleon and Berlin*, 39–41, and quote, 44.

13. Clark, *Iron Kingdom*, 363; Leggiere, *Napoleon and Berlin*, 45–47.

14. Chandler, *Campaigns*, 851–52; Leggiere, *Napoleon and the Struggle*, Vol. 1, chapter 2; Leggiere, *Napoleon and Berlin*, 41.

15. Leggiere, *Napoleon and Berlin*, 43; Leggiere, *Napoleon and the Struggle*, Vol. 1, chapter 2.

16. Leggiere, *Napoleon and Berlin*, 47; Leggiere, *Napoleon and the Struggle*, Vol. 1, chapter 2.

17. Leggiere, *Napoleon and Berlin*, 47; Leggiere, *Napoleon and the Struggle*, Vol. 1, chapter 2.

18. Clausewitz, "1812," *HPW*, 199; Louise Radziwill, diary entry for Mar. 14, 1813, Louise Radziwill, *Forty-Five Years of My Life (1770–1815)*, A. R. Allinson, trans., Princess Radziwill, ed. (New York: McBride, Nast & Co., 1912), 348; Paret, *Clausewitz*, 232.

19. Barclay de Tolly to Scharnhorst, Mar. 14/26, 1813, no. 39, Fond 846, Opis' 16, Delo 3947, part 2, Roll 80, RGVIA, transcribed by Margarete Ritzkowsky (there is another note mentioning Clausewitz in this file but it is virtually unreadable, neither have been published: [Barclay de Tolly] to Wittgenstein, Mar. 14/26, 1813, ibid.); Clausewitz to Marie, Mar. 26, 1813, *Leben*, 2:68–70.

20. Clausewitz to Marie, Mar. 25, 26, 1813, *Leben*, 2:68–70; Scharnhorst to Clausewitz, Mar. 21, 1813, *Scharnhorsts Briefe*, 1:463; Scharnhorst to his daughter, Mar. 19, 1813, Klippel, *Scharnhorst*, 3:692–93, and 3:703.

21. Clausewitz to Marie, Apr. 1, 4, 1813, *Leben*, 2:70–73; Rudolf von Caemmerer, *Clausewitz* (Berlin: B. Behr, 1905), 44–45.

22. Paret, *Clausewitz*, 232; Clausewitz to Marie, Apr. 4, 18, 1813, *Leben*, 2:72–73, 75–76; Prince Wilhelm to the crown prince, Mar. 30, 1813, and Princess Charlotte to the crown prince, Apr. 20, 21, 1813, *Hohenzollernbriefe*, Granier,

ed., 7–8, 31–32; [E. M. Arndt], *Zwei Worte über die Enstehung der Teutschen Legion* (n.p., 1813).

23. King Frederick William quoted in Paret, *Yorck*, 171; Clausewitz to Marie, Apr. 9, 1813, *Leben*, 2:74–75. See also: Clausewitz to Marie, Apr. 22, 1813, *Leben*, 2:76–77.

24. Paret, *Yorck*, 209, 218; Leggiere, *Napoleon and Berlin*, 49.

25. Leggiere, *Napoleon and Berlin*, 49; Leggiere, *Napoleon and the Struggle*, Vol. 1, chapter 2.

26. Clausewitz to Marie, Apr. 25, 1813, *Leben*, 2:77–79.

27. Leggiere, *Napoleon and Berlin*, 49–50, 53.

28. Ibid., 50–51; Leggiere, *Napoleon and the Struggle*, Vol. 1, chapter 3; Chandler, *Campaigns*, 881–82; J. F. C. Fuller, *A Military History of the Western World*, Vol. 2, *From the Defeat of the Spanish Armada, 1588, to the Battle of Waterloo, 1815* (New York: Funk and Wagnalls, 1955), 2:460.

29. Chandler, *Campaigns*, 882–84; Leggiere, *Napoleon and the Struggle*, Vol. 1, chapter 3; Leggiere, *Blücher*, 232–34.

30. Fuller, *Military History*, 2:460–61; Leggiere, *Blücher*, 234.

31. Chandler, *Campaigns*, 886.

32. Ibid., 886–87; Leggiere, *Blücher*, 234.

33. Clausewitz to Marie, May 18, 28, 1813, *Leben*, 2:82–84.

34. Carl von Clausewitz, *The Campaign of 1813 to the Armistice*, Niels Nielsen, trans. (Unpublished Manuscript, 2013) (hereafter, Clausewitz, *1813*), 16.

35. Napoleon quoted in Chandler, *Campaigns*, 887; Clausewitz to Scharnhorst, [c.6] May, 1813, Klippel, *Scharnhorst*, 3:733–34.

36. Leggiere, *Napoleon and Berlin*, 50–52; Chandler, *Campaigns*, 888; Leggiere, *Blücher*, 243.

37. Fuller, *Military History*, 2:461; Chandler, *Campaigns*, 888–90.

38. Clausewitz to Marie, May 8, 1813, *Leben*, 2:80–82.

39. Pertz-Delbrück, *Gneisenau*, 2:615; August Ludwig Ferdinand Nostitz-Rieneck, "Das Tagebuch des Generals der Kavallerie Grafen von Nostitz," in Großen Generalstabe, ed., *Kriegsgeschichtliche Einzelschriften*, No. 5 (Berlin: Mittler, 1884), 48; Clausewitz to Marie, May 18, 1813, *Leben*, 2:82–83.

40. Clausewitz, *1813*, 18.

41. Clausewitz to Marie, May 18, 1813, *Leben*, 2:82–83; Clausewitz, *1813*, 17.

42. Chandler, *Campaigns*, 890–91; Leggiere, *Blücher*, 243.

43. Chandler, *Campaigns*, 891–93, 895–96; Fuller, *Military History*, 2:461; Leggiere, *Blücher*, 244; Leggiere, *Napoleon and the Struggle*, Vol. 2, chapter 3; Preisdorff, ed., *Soldatisches*, 66.

44. Chandler, *Campaigns*, 894–95; Leggiere, *Blücher*, 247.

45. Clausewitz, *1813*, 24; *OW*, 267; Preisdorff, ed., *Soldatisches*, 66.

46. Clausewitz, *1813*, 25.

47. Leggiere, *Blücher*, 250; Chandler, *Campaigns*, 897; Leggiere, *Napoleon and the Struggle*, Vol. 1, chapter 9; Clausewitz to Marie, May 28, 1813, *Leben*, 2:83–84, and notes; Clausewitz to Scharnhorst, May 28, 1813, *Verstreute kleine Schriften*,

201–03; J. E. Marston, *The Life and Campaigns of Field-Marshal Prince Blücher of Wahlstaat* (London: Sherwood, Neely, and Jones, 1815), 31–34; Clausewitz, *1813*, 25–27.

48. Petre, *Napoleon's Last Campaign in Germany*, 149; Clausewitz to Marie, May 31, 1813, *Leben*, 2:85–86.

49. Petre, *Napoleon's Last Campaign in Germany*, 145–46, 152; Chandler, *Campaigns*, 897; Fuller, *Military History*, 2:464; Clausewitz, *1813*, 28.

50. Clark, *Iron Kingdom*, 365; Clausewitz to Marie, June 4, 1813, *Leben*, 2:87.

51. Fuller, *Military History*, 2:464–65; Chandler, *Campaigns*, 897–98; Clausewitz, *1813*, 28.

52. Clausewitz to Marie, June 30, 1813, *Leben*, 2:88; Klippel, *Scharnhorst*, 3:750; Paret, *Clausewitz*, 235–36, 239. Paret identifies the documents: August Neidhardt von Gneisenau and Clausewitz, "Nachruf," and "Neckrolog," June 1813, Pertz-Delbrück, *Gneisenau*, 3:32–37; "Die Erklärung des Oberst-Lieutenants von Clausewitz," [c. June 1813], ibid., 3:688–89; "Ueber den Parteigängerkrieg des Majors v. Boltenstern. (Verfaßt vom Oberstlieutenant v. Clausewitz.)," July 1813, ibid., 3:389–92.

53. Paret and Moran commentary, *HPW*, 85–87; Carl von Clausewitz, "On the Life and Character of Scharnhorst," *HPW*, 100, 106.

54. Clausewitz to Gneisnenau, June 20, 1813, *Schriften* 2/1:146–48; Paret, *Clausewitz*, 240; Clausewitz, *1813*, 2, 4–5. Clausewitz's original 1813 study appeared as: [Carl von Clausewitz], *Der Feldzug von 1813 bis zum Waffenstillstand* (Glatz, 1813). It also appears in Clausewitz's collected works: Carl von Clausewitz, "Der Feldzug von 1813 bis zum Waffenstillstand," *HW* (1862) 7:215–72. There is also a supplement: Carl von Clausewitz, "Historische Materialien von Strategie: Ueber den Feldzug von 1813," *HW* (1862), 7:273–80.

55. Clausewitz, *1813*, 16, 17, 29; Paret, *Clausewitz*, 240.

56. Marie to Gneisenau, June 25, 1813, *Leben*, 2:27–28; Heinrich and Amalie von Beguelin, *Denkwürdigkeiten von Heinrich und Amalie von Beguelin aus den Jahren 1807–1813, nebst Briefen von Gneisenau und Hardenberg*, Adolf Ernst, ed. (Berlin: Julius Springer, 1892), 275, 285, quoted in Paret, *Clausewitz*, 239 fn. 41.

57. Clausewitz to Marie, June 10, 11, 1813, *Leben*, 2:87–88; Pertz-Delbrück, *Gneisenau*, 3:16–17; Priesdorff, ed., *Soldatische*, 68.

58. Hardenberg to Gneisenau, June 24, 1813, and Gneisenau to Eichhorn, Aug. 16, 1813, Pertz-Delbrück, *Gneisenau*, 3:28–29, 95; Clausewitz to Marie, June 31 [*sic*], July 6, 1813, *Leben*, 2:89–91.

CHAPTER 8

1. Clark, *Iron Kingdom*, 365; Leggiere, *Napoleon and Berlin*, 126–27.

2. Henry Kissinger, *A World Restored* (Gloucester, MA: Peter Smith, 1973), 74–75; Leggiere, *Napoleon and Berlin*, 122–23.

3. Schroeder, *Transformation*, 470–72; Kissinger, *A World Restored*, 76–77; Clark, *Iron Kingdom*, 365.

4. Schroeder, *Transformation*, 472–73; Kissinger, *A World Restored*, 77–82; Clark, *Iron Kingdom*, 366.

5. Clark, *Iron Kingdom*, 366; Ross, *European*, 333.

6. Ross, *European*, 335; Clark, *Iron Kingdom*, 366; Gordon A. Craig, "Problems of Coalition Warfare: The Military Alliance against Napoleon, 1813–1814," in *The Harmon Memorial Lectures in Military History, 1959–1987*, Harry W. Borowski, ed. (Washington, DC: Office of Air Force History, 1988), 326, 328; Petre, *Napoleon's Last Campaign in Germany*, 26; Lieven, *Russia*, 340, 355.

7. Schroeder, *European*, 478; Leggiere, *Napoleon and Berlin*, 121–22, 124, 127; Michael V. Leggiere, *The Fall of Napoleon*, Vol. 1, *The Allied Invasion of France, 1813–1814* (Cambridge: Cambridge University Press, 2007), 5; Craig, "Coalition," 332–33; Lieven, *Russia*, 358-59.

8. Craig, "Coalition," 326; Violette M. Montagu, *Eugène de Beauharnais: The Adopted Son of Napoleon* (London: John Long, 1913), 284.

9. Craig, "Coalition," 326, 328.

10. Ibid., 330; Lieven, *Russia*, 369.

11. Craig, "Coalition," 331.

12. Ibid., 331–32; Lieven, *Russia*, 369; Carl von Clausewitz, "Historical Material on Strategy: On the Campaign of 1813," Niels Nielsen, trans. (Unpublished Manuscript, 2012), 3. The original text: Carl von Clausewitz, "Historische Materialien von Strategie: Ueber den Feldzug von 1813," *HW* (1862), 7:273–80.

13. Craig, "Coalition," 326; Leggiere, *The Fall of Napoleon*, 8–9; Lieven, *Russia*, 363.

14. Craig, "Coalition," 330–331; Leggiere, *The Fall of Napoleon*, 9; Leggiere, *Napoleon and Berlin*, 129; Leggiere, *Blücher*, 259–60.

15. Gabrielle Venzky, *Die Russisch-Deutsche Legion in den Jahren 1811–1815* (Wiesbaden: Harrassowitz, 1966), 90; Clausewitz to Marie, June 31[sic], July 6, 1813, *Leben*, 2:89–91.

16. Clausewitz to Gneisenau, Aug. 4, 1813, *Schriften*, 2/1:148–50.

17. Clausewitz to Marie, Aug. 12, 14, 1813, *Leben*, 2:91–92.

18. [Ludwig Georg Thedel von Wallmoden-Gimborn], *Der Feldzug des Corps des Generals Grafen Ludwig von Wallmoden-Gimborn an der Nieder-Elbe und in Belgien, in den Jahren 1813 und 1814* (Altenburg: Pierer, 1848), 12–13, 13n.; Clausewitz to Marie, June 31[sic], 1813, *Leben*, 2:89–90; Charles William Vane, *Narrative of the War in Germany and France in 1813 and 1814* (London: Colburn and Bentley, 1830), 80.

19. Lowe to Bathurst, Report on the Russo-German Legion and other German Troops, Sept. 5, 1813, *Lowe Papers*, Add 20111; Legion Russe-Allemande, Rapproachment des differentes Nations, dont consiste Le 1er Regiment

d'Hussards, and le 2nd Batallion d'Infantry, undated [1813], *Lowe Papers*, Add 20193.

20. Clark, *Iron Kingdom*, 366; Leggiere, *Napoleon and Berlin*, 134–35.

21. Leggiere, *Napoleon and Berlin*, 136–37.

22. Clausewitz, "Historical Material," 2.

23. [Wallmoden], *Feldzug*, 16; Bernadotte to Wallmoden, Aug. 9, 1813, [Johan Karl XIV] [Bernadotte], *Recueill des Ordres de Mouvement, Proclamations et Bulletins de S.A.R. le Prince Royal de Suède, Commandant en Chef l'Armée Combinée du Nord de l'Allemagne en 1813 et 1814* (Stockholm: Eckstein, 1839), 72–74; Clausewitz to Marie, Aug. 15, 1813, *Leben*, 2:92–93.

24. Leggiere, *Napoleon and Berlin*, 131, 137–140.

25. Ross, *European*, 335–36; Clark, *Iron Kingdom*, 366–67.

26. Clark, *Iron Kingdom*, 366–67; Ross, *European*, 335–36; Leggiere, *Napoleon and Berlin*, 136–37, 173, 189; Chandler, *Campaigns*, 905–06.

27. Petre, *Napoleon's Last Campaign*, 102, 165–67; Leggiere, *Napoleon and Berlin*, 189; James Lawford, *Napoleon: The Last Campaigns, 1813–1814* (New York: Crown, 1977), 49; Ross, *European*, 336.

28. Leggiere, *Blücher*, 284-85; Leggiere, *Napoleon and Berlin*, 193.

29. Leggiere, *Napoleon and Berlin*, 192–93, 209–11, 216–19, 223; Leggiere, *Blücher*, 285-87.

30. Leggiere, *Napoleon and Berlin*, 218.

31. Ibid., 230; Leggiere, *Blücher*, 288-89.

32. Chandler, *Campaigns*, 916; Ross, *European*, 337; Leggiere, *Napoleon and Berlin*, 228, 244; Lieven, *Russia*, 425, 429.

33. [Wallmoden], *Feldzug*, 16–17.

34. [Wallmoden], *Feldzug*, 18; North Ludlow Beamish, *History of the King's German Legion* (London: Boone, 1837), 2:175.

35. Beamish, *Legion*, 2:176–77; [Wallmoden], *Feldzug*, 20–21.

36. Clausewitz to Marie, Aug. 20, Sept. 1, 1813, *Leben*, 2:93–96. The dispatch is Napoleon to Davout, Aug. 8, 1813, *Correspondence de Napoleon 1er* (Paris: Plon, 1868), 26:13–18, but Clausewitz does not quote it exactly.

37. [Wallmoden], *Feldzug*, 22–23; Beamish, *Legion*, 2:180–82.

38. [Wallmoden], *Feldzug*, 23–27.

39. Wilhelm von Schramm, *Clausewitz: Leben und Werk* (Esslingen am Neckar: Bechtle, 1976), 441–45; Strachan, *Clausewitz's On War*, 62; Clausewitz to Marie, Aug. 27, 1813, *Leben*, 2:94–95.

40. [Wallmoden], *Feldzug*, 23, 29; Leggiere, *Napoleon and Berlin*, 173, 337 n.23; Ross, *European*, 336; Beamish, *Legion*, 2:188.

41. Chandler, *Campaigns*, 916; Ross, *European*, 337; Leggiere, *Blücher*, 288–89.

42. Chandler, *Campaigns*, 916–17.

43. Ibid., 918–19; Leggiere, *Napoleon and Berlin*, 259–62.

44. Chandler, *Campaigns*, 921–22; Ross, *European*, 338.

45. Ross, *European*, 338–40.

46. Craig, "Coalition," 333; Ross, *European*, 340; Clausewitz, "Historical Material," 2.

47. Clausewitz to Marie, Aug. 27, Sept. 1, 1813, *Leben*, 2:94–96.

48. Ibid.

49. [Wallmoden], *Feldzug*, 28–30; Clausewitz to Marie, Sept. 4, 1813, *Leben*, 2:96–97.

50. [Wallmoden], *Feldzug*, 31; Clausewitz to Marie, Sept. 12, 1813, *Leben*, 2:98–100.

51. [Wallmoden], *Feldzug*, 31–32, 34; Clausewitz to Marie, Sept. 19, 1813, *Leben*, 2:100–01; Pertz-Delbrück, *Gneisenau*, 3:386–87; Beamish, *Legion*, 2:190–92.

52. [Wallmoden], *Feldzug*, 35; Barthold von Quistorp, *Geschichte der Nord-Armee im Jahr 1813* (Berlin: Mittler, 1894), 2:360; Pertz-Delbrück, *Gneisenau*, 3:386–87 (this source transposes the directions of Wallmoden's attacking units); Beamish, *Legion*, 2:194–95.

53. Beamish, *Legion*, 2:195–97; Pertz-Delbrück, *Gneisenau*, 3:386–87; Clausewitz to Marie, Sept. 19, 1813, *Leben*, 2:100–01.

54. [Wallmoden], *Feldzug*, 39; Beamish, *Legion*, 2:198; Clausewitz to Marie, Sept. 19, 1813, *Leben*, 2:100–01.

55. Clausewitz to Marie, Sept. 19, 1813, *Leben*, 2:100–01; Pertz-Delbrück, *Gneisenau*, 3:386–87.

56. Clausewitz to Marie, Sept. 21, 1813, *Leben*, 2:102–03.

57. [Wallmoden], *Feldzug*, 42–44; Lowe to Bamberg, Oct. 1, 1813, *Lowe Papers*, Add 20111; Clausewitz to Gneisenau, Sept. 30, 1813, *Schriften*, 2/1:150–52.

CHAPTER 9

1. Paret and Moran in *HPW*, 205; Clausewitz, "1814," 19.

2. Lieven, *Russia*, 458–59; Schroeder, *European*, 488; Leggiere, *The Fall of Napoleon*, 14; Harold Blanton, "The Military and Diplomatic Defeat of Napoleon in 1814: The Critical Phase" (MA Thesis: Florida State University, 1994), 36.

3. Lieven, *Russia*, 460–67.

4. Ibid., 468–71; Ross, *European*, 342–43; Leggiere, *The Fall of Napoleon*, 50.

5. Ross, *European*, 342–43; Blanton, "Military," 36–37; Schroeder, *European*, 484; Leggiere, *The Fall of Napoleon*, 51–52, 59–61.

6. Craig, "Coalition," 334.

7. Lieven, *Russia*, 472–74.

8. Carl von Clausewitz, "Strategic Critique of the 1814 Campaign" (hereafter "1814"), Niels Nielsen, trans. (Unpublished Manuscript, 2012), 22–23. The original: Carl von Clausewitz, "Strategische Kritik des Feldzuges von 1814 in Frankreich," *HW*, 7:307–404. There is a partial English translation: *HPW*, 207–19. There is also Clausewitz's shorter take on the

campaign, "Übersicht des Feldzugs von 1814 in Frankreich," *HW* (1862), 7:281–306.

9. Craig, "Coalition," 335; Leggiere, *The Fall of Napoleon*, 35–37, 200–01, 224; Leggiere, *Blücher*, 321; Lieven, *Russia*, 478; Chandler, *Campaigns*, 948–49.

10. Clausewitz, "1814," 23; *OW*, 595.

11. Clausewitz, "1814," 24–25, 27; *OW*, 161.

12. Clausewitz, "1814," 29.

13. [Wallmoden], *Feldzug*, 44–47; Beamish, *Legion*, 2:202–03.

14. [Wallmoden], *Feldzug*, 49; Clausewitz to Gneisenau, Oct. 22, 1813, *Leben*, 2:48–49; *Schriften*, 2/1:152.

15. The map, dated October 1813, which mentions "Lieutenant-Colonel Klousewitz," is here: WO 78–25–1, National Archives, London.

16. Clausewitz to Gneisenau, Nov. 1, 1813, in Leggiere, *The Fall of Napoleon*, 555–56; *OW*, 596.

17. Clausewitz to Gneisenau, Nov. 1, 1813, Leggiere, *The Fall of Napoleon*, 555–56.

18. Scott, *Bernadotte*, 120, 122–23.

19. Clausewitz to Nostitz, Nov. 5, 7, 1813, *Schriften*, 2/1:196–97; Leggiere, *The Fall of Napoleon*, 146–47.

20. Clausewitz to Nostitz, Nov. 8, 1813, *Schriften*, 2/1:199–200.

21. Clausewitz to Gneisenau, Nov. 10, 1813, *Schriften*, 2/1:156; Marie to Gneisenau, Nov. 26, 1813, *Leben*, 2:58–59.

22. [Wallmoden], *Feldzug*, 50; Beamish, *Legion*, 2:203; Scott, *Bernadotte*, 122–23, 126; Clausewitz to Marie, Nov. 16, 1813, *Leben*, 2:103.

23. Clausewitz to Lieutenant Colonel von Bergen and Aide de Camp General au Lewin, Nov. 23, 1813, *Lowe Papers*, ADD 20191; Desmond Gregory, *Napoleon's Jailer, Lt. Gen. Sir Hudson Lowe: A Life* (Madison: Associated University Press, 1996), 87.

24. Scott, *Bernadotte*, 126; [Wallmoden], *Feldzug*, 50.

25. Gneisenau to Clausewitz, Nov. 16, 30, 1813, *Leben*, 2:52–55, 104; Pertz-Delbrück, *Gneisenau*, 3:557.

26. John G. Gallaher, *The Iron Marshal: A Biography of Louis N. Davout* (Carbondale: Southern Illinois University Press, 1976), 283–84; [Wallmoden], *Feldzug*, 50–56; Scott, *Bernadotte*, 128–29.

27. Scott, *Bernadotte*, 128–129; [Wallmoden], *Feldzug*, 56–61; Memoir from General Wallmoden, Nov. [?] 1813, in Charles William Vane, *Narrative of the War in Germany and France in 1813 and 1814* (London: Colburn and Bentley, 1830), 383–85; Beamish, *Legion*, 2:208–11; Clausewitz to Marie, Dec. 4, 13, 1813, *Leben*, 2:104–07; Bernhard Schwertfeger, *Geschichte der Königlich Deutschen Legion, 1810–1816* (Hannover and Leipzig: Hahn'sche, 1907), 1:536.

28. [Wallmoden], *Feldzug*, 61–62; Schwertfeger, *Geschichte*, 536; Clausewitz to Marie, Dec. 13, 1813, *Leben*, 2:105–07; Clausewitz to Gneisenau, Dec. 14, 1813, *Leben*, 2:55–57.

29. [Wallmoden], *Feldzug*, 62;.C. F. von Höegh, "Bericht von dem Treffen bei Sehedtedt am 10ten December 1813 zwischen den dänischen und alliirten [*sic*] Truppen," *Militairische Blätter*, Vol. 2 (July–Dec. 1820), 282–84. This includes Hessen's account of the battle.

30. Höegh, "Bericht," 284–87.

31. [Wallmoden], *Feldzug*, 62; Clausewitz to Gneisenau, Dec. 14, 1813, *Leben*, 2:55–57; Höegh, "Bericht," 287–88.

32. Höegh, "Bericht," 288–89.

33. Schwertfeger, *Geschichte*, 1:538; [Wallmoden], *Feldzug*, 63.

34. Clausewitz to Gneisenau, Dec. 14, 1813, *Leben*, 2:55–57; Clausewitz to Marie, Dec. 13, 1813, *Leben*, 2:105–07; Venzky, *Legion*, 105.

35. Venzky, *Legion*, 105.

36. Höegh, "Bericht," 289; Venzky, *Legion*, 105; Wallmoden, *Feldzug*, 63.

37. Clausewitz to Marie, Dec. 13, 1813, *Leben*, 2:105–07; Höegh, "Bericht," 290–92; Venzky, *Legion*, 105. In a letter to Gneisenau, Clausewitz says five battalions instead of four.

38. Höegh, "Bericht," 292 and note; [Wallmoden], *Feldzug*, 64; Clausewitz to Marie, Dec. 13, 1813, *Leben*, 2:105–07.

39. Höegh, "Bericht," 293–94, 294n. The various sources give *three* different incidents of Wallmoden almost being captured during the fight for Sehestedt.

40. Schwertfeger, *Geschichte*, 1:538; [Wallmoden], *Feldzug*, 64; Höegh, "Bericht," 345; Venzky, *Legion*, 106.

41. Clausewitz to Marie, Dec. 13, 1813, *Leben*, 2:105–07; Clausewitz to Gneisenau, Dec. 14, 1813, *Leben*, 2:55–57.

42. *OW*, 193.

43. *OW*, see espec. 117.

44. Chandler, *Campaigns*, 948; Leggiere, *The Fall of Napoleon*, 189; Leggiere, *Blücher*, 321; Craig, "Coalition," 335; Ross, *European*, 341; Lieven, *Russia*, 474.

45. Lieven, *Russia*, 475–76.

46. Blanton, "Military," 26–27; Clausewitz, "1814," 22.

47. Ross, *European*, 346; Leggiere, *The Fall of Napoleon*, 75.

48. Craig, "Coalition," 335–37; Blanton, "Military," 27–28.

49. Craig, "Coalition," 338–39; Gneisenau to Radetzky, and Gneisenau to Knesebeck, both Jan. 15, 1814, Leggiere, *The Fall of Napoleon*, 566–68; *OW*, 163.

50. Ross, *European*, 347–48; Craig, "Coalition," 338–39.

51. Blanton, "Military," 42, 48–54.

52. [Wallmoden], *Feldzug*, 66; Clausewitz to Gneisenau, Dec. 14, 1813, *Leben*, 2:55–57; Stülpnagel to Gniesenau, Dec. 15, 1813, Pertz-Delbrück, *Gneisenau*, 3:584–85; Paret, *Clausewitz*, 243.

53. Gneisenau to Clausewitz, Jan. 4, 1814, Pertz-Delbrück, *Gneisenau*, 4:143–45.

54. Scott, *Bernadotte*, 129–38, 144; [Wallmoden], *Feldzug*, 67–69.

55. Scott, *Bernadotte*, 150–51.

56. [Wallmoden], *Feldzug*, 69–70; Beamish, *Legion*, 2:217–18.

57. Ross, *European*, 346; Craig, "Coalition," 338; Lieven, *Russia*, 481; Blanton, "Military," 28–29; Leggiere, *Blücher*, 321.

58. Lieven, *Russia*, 479.

59. Blanton, "Military," 30; *OW*, 163.

60. Ross, *European*, 348–349; Craig, "Coalition," 339; Lieven, *Russia*, 486–91; Blanton, "Military," 30, 55.

61. Clausewitz, "1814," 39, 42–43.

62. *OW*, 162.

63. Craig, "Coalition," 340; Ross, *European*, 349–50.

64. Blanton, "Military," 55 and fn. 1, 56–57.

65. Ibid., 56–60, 66–67; Clausewitz, "1814," 40.

66. Lieven, *Russia*, 497–98.

67. Blanton, "Military," 60, 68–69, 147–48; Chandler, *Campaigns*, 983.

68. Clausewitz, "1814," 39; Clausewitz to Marie, Mar. 6, 1814, *Leben*, 2:108–09; Blanton, "Military," 74–76.

69. Blanton, "Military," 62, 76–77, 95–97.

70. Lieven, *Russia*, 499–503; Ross, *European*, 351–53; Blanton, "Military," 118–19, 127–28; Clausewitz, "1814," 44, 55.

71. Clausewitz, "1814," 39–40; Blanton, "Military," 85–86, 88; Ross, *European*, 350–51.

72. [Wallmoden], *Feldzug*, 71–72; Clausewitz to Marie, Feb. 27, 1814, *Leben*, 2:107–08.

73. Holstein to Alexander, Mar. 14, 1814, and second note [Mar. 14, 1814], Fond 846, Opis' 16, Delo 3591, Roll 53, *RGVIA*; [Wallmoden], *Feldzug*, 73; A. V. Weingarten, "Geschichte des Armeekorps unter den Befehlen des Generallieutenants Grafen von Wallmoden-Gimborn und der Nieder-Elbe und in den Niederlanden, von April 1813 bis zum Mai 1814," *Öestreichische militärische Zeitschrift*, No. 8, J.B. Scheis, ed. (Wien: Anton Strauß, 1827), 240–41.

74. Weingarten, "Geschichte," 239–41; Clausewitz to Marie, Mar. 17, Apr. 2, 1814, *Leben*, 2:110–11, 113–15.

75. Weingarten, "Geschichte," 243; Clasusewitz to Marie, Mar. 17, 22, 23, Apr. 2, 1814, *Leben*, 2:110–15.

76. Clausewitz to Marie, Mar. 22, 23, 1814, *Leben*, 2:111–12.

77. [Wallmoden], *Feldzug*, 73–74; Clausewitz to Marie, Apr. 2, 1814, *Leben*, 2:113–15; Maurice Weil, *La Campagne de 1814: D'après les Documents des Archives Impériales et Royales de la Guerre à Vienne: La Cavalerie des Armées Alliées Pendant la Campagne de 1814* (Paris: Librairie Militaire de L. Baudin, 1896), 4:341.

78. [Wallmoden], *Feldzug*, 74; Weil, *Campagne*, 4:323–26, 330, 333–35.

79. [Wallmoden], *Feldzug*, 75; Weil, *Campagne*, 4:335–37, 339.

80. Clausewitz to Marie, Apr. 2, 1814, *Leben*, 2:113–15; [Wallmoden], *Feldzug*, 75–76; Weil, *Campagne*, 4:340.

81. Clausewitz to Marie, Apr. 2, 1814, *Leben*, 2:113–15.

82. Lieven, *Russia*, 503; Chandler, *Campaigns*, 993–94; Clausewitz, "1814," 44.

83. Chandler, *Campaigns*, 994–98; Ross, *European*, 354.

84. Clausewitz, "1814," 62.

85. Lieven, *Russia*, 506–08; Clausewitz, "1814," 63.

86. Lieven, *Russia*, 509–16; Ross, *European*, 354–55.

87. Clausewitz, "1814," 43.

88. Weingarten, "Geschichte," 251; Clausewitz to Marie, Mar. 15, Apr. 4, 1814, *Leben*, 2:109–10, 115–16.

89. Ross, *European*, 356; Clausewitz to Marie, Apr. 11, 12, 1814, *Leben*, 2:117–19; Clausewitz to Gneisenau, Apr. 22, 1814, Pertz-Delbrück, *Gneisenau*, 4:238–39; *Schriften*, 2/1:160–61; Gneisenau to Frau von Clausewitz, May 5, 1814, Pertz-Delbrück, *Gneisenau*, 4:249–51.

90. Weingarten, "Geschichte," 259; Venzky, *Legion*, 112; Kleist von Nollendorf announcement, July 22, 1814, *Leben*, 2:62–63.

CHAPTER 10

1. Clausewitz to Boyen, Oct. 29 and [Oct. 30?], 1814, in Klaus Hilbert, "Ergänzungen zum Lebensbild des Generals Carl von Clausewitz," *Militärgeschichte*, Vol. 20 (1981), 212; Gneisenau to Clausewitz, Dec. 12, 1814, Pertz-Delbrück, *Gneisenau*, 4:301–03.

2. Paret, *Clausewitz*, 245; Clausewitz to Gneisenau, Dec. 21, 24, 1814, Feb. 9, 27, 1815, Pertz-Delbrück, *Gneisenau*, 4:303–05, 316–17, 323–25; Hahlweg, *Schriften*, 2/1:161–70.

3. Schroeder, *Transformation*, 548; Ross, *European*, 368.

4. Schroeder, *Transformation*, 549.

5. Ibid., 550–51.

6. Ross, *European*, 369.

7. Chandler, *Campaigns*, 1015 (Chandler's discussions of Prussian actions during the 1815 campaign have been overcome by more recent scholarship); Ross, *European*, 370; Michael V. Leggiere, "Friedrich Wilhelm von Bülow and the Campaign of 1815" (MA Thesis, Florida State University, 1992), 64.

8. Chandler, *Campaigns*, 1015; Leggiere, "Bülow," 64; Gregory W. Pedlow, "Wellington versus Clausewitz," in Christopher Bassford, Daniel Moran, and Gregory Pedlow, trans. and ed., *On Waterloo: Clausewitz, Wellington, and the Campaign of 1815* (www.clausewitz.com, 2010), 267.

9. Chandler, *Campaigns*, 1015–17; Ross, *European*, 370–71.

10. Clausewitz to Gneisenau, Mar. 17, 1815, Pertz-Delbrück, *Gneisenau*, 4:475–77; *Schriften*, 2/1:171–73; Preisdorff, ed., *Soldatisches*, 66.

    Conclusively dating Clausewitz's official reentry into the Prussian army is difficult. The surviving sources are not clear, and the fact that Clausewitz was still wearing a Russian uniform in March 1815 muddies the historiographical waters.

Schwartz gives the date of Clausewitz's commission as a Prussian colonel as April 11, 1814. Paret agrees with this date. Hahlweg dates Clausewitz's appointment to colonel in the Prussian army from March 30, 1815. Olaf Rose gives the same date. Preisdorff gives March 30, 1815, as the date Clausewitz was appointed a colonel on the General Staff. Preisdorff also says that Clausewitz returned to Prussian service as a colonel after the 1814 peace, which would mean after May 30. This is later than Schwartz's April 11, 1814, date. Does appointment to the General Staff mean reentry to the army on that date? See: Paret, *Clausewitz*, 244 and fn. 57; Schwartz, *Leben*, 2:62; Hahlweg, *Clausewitz*, 40; Olaf Rose, *Carl von Clausewitz: Wirkungsgeschichte seines Werkes in Rußland und der Sowjetunion, 1836–1991* (Munich: R. Oldenbourg, 1995), 20; Preisdorff, ed., *Soldatisches*, 66, 68.

Paret and Schwartz wonder whether Clausewitz ever sent the letter to Frederick William mentioned at the conclusion of chapter 9 in which Clausewitz planned to ask the king to specifically readmit him to the army. This argument is reinforced by a note Clausewitz posted to Gneisenau not long after in which Clausewitz mentioned that if the Legion entered Prussian service he would ask the king via his highness's adjutant whether the king wanted him back. See Paret, *Clausewitz*, 244; Clausewitz to Marie, Apr. 11, 12, 1814, *Leben*, 2:117–19, and *Leben*, 2:62; Clausewitz to Gneisenau, Apr. 22, 1814, Pertz-Delbrück, *Gneisenau*, 4:238–39; *Schriften*, 2/1:160–61.

It is also possible that Clausewitz did indeed send the aforementioned letter and then simply continued serving—technically—as a Russian liaison officer. We can only argue something on this line because we know from a March 17, 1815, note from Clausewitz that he was at this time still wearing a Russian uniform. Preisdorff's date of March 30, 1815, seems the most likely one for both Clausewitz's reentry into the Prussian army and his appointment to the General Staff. See Clausewitz to Gneisenau, Mar. 17, 1815, Pertz-Delbrück, *Gneisenau*, 4:475–77; *Schriften*, 2/1:171–73; Preisdorff, ed., *Soldatisches*, 66.

11. Clausewitz to Gneisenau, Apr. 9, 1815, Pertz-Delbrück, *Gneisenau*, 4:490; Hahlweg, *Schriften*, 2/1:176–77, 176, fn. 1; Clausewitz to Gneisenau, Dec. 21, 1814, Pertz-Delbrück, *Gneisenau*, 4:303–04; Peter Hofschröer, *Waterloo 1815: Wavre, Placenoit, and the Race to Paris* (Barnsley, UK: Pen & Sword, 2006), 35; Clark, *Iron Kingdom*, 388; Pedlow, "Wellington versus Clausewitz," 259 fn. 3.

12. Preisdorff, ed., *Soldatisches*, 68.

13. Clausewitz to Marie, May 14, 1815, *Leben*, 2:139; Herman von Petersdorff, *General Johann Adolph Freiherr von Thielmann, ein Charakterbild aus der napoleon-sichen Zeit* (S. Hirzel: Leipzig, 1894), 288.

14. Hofschröer, *Waterloo 1815: Wavre*, 47; Schroeder, *Transformation*, 536; Petersdorff, *Thielmann*, 292; Clausewitz to Marie, May 17, 20, 23, 1815, *Leben*, 2:140–43. These notes also cover the preceding paragraph.

15. Clausewitz to Marie, June 15, 1815, *Leben*, 2:144.

16. Chandler, *Campaigns*, 1020.

17. Ibid., 1018, 1023.

18. *OW*, 310; Chandler, *Campaigns*, 1027; Pedlow, "Wellington versus Clausewitz," 264–65; Clausewitz to Marie, July 3, 1815, Bassford, et al., *On Waterloo*, 23.

19. Chandler, *Campaigns*, 1027–31; Leggiere, *Blücher*, 389.

20. Chandler, *Campaigns*, 1029–30.

21. Pedlow, "Wellington versus Clausewitz," 270–71; Chandler, *Campaigns*, 1031–32; Peter Hofschröer, *Waterloo 1815: Quatre Bras & Ligny* (Barnsley, UK: Pen & Sword, 2005), 41.

22. Chandler, *Campaigns*, 1032–33.

23. Ibid., 1034–36, 1038.

24. Leggiere, *Blücher*, 390; Clausewitz, "1815," 104.

25. Leggiere, *Blücher*, 389–90; Leggiere, "Bülow," 69, 71–74; *OW*, 329.

26. Chandler, *Campaigns*, 1038–39; Clausewitz, "1815," 100; Petersdorff, *Thielmann*, 293–94; maps.

27. Leggiere, *Blücher*, 390; Chandler, *Campaigns*, 1040.

28. Chandler, *Campaigns*, 1041–42.

29. Ibid., 1043.

30. Clausewitz, "1815," 116; Leggiere, *Blücher*, 395; Petersdorff, *Thielmann*, 293.

31. Chandler, *Campaigns*, 1044.

32. Ibid., 1044–45.

33. Ibid., 1045–46; Leggiere, *Blücher*, 399–401.

34. Petersdorff, *Thielmann*, 293–94; Clausewitz, "1815," 117–18; Oscar von Lettow-Vorbeck, *Geschichte der Befreiungskriege, 1813–1815: Napoleons Untergang, 1815* (Berlin: Mittler, 1904), 1:339.

35. Chandler, *Campaigns*, 1046–47; Leggiere, *Blücher*, 401.

36. Clausewitz, "1815," 118–20.

37. For a discussion of this, see Paret, *Clausewitz*, 248.

38. Petersdorff, *Thielmann*, 294.

39. Chandler, *Campaigns*, 1047–49.

40. Ibid., 1050–53, 1056.

41. Clausewitz to Marie, July 3, 1815, in Bassford, et al., *On Waterloo*, 23; Lettow-Vorbeck, *Geschichte*, 1:469; Clausewitz to Marie, June 17, 1815, *Leben*, 2:144–45.

42. Hofschröer, *Waterloo 1815: Wavre*, 10–11, 13; Leggiere, *Blücher*, 402.

43. Clausewitz to Marie, July 3, 1815, Bassford, et al., ed., *On Waterloo*, 23–24.

44. Hofschröer, *Waterloo 1815: Wavre*, 18; Leggiere, *Blücher*, 403; Clausewitz, "1815," 132; Clausewitz to Marie, July 3, 1815, Bassford, et al., ed., *On Waterloo*, 24.

45. Clausewitz to Marie, July 3, 1815, Bassford, et al., ed., *On Waterloo*, 24; Hofschröer, *Waterloo 1815: Wavre*, 23; Clausewitz, "1815," 132.

46. Chandler, *Campaigns*, 1058–60.

47. Ibid., 1064–65.

48. Leggiere, *Blücher*, 403; Lettow-Vorbeck, *Geschichte* 1:460.

49. Chandler, *Campaigns*, 1062–63, 1066–67.

50. Hofschröer, *Waterloo 1815: Wavre*, 14; Chandler, *Campaigns*, 1069.

51. Hofschröer, *Waterloo 1815: Wavre*, 19, 23, 27; Leggiere, *Blücher*, 404; Lettow-Vorbeck, *Geschichte* 1:460; Clausewitz, "1815," 136.

52. Hofschröer, *Waterloo 1815: Wavre*, 64, 66.

53. Chandler, *Campaigns*, 1069, 1071; Clausewitz, "1815," 180–81.

54. Hofschröer, *Waterloo 1815: Wavre*, 23, 34, 67–68; Petersdorff, *Thielmann*, 296; Clausewitz, "1815," 147–148, 153; Clausewitz to Marie, July 3, 1815, Bassford, et al., ed., *On Waterloo*, 24–25.

55. Peter Hofschröer, *1815: The Waterloo Campaign. The German Victory: From Waterloo to the Fall of Napoleon* (London: Greenhill, 1999), 158; Petersdorff, *Thielmann*, 296–97; Clausewitz, "1815," 154.

56. Peter Hofschröer, *1815*, 158–59; Clausewitz, "1815," 153.

57. Clausewitz, "1815," 154.

58. Ibid.; Petersdorff, *Thielmann*, 297–98; Hofschröer, *1815*, 159.

59. Hofschröer, *1815*, 158; Hofschröer, *Waterloo 1815: Wavre*, 16–17.

60. Hofschröer, *Waterloo*, 68–69.

61. Hofschröer, *1815*, 162–63; Petersdorff, *Thielmann*, 298; Hofschröer, *Waterloo 1815: Wavre*, 68, 70.

62. Hofschröer, *1815*, 68; Clausewitz, "1815," 155–56; Clausewitz to Marie, July 3, 1815, Bassford, et al., ed., *On Waterloo*, 25; Hofschröer, *1815*, 163–64; Petersdorff, *Thielmann*, 299.

63. Fuller, *Military* 2:523–24, 527; Chandler, *Campaigns*, 1064.

64. Chandler, *Campaigns*, 1063, 1065, 1067; Fuller, *Military*, 2:523.

65. Fuller, *Military*, 2:523–24.

66. Ibid., 2:526, 528–29.

67. Ibid., 2:529–33.

68. Ibid., 2:530, 534.

69. Ibid., 2:534–38; Clausewitz, "1815," 173–74.

70. Hofschröer, *Waterloo 1815: Wavre*, 70; Clausewitz, "1815," 156; Petersdorff, *Thielmann*, 300; Clausewitz to Marie, July 3, 1815, Bassford, et al., ed., *On Waterloo*, 25.

71. Hofschröer, *Waterloo*, 73; Clausewitz, "1815," 156; Clausewitz to Marie, July 3, 1815, Bassford, et al., ed., *On Waterloo*, 25; Hofschröer, *1815*, 169–70.

72. Thielmann quoted in Hofschröer, *1815*, 170; Paret, *Clausewitz*, 249.

73. Gneisenau to Clausewitz [July 22, 1815], Pertz-Delbrück, *Gneisenau*, 4:587–88.

74. Clausewitz, "1815," 157; Hofschröer, *Waterloo 1815: Wavre*, 71, 79; Clausewitz to Marie, July 3, 1815, in Bassford, et al., ed., *On Waterloo*, 24; Chandler, *Campaigns*, 1091.

75. The controversy is discussed in Paret, *Clausewitz*, 250 and fn. 80.

76. Hofschröer, *1815*, 171; F.A.L von der Marwitz, *Aus dem Nachlasse Friedrich August Ludwig's von der Marwitz* (Berlin: Mittler, 1852), 2:121; Ludwig von Reiche, *Memoiren des könlich preußischen Generals der Infanterie Ludwig von Reiche*, Louis von Weltzien, ed. (Leipzig: Brockhaus, 1857), 2:224; Petersdorff,

Thielmann, 300. See also Raymond Aron, *Penser la guerre, Clausewitz* (Paris: Gallimard, 1976), 1:60.

77. Hofschröer, *1815*, 171.

78. Paret, *Clausewitz*, 250; Bassford, "Jomini and Clausewitz,"1.

79. Quoted in Paret, *Clausewitz*, 431.

80. Clausewitz to Marie, Dec. 14, 1813, Apr. 2, 1814, *Leben*, 2: 55–57, 113–15; Clausewitz to Marie, July 3, 1815, Bassford, et al., ed., *On Waterloo*, 25; Clausewitz to Gneisenau, Sept. 11, 1815, Pertz-Delbrück, *Gneisenau*, 4:629; *Schriften*, 2/1:189–90.

81. Hofschröer, *Waterloo 1815: Wavre*, 75–76.

82. Fuller, *Military*, 2:539; Hofschröer, *Waterloo 1815: Wavre*, 74–75, 80–81; Clausewitz, "1815," 203.

83. Clausewitz, "1815," 203; Chandler, *Campaigns*, 1094; J. Christopher Herold, *The Age of Napoleon* (New York: American Heritage, 1963), 398–99; Chandler, *Campaigns*, 1094–95; Esdaile, *Napoleon's Wars*, 560.

84. Hofschröer, *Waterloo 1815: Wavre*, 80; Clausewitz, "1815," 198; Clausewitz to Marie, June 23, 1815, *Leben*, 2:146; Clausewitz to Marie, July 7, 1815, Bassford, et al., ed., *On Waterloo*, 27.

85. Clausewitz, "1815," 206; Clausewitz to Marie, June 29, 1815, *Leben*, 2:146–48; Clausewitz to Marie, July 3, 1815, Bassford, et al., ed., *On Waterloo*, 26.

86. Clausewitz to Marie, June 29, 1815, *Leben*, 2:146–48; Clausewitz to Marie, July 3, 1815, in Bassford, et al., ed., *On Waterloo*, 26.

87. Hofschröer, *Waterloo 1815: Wavre*, 83, 86.

88. Clausewitz, "1815," 207–08; Hofschröer, *Waterloo 1815: Wavre*, 86.

89. Schroeder, *Transformation*, 553.

90. Hofschröer, *Waterloo 1815: Wavre*, 87, 95.

91. Clausewitz, "Fortsetzung meines Tagebuch," July 7, 1815, *Leben*, 2:159; Clausewitz to Marie, July 12, 1815, *Leben*, 2:161–64.

92. Clausewitz to Marie, July 12, 24, 30, 1815, *Leben*, 2:166–69; Clausewitz to Gneisenau, July 24, 1815, Pertz-Delbrück, *Gneisenau*, 4:590–91; *Schriften*, 2/1:181–83.

CHAPTER 11

1. Priesdorff, ed., *Soldatisches*, 68; Paret, *Clausewitz*, 256–57; *Leben*, 2:172–73.

2. Paret, *Clausewitz*, 257–58, 260–66; *Leben*, 2:176 notes.

3. Paret, *Clausewitz*, 266–67; Goerlitz, *The German General Staff*, 57; Clausewitz to Gneisenau, Apr. 30, 1817, *Schriften*, 2/1:266; Priesdorff, ed., *Soldatisches*, 68.

4. Paret, *Clausewitz*, 270–71; Caemmer, *Clausewitz*, 68; Clausewitz to Gneisenau, Dec. 11, 30 (two notes), 1817, *Schriften*, 2/1:305–06, 310–14.

5. Priesdorff, ed., *Soldatisches*, 68; *Leben*, 2:198; Clausewitz to Gneisenau, May 20, 1818, *Schriften*, 2/1:338–39; Paret, *Clausewitz*, 271–74.

6. Priesdorff, ed., *Soldatisches*, 68; Paret, *Clausewitz*, 271–74; White, *Scharnhorst*, 202.

7. Paret, *Clausewitz*, 276–78. As Paret notes, Clausewitz's surviving curriculum texts appear in Ludwig von Scharfeort, *Die Königlich Preussische Kriegsakademi, 1810–1910* (Berlin: Mittler, 1910).

8. Paret, *Clausewitz*, 272, 275–79.

9. Ibid., 279–81.

10. Priesdorff, ed., *Soldatisches*, 66; Alexander I, Petersburg, June 30, 1822, *Leben*, 2:65; Hugh Smith, *On Clausewitz: A Study of Military and Political Ideas* (New York: Palgrave/Macmillan, 2004), 16; Paret, *Clausewitz*, 284, 323–24.

11. Èugène Reventlow to Rosenkrentz, Nov. 27, 1819 (received Dec. 3, 1819), Dpt. F.u.A. 1771–1848, Preussen II, Depecher 1819, Rigsarkivet, Copenhagen; Bernstorff to Clausewitz, Nov. 21, 1823, *Leben*, 2:258; Harald Müller, "Die Karlsbader Beschlüsse und Clausewitz," *Jahrbuch für Geschichte*, Vol. 36 (1988), 11–25; Peter Paret, "Bemerkungen zu dem Versuch von Clausewitz, zum Gesandten in London Ernannt zu Werden," *Jahrbuch für Geschichte Mittel- und Ostdeutschlands*, Vol. 26 (1977), 161–72; Paret, *Clausewitz*, 270, 319–23; Clausewitz to Gröben, Dec. 26, 1819, in Eberhard Kessel, "Zu Boyens Entlassung," *Historische Zeitschrift*, Vol. 175, No. 1 (1953), 51.

12. Arndt to Schliermacher, Jan. 17, 1818, in Ernst Moritz Arndt, *Ein Lebensbild in Briefen*, Heinrich Meisner and Robert Geerds, ed. (Berlin: Georg Reimer, 1898), 170–71; Paret, *Clausewitz*, 323; Priesdorff, ed., *Soldatisches*, 68; Clausewitz's many letters to Gneisenau from 1816 to 1828, *Schriften*, 2/1, espec. 266, 288, 446–47, 452, 455, 460, 467, 481, 490, 548.

13. Clausewitz to Marie, May 18, 1821, *Leben*, 2:252–54.

14. Schering, *Geist und Tat*, 151; Paret, *Clausewitz*, 307–10; [Friderici], *Was sich die Offiziere im Bureau erzählten*, 36–37, 42. For more on Clausewitz's time at the War College see, ibid., 38–43.

15. Paret and Moran notes, *HPW*, 224; Clausewitz, "Scharnhorst," *HPW*, 106; Paret, *Clausewitz*, 267–68, 282. The originals: Clausewitz, "Über das Leben und den Charakter von Scharnhorst," *Verstreute kleine Schriften*, 205–41; on defending the Rhine and Trier, and a piece on roads: *Schriften*, 2/2:1120–33; on the Prussian military situation on the Rhine: "Bemerkung zu dem Memoir des G[eneral] L[eutnant] H[ake] über usnere militärischen Einrichtungen am Rhein," and "[Anlage]," Feb. 3, 1818, *Schriften*, 2/1:317–24; on the territorial issue: "Über den Gedanken eines Ländertauschs zür Verbindung der Ost- und Westmasse der Preußischen Monarchie noach den Befreigungskriegen, 20. Januar 1818," *Verstreute kleine Schriften*, 267–74. Also see Eberhard Kessel, "Clausewitz über den Gedanken eines Ländertauschs zur Verbindung der Ost- und West-Masse der Preußischen Monarchie nach den Befreigungskriegen," *Forschungen zur Brandenburgischen und Preussischen Geschichte*, LI (1939), 371–77, especially 373–77 for Clausewitz's Jan. 20, 1818, report.

16. Carl von Clausewitz, *Carl von Clausewitz: Two Letters on Strategy*, Peter Paret, and Daniel Moran, ed. and trans. (Fort Leavenworth, KS: US Army Command and General Staff College, Combat Studies Institute, 1984), 1–3,

22; Clausewitz to Gneisenau, Feb. 9, 1815, Pertz-Delbrück, *Gneisenau*, 4:316–17; *Schriften*, 2/1:165–68, 166 fn. 4. The originals: Clausewitz, *Verstreute kleine Schriften*, 493–527.

17. Clausewitz to Roeder, Dec. 22, 1827, in Clausewitz, *Two Letters*, 21–22, 24.

18. Smith, *On Clausewitz*, 15; Carl von Clausewitz, "Our Military Institutions," *HPW*, 316–28; "On the Political Advantages and Disadvantages of the Prussian *Landwehr*," *HPW*, 331–34. The originals: "Unsere Kriegsverfassung," *Verstreute kleines Schriften*, Hahlweg, ed., 275–99, and "Ueber die politischen Vortheile und Nachtheile der Preußischen Landwehr-Einrichtung," *Schriften*, 2/1:367–72; Clausewitz, *Politische Schriften*, Rothfels, ed., 242. See also Clausewitz, "[Bemerkungen zum Aufsatz des Prinzen August von Preußen über die preußische Landwehr,]" Oct. 10, 1820, *Schriften*, 2/1:397–99.

19. Paret and Moran comments, *HPW*, 304–06, and the text, "On the German Federal Army," 306–12. The original: "Deutsche Militär Verfassung," *Schriften*, 2/2:1141–51.

20. Paret, *Clausewitz*, 298–306; Paret and Moran notes, *HPW*, 333–38; Clausewitz, "Agitation," *HPW*, 338–68, espec. 339. The original: "Umtriebe," *Leben*, 2:200–44.

21. Clausewitz to Gneisenau, July 5, 1815, *Schriften*, 2/1:179–80; Heuser, *Reading Clausewitz*, 10; Peter Paret, "Clausewitz and Schlieffen as Interpreters of Frederick the Great: Three Phases in the History of Grand Strategy," *Journal of Military History* 76 (July 2001), 845.

22. Clausewitz, "1814," 20; *OW*, 132; Moran, "Clausewitz on Waterloo," 246 fn. 18.

23. Paret and Moran comments, *HPW*, 30–31; Carl von Clausewitz, "Nachrichten über Preussen in seiner grossen Katastrophe," in Großen Generalstabe, ed., *Kriegsgeschichtliche Einzelschriften*, Vol. 10 (Berlin: Mittler, 1888), 417–548; Clausewitz, "Bemerkungen auf der Reise nach Marienbad im Juli 1825," *Leben*, 2:269–88.

24. Paret, *Clausewitz*, 343–44; Clausewitz, "Observations," *HPW*, 40, 73.

25. Smith, *On Clausewitz*, 16; Clausewitz, "1812," *HPW*, 41, 110, 157, 201.

26. Dan Moran, "Clausewitz on Waterloo: Napoleon at Bay," in Bassford, et al., trans. and ed., *On Waterloo*, 237; Bassford, "Introduction," in ibid., 6; Clausewitz, "1815," in ibid., 190. Clausewitz's study of 1815 is available in two English translations, Bassford, et al., trans. and ed., "1815," *On Waterloo*, and Carl von Clausewitz, *On Wellington: A Critique of Waterloo*, Peter Hofschröer, trans. and ed. (Norman: University of Oklahoma Press, 2010). The original: Carl von Clausewitz, "Der Feldzug von 1815 in Frankreich," *HW* (1862), Vol. 8.

27. Paret, *Clausewitz*, 330, 333. For an excerpt in English, see Carl von Clausewitz, "Observations on the Wars of the Austrian Succession," *HPW*, 21–29. The

original: "Die Feldzüge Friedrich des Grossen von 1741–1762," *HW* (1863), 10:26–214.

28. Carl von Clausewitz, "Some Comments on the War of the Spanish Succession after Reading the Letters of Madame de Maintenon to the Princess des Ursins," *HPW*, 15–18. The original: "Einige Bemerkungen zum spanischen Erbfolgekriege bei Gelegenheit der Briefe der Madame de Maintenon an de Prinzessin des Ursins," *HW* (1862), 9:231–35.

29. Paret, *Clausewitz*, 334, 342–43, 343n. 25; Carl von Clausewitz, "Der Feldzug von 1796 in Italien," *HW* (1858) Vol. 4; Carl von Clausewitz, "Der Feldzüge von 1799 in Italien und der Schweiz," *HW* (1858), Vols. 5 and 6; Carl von Clausewitz, *Sobieski*, in *HW* (1863) 10:1–12; Carl von Clausewitz, "Der Feldzug des Herzogs Carl Wilhelm Ferdinand von Braunschweig, 1787," *HW* (1863), 10:255–320.

30. On the Vendée: "Historische Materialien zur Strategie. Der Krieg in der Vendée, 1793," *HW* (1863), 10:273–96; on the Russo-Turkish War: "Feldmarschal Münich," *HW* (1863), 10:13–24.

31. Michael Handel, "Introduction," in Michael Handel, ed., *Clausewitz and Modern Strategy* (London: Frank Cass, 1986), 4. For Handel's interpretation of Clausewitz and his ideas, especially in relation to those of other theorists, see his *Masters of War: Classical Strategic Thought*, 3rd ed. (London: Frank Cass, 2001).

32. Paret, *Cognitive*, 140, 54–55; Paret, *Clausewitz*, 150; Echevarria, *Clausewitz and Contemporary War*, 3–4, 22–25; Ghyczy, et al., *Clausewitz on Strategy*, 22; Smith, *On Clausewitz*, 61; "By Marie von Clausewitz to the Posthumous Edition of Her Husband's Works, Including *On War*" (hereafter "By Marie von Clausewitz"), *OW*, 65–66; Clausewitz to Marie, Apr. 9, 1807, *Leben*, 1:265–67.

33. White, *Scharnhorst*, 11–12; Smith, *On Clausewitz*, 57, 59, 60.

34. "By Marie von Clausewitz," in *OW*, 65–66. The original 1832–34 version of *Vom Kriege* (which first saw publication as the first three volumes of Clausewitz's *Hinterlassene Werke*) is available online at www.clausewitz.com. The authoritative modern version: Carl von Clausewitz, *Vom Kriege*, Werner Hahlweg, ed. (Bonn: Dümmlers Verlag, 1980).

35. "On the Genesis of His Early Manuscript on the Theory of War, Written around 1818," *OW*, 63; Author's Preface, "To an Unpublished Manuscript on the Theory of War, Written between 1816 and 1818," in *OW*, 61–62. See also *OW*, 140.

36. "Note of 10 July 1827," *OW*, 69–70; "Unfinished Note, Presumably Written in 1830," *OW*, 70.

37. Ghyczy, et al., *Clausewitz on Strategy*, 7; Jon Tetsuro Sumida, *Decoding Clausewitz: A New Approach to On War* (Lawrence: University of Kansas Press, 2008), xiv–xv, 2; Azar Gat, *A History of Military Thought: From the Enlightenment to the Cold War* (Oxford: Oxford University Press, 2001), 257–65; Moran, "Clausewitz on Waterloo," in Bassford, et al., trans. and ed., 240–41 fn. 8.

Gat's discussion, unfortunately, does not sufficiently distinguish between the theoretical concept of "absolute war" and an actual war fought for an unlimited political objective. See also note 43 below.

38. "Note of 10 July 1827," *OW*, 70.

39. For a concise discussion of the misreading of Clausewitz, see Christopher Bassford, "John Keegan and the Grand Tradition of Trashing Clausewitz," *War and History*, Vol. 1, No. 3 (November 1994), available online at: http://www.clausewitz.com/readings/Bassford/Keegan/.

40. *OW*, 579, 582, 593.

41. OW, 605–06; Handel, *Masters of War*, 327–28.

42. *OW*, 605–06.

43. *OW*, 580, 582. See also *OW*, 488–89, 501, 581, 606. This confusion related to "absolute war" takes many forms. For example, W. B. Gallie, whose analysis of Clausewitz's text is fascinating reading, takes Clausewitz's discussion of "absolute war" and applies it to Clausewitz's 1827 letter in which Clausewitz says that wars are fought for either unlimited political objectives (what today we would call "regime change") or limited political objectives (something less than this) and insists that a war fought for an unlimited aim is an "absolute war." This is not what Clausewitz argued, W. B. Gallie, *Philosophers of Peace and War: Kant, Clausewitz, Marx, Engels, and Tolstoy* (Cambridge: Cambridge University Press, 1977), 57.

44. Smith, *On Clausewitz*, 16.

45. *OW*, 75.

46. *OW*, 86–87, 92; Dan Moran, "Strategic Theory and the History of War," (Monterey: Naval Postgraduate School, 2001), 1.

47. *OW*, 585–86.

48. *OW*, 69, 88–89; Jomini, *Art of War*, 12–34; OW, 602. I am indebted to Alaric Searle for this point on Jomini.

49. *OW*, 184, 186, 605.

50. White, *Scharnhorst*, 96; *OW*, 85–86, 101.

51. *OW*, 117, 140.

52. Clausewitz, *Strategie*, 27–28. For other positive comments on intelligence, see *OW*, 373, 397–98, 424, 436. I am indebted to my colleague Michael Jones for the larger point of this discussion.

53. *OW*, 140.

54. *OW*, 114–15, 120–21.

55. *OW*, 119, 122.

56. *OW*, 76–79, 149.

57. Christopher Bassford, "The Primacy of Policy and Trinity in Clausewitz's Thought," in Hew Strachan and Andreas Herberg-Rothe, ed., *Clausewitz in the Twenty-First Century* (Oxford: Oxford University Press, 2007), 77; *OW*, 89.

58. Bassford, "The Primacy of Policy," 77; *OW*, 89.

59. *OW*, 76, 262; Moran, "Strategic Theory," 7.

60. *OW*, 95, 128, 579.

61. *OW*, 84, 357, 488.

62. *OW*, 358, 600. See also *OW*, 217, 220.

63. Clausewitz, "1812," *HPW*, 120.

64. *OW*, 486, 595–96, 618.

65. Some other references to the "center of gravity" in *On War* also lead one to conclude that the concept generally applies to today's current operational level of war. See *OW*, 485–86, 488, 489, 491. An added wrinkle to this is that there is one place in the text where he uses the term "center of gravity" that could be read as tactical in nature: "The major battle is therefore to be regarded as concentrated war, as the center of gravity of the entire conflict or campaign." *OW*, 258.

66. *OW*, 128, 200, 205, 177–79.

67. *OW*, 577–637, espec. 577, 617.

68. *OW*, 596, 599–600.

69. *OW*, Jolles, trans., 153–54; *OW*, 194–95.

70. Moran, "Strategic Theory," 13; *OW*, 479, 481. See also *OW*, 288.

71. *OW*, 100–12, 136; *OW*, Jolles, trans., 31; Carl von Clausewitz, *On War*, J. J. Graham, trans., Anatol Rapport, ed. (Harmondsworth, Middlesex, UK: Penguin, 1968), 138; Kant quoted in Smith, *On Clausewitz*, 190.

72. *OW*, 101–02, 578.

73. *OW*, 100–12.

74. *OW*, 632–33. See also *OW*, 140.

75. John E. Tashjean, "The Short-War Antinomy Resolved: or, From Homer to Clausewitz," *Defense Analysis*, 8:2 (1992), 169–70; *OW*, 528.

76. *OW*, 570, 572–73.

77. *OW*, 80, 291, 582.

78. Clausewitz to Gneisenau, Dec. 20, 1829, Aug. 20, July 31, 1830, *Schriften*, 2/1:572–73, 580–81, 583–85; Paret, *Clausewitz*, 325–26; "By Marie von Clausewitz," in *OW*, 66; Priesdorff, ed., *Soldatisches*, 66, 70; F. von Meerheimb, "Carl von Clausewitz. Vortrag, gehalten in der militärischen Gesellschaft zu Berlin am 23. October 1874," *Jahrbücher für die Deutsche Armee und Marine*, G. von Marées, ed., Vol. 3 (Oct.-Dec., 1874), 233; *Leben*, 2:294–95.

79. Carl von Clausewitz, "Europe since the Polish Partition," *HPW*, 372–76, espec. 373–74. The original: "Die Verhältnisse Europa's seit der Theilung Polens," *Leben*, 2:401–07.

80. "On the Basic Question of Germany's Existence," *HPW*, 378–84. The original: "Zurückführung der vielen politischen Fragen, welche Deutschland beschäftigen, auf die unserer Gesamtexistenz," *Leben*, 2:408–17.

81. Paret and Moran notes, *HPW*, 377–78; Peter Paret, "An Anonymous Letter by Clausewitz on the Polish Insurrection of 1830–1831," *Journal of Modern History*, Vol. 42, No. 2 (June 1970), 187–90; Clausewitz to Marie, Aug. 2, 20, 1831, *Leben*, 2:375–76, 384–85. See also Peter Paret, *Understanding War: Essays on*

Clausewitz and the History of Military Power (Princeton: Princeton University Press, 1992), 199–205.

82. Paret, *Clausewitz*, 402–05. For the originals, see: Clausewitz, "Betrachtungen über einen künftigen Kriegsplan gegen Frankreich, 1830," and "I. Promemoria über einen möglichen Krieg mit Frankreich; II. Einige Gesichtspunkte für einen gegen Frankreich bevorstehenden Krieg, 1830/31," *Verstreute kleine Schriften*, Hahlweg, ed., 533–63, 567–601.

83. "By Marie von Clausewitz," in *OW*, 66; *Leben*, 2:295; Smith, *On Clausewitz*, 17; Clausewitz letters to Marie during his deployment, *Leben*, 2:318–400; "Tagebuch Clausewitz's vom 7. September 1830 bis zum 9. März 1831," *Leben*, 2:298–318, see espec. 302–03 for his deployment preparations; E. von Conrady, *Leben und wirken des Generals der Infanterie und kommandirenden Generals des V. Armeekorps, Carl von Grolman* (Berlin: Mittler, 1894), 3:124.

84. Clausewitz to Gneisenau, Nov. 13, 1830, *Schriften*, 2/1:591–95; Heinrich von Brandt, *Aus Leben des Generals der Infanterie z. D. Dr. Heinrich von Brandt*, vol. 2, *Leben in Berlin, Ausstand in Polen, Sendung nach Frankreich, 1828–1833*, H. von Brandt, ed. (Berlin: Mittler, 1869), 2:107–08; see also Clausewitz's numerous letters, *Leben*, 2:318–400.

85. Paret, *Clausewitz*, 421–26; *Leben*, 2:297; Clausewitz to Marie, June 14, 16, Aug. 23 (two notes), 1831, *Leben*, 2:353–57, 385–86; Clausewitz's "Tagebuche," ibid., 2:286–89.

86. *Leben*, 2:297–98; Clausewitz to Marie, Sept. 16, 21, 1831, ibid., 2:397–400; Paret, *Clausewitz*, 427–28.

87. Smith, *On Clausewitz*, 18; Paret, *Clausewitz* (2007), xvi; "By Marie von Clausewitz," *OW*, 66.

88. Caroline v. Rochow to Klara v. Pfuel, Nov. 22, 1831, in Caroline v. Rochow geb. v.d. Marwitz and Marie de la Motte-Fouqué, *Von Leben am preußischen Hofe, 1815–1852*, Luise v.d. Marwitz, ed. (Berlin: Siegfried Mittler, 1908), 234–36; Marie quoted in Paret, *Clausewitz*, 431.

89. "By Marie von Clausewitz," *OW*, 66; Marie quoted in Paret, *Clausewitz*, 431.

90. Quotes and material, Smith, *On Clausewitz*, 18.

91. "By Marie von Clausewitz," *OW*, 65; Strachan, *Clausewitz's On War*, 69–70.

92. Strachan, *Clausewitz's On War*, 69–70.

CONCLUSION

1. Peter Paret, "Clausewitz: A Bibliographical Survey," *World Politics*, Vol. 17, No. 2 (Jan. 1965), 285; Hew Strachan, "Clausewitz and the Dialectics of War," in *Clausewitz in the Twenty-First Century*, 19; Heuser, *Reading Clausewitz*, 12–13.

2. Heuser, *Reading Clausewitz*, 12–13; Bassford, "Jomini and Clausewitz," 1, 6–8.

3. Heuser, *Reading Clausewitz*, 14; Strachan, *Clausewitz's On War*, 10–11.

4. Sir Julian Corbett, *Some Principles of Maritime Strategy* (Annapolis: Naval Institute Press, 1988). Originally published in 1911.

5. Heuser, *Reading Clausewitz*, 18–19, 143–44.

6. Ibid., 19, 21.

7. Ibid., 20–22.

8. Ibid., 17.

9. Harry G. Summers Jr., "Foreword," in *War, Politics, and Power: Selections from On War, and I Believe and Profess: Karl von Clausewitz*, Edward M. Collins, trans. and ed. (Regnery: Washington, 1997), x, xiv–xv. I am indebted to Brandon Little for pointing out this source.

10. Bassford, *Clausewitz in English*, 203; Harry G. Summers Jr., *On Strategy: A Critical Analysis of the Vietnam War* (Novato, CA: Presidio, 1982); Summers, "Foreword," ibid., xvi.

11. Bassford, *Clausewitz in English*, 204; Michael Howard, "Foreword: Clausewitz *On War*: A History of the Howard-Paret Translation," in *Clausewitz in the Twenty-First Century*, v–vii.

12. Bassford, *Clausewitz in English*, 204; Handel, *Masters of War*, 307–26, see 310–11 for the text of the Weinberger Doctrine.

13. Moran, "Strategic Theory," 7.

14. Gallie, *Philosophers*, 37, 42; Paret, *Cognitive*, 116–17.

15. *OW*, 229.

16. For a concise examination of the modern relevance of Clausewitz's ideas in *On War*, see Smith, *On Clausewitz*, 244–50.

17. For additional examination of the modern relevance of Clausewitz's ideas in *On War*, see ibid., 257–71; Hew Strachan and Andreas Herberg Rothe, "Introduction," in *Clausewitz in the Twenty-First Century*, 1.

18. Heuser, *Reading Clausewitz*, 194; Smith, *On Clausewitz*, 70.

19. *HW*, 7:311 (1862), quoted in Ghyczy, et al., *Clausewitz on Strategy*, 185; Smith, *On Clausewitz*, 69.

Select Bibliography

Full citations for the sources used appear in the notes. The seemingly annually exponential increase in publications on Clausewitz and his produce make any bibliography obsolete before its publication. The definitive Clausewitz bibliography is maintained by Dr. Christopher Bassford and the other Clausewitzian bibliographical geniuses at www.clausewitz.com. But listing the most important material is necessary.

I have divided the sources into two classes: "archival" and "other." "Archival" is self-explanatory. "Other" generally means the key primary sources by Clausewitz himself, important secondary sources generally containing primary source material related to Clausewitz, and the more well-known or useful works about Clausewitz that focus upon or include biographical information.

There is no complete collection of Clausewitz's papers and publications. Undoubtedly, the dispersion of some and the destruction of other of his papers during the Second World War has greatly contributed to this. Most of the surviving primary material by and related to Clausewitz is printed within other, sometimes nineteenth-century works. If one has Clausewitz's *Hinterlassene Werke*, the two volumes of his biography by Karl Schwartz, and the four volumes published by the staggeringly industrious Werner Hahlweg, he or she possesses the majority of Clausewitz's surviving known works, but by no means all.

After this book had gone into production Vanya Eftimova Bellinger, who is writing a biography of Marie von Clausewitz, brought to my attention the discovery of what seems to be a complete set of correspondence between Carl and Marie von Clausewitz. Ms. Bellinger believes the collection adds little to the published Clausewitz letters, but there are many from Marie that were previously unknown and she has been kind enough to supply me with a few details from these. Ms. Bellinger is writing a biography of Marie von Clausewitz and will undoubtedly present us with an original and revealing portrait of Marie's critical role in the evolution and creation of Clausewitz's work, as well as some additional insights on Clausewitz himself.

ARCHIVAL SOURCES

Denmark. Rigsarkivet. Copenhagen. Dpt. F.u.A. 1771–1848, Preussen II, Depecher 1819.

Great Britain. British Library. The Papers of Sir Hudson Lowe. ADD 20111, 20191, 20193.

Great Britain. National Archives. Public Record Office. Kew. London. Map. Oct. 1813. WO 78–25–1.

Russia. Rossiinskii Gusudarstvennyi Voenno-Istoricheskii (RGVIA). *The Napoleonic Wars, 1805–1815: Military Science Archive at the Russian State Military History Archive*. Woodbridge, CT: Primary Source Microfilm, 2002. 90 rolls. Fond 846, Opis' 16, Delo 3591, Roll 53, Delo 3947, part 2, Roll 80.

OTHER SOURCES

Aron, Raymond. *Penser la guerre, Clausewitz*. Paris: Gallimard, 1976.

Bassford, Christopher. *Clausewitz in English: The Reception of Clausewitz in Britain and America, 1815–1945*. Oxford: Oxford University Press, 1994.

———, Daniel Moran, and Gregory Pedlow, trans. and ed., *On Waterloo: Clausewitz, Wellington, and the Campaign of 1815*. www.clausewitz.com, 2010.

Caemmerer, Rudolf von. *Clausewitz*. Berlin: B. Behr, 1905.

Clausewitz, Carl von. *Ausgewählte militärische Schriften*. Gerhard Förster, Dorothea Schmidt, and Christa Gudzent, eds. Berlin: Militärverlag der Deutschen Demokratischen Republik, 1981.

———. "Bemerkungen über die reineung angewandte Strategie des herrn von Bülow." *Neue Bellona*, IX, No. 3 (1805): 252–87.

———. *The Campaign of 1812 in Russia*. Foreword by Sir Michael Howard. New York: Da Capo, 1995.

———. *The Campaign of 1813 to the Armistice*. Niels Nielsen, trans. Unpublished Manuscript, 2013.

———. *Der Feldzug von 1813 bis zum Waffenstillstand*. Glatz, 1813.

———. *Geist and Tat*. W. M. Schering, ed. Stuttgart: Alfred Kröner, 1941.

———. *Hinterlassene Werke des Generals Carl von Clausewitz über Krieg und Kriegführung*. 10 vols. Berlin, 1832–37; 2nd ed., 1857–63.

———. *Historische Briefe über de großen Kriegsereignisse im Oktober 1806*. Joachim Niemeyer, ed. Bonn: Dümmlers, 1977.

———. *Historical and Political Writings*. Peter Paret and Daniel Moran, ed. and trans. Princeton: Princeton University Press, 1992.

———. "Historical Material on Strategy: On the Campaign of 1813." Niels Nielsen, trans. Unpublished Manuscript, 2012.

———. *Karl und Marie von Clausewitz: Ein Lebensbild in Briefen und Tagebuchblättern*. Karl Linnebach, ed. Berlin: Warneck, 1916.

———. "Kriegsartikel für die Unter-Officiere und gemeinen Söldaten (der königl. preussischen Armee).... Verordnung wegen der Militär-Strafen. Verordnung wegen Bestrafung der Officiere....Reglement über die Besetzung der Stellen der Port-epée Fähnriche und über die Wahl zum

Officier…" *Jenaische Allgemeine Literatur-Zeitung*, No. 238 (Oct. 11, 1808): 65–68.

———. Letter to the editor [part 1], Dec. 19, 1806. "Historische Briefe über die großen Kriegs-Ereignisse im October 1806." *Minerva*, No. 1 (Jan. 1807): 1–21.

———. Letter to the editor [part 2], Dec. 19, 1806. "Historische Briefe über die großen Kriegs-Ereignisse im October 1806." *Minerva*, No. 2 (Feb. 1807): 193–209.

———. Letter to the editor, Feb. 19, 1807. "Historische Briefe über die großen Kriegs-Ereignisse im October 1806." *Minerva*, No. 4 (Apr. 1807): 1–26.

———. "Nachrichten über Preussen in seiner grossen Katastrophe." In Großen Generalstabe, ed. *Kriegsgeschichtliche Einzelschriften*. Vol. 10. Berlin: Mittler, 1888, 417–548.

———. "Notes on the Jena Campaign," and "Notes on Prussia in Her Grand Catastrophe of 1806," and "Prince August's Batalion in the Battle of Prenzlau." Colonel Conrad H. Lanza, ed. and trans. Command and General Staff School. *Jena Campaign Sourcebook*. Fort Leavenworth, KS: The General Service Schools Press, 1922.

———. "On the Life and Character of Scharnhorst" (1817). In Peter Paret and Daniel Moran, ed. and trans. *Historical and Political Writings*. Princeton: Princeton University Press, 1992, 88–109.

———. *On War*, J. J. Graham, trans. Anatol Rapport, ed. Harmondsworth, Middlesex, UK: Penguin, 1968.

———. *On War*. Michael Howard and Peter Paret, ed. and trans. Princeton: Princeton University Press, 1984.

———. *On War*. O. J. Matthijs Jolles, trans. Washington, DC: Combat Forces Press, 1943, 1950, 1953.

———. *On Wellington: A Critique of Waterloo*. Peter Hofschröer, trans. and ed. Norman: University of Oklahoma Press, 2010.

———. *Politische Schriften und Briefe*. Hans Rothfels, ed. Munich: Drei Masten Verlag, 1922.

———. *The Principles of War*. Hans W. Gatzke, ed. and trans. Harrisburg, PA: Stackpole, 1960.

———. *Schriften—Aufsätze—Studien—Briefe*. Werner Hahlweg, ed. 2 vols (in 3). Göttingen: Vandenhoeck & Ruprecht, 1966.

———. "Strategic Critique of the 1814 Campaign." Niels Nielsen, trans. Unpublished Manuscript, 2012.

———. *Strategie aus dem Jahr 1804, mit Zusätzen von 1808 und 1809*. Eberhard Kessel, ed. Hamburg: Hanseatische Verlagsanstalt, 1937.

———. *Strategy: From the Year 1804, with Addenda of 1808 and 1809*. Marc F. Guarin, trans. Unpublished manuscript, 2012. Based upon the text: Carl von Clausewitz. *Strategie, aus dem Jahr 1804, mit Zusätzen von 1808 und 1809*. Eberhard Kessel, ed. Hamburg: Hanseatische Verlagsanstalt, 1937.

———. *Carl von Clausewitz: Two Letters on Strategy.* Peter Paret and Daniel Moran, ed. and trans. Fort Leavenworth, KS: US Army Command and General Staff College, Combat Studies Institute, 1984.

———. *Verstreute kleine Schriften.* Werner Hahlweg, ed. Osnabrück: Biblio, 1979.

———. *Vom Kriege.* Werner Hahlweg, ed. Bonn: Ferd. Dümmlers, 1980.

Clausewitz, Marie von. "Erinnerung an den General Clausewitz und sein Verhältniss zu Scharnhorst." In Leopold Ranke, ed. *Historisch-politische Zeitschrift.* Hamburg: Friedrich Perthes, 1832, 1:213–22.

Fabian, Franz [Franz Mielke]. *Clausewitz: Sein Leben und Werk.* Berlin: Ministeriums für Nationale Verteidigung, 1957.

Hahlweg, Werner. "Clausewitz bei Liddell Hart: Ein unbekannter Clausewitz-Brief in Wolverton Park." *Archiv für Kulturgeschichte*, Vol. XLI, No. 1 (1959): 100–05.

———. *Carl von Clausewitz. Soldat, Politiker, Denker.* Göttingen, Musterschmidt-Verlag [1957].

———. *Lehrmeister des Kleinen Krieges: Von Clausewitz bis Mao Tse-Tung und (Che) Guevara.* Darmstadt: Wehr und Wissen Verlagsgesellschaft, 1968.

Hilbert, Klaus. "Ergänzungen zum Lebensbild des Generals Carl von Clausewitz." *Militärgeschichte*, No. 20 (1981): 208–13.

Jomini, Henri-Antoine de. *The Art of War.* G. H. Mendell and W. P. Craighill, trans. Philadelphia: Lippincott, 1862; Reprint, Westport, CT: Greenwood Press, 1978.

Kessel, Eberhard. "Clausewitz über den Gedanken eines Ländertauschs zur Verbindung der Ost- und West-Masse der Preußischen Monarchie nach den Befreiungskriegen." *Forschungen zur Brandenburgischen und Preussischen Geschichte*, Vol. LI (1939): 371–77.

———. "Zu Boyens Entlassung." *Historische Zeitschrift*, Vol. 175, No. 1 (1953): 41–54.

Meerheimb, F. von. "Carl von Clausewitz. Vortrag, gehalten in der militärischen Gesellschaft zu Berlin am 23. October 1874." *Jahrbücher für die Deutsche Armee und Marine.* G. von Marées, ed. Vol. 3 (Oct.–Dec. 1874): 225–55.

Moran, Daniel. "Clausewitz and the Revolution." *Central European History*, Vol. 22, No. 2 (June 1989): 183–99.

Paret, Peter. "An Anonymous Letter by Clausewitz on the Polish Insurrection of 1830–1831." *Journal of Modern History*, Vol. 42, No. 2 (June 1970): 184–90.

———. "Bemerkungen zu dem Versuch von Clausewitz, zum Gesandten in London Ernannt zu Werden." *Jahrbuch für Geschichte Mittel- und Ostdeutschlands.* Vol. 26 (1977): 161–72.

———. "Clausewitz." In *Makers of Modern Strategy: From Machiavelli to the Nuclear Age.* Princeton: Princeton University Press, 1986, 186–213.

———. "Clausewitz: A Bibliographical Survey." *World Politics*, Vol. 17, No. 2 (Jan. 1965): 272–85.

————. *Clausewitz and the State: The Man, His Theories, and His Times.* Princeton: Princeton University Press, 1985, 2007.

————. 'Clausewitz: "Half against my will, I have become a Professor,"' *Journal of Military History* 75 (Apr. 2011): 591–601.

————. *The Cognitive Challenge of War: Prussia 1806.* Princeton: Princeton University Press, 2009.

_____. "Translation, Literal or Accurate." *The Journal of Military History* 78 (July 2014): 1077–80.

————. *Understanding War: Essays on Clausewitz and the History of Military Power.* Princeton: Princeton University Press, 1992.

————. *Yorck and the Era of the Prussian Reform, 1807–1815.* Princeton: Princeton University Press, 1966.

Parkinson, Roger. *Clausewitz: A Biography.* New York: Stein and Day, 1971.

Preußen, August von. "Aus dem kriegsgeschichtlichen Nachlasse seiner Königlichen Hoheit des Prinzen August von Preußen: Feldzug 1806." In *Kriegsgeschichtliche Einzelschriften.* Großen Generalstabe, ed. Berlin: Mittler, 1883, 2:10–34.

Pertz, G. H. and Hans Delbrück. *Das Leben des Feldmarschalls Grafen Neidhardt von Gneisenau.* Berlin: Reimer, 1864–80. 5 vols.

Priesdorff, Kurt von, ed. *Soldatisches Führertum.* Vol. 8. Hamburg: Hanseatische Verlagsanstalt, [1938].

Roques, P. *Le Général de Clausewitz: Sa Vie et sa Théorie de la Guerre.* Paris: Berger-Levrault, 1912.

Rose, Olaf. *Carl von Clausewitz: Wirkungsgeschichte seines Werkes in Rußland und der Sowjetunion, 1836–1991.* Munich: R. Oldenbourg, 1995.

Rothfels, Hans. "Clausewitz." In *Makers of Modern Strategy: Military Thought from Machiavelli to Hitler.* Edward Earle Meade, ed. Princeton: Princeton University Press, 1943, 93–113.

————. *Carl von Clausewitz, Politik und Krieg: Eine ideengeschichtliche Studie.* Berlin: Dümmlers, 1920.

————. "Ein Brief von Clausewitz an den Kronprinzen Friedrich Wilhelm aus dem Jahre 1812," *Historische Zeitschrift.* CXXI (1919): 282–86.

————. "Ein kunsttheoretisches Fragment von General von Clausewitz." *Deutsche Rundschau* CLXXIII, No. 3 (1917): 373–82.

Scharnhorst, Gerhard Johann David von. *Scharnhorsts Briefe: Privatbriefe.* Karl Linnebach, ed. Munich: G. Mueller, 1914.

Schössler, Dietmar. *Carl von Clausewitz.* Hamburg: Rowohlt, 1991.

Schramm, Wilhelm von. *Clausewitz: Leben und Werk.* Esslingen am Neckar: Bechtle, 1976.

Schwartz, Karl. *Leben des Generals Carl von Clausewitz und der Frau Marie von Clausewitz.* 2 Vols. Berlin: Dümmlers, 1878.

Stark, Klaus T. *Carl von Clausewitz.* Lutherstadt Eisleben, Germany: Projekte-Verlag Cornelius, 2014.

Index